D1231500

THE LORDS OF CREATION

Frederick Lewis Allen was born in Boston, studied at Groton and Harvard University, and was assistant and associate editor of *Harper's* magazine for eighteen years, then the magazine's sixth editor-in-chief for twelve years. His best-known books were *Only Yesterday*, *Since Yesterday*, and *The Big Change*. He died in 1954.

THE LORDS
OF CREATION

By

FREDERICK LEWIS ALLEN

Q

QUADRANGLE PAPERBACKS
Quadrangle Books / Chicago

SECOND PRINTING

First QUADRANGLE PAPERBACK edition published 1966 by Quadrangle Books, Inc., 12 East
Delaware Place, Chicago 60611. Manufactured in
the United States of America.

To A. R. A.

CONTENTS

PREFACE

THIS book is an attempt to tell the story of the immense financial and corporate expansion which took place in the United States between the depression of the eighteen-nineties and the crisis of the nineteen-thirties; to show how profoundly it altered the circumstances and quality of American life, why and how it ended in collapse, and what the collapse meant to all of us.

One reason why I decided to make this attempt was that the theme seemed to me to be vitally important. One need not accept *in toto* the economic theory of history to recognize that in our recent American history the economic thread has become a rope to which almost everything else in our lives appears to be attached. I do not believe that anybody can understand how the United States reached its present predicament without some sort of understanding of the economic processes, and particularly the almost revolutionary financial processes, which were at work during the great age of financial expansion. In a very real sense, this story is the story of forces which dictated the terms of American life yesterday and today. The theme is important also because of the pervasive social influence—in the broadest sense—of the financial and industrial leaders; for they largely constituted our American upper class, and their standards and ideas tended to permeate the whole population.

Another reason why I decided to make the attempt was that although thousands of volumes had been written upon one phase of this subject or another, nobody else had told this story as a whole, with an eye not merely to the economic facts and figures, but also to their dramatic and human interest and their social significance.

There seemed to me to be room for a volume which would be true to the facts, in so far as they could be determined; which would survey the whole subject and yet enliven it by recounting in detail certain characteristic and exciting episodes; which would give some impression of the conflict and suspense of the market place, the personal quality of the people involved, and the influence which they exercised; and which would be as impartial as a writer not immune to prejudices and misconceptions could make it.

A very large order, I am afraid; in the two years during which I have been engaged in trying to fill it I have been constantly aware of its size. Research upon such a topic could be endless; almost every chapter of this book has been the subject of previous books, articles, reports, to the point not merely of fatigue but of dismay to the historian who is trying to piece together the connected story without spending several lifetimes upon it. A great deal of essential material is missing; some, of course, has been diligently concealed. Of the material which is available, much is so biased, either for or against the financiers, that a writer who tries to umpire the disputed points has many opportunities to go astray. For possible errors or lapses of understanding I can only plead these difficulties as a partial excuse.

Yet I might add that I have found the task continuously and absorbingly interesting. I should be very glad if I were able to communicate some of this interest to at least some readers.

My principal sources and obligations are set forth in the Appendix.

F. L. A.

Chapter One

MORGAN CALLS THE TUNE

ON THE evening of the 12th of December, 1900, two gentlemen of New York gave a large dinner to Charles M. Schwab, the energetic young president of Andrew Carnegie's great steel company.

The dinner was private and unpublicized; as one turns the yellowed and brittle pages of the *New York Times* of the following morning, one finds no mention of it whatever. The two most striking events of December the twelfth, 1900, to judge from the front-page headlines of the *Times*, were an advantage gained by DeWet, the Boer general, over the British in the war in South Africa, and an accident in a six-day bicycle race in Madison Square Garden. Yet the Schwab dinner at the University Club on Fifth Avenue was one of those events which direct the destinies of a nation.

For at this dinner John Pierpont Morgan, by common consent the leader of the financial forces of the day, sat at Schwab's right hand; and it was Schwab's irresistible persuasiveness as an after-dinner speaker which convinced Morgan that the time had come to organize the United States Steel Corporation, and thus to strike the resounding keynote of the theme of American financial and economic life for more than thirty years to come.

A new century was beginning; but more than that, a new era for America was beginning. The dragging business depression which had blighted the country after the panic of 1893 had come to an end in 1897; bumper wheat crops in the United States and simultaneous crop

failures in Europe had turned the tide that summer—
almost precisely as they had turned it in 1879, at the
end of a previous span of lean years. (Here is an ironical
circumstance for the contemplation of those who preach
the economic interdependence of nations: that recovery
in America should twice have been hastened by catastrophic conditions abroad!) New industrial processes
were ready for development; the age of mass production,
the electrical age, were on their way. The amiable
William McKinley sat in the White House; Senator
Mark Hanna, to whom the welfare of big business and
the welfare of the country were almost indistinguishable,
stood behind McKinley, ready with encouragement and
advice; business men felt sure that the affairs of the
United States would be managed with a conservative regard for the rights and privileges of property. The boom
which began in 1897 was only momentarily interrupted
by the outbreak of the Spanish War. Prosperity had returned.

But it had returned to a very different country from
the America of the eighties and early nineties.

The frontier had now for many years been closed. No
longer could Americans depend upon hopeful expansion
into the free lands beyond the plains as a safety-valve for
the pressure of industrial competition. Two alternatives
confronted a nation accustomed to restless growth: conquest beyond the seas, and intensive economic development within its natural boundaries.

The idea of outward conquest had been given a powerful impetus by the *opera-bouffe* victory in the Spanish
War, which had bestowed upon a surprised country a
group of islands across the Pacific. The troops were
hardly back from Cuba, the echoes of "There'll Be a
Hot Time in the Old Town Tonight" were still floating
on the air, and Admiral George Dewey was still the

nation's adored hero, when Rudyard Kipling wrote "The White Man's Burden," and its lines became familiar almost overnight. To many enthusiastic citizens it seemed as if American shoulders were built for that burden. President McKinley told a group of Methodists that we must accept sovereignty over the Philippines "to educate the Filipinos, and uplift and civilize and Christianize them"; to another less pious audience he said that the Philippines offered a "commercial opportunity to which American statesmanship could not be indifferent." Early in 1900 Senator Beveridge was proclaiming that America must follow the judgment of the Master: "Ye have been faithful over a few things; I will make you ruler over many things." It is true that a considerable body of American opinion was very dubious about our sacred duty to our "little brown brother" and hated the whole imperial conception; but McKinley and his mentors chose "expansion" as the issue of the 1900 campaign against Bryan, and it was a winning issue. The mood of the day was confident; in the flush of victory most Americans probably believed that their country could easily assume dominion over palm and pine if she chose to take the trouble.

As it happened, no further direct expansion of American territory was destined to take place; but the new and intoxicating idea that America was now an imperial power, fit to assume the obligations of a great force in world affairs, had striking financial and economic effects. For the first time in history, America was now lending money to Europe in quantity: between 1899 and 1902, New York took over two hundred million dollars of the British Exchequer loans to finance the Boer War. American foreign trade was growing, the captains of industry had begun to dream extravagant dreams of the capture of foreign markets, and on both sides of the Atlantic there was talk of the possibility that New York might displace London as the financial center of the world. The national ego was enlarging. America was enjoying the responsibilities and releases of maturity.

Meanwhile, however, the intensive development of the national economy was proceeding still more rapidly. In the three or four years immediately preceding that dinner at the University Club when Morgan and Schwab sat cheek by jowl, the organization and character of American business had been undergoing a profound change, with consequences which were to reach into the daily lives of millions.

This change had been in preparation for a very long time. To understand the nature of it and the reasons for it we must go back to the days when the name of Pierpont Morgan was unknown outside of Wall Street and Charles M. Schwab was a little boy playing about his father's livery stable in a village in the Alleghany Mountains.

§ 2

In the eighteen-seventies and eighteen-eighties the accepted principle of American business was free competition. Almost everybody believed in laissez-faire; the ideal economic order, it was generally thought, was a sort of endless game which anybody could enter, with the government serving as referee and intervening only to prevent flagrant holding and roughing. At the beginning of this period most businesses were small, few did business on a national scale; and if a competitor became crippled in the game, there were always other fields in the West where he could begin again unhandicapped. The standards of fair play were low, for the referee was often not only absent-minded but venal: the economic history of those years is full of stories of piratical methods in the fight for business advantages and markets. But the ideal of free competition was not seriously disputed.

In business as in a game, however, the score does not always remain at a tie; and in this particular game there were sometimes so many players and the play was so fierce that heads were broken. During the eighteen-eighties competition among the railroads, for example, got completely out of hand; it was easy for daring and unscrupulous plungers to build new lines simply as a form of economic blackmail—in order to be bought off by their competitors in self-defense; at one time there were five lines bidding against each other for the traffic between New York and Chicago, two more were under construction, and the passenger fare for the through trip had been beaten down to the ruinous figure of one dollar. During the oil boom in Western Pennsylvania some years earlier, so many fortune-seekers had rushed to sink oil wells that the price of oil dropped to the depths, carrying men down with it to bankruptcy. In such situations, some device for limiting competition seemed to be necessary. It was provided, not by the law, but by agreements among groups of the competitors themselves—agreements to share privileges, maintain prices, and choke off cut-throat attacks on the part of their rivals.

In the oil industry the control of competition was provided by a severe young man named John D. Rockefeller, who had run his little refining business in Cleveland with such calculating efficiency, had bought out his immediate competitors with such boldness, and had wrung secret privileges from the railroads with such shrewdness, that shortly he was able to dictate to the industry. No impartial referee would have sanctioned some of the practices which had enabled Rockefeller to gain supremacy. Early in the eighteen-seventies his Standard Oil Company and a number of others had joined forces in setting up an association euphemistically known as the South Improvement Company, and had thus secured from a number of railroads (by threatening to take their freight business elsewhere) not only rebates on their freight charges but what were known as "drawbacks"; in other words, the Rockefeller group had forced the railroads to hand back to them secretly not only a part of the freight charges which the Rockefeller group themselves had paid (in accordance with the published rates), but also a part of what their competitors had paid! No competitor could long exist under such a crushing handicap. The South Improvement Company was short-lived, for when its devices were discovered there arose a howl of protest which echoes to this day; but by that time the pious Mr. Rockefeller had become too mighty a force in the oil industry to be resisted. He had the market in his grip; presently he had a large number of refining companies at his mercy; and by 1879 he was ready to deal the principle of free competition a thumping blow.

A lawyer named Samuel C. T. Dodd provided him with the means of doing it. Dodd invented a way of bringing forty separate oil companies into a compact group under unified management. The shareholders in all these forty companies turned their stock over to a group of nine trustees, consisting of Rockefeller and his associates, and received, in return, trust certificates which entitled them to their dividends. The nine trustees, thus having full voting power over each of the forty companies, could do exactly as they pleased with the direction of each, operating them as a gigantic but flexible unit and confronting their competitors with their colossal collective power. Ordinary trade agreements between business rivals on prices and on the division of markets were usually made only to be broken; as a big industrialist testified many years later, they often lasted only until one of the conferees could get to a telegraph office or a telephone; but the decisions of these trustees were unbreakable. The first trust had been born.

Now if there was one thing which American public opinion, devoted as it was to the ideal of free competition, would not tolerate, it was monopoly; and when the truth about this trust leaked out—which of course it did, despite the bland statements of Rockefeller and his associates that they were not connected with any oil concern but the Standard Oil Company of Ohio—there was a great public outcry. The small business man saw with acute dread the possibility that some day he might be forced out of business by such a trust. Consumers realized that trusts might be able to force upward the prices of essential commodities and thus take toll of a helpless population. Lovers of fair play were outraged by the spectacle of an economic game in which one player appeared to be a giant equipped with brass knuckles. During the eighteen-eighties a great many other trusts were formed, for the instinct of self-preservation and the acquisitive instinct combined forces to draw men into such combinations; soon there appeared a sugar trust, a rubber trust, a butcher trust, a whiskey trust, a cottonseed oil trust, and many more; but the outcry grew to such volume that in 1888 all the political parties denounced the trusts in their platforms, and in 1890 Congress passed, with only slight opposition, an act prohibiting "combination in restraint of trade"—the famous Sherman Act.

Shortly afterward the Standard Oil Trust was forced to dissolve (or rather, to appear to dissolve).

Apparently the Dodd form of industrial combination, a rather awkward form at best, was doomed. But the desire for combination remained and became intensified. The score in the game of business refused to remain at a tie. The trend of American economic life was in the direction of integration and consolidation. Business units were becoming larger; more and more businesses were becoming national in scope. How could it be otherwise, with the transportation and communication systems of the country binding Maine and California ever more closely together, and with banks and private fortunes growing, and business ambition rampant? And, as it happened, already a way of achieving combination legally was at hand.

§ 3

In the year 1888 the Governor of New Jersey, becoming concerned over the finances of the state, had consulted a New York lawyer named James B. Dill. What could New Jersey do to bring more income into the state treasury? Dill suggested passing a law which would permit companies incorporated in New Jersey to hold the stock of other corporations. Such a law was duly passed, to the immense benefit of the state treasury, which fattened—as other state treasuries were later to fatten—on the fees resulting from an extension of the privileges of property. Thus, even before the passage of the Sherman Act, holding companies were given legal sanction. (Heretofore it had generally been held illegal for one corporation to own the stock of another except by special legislative permission, and only a few scattered companies had secured such permission.)

If a man wanted to bring forty companies under a central control, he now no longer had to attempt personally to buy 51 per cent of the stock of each (a colossal task). He could induce the owners of the various companies to exchange their shares for the shares of a newly-formed New Jersey holding corporation (or to sell their properties to it) ; he could induce the public to buy stock in the holding corporation; and thus, with financial assistance from the public, he could bring the forty concerns into an effective centrally-administered unit. Whether such a holding company would be adjudged a conspiracy in restraint of trade by the Federal Government under the Sherman Act was uncertain; but the Government was apparently not taking the enforcement of the Sherman Act very seriously, and anyhow the holding company device was secure against interference by the New Jersey authorities. Presently there was a rush to New Jersey to form holding companies.

It was not necessary for these companies actually to conduct their business in the state; their legal domicile within the boundaries of New Jersey was usually one of those painstaking fictions beloved of lawyers. A corporation needed only to hang its hat there, so to speak: to appoint someone in a trust company in Hoboken or Jersey City as its agent, and to hold its annual stockholders' meetings in his office. The rush to Hoboken was somewhat delayed by the depression which began in 1893, but by 1897, when the skies cleared, it was under way again in dead earnest. Already other states, jealous of New Jersey's new-found source of revenue, had moved to emulate her. Combination through the medium of the holding company—or through the medium of a company which bought the properties of its constituents instead of buying their shares—became the order of the day. And thus began that new industrial era which was to approach its maturity on the night when Morgan and Schwab dined together.

It began recklessly and flamboyantly. For not only did the increasing pressure and ferocity of competition make capitalists eager to join forces; the discovery had also been made that the formation and financing of holding companies offered the easiest way to get rich quickly that had ever legally existed in the United States. Accordingly a new species of financier appeared upon the scene, a man part economic statesman and part gambler—the promoter. The promoter made a business of bringing together the owners of competing concerns. He persuaded them to exchange their stock (on very generous terms) for the shares of a new holding company; he distributed the rest of the bonds and shares of the holding company to an eager investing public; and then he often so manipulated these shares on the stock exchanges as to reap fortunes for all those on the inside, including himself (for generally the promoter was assigned a goodly portion of the stock of the holding company for his services in bringing about the alliance).

Many of the promoters had no special knowledge of the industries in which they intervened as matchmakers. A man might bring together a group of steel companies in January, a group of woolen companies in August, and a group of match companies in December. What he needed was not specialized knowledge, but persuasive salesmanship, coupled with the ability to command the millions and the investment-sales machinery of a large banking house, and to command also the services of astute corporation lawyers and stock-market operators. Having launched his holding company, pocketed his stock, and arranged to distribute part or all of it through the stock market, the promoter might pass on to fresh woods and pastures new.

What made these enterprises vastly profitable to the promoters and also to the owners of the various companies which were combined was the lavish way in which it was possible to do the financing. Obviously, the owners of successful businesses would not sell out unless they received a very handsome price. But they need not be paid this price in cash; they could be paid it in stock of the new holding company. Common stock was issued in huge quantities and exchanged on inflated terms. For instance, when the Consolidated Steel and Wire Company (itself a combination of steel companies) was taken over by the American Steel and Wire Company of Illinois, the holder of a single hundred-dollar share of Consolidated Steel was handed $175 worth of preferred stock and $175 worth of common stock of the new company—a total of $350 worth; and when the new company in its turn was taken over by a yet larger combination, the American Steel and Wire Company of New Jersey, the stockholder received (for these same shares) $175 worth of preferred and $315 worth of common in the New Jersey concern. His hundred-dollar certificate had in a brief space of time been converted by the legerdemain of the promoter into certificates of a face value of four hundred and ninety dollars!

Now obviously there must have been a joker in such a deal, and there was. It lay in the nature of the "face value" of the certificates. Logically it should have made no difference whatever whether a man held "one hundred dollars' worth" of stock or "four hundred and ninety dollars' worth" of stock, provided they represented the same proportionate share in the earnings of the industry. Money is not thus manufactured out of thin air—at least in the realm of logic. But in point of fact the cash gain could be made actual and substantial. For the new combination *might* be able to earn enough, through the economies and the bargaining power which it was able to bring to its members, to make real the promise implied in that optimistic face value; at any rate, there was always the hope that it might, and at certain rosy seasons hope can be sold for cash in the speculative markets; and anyhow, to a large investing public the phrase "$100 par value" on a certificate meant something a good deal more solid than pure fancy. In the realm of fact, you could sell $490 worth of shares for a good deal more than you could sell a single $100 share. And so the certificates were lavishly printed and handed about, and in due course quantities of them were sold on the exchanges, and the promoter and the other participants cleaned up.

The process of thus "watering" stock was by no means new, of course. It had got its name two generations before. As a young cattle drover, Daniel Drew had been accustomed to give his cattle insufficient water on the way from upper New York State down to the City of New York, and then, just before the metropolitan purchasing agents were to meet him in Harlem to weigh the cattle and pay for them by weight, Drew had led the beasts to the trough and let them drink their fill—and had profited accordingly in the purchase price. Later, when as a notorious speculator and railroad manipulator Drew discovered how much money could be made by printing extra stock and selling it, he wittily called this process "watering the stock." But though the process was an old one, the formation of holding companies in the late nineties offered the vastest opportunity to take advantage of it yet known—and this time the methods used were perfectly legal. The ultimate value of such stock was, of course, highly problematical; suffice it to say here that a gain in efficiency of operation and a period of prosperity will soak up a great deal of water, or for a time appear to; and that at the turn of the century there were plenty of hopeful buyers ready to take surplus stock off the promoters' hands.

So rapidly did the promoters work that by 1900 the census showed that there were no less than 185 industrial combinations in existence, with a total capitalization of three billion dollars—one-third of all the capital invested in manufacturing enterprises in the whole country. Charles R. Flint, the "father of the trusts"; Judge William H. Moore and his brother James; H. H. Rogers, William Rockefeller, and other members of the Standard Oil group of millionaires, behind whom stood James Stillman with the additional funds of the National City Bank of New York; Elkins, Widener, and other combiners of gas and electric light companies; "Bet-a-Million" Gates, Reid, Morse, Addicks—these were only a few of the more conspicuous and daring promoters. And Pierpont Morgan himself, the monarch of Wall Street, took a conspicuous part in the movement, putting the rich resources of his private banking house and the bulwark of his prestige behind a number of ambitious combinations.

The center of gravity of American industrial control was moving, and the direction of its motion was immensely significant. It was moving toward Wall Street. The reins which guided the great industries of the country were gradually being taken into the hands of bankers and financiers who could finance these immense holding-company operations and distribute stock by the millions of shares.

From wide-eyed young bank clerks in Wall Street the miracle-workers of this new dispensation commanded an awed respect like that which the new-era financiers of 1929 were to command a generation later. Meanwhile the outside public looked on in mingled admiration and alarm and bewilderment. They feared the power which was now concentrating in downtown New York and the other financial centers of the country, they watched with dismay the inroads being made on the domain of free competition, and yet the processes of change were so multiple, so obscure, and so baffling that they did not know what to do.

§ 4

The epidemic of promotion and consolidation struck
the vast steel industry in 1898, the year of the Spanish
War. John W. Gates, a jovial buccaneer of finance with
the confidence and daring of a born gambler, brought together a quantity of wire and nail companies in the
American Steel and Wire Company of New Jersey. Gates
and Morgan arranged another big combination, the Federal Steel Company. Morgan arranged two more without
Gates's intermediation, the National Tube Company and
the American Bridge Company. And Judge William H.
Moore and his brother, who as promoters roved at large
from the biscuit industry to the steel industry and back
to the chewing-gum industry, formed a whole fleet of
combinations in steel—the American Tin Plate Company, the American Steel Hoop Company, the American
Sheet Steel Company, and the National Steel Company.

It seems incredible that within the space of hardly
more than two years the investing and speculative public
should have been able to ingest the flood of securities resulting from this mania of combination and recapitaliza-
tion; and to tell the truth, there were moments when the
investors seemed to gag a little. But by the summer of
1900 a considerable part of the huge and hitherto disorganized steel industry was mobilized into these eight
new groups.

Yet there was one glaring exception to the rule of
combination, one company outside the fold which was
more powerful than any company or group of companies
within it. It was headed by Andrew Carnegie, the sharp-
eyed little Scotchman who had been born in a weaver's
cottage at Dunfermline, had begun his business life as a
bobbin-boy in a Pittsburgh cotton mill, and had become

the ablest steel manufacturer and the richest man in the world. Carnegie hated Wall Street methods, hated stock-watering; he set the par value of the shares of his company at a thousand dollars in order that they would not be dealt in on the Stock Exchange, and that his partners might not be working with an uneasy eye on the rise and fall of security prices. The Henry Ford of his day, Carnegie believed in competition, not combination; and when he competed he fought to a finish and won. For he was a brilliant judge of business capacity, he surrounded himself with able technicians, and he conducted his battles for markets with brilliant strategy and without compunction.

The Carnegie Steel Company had made for itself an impregnable position in the industry. Through the Oliver Iron Mining Company it controlled its own mines in the rich Mesabi Range; through H. C. Frick's coke company it controlled the coke that it needed; and it also controlled steamships and railroads. Furthermore it dominated the production of crude steel. The sprawling aggregations of steel companies which had been brought together by Gates and Morgan and the Moores were nearly all engaged in the making of finished products—rails, beams, steel plate, wire, and what not. For the crude steel which served as the raw material for their operations, they depended upon a department of the industry in which the little Scotchman from Pittsburgh was supreme. That fact gave him a huge advantage in competition with them. Carnegie's mills were amazingly efficient; if, when a new one was being built, some new way of cutting costs of production was pointed out to him, he was quite ready to tear the mill down and rebuild it; he could undersell his competitors; and having no army of holders of watered stock to worry about, he stood quite ready to forego present profits in a price-war if one should be declared.

In the summer of 1900 the battle between Carnegie and the new combinations in the steel industry was definitely joined. Gates and Moore and the other leading spirits in the new steel combinations decided that they could no longer tolerate the sort of venomous competition which Carnegie had been giving them, and threatened to produce their own crude steel.

To Carnegie this threat was a declaration of war. When it was made he was idling at Skibo Castle in Scotland, enjoying one of those extensive leisure periods of his which are so seldom mentioned by the exponents of success through hard work. At once he prepared his forces for action. He wrote to young Schwab, his chief executive, quoting Richelieu's advice: "First, all means to conciliate; failing that, all means to crush." He authorized Schwab to build a new twelve-million-dollar tube plant at Conneaut on Lake Erie—a direct challenge to Morgan's National Tube Company. The situation at Conneaut was ideal for a huge steel plant; much too ideal for the peace of mind of Carnegie's industrial rivals. He instructed Schwab to acquire further land at Conneaut on which he might build huge factories for other finishing works—factories which would directly compete with his adversaries. "No use going half way across a stream," he advised his associates; "should aim at finished articles only."

Nor was this all. Feeling that the freight rates charged by the Pennsylvania Railroad for carrying his steel to the seaboard were unduly high, Carnegie gave aid and comfort to George Gould, who had bought control of the Western Maryland Railroad and needed only to build 157 miles of track, from Pittsburgh to Cumberland in

Maryland, to have an alternative route to the sea which Carnegie would patronize.

Carnegie possessed all the implements for conquest. Clearly he meant to fight, even if fighting meant driving his competitors to the wall. As reports of his huge plans began slowly to leak out, there was consternation among the hosts of Moore and Gates and Morgan. The prospect which confronted them was formidable.

There was, however, another element in the situation to be taken into account. Carnegie had long wanted to retire. More than thirty years before, at the age of thirty-three, he had written a memorandum, carefully kept thereafter, in which he declared his intention of not making too much money. "The amassing of wealth," he had written, "is one of the worst species of idolatry, no idol more debasing. To continue much longer overwhelmed by business cares and with most of my thoughts wholly upon the way to make more money in the shortest time, must degrade me beyond hope of permanent recovery." He had continued, it is true, to amass wealth, contenting himself, as time went on, with taking six months of vacation each year and thereby perhaps escaping in some measure the degradation which he had feared; but always he had looked forward to the day when he might leave business forever and devote himself to giving away what he had amassed—running the money-making machine in reverse, as it were. He was now approaching his sixty-fifth birthday. His associates knew well that he was thinking of retiring. His plans for a mighty price war in the industry were probably thus made with a double purpose, which may be expressed in a paraphrase of the text from Richelieu which he had used as his call to battle: First, by all means to frighten his competitors into buying him out; failing that, by all means to crush them.

What were the competitors to do? Mobilize a combina-

tion large enough to defeat Carnegie? Impossible: even
if their scattered forces could be assembled, he would still
occupy a very strong position; he would still have his grip
on the production of crude steel. In the words of William C. Temple, a steel manufacturer, "The cooks who
were preparing this meal . . . found that they had prepared and were ready to bake the finest plum pudding
ever concocted financially, but that Mr. Carnegie had all
the plums." Well then, could they buy out Carnegie?
But a combination of steel companies which would include Carnegie would have to be so enormous that one
could hardly contemplate it seriously. Only one man
could conceivably command the mobile capital, the prestige, and the influence with banks and investment houses
to attempt to create such a combination—Pierpont Morgan; and Morgan would not venture it. Gary suggested
it to him but received no encouragement. "I would not
think of it," said Morgan. "I don't believe I could raise
the money." And there the matter lay, while Schwab and
shrewd old Andy studied the blueprints for the Conneaut
mills.

Election Day, 1900, came and went. McKinley and
Mark Hanna and expansion won; Bryan was submerged
again. Big business rejoiced; for four years more it would
be able to feast on the fat of the land. Sound money, a
high tariff, a conservative Senate under Mark Hanna's
influence, and an Attorney General who would regard
business combinations with a near-sighted eye: what
more could one want?

The stock market leaped with delight; the total sales
for the day after Election Day of 1900 were 1,418,735
shares, the second largest in the history of the New York
Stock Exchange. A front-page news story in the conservative *New York Tribune* of November 8, 1900, began its
account of the excitement in Wall Street with a paean of

triumph: "Upon the issue of the national election of Tuesday, it was everywhere recognized by thinking men, depended the restoration of business confidence, the existence of which is a vital element of commercial and industrial activity and enterprise, and the integrity of which was so desperately assailed and so gravely impaired by the nomination of William J. Bryan at Kansas City. That confidence has now been re-established" . . . The weather-vanes of politics took notice of the direction in which the winds of opinion were so surely blowing. Even Governor Theodore Roosevelt of New York, finishing out his term at Albany and preparing to endure four years of dreadful inactivity in the Vice-Presidency to which he had just been elected, bent to the prevailing wind: the future champion of trust-busting actually gave a dinner to Pierpont Morgan, a dinner which, as he confided to Root, represented "an effort on my part to become a conservative man in touch with the influential classes."

It was just at this juncture—as the warm sun of political approval promised to shine steadily upon the influential classes, and as Carnegie threatened to plunge the steel industry into virtual civil war—that J. Edward Simmons and Charles Stewart Smith invited Charles M. Schwab, Carnegie's right-hand man, to be their guest of honor at dinner at the University Club.

§ 5

It has been assumed by many people that Carnegie engineered the Schwab dinner of December 12, 1900, as a Machiavellian means of bringing Morgan and Schwab together for negotiation; but such an assumption perhaps gives too much credit to Carnegie's accuracy of foresight and too little credit to chance. The evidence is simply

that Simmons and Smith and a party of other New Yorkers had been visiting Pittsburgh and had been lavishly
entertained there by Schwab, and that they wished to
return the compliment. But can it be doubted that
Schwab saw a great opportunity before him when he
found that Morgan was to be at the dinner?

The livery-stable keeper's son had come far since the
days when he had used to bring the horse and wagon
round to the Carnegies' cottage of a summer afternoon.
Step by step young Schwab had risen in the steel business,
and now at the age of thirty-eight he was president of
Carnegie's company—and here were eighty of the leading
financiers of New York gathered to do him honor, and
at his right hand sat Morgan himself, the titan of American finance—massive, jovial, friendly, alert to hear him
speak.

Schwab spoke. The voice that Carnegie had delighted
to hear in the summer evening at Cresson Springs, when
the stableman's son had sung for the guests on the Carnegies' porch, could be eloquent in speech as well as in
song, and it was eloquent now. Schwab had intended to
speak for only a few minutes, but he was on his feet for
an hour; and presently it appeared that his theme was to
be a bold one, intended primarily for the ear of the man
beside him.

Schwab talked of the immense future in world trade
which lay before the steel industry of America—if only it
were properly organized and operated. He made it clear
that proper organization and operation implied three
things: first, specialization—one mill or group of mills
concentrating on a single product such as rails, another
mill or group of mills concentrating on another single
product; second, integration—the control by a single authority of all the processes of steel-making from the mining of the ore down to the completion of the finished

product; and third, the translation of economy in operation into lower prices. The Carnegie company had gone far in achieving economies, he explained, but only a steel company larger by far than Carnegie's could achieve the necessary integration and thus capture the world trade which was waiting for it. Meanwhile the practice of throttling competition by pools and trade agreements and little monopolies and then jacking up prices to win a quick and easy profit was ruining the chances for American supremacy in steel. The day for that sort of thing was past, Schwab insisted. A huge concern such as he proposed would not descend to such methods. It would enforce not higher prices but low ones, for the sake of expanding its markets at home and abroad.

Morgan listened hard, his expression unmoved, his piercing eyes fixed upon his plate, as Schwab rebuked by implication the methods of Gates and the Moores and the other promoters in the steel industry who had doubled and tripled their prices as soon as their monopolistic holding-company control permitted them to. Morgan himself had countenanced such methods; the rebuke was aimed at him too. He was a man capable of volcanic anger, but he showed no anger now. "After the cheers had subsided he took Schwab by the arm and led him to a corner." (I quote from Burton J. Hendrick's excellent biography of Carnegie.) "For half an hour the two men engaged in intimate conversation. The banker had a hundred questions to ask, to which Schwab replied with terseness and rapidity. The talk ended, Morgan left for his home and Schwab took the midnight train for Pittsburgh. The germ that resulted in the world's largest corporation had been implanted."

During the next few days Morgan's mind was full of what Schwab had said. He kept speaking of it to his partners. The reason why he was so deeply impressed may easily be surmised. It was not merely that the launching of a super-corporation in steel would be the most ambitious financial project which he or any other American banker had ever undertaken, and, if successful, one of the most profitable. Morgan was a promoter, it was true, who could speak the language of the Gateses and Moores and Rogerses, but he was much more than this. He could take a large view. In his re-organization of railroads and his mediation between the conflicting interest; of railroad barons, he had taken his profits in millions with the best of them, but always he had sought harmony, conciliation in the interest of all, coördination of competing railroads into coherent regional patterns. This passion of his for order, for the smooth-running economic machine, was ready-made for the acceptance of what Schwab had to suggest. For Schwab, with his talk of specialization, integration, and price reduction, was expounding the philosophy of orderly mass production: the notion of a single economic unit reaching from the raw material all the way to the finished product; the notion of the assembly line; the notion of low cost, low prices, and profits through vastly increased sales. It was in essence what we have come to call the Ford idea—though Henry Ford was then merely the chief engineer of the feeble Detroit Automobile Company, and the largest automobile company in the United States was turning out only four hundred cars a year.

Furthermore, Schwab's talk of the capture of foreign markets, though one might dismiss it as merely a sample of the resounding expansion talk of the moment, was well devised to appeal to Morgan. For Morgan could think in international terms. His whole training as the son of an American banker in London, as a dealer in foreign exchange, as a distributor of American securities in Europe and European securities in America, prepared him to see American industries in terms of the trade of the world. Criticize Schwab's speech though one may as chiefly a spread-eagle appeal to the American business man's lust for size, for power, and for profit, nevertheless it looked toward a sort of industrial combination more disciplined than the gross money-making machines which the incorporation-mill at Trenton was turning out by the score; and it is only reasonable to assume that Morgan, who was not without public spirit, felt the difference.

Morgan's intuition told him that Schwab was right, that a great steel combination such as had seemed impossible a few weeks before was possible after all, that this moment of supreme business confidence was the moment to move; and that the first requirement was to eliminate from the industry Schwab's own chief—to buy out Andrew Carnegie.

After a few days of thought Morgan called in John W. Gates, a sharp customer but a necessary ally and a worldly-wise negotiator. How should one approach Carnegie? he asked Gates. "Through Schwab," Gates instructed him; Schwab was Carnegie's white-headed boy, the one man who had real influence with the old Scotchman. Get Schwab to come to New York and see me, said Morgan.

Out in Pittsburgh Schwab received Gates's long-distance call with elation. Yet he realized that his situation was equivocal. What would old Andy say if he discovered that his subordinate had been negotiating with Morgan? He had best be a little careful. So he suggested an "accidental" meeting with Morgan. Presently Gates gave him his instructions. If Schwab chanced to be at the Bellevue Hotel in Philadelphia the next day, Morgan would be there too.

Fortified with facts and figures, Schwab packed his bag and took the night train from Pittsburgh to Philadelphia. He went to the Bellevue. No sign of Morgan. But a telephone call came through. It was Gates again. Morgan had a cold, it was snowing in New York, and the doctor wouldn't let Morgan go out. Now that Schwab had come this far, couldn't he continue to New York and talk with Morgan at his home? Schwab duly went to New York, dined with Gates at the Manhattan Club, and proceeded with him at nine o'clock in the evening to the big brownstone house at the corner of Madison Avenue and Thirty-sixth Street.

Four men conferred that night in the library of Pierpont Morgan's home. Their diversity was suggestive of the diversity of the human elements in the overlordship of industry. Morgan had called in to support him a partner, Robert Bacon. One of the handsomest Americans of his day, Bacon was a gentleman of substance and cultivation and charm, an Overseer of Harvard University, a future Secretary of State and Ambassador to France: a fine though not brilliant product of the tradition which sent into Wall Street a large proportion of the well-born, personable young college graduates of each generation.

Schwab stood for something quite different. He was self-made. A congenital optimist, an orator, a hearty young man who called hundreds of his employees by their first names, he was nevertheless a hard-headed man at figures and an authority on the technical processes of steelmaking. His friendliness and his eloquence were dedicated to salesmanship. He might be roughly classified as a Babbitt of the 1900 model: a representative of that zeal for efficiency, that pushfulness, that limited but intense vision, which led men to build bigger and bigger businesses as if under some blind inner compulsion.

John W. Gates represented still another influence in the industrial world of the day—that of the gambler. He too was self-made; he had begun life in poverty in an Illinois village. His rise to success in the barbed-wire business had been the result of aggressiveness, shrewdness, and unscrupulousness. Gates was always gambling: once he was said to have spent a morning on a railroad train betting with an associate on the raindrops coursing down the sooty window of the car—at a thousand dollars a race; on another occasion he was said to have lost a quarter of a million dollars in a prolonged poker game at the Waldorf-Astoria with a group of other Wall Street plungers. He was a good fellow and a remorseless trader: the sort of man who will sit up all night at a friend's bedside and then destroy the man financially the next day. Business, to him, was a poker game in which any sort of trick was permissible—if you could get away with it. He had built up his huge combination of wire companies by stock-watering and manipulation, and only a few months before the conference at Pierpont Morgan's he had been charged with closing thirteen wire mills and issuing pessimistic statements about the steel business in order to clean up on a short sale in the stock of his own company. Gates represented the purely predatory influence which was dominant in many consolidations of the day.

Finally, there was Morgan, an aristocrat like Bacon, an optimist like Schwab, a man who distrusted Gates yet made use of his practical knowledge of the technique of promotion: a man who combined some of the qualities of each of the other men and yet outmastered all of them: an embodiment of sheer force, a man of whom the financial and industrial community stood in awe, partly because of the ramifying power of his banking house, partly because they felt him and his word to be solid as a rock, partly because of the overwhelming authority that expressed itself in his few gruff words, his swift and far-reaching decisions, his piercing eyes. The other men sitting in his library that night represented types; Morgan was unique.

Hour after hour the men talked. Schwab had a list of all the companies which might be brought into the big combination; he explained why this one was needed and why that one was not; he specified purchase prices; Morgan plied him with incessant questions, battered the project into practical financial shape as the talk progressed. Finally the conference ended.

"The sun was now streaming into the library windows," writes Hendrick in his life of Carnegie. . . . "Morgan brought matters to a close by rising.

" 'Well,' he said to Schwab, 'if Andy wants to sell, I'll buy. Go and find his price.' "

One may imagine Schwab's delight as he walked out into Madison Avenue that early winter morning. The great project had gained Morgan's approval, almost precisely as he had laid it out. But an obstacle still remained —Carnegie. What if Andy should have changed his mind? The next step required caution.

Schwab did a shrewd thing. He consulted Mrs. Carnegie.

She advised him to invite Andy to play golf and to break the news to him after the game. Schwab did so. The two men made the frosty round of the St. Andrews links in the Westchester hills, and then Schwab told his story.

The little white-bearded Scotchman was at first cast into gloom at the prospect of retirement. For thirty years he had planned to retire, but now that the gates of a financial Valhalla stood open before him, he saw them with a heavy heart, for he loved the fight. But he did not say no. He asked only to be given a little time to think the proposal over. Schwab knew then that he had won.

The next day Carnegie discussed the sale again with Schwab, wrote his price—expressed in terms of exchange of Carnegie stocks and bonds for securities of the new corporation—in pencil on a slip of paper, and gave it to Schwab. Schwab took the paper down to Wall Street and showed it to Morgan. One glance, and Morgan said, "I accept," and the thing was done.

So completely informal were the negotiations, in fact, that it was not until weeks later, after the public announcement of the formation of the Steel Corporation had been made, that Morgan suddenly realized that he did not have Carnegie's acceptance in writing—that technically he had sold the Carnegie Company short—and hurriedly sent his lawyer to Carnegie to sign a paper concluding the deal.

§ 6

The months of January and February, 1901, went by, and not until the latter part of February did the public have an inkling of what was afoot. Conferences were being held daily at the Morgan offices, where Judge Gary, of the Federal Steel Company, installed as Morgan's trusted agent, was bringing into line the other big steel companies which were needed for the merger.

One by one they came in. Gates, of course, tried at the last moment to hold out for an impossible price, and capitulated only when Morgan came into the room where Gates and his friends had been bargaining with Gary for hours, and said sternly, "I am going to leave this building in ten minutes. If by that time you have not accepted our offer, the matter will be closed. We will build our own wire plant." At this threat Gates accepted Morgan's terms; an acceptance which so delighted Morgan that—as Gary later told his biographer—the banker went home as exuberantly as "a boy going home from a football game."

At last the negotiations were completed, and the

United States Steel Corporation became a reality. On the third of March, 1901, as the crowds were gathering in Washington for the triumphant inauguration of Mc-Kinley and Roosevelt, there appeared in the papers an advertisement addressed to the stockholders of Federal Steel, National Steel, National Tube, American Steel and Wire of New Jersey, American Tin Plate, American Steel Hoop, and American Sheet Steel, informing them that the United States Steel Corporation had been "organized under the laws of the State of New Jersey, with power, among other things, to acquire the outstanding preferred stocks and common stocks of the companies above named, and the outstanding bonds and stocks of the Carnegie Company."

The biggest of all giant holding companies had been born. Carnegie was out of the steel industry. Gates was on his way out—for Morgan sternly refused to make him a director of the Steel Corporation. Hundreds of steel companies—the Tin Plate group alone was a combination of 265 plants—were being brought under a single control; the fate of 168,000 steel workers, the production of half the steel used in the United States, now hung on the decisions of one man.

§ 7

The distribution of the shares of the new corporation to those who had joined forces in it was done on a lavish scale. Carnegie, distrustful as ever of Wall Street methods and watered stock, insisted upon being paid in bonds, but the shareholders of the other constituent companies were paid for their holdings in these companies by being assigned preferred stock and common stock in United States Steel, and the terms of some of the various agreements rewarded them very generously for coming into the alliance.

A stockholder in one of the Moore concerns, for example, received $145 worth (par value) of Steel Corporation stock for each $100 worth (par value) of common stock in the original company. A man who in 1897 had owned a $100 certificate of stock in the Consolidated Steel Company, and, as we have already seen, had subsequently exchanged it for stock to the par value of $490 in the American Steel and Wire Company of New Jersey, now found that he possessed, in Steel Corporation stock, certificates of a par value not of $100 or even $490, but of $564.37.

It took an enormous amount of stock to meet the requirements of the agreements which Morgan had made with the already heavily capitalized components in his scheme. When two more big companies had been added to the collection—Morgan's American Bridge Company and John D. Rockefeller's Lake Superior Consolidated Iron Mines—and when the Morgan syndicate had taken for its services a block of stock with a par value of nearly one hundred and thirty millions, the capitalization of this greatest corporate monster in history reached breathtaking dimensions. It had underlying and miscellaneous obligations to meet of 81 millions; it issued 303 millions in corporate bonds, all of which went to the owners of the Carnegie properties and about two-thirds of which went to wily old Andrew himself; and it issued also no less than 510 millions in preferred stock and 508 millions in common stock, making its total capitalization some 1402 millions—over a billion and a third of dollars!

No wonder the public gasped. No such immense financial operation had ever before been witnessed.

How much of this immense figure represented the actual value of the steel factories and other properties

taken over by United States Steel? Ten years later the
Commissioner of Corporations issued a report in which
this question was very carefully answered. His investigators attempted to arrive at the real value of the Steel
Corporation investment in three ways. First, they traced
back the financial history of the constituent companies
in the effort to find out what they represented in money
actually invested, and arrived at a figure of 676 millions.
Second, they added together the market values of the constituents' shares and arrived at 793 millions. Third, they
made detailed estimates of the physical value of the
various properties and arrived at 682 millions. Striking
a rough average of these figures, the Commissioner decided that the fair market value of the properties of the
Steel Corporation in 1901 was in the neighborhood of
700 millions. And the bonds and stock issued amounted
to 1402 millions!

According to these figures, the bonds and preferred
stock alone more than covered the total value of the
properties; all the common stock, and for that matter
a part of the preferred stock, was sheer water—in other
words, a huge collection of paper certificates representing not actual property but the hope of rewards through
huge profits. The common stock might thus be regarded
as a bonus, thrown in to sweeten the bargains with the
Gateses and Moores and their allies and the other stockholders and promoters who had made the organization
of the Steel Corporation possible.

This estimate of value by the Commissioner of Corporations was made, however, as his report explicitly
stated, without giving consideration to any "merger,
integration or monopolistic factors arising from the combination of 1901." In other words, it took no account of
the fact that by combining, these innumerable steel companies were able to operate more effectively, more eco-

nomically, and with less fear of competition than before: that their earning power was immensely enhanced. The orthodox Wall Street view of the capitalization of the Steel Corporation was that these factors of efficiency and partial monopoly must be taken into account; that if a combination of factories could earn twice as much as the factories could earn separately, they were of course worth twice as much; that their owners deserved the increased income which resulted from their ingenuity and far-sightedness in putting the factories together; and that if the stock certificates which they received represented a capital sum twice as big as before, these certificates there-fore represented not watered value but real value—a legitimate payment.

As to the Steel Corporation, the Wall Street argument was later supported by the fact that the Corporation was actually able to earn a return upon its common stock: that it not only paid a dividend of four dollars a share in its very first year, with nearly forty-four millions to spare, but was able to continue its dividends with few inter-ruptions for a long time thereafter. (There was one pro-longed and frightening interruption in the Corporation's early years.) If the proof of a pudding is in the eating, ran the Wall Street argument, then in this case the size of the common stock issue was ultimately justified.

The question at issue is a large one; it has been de-bated hundreds of times with regard to dozens of incor-porations for over a generation, for the Steel Corporation pattern of financing was followed again and again, with varying results, from that day on. Men and women will doubtless arrive at their own answers in accordance with their social convictions and prejudices. One aspect of the matter, however, may be suggested here. What made these vast combinations possible and profitable? Not simply the wisdom or daring of their owners and pro-

moters, but also a number of other factors: the spread
of population, the growth of cities and general urbanization of American life, the influx of immigration, the new
efficiency of communication, the engineering skill which
went into the design of new machinery, the labor of hundreds of thousands of workers: in short, the growth of
the country and the advance of the machine age. If at
one fell swoop a group of promoters and stockholders
took advantage of these factors to consolidate a number
of companies, were all—or nearly all—of the resulting
profits legitimately theirs? And if not, was it quite proper
so to increase the capitalization of the new company that
it would be obliged to hand out to its owners and promoters—or to those who had bought their shares—all or
nearly all of these possible profits, in order to justify its
financial set-up? In theory the advantages derived from
combination might have been distributed to labor in
higher wages or to the general public in the form of
lower prices; in practice they were almost completely
absorbed by capital—and to a large extent by the promoters—and the lavish issue of stocks was the method
through which this was done.

In these latter days, when a large public has learned
to think in terms of national purchasing power, the question whether such devices are legitimate clamors for answer; but in 1901 the end results of the financial methods
which were illustrated in the formation of the Steel Corporation, and were given sanction and prestige by its
success, were not visible. The outburst of public dismay
which greeted the announcement of the formation of the
Steel Corporation was not directed in any large degree
at the financial methods by which the operation made
money for those on the inside. An outburst there was,
not only in the United States but abroad, but what
frightened the general public was mostly the sheer size

of the new concern, the thought of the concentration of power which it involved, the thought of what such power might do to snuff the little business concern out of existence, the thought that Pierpont Morgan might gradually take all American industry within his ample grasp.

The London correspondent of the *New York Tribune* cabled that the British mercantile community was "appalled by the magnitude of the American Steel combination headed by J. P. Morgan." President Hadley of Yale, in an address shortly after the Morgan announcement, said that if trusts were not "regulated by public sentiment," the country could expect "an emperor in Washington within twenty-five years." That aptest commentator of the day, Finley Peter Dunne's "Mr. Dooley," described Morgan as now being able to say to one of his office boys, "Take some change out iv th' damper an' r-run out an' buy Europe f'r me." Other critics of the steel combination feared that labor would now learn a lesson from capital, organize and seize the power from capital, and plunge the country into socialism. But of intelligent criticism of the corporate mechanism and the way in which it distributed the financial gains from such a deal there was comparatively little.

Meanwhile, however, the gains were being made. James R. Keene, a stock-market operator of uncanny ability, was engaged to "make a market" in Steel Corporation stock on the Exchange, and presently, with the aid of his buying and selling, the shares were changing hands in large quantities—the preferred at prices ranging between ninety and a hundred dollars a share, and the common between forty and fifty dollars a share. Speculators leaped in to buy; investors followed, large and small; and presently the stock of the new concern was the center of a bull market of increasing proportions.

Into this frenzied market, in which—almost as in 1928

and 1929—clerks and shopkeepers were staking their savings, the millions of shares which had been handed out to the stockholders of the constituent companies and to the promoters and their associates began gradually to be fed. The stock was being "distributed" to the public, and the insiders were taking their profits—in hundreds of dollars, in thousands, and in millions. For example, you may recall that the Morgan syndicate had been paid for its services not in cash but in stock—a large block, amounting to nearly 1,300,000 shares. This stock had to be "distributed." The result of the distribution was a profit to the syndicate, over and above all expenses, of sixty-two and a half million dollars, of which the House of Morgan took as its own share considerably more than twelve and a half million.

Keene's manipulative operations were fulfilling the triple function of providing a steadying influence for the market price, of advertising Steel common on the ticker tape and in brokers' offices and on the financial pages and wherever speculators and investors gathered, and of providing plenty of buyers for those who had been allotted stock and wished to unload and gather in their cash.

Meanwhile, also, across the street from the humming Stock Exchange, Morgan, with the righteous Gary to assist him in matters of policy and the entranced Schwab to supervise the processes of steel-making in scores of mills, began to face the vast problem of making his enterprise actually succeed.

§ 8

It was a long time before Morgan and Gary succeeded in bringing into some sort of line the discordant methods and policies of all the companies now linked together under their suzerainty, or even the conflicting influences within the directorate itself. But a strike called by the Amalgamated union during the first precarious summer brought forth a resolution by the Board which prefigured the Corporation's attitude toward labor organizations for a generation to come: a resolution "that we are unalterably opposed to any extension of union labor and advise subsidiary companies to take a firm position when these questions come up, and say that they are not going to recognize it." Capital might combine; labor might not.

The relationship between the management and the workmen was destined to remain feudal. Whenever a Steel Corporation official thereafter found himself on the witness stand and the embarrassing matter of the twelve-hour day or the seven-day week was brought up, he always expressed acute distress at the fact that the Corporation had not yet succeeded in doing away with this barbarous condition and said that it was about to do so— but the years dragged on and the twelve-hour day and the seven-day week remained, to the disgrace of American industry. It must be admitted that the Steel Corporation maintained conditions no worse than its competitors and probably a little better; that the trend of wages was haltingly upward during the first decade of the Corporation's life; and that the labor policy of the Corporation was further mollified by such devices as a plan for the purchase of stock by employees on reasonable terms. The unsentimental essence of that policy, however, was: Pay what you have to pay in wages but keep absolute control in your own hands, and remember that profits come first.

As for the policy of the Corporation with regard to prices, there was at least a trend in the direction so rapturously pointed out by Schwab in his University Club speech. Previous consolidations in the steel industry had been followed by a gleeful marking up of prices; no such advance took place during the Steel Corporation's first year, and during the next decade prices in general moved somewhat downward. Bearing in mind the perpetual danger of prosecution under the Sherman Act, the company prudently refrained from overtly dictating prices to the rest of the industry. But it was noticeable from time to time that after Gary's lavish dinners to the steel producers of the country, prices throughout the industry had a curious way of moving in concert.

As to the ethics of corporate management, Gary's policy, fully backed by the omnipotent Morgan, was strict. To the amazement of plungers on the Board of Directors such as H. H. Rogers, who had been accustomed to make good use on the Stock Exchange of advance inside information on earnings and dividend decisions, Gary insisted on keeping all information of this sort from the directors of the Steel Corporation until the regular directors' meetings, on holding these meetings after the stock market had closed for the day, and on giving the information immediately to the press. So opposed was Gary, in fact, to the whole atmosphere of private speculation which surrounded the direction of corporations— and has surrounded it very often to this day—that he even lectured the members of the Board on one occasion on their lamentable custom of matching for the twenty-dollar directors' fees of absent members. It was not simply that Gary's Methodist soul revolted at gambling; he thought of the directors of corporations as trustees, and anything which detracted from the dignity of their fiduciary attitude offended him—as, he was well aware, it offended a suspicious public.

In short, the policy of the Steel Corporation, as time went on, was the result of a number of forces: the Morgan preference for discipline and restraint; the ethical severity of Gary, and his further insistence upon maintaining an

appearance of virtue even where virtue itself was too
much to expect of greedy men; the accepted American
doctrine that the end and justification of business was
profit, and the more of it the better; and the Bourbonism
of Wall Street's attitude toward the laboring classes. The
gulf between capital, as represented by boards of directors sitting in the splendid comfort of New York offices,
and labor, as represented by Polacks and Hunkies slaving
twelve hours a day in roaring mills, was widening, and
the Corporation helped to widen it. But on the other
hand the Gary-Morgan attitude of restraint was an un-
doubted influence against irresponsible corporate plundering. It sobered and thus prolonged the new era of industrial concentration.

§ 9

To the men at the blast-furnaces of Pittsburgh the
coming of the Steel Corporation on April first, 1901,
meant no immediate change; it is probable that many
of them were quite unaware that they now had new
masters. But with the men at the top it was quite different.

Old Andrew Carnegie, his long dream now realized,
sailed for the Riviera even before the Corporation began
operations. His specially constructed vault in Hoboken
now held something like three hundred million dollars
in bonds. It was his delight to live in baronial splendor
at Skibo on the coast of his beloved Scotland, where he
had built a castle with medieval battlements, Pittsburgh
steel girders, Westinghouse dynamos, and a covered
swimming-pool with artificially heated water; to have
a bagpiper wake him and his guests at eight in the morning by skirling from a far distance up to the great house
and around it; to have an organist play for him through-

out the breakfast hour; to construct a miniature water-fall to tinkle outside his bedroom window. At this castle —in some respects so much like a small boy's dream come true—Carnegie entertained the mighty of the earth, states-men, British noblemen, distinguished men of letters; and they came gladly, for their host was not merely a man of millions but a man also of broad understanding and gay humor. But the turrets of Skibo and the fine yacht and the massive house at Fifth Avenue and Ninety-first Street, New York, where Carnegie spent his winters, took only a trifling part of his great fortune. Years before, he had resolved to give away most of what he had earned; and this he now did with unexampled thoroughness and, on the whole, with remarkable wisdom—all the time reveling in the applause which greeted his successive benefactions.

When Carnegie died in 1919 it was found that he had given away nine-tenths of his colossal fortune. An extra-ordinary creature, this little rosy old man, twinkling about his vast Scottish demesne, and giving away with such glee and such discretion the fruits of a lifetime of completely merciless competitive acquisition. Could such acquisition and such generosity have been combined in any one man in any other era of the world's history?

At an extreme from Carnegie stood Gates. First and last a gambler, he continued to plunge in and out of the speculative markets of Wall Street and in and out of the managements of railroads and industrial corporations, fighting for mastery, hating his opponents in the specula-tive game with a rousing hate; sitting by the hour at a bridge table conveniently near the Waldorf-Astoria bar, and playing with such abandon that the story is told of a young man who found himself in a game with Gates, heard with some trepidation that the stakes were "ten a point," thought this meant ten cents, and turned pale when he discovered the next day in his mail a check for thirty-three thousand dollars—his winnings. Gates conformed sufficiently to the millionaire pattern of the time to collect Corots and Meissoniers, but he gave away no libraries, endowed no observatories; with diamond studs in his shirt-front and three diamonds in each suspender buckle he flaunted himself in brokerage offices and at the Waldorf bar, winning fortunes and losing them.

More typical of his generation, perhaps, than either of these men in his disposition of his millions was Frick, who after being bought out of his share in the Carnegie steel business in 1900 divided his time of retirement in almost equal parts among his investments, his collection of Old Masters, and a spacious leisure in his palace on Fifth Avenue—a mile from Carnegie's—or at his ample country estate on the Massachusetts shore. It was Frick who threw a side-light on art-collecting with his reference to railroad securities as "the Rembrandts of investment."

Somewhat typical, also, was Schwab, who built himself a French chateau on Riverside Drive, and played on the great organ which he had built into it, and gave away millions, and speculated with other millions; and after he had slid out of the presidency of United States Steel, became the head of a company of his own, the Bethlehem, and grew into a somewhat heavier, somewhat more florid, somewhat less glowing orator at innumerable business men's banquets over a quarter of a century, until at last in the depression of the nineteen-thirties his easy optimism came to seem like the standard product of an age gone by.

Typical of one sort of new millionaire, perhaps, was a naïve Carnegie partner whose millions from the deal of 1901 so went to his head that when the Metropolitan Opera visited Pittsburgh he rose in his box during the intermission and in full view of the assembled elect of the city, graciously draped about his wife's neck a pearl necklace. Pearl necklaces, Rembrandts, pipe organs, vast residences with expensive lawns; membership in clubs whose exclusiveness was constantly subject to the pressure of new-found millions; invitations to Assemblies with gorgeous cotillions: appeals from universities and museums and hospitals for benefactions; the awe of the multitudes,—all these, in varying proportions, came to the beneficiaries of those exchanges of certificates of stock which accompanied the consolidation of American industry.

And Morgan?

He too was a princely giver, though not on Carnegie's scale; and a princely collector of recognized treasures of art, on a scale far larger than Frick's. Morgan bought medieval armor, Chinese porcelains, rare old books and manuscripts, tapestries, miniatures, jewels, and paintings, paintings, paintings, of every age and every school except his own age and the American school; and though he built no palace on Fifth Avenue, he was soon to build, next to his substantial brownstone house, a palace of white marble for his books and his masterpieces. But always he defied classification, this gruff man of heavy silences and sudden boyish humor and thundering authority: so American in his optimism, his rough practicality, his instinct for dealing with American business men; in his reserve, so like the English among whom he liked to live; in his lust for the collection of the treasures of the earth, so like a conquering Renaissance prince.

Morgan now carried a load of responsibility such as none of these other millionaires had ever carried. Already he had gained dominion over many railroads and industrial corporations and his influence was felt through a great network of banks, and now he had become also the power behind half the steel industry of the country. When he was asked in the Pujo inquiry whether he had named the Board of Directors of the Steel Corporation, he answered solidly, "I am willing to assume the final responsibility, if that will answer your question. . . . I say that whatever was done, if passing upon it and approving it is equivalent to making it, I did it." And again, when Samuel Untermyer asked him, "Is anybody nominated for it [the Board] against your protest?" he answered, "Not against my protest." Morgan had brought the Steel Corporation to birth, his House had made over twelve and a half millions fathering it, and he intended to stand by it.

Other consolidations almost as grandiose were being planned in Morgan's office, for now his position in the financial and industrial world was more mighty than ever. But in the meantime he must have rest. So in April, 1901, only a few weeks after Carnegie's sailing for the Riviera, Morgan also sailed—for a holiday at Aix-les-Bains, from which he was to be rudely jolted by a frontal attack from an unexpected quarter.

Chapter Two

THE HARRIMAN CHALLENGE

IN THE early spring of 1899, a small, unassuming-looking man with sharp eyes and a drooping mustache called upon Dr. C. Hart Merriam, the chief of the United States Biological Survey in Washington, and asked for his help in organizing a scientific expedition to Alaska. He said that his name was Harriman—E. H. Harriman—and that he was a railroad man. The name meant nothing to Doctor Merriam. After Harriman left, Merriam telephoned to a railroad official of his acquaintance to find out who his caller might be.

The subsequent story of the Harriman Alaska Expedition need not concern us here. What is noteworthy for us is that in 1899 a well-informed citizen had never heard of Harriman. Doctor Merriam's ignorance was by no means exceptional; at that moment the little giant of American railroading was virtually unknown outside of Wall Street and the railroad business. Yet within twenty-six months he was to engage in a financial adventure of unparalleled boldness which was to lead to a disastrous panic on the stock exchange, and within a few more years his power was to grow to such dimensions that men would be asking one another whether he would not soon control every railroad in the country.

Few Americans have risen so swiftly to dominion; and the manner in which Harriman rose was significant of the man, the country, and the time. Edward Henry Harriman came of a substantial New York family and had the aid of wealthy and influential friends in his early career, but his father, an Episcopal clergyman, was always hard pressed for money, and the boy Edward Henry not only did not go to college, but left school at fourteen to become a messenger for a firm of stockbrokers in Wall Street. He learned the business from the ground up, set up his own firm, speculated successfully, married the daughter of the president of a small railroad, and two years later went into railroading himself by the Wall Street entrance—by buying a small, run-down road, improving it, and selling it at a handsome profit. In 1883, at the age of forty-five, he became a director of the Illinois Central, and soon he was its vice-president, thus extending his knowledge of actual railroad operation. But until the eighteen-nineties Harriman was primarily known as a shrewd player of the financial game of buying low and selling high; a cool speculator, greedy for power; a sharp young man who belonged to fashionable clubs, had accumulated riches, liked to hunt and fish in the Adirondacks and race his fast trotters on the Speedway, exercised his generous instincts by organizing a boys' club in the slums, but showed no readily visible signs of economic statesmanship.

The history of American railroading during the years of unbridled national expansion between the Civil War and the eighteen-nineties had been magnificent and scandalous: magnificent in the bold vision of its promoters, in the engineering skill which threw lines of iron across the continent and through the snowy passes of the Rockies, in the irresistible conquest of district after district for an expanding civilization; scandalous in the sordid abuse of the privileges extended to the railroad barons by the federal government, in the corruption of state legislatures by tax-dodging railroad corporations, in the granting of secret rebates to favored industrial concerns, in the arbitrary raising of freight rates on short-haul traffic to enable the roads to set low rates on the long hauls where they faced fierce competition, and above all in the watering and manipulation of their securities. The railroads were then the largest economic units in the country, and as such were usually financed by bankers and capitalists in New York, Boston, and Philadelphia, who often knew little about the local problems of the farmers and homesteaders whom the roads served, and cared less. Some of the railroad barons, such as James J. Hill of the Great Northern, had a far-sighted sense of the opportunity for solid gain which lay in developing the communities dependent upon their lines; but for every Hill, great or small, there was a Jay Gould, buying roads, plundering them financially for the benefit of his own pocket, and then washing his hands of them; or a financial blackmailer like the promoters of the West Shore line, building roads parallel to existing lines for the sheer purpose of threatening them with ruin and being bought out at fancy prices.

Only the rapid growth of the country and the increasing efficiency of metal and steam had prevented recurrent disaster for the roads, for as a result of irresponsible absentee ownership and speculative plundering, by 1890 the railroad system of the country, by and large, was overbuilt and overcapitalized (and thus overloaded with debt). When the panic of 1893 dragged the country down into depression, the number and extent of railroad failures was dismaying. According to Alexander Dana Noyes, in the year 1894 at least 61 per cent of the outstanding shares of American railroads were receiving no dividend whatever, and 25 per cent of them represented bankrupt roads. In the West, where the iron horse had made its most splendid conquests, three great roads were in the hands of receivers: the Union Pacific, the Northern Pacific, and the Santa Fé.

It was at this moment that Harriman saw his opportunity. Morgan, banker for a number of the big roads, had been a member of the Brice committee that had tried to reorganize the Union Pacific and had given it up as a bad job. Jacob Schiff, the head of the smaller private banking house of Kuhn, Loeb & Co., took the task over, but he discovered that somebody in Wall Street—he could not make out who—was throwing obstacles in his way, arousing opposition to his plan, turning creditors of the road against it.

The story is that Schiff went to Morgan and asked him if he was responsible for the opposition. No, said Morgan; he was no longer interested in the Union Pacific; but he would find out who was making the trouble. Later he reported that it was "that little fellow Harriman." "You want to look out for him," said Morgan. Schiff saw Harriman, who blandly admitted that he had been throwing monkey wrenches into Schiff's machinery of reorganization because he intended to reorganize the Union Pacific himself. Ultimately a treaty was made: Schiff would go ahead without opposition from Harriman, and Harriman would have a place on the executive committee of the road when it was freed from bankruptcy.

There was nothing in this episode to indicate that Harriman, thus bludgeoning his way into authority, was anything more than a ruthless Wall Street operator. But when at the end of 1897 the reorganized Union Pacific began operations, Harriman disclosed another personality. His knowledge of railroading proved to be immense and practical, his judgment swift and sure, his sense of the possibilities of the Union Pacific bold and strategic. The road ran from Omaha across the Rocky Mountains to Ogden, Utah, connecting there by means of the Central Pacific and the Oregon Short Line with the principal cities of the Pacific Coast. Harriman saw that if it were equipped to handle heavy freight rapidly and economically, it might secure a great share of the traffic moving from coast to coast; and that with prosperity returning—as it already was—and the Far West growing, and trade with the Orient expanding, this traffic would gain in volume and importance. But the road, long bankrupt, was in very bad shape to take advantage of these opportunities. It must be completely modernized.

To decide what improvements were necessary, Harriman went on a long slow inspection tour of the line, in a private train pushed by a locomotive at the rear, with an observation platform out in front. Day after day, week after week, he sat on that platform with his subordinate officials.

One of the division superintendents, it is said, had been worried for years by the fact that on a certain curve a signal tower was hidden from the engineer's eye by a water tank. He had often recommended that the water tank be moved, but his pleas had been disregarded. When Harriman's train passed this point the little bespectacled man was talking about something else and apparently noticed nothing. When finally the special train pulled off on a siding and the company sat down to dinner, Harriman said nothing about the condition of the road until the meal was ended. Then he suggested to his officials that they come down to business, and at once began a detailed account of the changes needed in that section of the line—grades to be altered, curves to be straightened, rails to be replaced, and so on; and at the proper place in his account he said that the water tank which obstructed the view of the signal must be moved immediately.

This story is of a piece with Julius Kruttschnitt's account of a change which Harriman later suggested when inspecting the Southern Pacific. As he and Kruttschnitt were walking along the line he picked up a track bolt and asked why the bolt protruded a fraction of an inch beyond the nut. Kruttschnitt said there was no reason except that bolts were always made so. Harriman asked how many bolts there were to a mile of track and then did some rapid figuring. "If you can cut an ounce off from every bolt, you will save fifty million ounces of iron," said he, "and that is something worth while. Change your bolt standard." Nothing escaped the little man's observation—rails, ties, ballast, rolling stock, curves, grades, signals, even the condition of the boards on the station platforms; costs, rates, charges.

As a result of Harriman's inspection trip in 1898, he recommended the expenditure of some twenty-five millions of dollars on the rehabilitation of the Union Pacific, and presently a gigantic work of reconstruction was under way: grades were reduced to enable heavy trains to climb the Rockies, curves were smoothed out, new heavy steel rails and new ballast were provided. The mountains echoed with the roar of dynamite as cliffs were ripped away; the steam shovels puffed, tunnels were drilled through primitive granite, ravines were filled; one hundred and fifty miles of old track were abandoned in the process; it might almost be said that a new road was built.

Harriman's assurance in planning these vast changes was complete, and he took a huge zest in the work. A banker tells of going to the little giant's office in New York and finding him standing at a long table littered with blue-print maps of the Union Pacific lines. For half an hour Harriman talked about his project, and finally he turned to the banker and said with his caustic humor, "You see, what I want to do is to put the road in such shape that if I were to die and you succeeded me, not even *you* would be able to undo my work!" Harriman's biographer, George Kennan, tells of the surprise of Harriman's former associates at his new zeal. "Ned Harriman!" they would say. "Why, I knew him years ago as a little 'two dollar' broker. What should he know about practical railroading?" He knew so much about practical railroading that within a few years he had transformed the Union Pacific from a badly broken-down road into a splendidly profitable and useful property.

Let it not be thought that Harriman had entirely changed his spots. He could still suck a big profit out of a railroad. He was interested at this period in other properties than the Union Pacific; one of these was the Chicago and Alton. He was the leading member of a group which bought and refinanced this road in 1899. They gained control by buying nearly all the common stock of the road, partly reimbursed themselves by calmly declaring a dividend of thirty per cent, issued so many bonds and so much stock that the bonded indebtedness of the road was increased nearly seven-fold and its total capitalization was tripled, and sold these bonds and this stock to the public at a large profit to themselves; their total profit on the refinancing of the road has been estimated variously at from four and a half millions to twenty-three millions.

It must be added that under Harriman's brilliant management the Chicago and Alton did not fall down under the huge load of debt with which he had saddled it; that on the contrary, it did well so long as he was running it; and that its rates were not raised but on the average lowered. Nevertheless the refinancing operation was a perfect example of the way in which the reorganizers of a railroad could seize for themselves at one swoop a great sum of money earned not merely by their own astuteness and skill, but also by the growth of the country over a long period, the conservatism of their predecessors, and the labors of their engineers, executives, workmen, and customers, for many years past and to come. Clarence Barron quotes Judge Lovett of the Southern Pacific as saying that when you engage in this sort of operation "you are taking the company's credit and transferring it to your own pocket." The whole process was quite legal, a plausible justification could be found for every step in it, and the consciences of those who engaged in it could easily be salved by the fact that they did not seem to be taking money from anybody in particular; yet theft it morally was. The mountain of debt under which the railroads have struggled in recent years is in considerable degree a monument to such performances.

Harriman may thus be regarded as two men in one—a sharp financier on the make, and an extraordinary railroad builder. He was also a man of Napoleonic ambition: an ambition which in the spring of 1901 was to push him into shattering conflict with the forces of Pierpont Morgan.

§ 2

Of the railroads which ran east and west across the Rocky Mountains, linking the central part of the country with the Pacific Coast region, three immediately concern us now.

First, and farthest to the south of the three, was Harriman's Union Pacific, which as we have seen ran from Omaha to Ogden, Utah, connecting there with railroads extending to the Coast. The Union Pacific was backed financially by Kuhn, Loeb & Co.

Second, and considerably north of it, was the Northern Pacific, which ran from St. Paul and Duluth through the farming country of North Dakota and the mining country of Montana to the Coast.

Third, and farthest north of the three, was James J. Hill's Great Northern, hard against the Canadian border.

These two latter roads, the Northern Pacific and the Great Northern, served virtually the same regions and were close neighbors; too close for comfort, in fact, had not their managements been allied. Morgan had tried to combine them a few years before so that the prosperous Great Northern might aid the Northern Pacific—just emerging from bankruptcy—by a sort of financial transfusion of blood, but the laws forbidding alliances between directly competing roads had prevented any such formal association. Both roads, however, did their banking with the House of Morgan. Hill was influential in both, the community of interest between them—to use Morgan's favorite phrase—was generally acknowledged, and both were known as Morgan roads or as Hill roads.

In the year 1900, the two groups of men in charge of these three railroads—Harriman and Jacob Schiff of Kuhn, Loeb on the one hand, representing the Union Pacific; and Hill and Morgan on the other hand, representing the Northern Pacific and Great Northern—both cast longing eyes upon another railroad to the east. This was the Chicago, Burlington, and Quincy, popularly known as the Burlington. It had a network of lines running through Illinois, Iowa, Missouri, and Nebraska; it connected with several other roads to the south and east; and better yet, it ran into Chicago. Morgan and Hill thought there would be great advantage in acquiring it for the Northern Pacific, chiefly because of the direct entrance into Chicago which it would give them; and Harriman wanted it for the Union Pacific for the same reason. Both groups therefore set about trying to purchase the Burlington.

Harriman tried first. But the stock of the Burlington was mostly held by thrifty New Englanders who saw no reason for parting with their holdings; Harriman's syndicate found that the shares came very hard, and by the end of 1900 the attempt had been abandoned. Harriman had other fish to fry at this moment, anyhow.

Even more important to his Union Pacific than an entrance into Chicago was an adequate entrance into San Francisco, which Union Pacific freight could reach only by traveling over an inadequate line which he did not control. This inadequate line, the Central Pacific, was controlled by the Southern Pacific; and Harriman was engaged in boldly buying control of the Southern Pacific in order to get the subsidiary which he thought he needed. How he did this need not detain us, except to remark that the hazardousness of the operation was characteristic of the man and his day: he got the money for the purchase by selling an issue of Union Pacific bonds backed partly by the common stock of another recently acquired road—certainly a dubious kind of security. Harriman succeeded in this enterprise, partly because the bonds themselves were convertible into common stock and thus appealed to the speculative instinct at a time when the speculative instinct was rampant, and partly because he later regenerated the Southern Pacific and made it pay; but it was essentially bull-market financing, of the sort that can be carried to success only on a tide of prosperity, and not all his imitators have been so fortunate.

Harriman was thus looking westward, not eastward, as the year 1901 began, and had abandoned, at least for the time being, his plan to buy the Burlington. But Hill was not thus diverted. Hill now went to work—and with a different result. During the early months of 1901 he succeeded in inducing the directors of the Burlington to sell. In April the deal was approved by the Burlington stockholders. Morgan and Hill had possession of the road.

Harriman was beaten. But his ambition was overwhelming; as Judge Lovett said of him later, "when he started upon a course nobody could swerve him from it." He had started to get the Burlington, and get it he would. Obviously he could not do it directly; so he decided to do it indirectly—*by buying the Northern Pacific, Morgan's and Hill's own road, right out from under their very noses!* He would do this not by arrangement with the board of directors, or by private negotiation with the large holders of stock, but in the open market on the New York Stock Exchange, and with all the rapidity and secrecy of which skillful stock-market operators are capable.

It is said that this buccaneering project was proposed to Harriman by John W. Sterling, the eccentric and secretive corporation lawyer who was the constant intimate adviser of James Stillman of the National City Bank: the same Sterling, by the way, whose financial profits were subsequently converted into majestic Gothic towers at Yale.

What Sterling proposed to Harriman was no petty operation. The Northern Pacific had 80 million dollars' worth of common stock and 75 millions of preferred stock outstanding, and both classes of stock had voting rights, the only difference between them in voting power being that the preferred stock might be retired any time after January 1, 1902, and thus lose its vote (though presumably it might meanwhile have its say as to whether it should be retired or not). Both the preferred and the common were selling on the market at somewhere near $100 a share. To acquire a 51 per cent interest in 155 million dollars' worth of stock would therefore take all of 78 millions—and more if the buying pushed the price up, as of course it would. Harriman was accustomed to using the credit of his own companies lavishly, as was shown in his Southern Pacific exploit, and he had wealthy backers, including not only Schiff and his banking house but men like James Stillman, whose National City Bank could draw upon the vast hoards of the Standard Oil men, and George Gould, inheritor of a fortune from the notorious Jay Gould; nevertheless the Southern Pacific purchasing operation was still incomplete, and to engage in another one at this moment required great temerity. Certainly this was straining the credit of the Union Pacific to the breaking point: taking a risk incommensurate with the probable advantage to the railroad or its stockholders.

Furthermore, in trying to seize the Northern Pacific, Harriman was raiding Pierpont Morgan's own preserve; Morgan had just organized the Steel Corporation that very spring, his prestige was high, and the weight of his enmity could be crushing.

But Harriman was counting upon the chance of catching Jupiter nodding. He knew or guessed that the Morgan-Hill forces and their friends held only 33 or 35 millions of Northern Pacific stock out of a total of 155; it generally was considered unnecessary for a group in the saddle to have an actual majority, and ninety-nine times out of a hundred it was actually unnecessary. Morgan himself had sailed for Europe; the handsome Robert Bacon was in charge at 23 Wall Street. The launching of the Steel Corporation only a few weeks before had stimulated a wild speculation in stocks; trading was so heavy and gains in prices under the manipulation of pools were so frequent that large purchases of Northern Pacific might possibly escape attention. As to the stock market boom which was then in progress, read this description and try to believe that it appeared not in 1928 or 1929— no, nor even in June or July of 1933—but in the *Commercial and Financial Chronicle* of May 11, 1901: "The most serious part of the recent situation lay in its indications that the fever of speculation was spreading to all ranks of society. It was coming to be believed that the conditions underlying this market's movement were so novel and unprecedented that old rules could no longer hold. From such conviction it was but one step to the belief that nothing could stop or reverse the upward movement of prices. . . . It is notorious that for weeks the smaller brokers' offices and the 'bucket shops' have been crowded with people of moderate means who were speculating with all the money they could control for a r se in stocks."

The moment was ripe for Harriman. The soaring confidence of the time was matched by his own. He gave an order to Kuhn, Loeb & Co. to buy Northern Pacific stock in quantity for the account of the Union Pacific railroad.

§ 3

Naturally the price rose. On Monday, April 22, Northern Pacific common had been quoted at 101; by Tuesday, April 30, it had risen to 117¼. To many of the men in the Morgan-Hill camp the climb in prices seemed to offer a delightful chance to sell blocks of their stock at a profit, and they did so—quite unaware of the destination of the shares. One man sold three and a half million dollars' worth, never suspecting what was afoot. The Northern Pacific board itself approved the sale of a block of shares held by one of its subsidiaries. Even the House of Morgan sold 10,000 shares which had happened to come into their hands.

But at the end of April old Jim Hill suspected that something was wrong. The rising price disturbed him. He was in Seattle at the moment, but he had a special train made up for him and went roaring across the continent, with a right of way over everything to the Mississippi River; and reaching New York on Friday, May 3, he went straight to the office of Jacob Schiff.

Here the two men confronted each other: the bulky, shaggy Scotch-Irish pioneer, with his immense shoulders and his great dome of a head and his unkempt country-man's attire; and the small, erect, precise German-Jewish banker with his impeccable garb and a flower in his but-tonhole. Hill asked Schiff what he was up to.

Already the Harriman-Schiff forces had accomplished their bold purpose—or very nearly so. Of the preferred shares of the Northern Pacific they had over 42 millions out of 75. Of the common shares they had over 37 mil-lions out of 80. Not quite half of the common, you will observe; but a clear majority of the two classes together—79 out of 155—which meant control unless in some way the preferred shares could legally be retired without get-ting a vote in the matter. Harriman, if not victorious, was at least on the verge of victory.

Exactly what transpired between Hill and Schiff at that meeting on Friday, May 3, 1901, is a matter of conflicting reports. The Hill version is that Schiff said that he and Harriman now controlled the Northern Pacific, but would like Hill to continue in the management with them. (This offer Hill subsequently denounced as a bribe.) The Schiff version, on the other hand, is that Schiff assured Hill that he had no idea of taking away from him the control of the road, but only of getting some say in the management, "to bring about the har-mony and community of interest which other means and appeals to him had failed to produce." According to Schiff's version, they talked again that evening at Schiff's house until after midnight, Schiff protesting that har-mony was what he wanted, not conquest, and Hill reply-ing that harmony could be achieved.

The Schiff version seems acceptable—if one remembers also that an olive branch extended by a man who has just raided your camp can be infuriating. Probably a peaceful compromise of the struggle would have been quite satisfactory to Schiff. He had enough votes, presumably, to force the Northern Pacific to give the Union Pacific whatever advantages it might wish in the use of the Burlington, and after all it was the Burlington which originally was at stake and not the Northern Pacific; and he must have realized the hazards of continuing the raid.

But peace without victory was not to Harriman's taste. Hazards meant nothing to him. He was all for conquest. The next morning he was ill in bed, but he picked up the telephone and called up Schiff's office to ask for the immediate purchase of 4 millions more of Northern Pacific common, which would lift his total from 37 to 41 (out of 80) and thus give him a clear majority of the common as well as the preferred. Schiff was not in the office and Harriman talked with a subordinate, but he hung up in the confidence that his order would be executed at once, and lay back content. As it happened, however, the peaceable Schiff was at the Synagogue that morning, his subordinates were unwilling to execute the order without his approval, and before he could be reached the short Saturday session of the Stock Exchange had come to an end. The stock was not bought.

Meanwhile Hill had gone to the Morgan offices and was conferring with the amazed partners there. Apparently his meditations in the small hours of the morning had persuaded him not to rely upon Schiff's protestations of peace. At his request a cablegram was sent to Pierpont Morgan, who was sunning himself at Aix-les-Bains in the foothills of the Alps, asking for permission to buy 15 millions of Northern Pacific common. Control of the preferred was already lost, but perhaps the common shares would have the legal power to retire the preferred and thus hold the command of the road; and as the Morgan-Hill forces still had some 26 millions of the common out of the total of 80, 15 more would give them a majority.

One can picture the blinding wrath of Morgan when the cablegram came into his hands by the shore of the Lac du Bourget. "I feel bound in all honor," he later testified, "when I reorganize a property and am morally responsible for its management, to protect it, and I generally do protect it." Yet here was a Morgan railroad being ripped right out of his protecting hands!

And it was worse than that. In launching the Steel Corporation Morgan had achieved vast prestige. This prestige was now imperiled. He had other great consolidations in progress—one of them an ambitious attempt to unite several big steamship lines. Even his success in the Steel venture was as yet unproved: the distribution of stock was only just begun and the organization of the company was still largely on paper. What a moment to admit defeat by little Harriman!

Furthermore, Harriman was now working hand in glove not only with Schiff but with Stillman and the Standard Oil millionaires. Surely they were behind this sudden raid, seeking domination in the railroad sphere, in which Morgan had thus far been the outstanding power. Perhaps they sought to destroy Morgan altogether. Was he who had bought off the warring Carnegie only a few months before to be defeated by the warring Rockefellers? Come what might, Harriman must be beaten.

Pierpont Morgan no more counted the hazards than did Harriman. He cabled his approval of the purchase of 15 millions of Northern Pacific common.

A little arithmetic will show how inevitable was the result of the Harriman raid and the Morgan decision—a result which might have been foreseen by anybody save men who wanted what they wanted and did not care whether the heavens fell in consequence. There were 80

millions of Northern Pacific common stock. The Harriman group already had 37. The Morgan-Hill group was
out to get 41. That left only something like two millions
for everybody else, including the remote stockholders
whose certificates were locked away and who did not
know what was going on, and the speculators who were
on the rampage in Wall Street. It stood to reason, furthermore, that as the price of Northern Pacific leaped upward
under competitive purchases, other speculators would
sell the stock short—in other words, sell shares which they
did not possess, expecting to repurchase them at lower
figures, and never dreaming that the shares which they
wanted to repurchase were being put under lock and key.
More stock would be sold than existed; in the phrase of
the Street, Northern Pacific common would be "cornered." Probably Schiff foresaw the danger of this; at any
rate, no more purchases were made by the Harriman
group. But the Morgan-Hill group went ahead regardless
of arithmetic and the inevitable.

§ 4

On Monday morning, May 6, brokers began purchasing for the Morgan-Hill forces in quantity. A single
broker, E. L. Norton, was reported to have bought 20
millions of Northern Pacific that day—more than enough
for the Morgan purposes if Norton or others had not also
been selling simultaneously to keep the price under some
sort of check. As it was, the price, which had been 110
at the close of the market on Saturday, was 114 at the
opening of the market on Monday, climbed during the
day to 133, and had dropped only to 127½ when the
gong brought trading to a close at three o'clock.

The leap in Northern Pacific stimulated speculation in
other securities. The bull-market hysteria of the preced-

ing week was intensified. The sessions of the Stock Exchange were being held in temporary quarters in the Produce Exchange building while its new home was under construction; visitors to the Produce Exchange gallery described a scene of the utmost confusion on the floor where stocks were changing hands: "a struggling mass of humanity . . . howling and shrieking as though a mob were let loose."

Not yet, however, was the tumult in Wall Street a front-page newspaper story. The *Times* reported it on page three.

On Tuesday the drama was further advanced. The inevitable was approaching. The Morgan forces were still buying; and as some of the speculators who had sold short began to guess their predicament and sought to buy to cover their sales, the price of Northern Pacific zigzagged crazily upward, touching 149¾ and closing at 143½, up 16 more points for the day. At the close of the market the Morgan purchases ceased: Morgan and Hill now had their 15 millions of stock. But the mischief had been done.

During the final hour of trading there was a premonition of trouble, and prices in general broke sharply. Rumors—as accurate as Wall Street rumors usually are—were flying about: Northern Pacific was about to give valuable rights to its stockholders, the Vanderbilts had got control of the road, there was a plot on somebody's part to "squeeze the shorts," Harriman had lost control of the Union Pacific; but by nightfall the truth was apparent to the brokers who gathered on the street corners and in the downtown cafés and in the corridors of the Waldorf and the other uptown hotels. Northern Pacific was cornered. It was rumored that Norton, the broker who had bought 20 millions of Northern Pacific on Monday, had lent 12½ millions of it to short sellers. That looked as if there were a lot of them—and little or no stock available for them to buy. It was a desperate situation for the "shorts": they had better buy Northern Pacific tomorrow, regardless of price, if they were to get it at all—even if this meant throwing overboard other stock to get the cash to buy it with.

Still, however, the *Times*'s chronicle of the affair was printed on an inside page. A reported corner in a single stock was not an event of the first importance.

On Wednesday there was no purchasing of Northern Pacific for Morgan and Hill, and of course there was none for Harriman. There was other purchasing, however—by frantic shorts trying to escape bankruptcy. Northern Pacific opened at 155, gyrated even more senselessly than on the preceding day, touched 180, and closed at 160, up 16½ points for the day. Meanwhile, however, everything else was dropping. Men were selling stock to raise the money to pay for Northern Pacific, and their sales were breaking the market. "Where before the cry had been only 'Buy, buy, buy,' it became 'Sell, sell, sell.' " Steel fell 7 points; Amalgamated Copper, 12; Union Pacific, 8½—and so on all along the line.

Till late on Wednesday night excited crowds of brokers surged about the corridors of the Waldorf, the gilded gathering-place of Wall Street bulls and bears; from Peacock Alley into the bar and from the bar to the billiard room they swarmed, discussing with sinking hearts what might happen on the morrow. The air was blue with tobacco smoke, the bar was doing heavy business, reporters were threading their way through the crowds, picking up fantastic tales of gains and losses. It was said that the shorts were being shown no mercy; Norton had been calling back certificates which he had previously lent to them. Apparently the Morgan group dared not lend their certificates for fear they would not get them back again. Harriman, it was said, was unrelenting. He sat in his big office in Pine Street and listened to men pleading with him for mercy, but he would not lend. He too was bent on control, and had no eyes for anything else.

The next day—Thursday, May 9—panic came in dead earnest, making all that had gone before seem as nothing. On that day Northern Pacific opened at 170, swung up to 200, seesawed down and up—and then, to the utter consternation of those who in hundreds of banks and brokers' offices were watching the ticker-tape chatter its news of disaster, pushed up to 320, to 650, to 700, and, on one sale, to 1000.

Meanwhile the prices of other securities cascaded as if the bottom would never be reached. Money was almost unobtainable and the interest rate in the call-loan market at the Exchange had jumped to 75 per cent. The babel on the Stock Exchange floor, the white faces of cornered shorts, the disheveled brokers fighting frantically for a chance to buy Northern Pacific at ruinous cost and to sell everything else before prices sank to zero: all these are implicit in this record of a few consecutive transactions in the common stock of Morgan's own baby, the six-weeks-old Steel Corporation, during the worst period of the collapse:

A sale of one thousand shares at 40; of 600 at 39½; 1500 at 39; 2,900 at 38½; 500 at 38. And then—

300 at 37
500 at 36
200 at 34½
100 at 34
400 at 32
1000 at 34½
100 at 34
200 at 32
500 at 31
800 at 32
200 at 30⅞
100 at 29¾
1000 at 29

4000 at 28
500 at 27
100 at 26

It was incredible. The message hammered out by the ticker did not make sense. Only a few days before, Steel had been selling at 54¾. Thousands of men had been speculating in the shares on margin, and the crash of prices meant ruin to them. Such a catastrophe must not continue. Something must be done immediately.

A little after noon it was done—about forty-eight hours too late. The ticker carried the news that the Morgan and Kuhn, Loeb firms had agreed not to demand immediate delivery of stock which had been sold short to them; and also that a number of banks had formed a pool for the relief of the money market, lending money at 6 per cent to men who a few minutes before had been clamoring for it at 75 per cent. The worst was over. In the last hour or two of trading there was a moderate recovery of prices, and Northern Pacific dropped from 1000 to 325. Later the contending groups, at the instigation of the alarmed Schiff, agreed to let the cornered shorts settle at the rate of $150 per share for Northern Pacific common. With that announcement the crisis ended. The next day there was recovery all along the line.

But meanwhile the damage done had been great. It had been a wild day in Wall Street. The volume of trading on the Exchange had probably been the greatest in its history; though the official total of sales was 3,071,805, a little less than the record set a few days before, it was agreed that many sales had gone unrecorded in the excitement.

Some of the frantic efforts made to get hold of Northern Pacific stock certificates for delivery had been picturesque: one certificate for 500 shares had ridden from Albany to New York on a special train engaged to transport it. At noon, half the brokerage firms in the Street had been technically bankrupt. The bold-face front-page headlines which shouted "DISASTER AND RUIN IN FALLING MARKET . . . LOSSES, UNTOLD MILLIONS" did not exaggerate. Thousands of families, their capital tied up in margin speculation, had lost everything. There were few men as fortunate as the visitor from Meriden, Connecticut, who had bought Northern Pacific at 84 some weeks previously, had taken the Yankee precaution of bringing with him to New York his certificate for 100 shares, and had succeeded in selling it Thursday noon for $700 a share, clearing over $60,000 without a stroke of work; or the Minnesota barber who owned 200 shares of Northern Pacific, and "when he heard the stock had reached 1,000 . . . dropped his razor in the cuspidor and locked up the shop." For every triumph such as these there were a hundred unchronicled tragedies.

To one unaccustomed to hearing great conservative newspapers speak out unreservedly about the errors of captains of finance, the editorial comments upon the Northern Pacific panic, as one turns back to them today, come with a shock of surprise. They were blistering. The *New York Times*, for instance, which had got off to a slow start in its editorial of Thursday by quoting from Bagehot's essay on Shelley, was fully awakened by Friday, describing the panic as "an exhibition of the use of vast power for private ends unrestrained by any sense of public responsibility," and charging the contending Wall Street groups with behaving "like cowboys on a spree, . . . shooting wildly at each other in entire disregard of the safety of the bystanders." Russell Sage said bluntly that the panic was "a result of hoggishness." That seemed to be the prevailing opinion, and the frank expression of it chastened the contestants for the control of the Northern Pacific.

The irrepressible Harriman, it is true, still felt the lust of battle; in the midst of the excitement he had come down with appendicitis, and the first thing he did on coming out of ether was to telephone to Hill: "This is Harriman. I wanted to tell you that the operation's over and I'm all right." Hill, too, took the débâcle lightly. Three days after the panic he came into the Kuhn, Loeb offices, and finding that Schiff was out, walked over to Felix Warburg's desk. "How is Schiff?" asked Hill. "Not very happy," answered Warburg. "He takes these things too seriously," said Hill. Schiff and the Morgan partners, however, were deeply chagrined at the devastation which their warfare had brought about. They realized that the armistice arrived at on Thursday, May 9, at the crisis of the panic, must be followed by a peace treaty.

In due course the treaty was made. Morgan, who now controlled a bare majority of the common stock of the Northern Pacific, was to be permitted to name the revised directorate of the road. The preferred stock, of which the Harriman forces held a majority, was to be retired. But Morgan had to give places on the Northern Pacific board to Harriman and his ally William Rockefeller, and Harriman also got a place on the Burlington board. Both groups were thus given representation; "community of interest" was thus achieved—at what cost!

To put the results of the peace treaty on a secure and unchallengeable basis, a holding company was formed in due course. This company was designed to be too immense ever to be conquered in a raid like Harriman's. The Northern Securities Company, as it was called, was to hold a majority of stock in the Northern Pacific and the Great Northern, and thus also was to control the Burlington indirectly; and on its board of directors were to sit ten Morgan-Hill men, three Harriman men, and two others belonging to neither group.

Was it peace without victory? Morgan was still dominant. His prestige was shaken, but survived. On the other hand he had been forced to give Harriman a place in the sun; and Harriman, with his Standard Oil backing, emerged from the struggle a man of new financial prowess. The one sure victor in the battle—a battle which from any broad social point of view, considering the railroads as public carriers rather than as pawns in a game of grab, appeared almost completely senseless—was the principle of consolidation and concentration of capital. The losers were the speculators and investors, large and small, who had been trapped between the contending armies.

And what of the effect of the episode on the financial and industrial world in general? On the afternoon of the panic many of the minor potentates of Wall Street had hastened to issue reassuring statements, such as that of President Kimball of the Seventh National Bank: "I do not think that the flurry in Wall Street today will be anything else but incidental. The prosperity of the country will not be affected." To a generation which recalls the synthetic optimism of more recent years, such a statement would seem less than convincing. President Kimball, however, was essentially right. Great as the speculative boom had been, it had not involved a fraction of the money or the men who were to be sucked into the boom of 1928-29; and the momentum of national growth was still tremendous. No depression followed the panic. Not even had the speculative movement been destroyed; it had merely been checked; by the end of May prices on the Exchange had regained most of their lost ground. Industrial and railroad combinations continued to be the order of the day.

The complacent McKinley still sat in the White House. Mark Hanna, the gruff Republican boss who saw eye to eye with the big industrialists and bankers, still had Mc-

Kinley's ear. The Sherman Act seemed almost to have been forgotten; in December, 1899, in the Addyston Pipe Company case, the Supreme Court had at last taken a strong position with regard to conspiracies in restraint of trade, yet in the seventeen months since that decision McKinley's Department of Justice had not brought a single action against any of the big business combinations. Senators were still deferential to the captains of industry; sometimes with good reason, as was later shown when the pilfered correspondence of John D. Archbold revealed how Archbold—a church trustee, a munificent donor to Syracuse University, and the executive head of the Standard Oil Company since John D. Rockefeller's virtual retirement—had subsidized public men right and left. The Industrial Commission appointed by the government to investigate the trusts had turned in a singularly innocuous report, revised in accordance with Archbold's wishes and secretly approved in advance of publication by him and perhaps by other industrialists. Big business was still securely in the saddle. Even a Northern Pacific panic could not change the new order.

§ 5

But a cloud was coming up the sky, at first no bigger than a man's hand.

On the 6th of September, 1901, President McKinley was shot by the anarchist Czolgosz. On the morning of the 14th of September he died; and Theodore Roosevelt of New York, who had believed his public career to be over when he was shunted into the Vice-presidency, became President of the United States.

The assassination of McKinley was a hard blow to Wall Street. What would the new President do? He was not radical, but he was young and impulsive. "I told William

McKinley it was a mistake to nominate that wild man,"
cried Mark Hanna to his friend Kohlsaat, ". . . now
look, that damned cowboy is President of the United
States!" Friends hastened to counsel Roosevelt that he
must do nothing which might disturb the equilibrium of
business. Hanna took the first opportunity to urge him
to "go slow," to listen to advisers but "reserve your decision." "I must frankly tell you," Roosevelt's brother-
in-law had written while McKinley lay dying, "that there
is a feeling in financial circles here that in case you become President you may change matters so as to upset the
confidence . . . of the business world, which would be
an awful blow to everybody—the West as well as the East
—as that means tight money." (A curious phenomenon
is the Wall Street mind, which can look with equanimity
upon the building of over-capitalized financial structures
like those of Morgan and Harriman, to say nothing of the
manipulations of men like John W. Gates and the speculative excesses and raids which lead to panics, and then
tremble at the least suggestion that the stability of these
structures may be examined and their legality possibly
put to the test!)

At first Roosevelt proceeded with obliging caution. He
had dreaded the thought that his arrival in the White
House might be the signal for a slump in the stock market. He conciliated Mark Hanna. He sought the advice of
Senator Aldrich and other stalwart conservatives. His first
message to Congress was cautious to the last degree; as
"Mr. Dooley" summarized the portions dealing with
business, " 'Th' trusts,' says he, 'are heejous monsthers
built up be th' enlightened intherprise iv th' men that
have done so much to advance progress in our beloved
country,' he says. 'On the wan hand I wud stamp thim
undher fut; on th' other hand not so fast.' " Wall Street

began to think very well of the "damned cowboy's" conservative wisdom.

And then, in February, 1902, the first blow fell. Without consulting Hanna or anybody else, Roosevelt instructed his Attorney-General to bring suit for the dissolution of the Northern Securities Company under the Sherman Act.

Morgan was at dinner in his big brownstone house on Madison Avenue when the news came. He expressed amazement to his guests that he had had no advance knowledge or warning of the suit. He went to Washington and saw the President. "If we have done anything wrong," said he, "send your man to my man and they can fix it up." Surely the Attorney-General and a Morgan lawyer ought to be able to adjust matters in quiet negotiation, without disturbing the markets as Roosevelt's impetuous decision had disturbed them! But Roosevelt was unmoved. Morgan asked whether Roosevelt intended to attack his other interests, such as the Steel Corporation. He seemed to fear a general offensive on the part of the government. No, said Roosevelt, unless "they have done something that we regard as wrong." He would not consider withdrawing the suit.

It may seem strange to one who considers the havoc wrought by the financial conflict over the Northern Pacific, that when a holding company was finally formed to reconcile the opposing forces and prevent such a thing from happening again, the government should act to dissolve it. But the dominant economic belief of the American people was still in free competition. Any idea of permitting such combinations and then regulating them in the public interest would have seemed dangerously socialistic. There were only two available alternatives—to let things alone or to dissolve the combinations. The Northern Securities Company was the first really im-

portant railroad holding company; it might be used for
the purchase of other roads and the formation of a big railroad trust, annihilating the principle of free competition.
Roosevelt's understanding of economic forces was uncertain, but he felt this danger; and vaguely he felt also that
the sovereignty of the government was at stake. If it did
not take measures to curb the rising plutocracy, it would
soon stand helpless before them. Undeterred by the alarm
of Wall Street—expressed in a flustered stock market—
Roosevelt proceeded with his first "trust-busting" project, which in due course was to win a Supreme Court decision dissolving the Northern Securities Company.

§ 6

Only a little over fourteen months had passed since
Morgan and Schwab had sat together at dinner at the
University Club, yet already the drama of twentieth-
century American capitalism was well advanced and many
of the principal performers had assumed their parts. Pierpont Morgan, by forming the largest corporation in the
world, had set an authoritative example of industrial combination under Wall Street auspices through the medium
of the heavily-capitalized holding company, the chief engine of twentieth-century financial power; and now he
was proceeding to fresh conquests. Harriman, rising from
obscurity, had established his technic of accumulating
and reconstructing railroads, had fought Morgan to a
draw, and was well on his way toward the completion of
his empire. The first twentieth-century wave of speculation had curled and broken; but the groundswell of
financial concentration still swept surely forward. Meanwhile governmental and public opposition to the financial powers had begun to take shape. The character of the
new economic era was becoming established.

Chapter Three

THE OVERLORDS

THE pell-mell rush to form huge industrial consolidations and to speculate in their securities—a rush
which did not slacken for long until late in 1902—had
distressing after-effects. Although a sharp recovery followed the Northern Pacific panic, the spree was bound in
time to bring a headache, and so it did: during the latter
part of 1902 and the whole of 1903, Wall Street and the
other financial centers suffered from a malady correctly
ascribed by Pierpont Morgan to "undigested securities."
(James J. Hill, improving on Morgan's phrase, remarked
that the securities which caused the trouble were "indigestible," and many of them surely were.)

Too much stock and too many bonds had been issued.
Not only had the formation of each holding company
called for the sale of quantities of stock to the investing
public, but when a railroad company or a manufacturing
company had purchased control of another concern to
further the ambitions of the men in control (as when the
Northern Pacific acquired the Burlington for Morgan
and Hill, or the Union Pacific acquired the Southern
Pacific for Harriman) this had usually meant the sale of
a new issue of stock or of bonds, thus adding to the supply
of securities outstanding without adding to the physical
properties. At last the purchasing power of the possible
buyers of securities was exhausted and they could take
no more.

The exhaustion was intensified by the effects of the
depredations of professional speculators and stock-market

manipulators throughout the boom. The fine art of organizing pools to buy and sell securities in huge bulk on the Stock Exchange and thus push stock prices up and down, taking profits along the way from the pockets of unorganized and unlucky speculators, had never before attained such perfection.

For example, let us watch James R. Keene in action. (Keene was the man whom the Morgan syndicate engaged to distribute the shares of the Steel Corporation by manipulation on the Exchange.) According to an entry made by Clarence Barron in his journal in 1900, Keene managed the pool formed by the brokerage house of Moore and Schley to manipulate the stock of the "whisky trust," and when the pool was organized "the question came up as to whether individual members of the pool could also operate on their own account. Mr. Keene said, 'Certainly, operate all you want to; buy it and sell it; . . . but just understand that I will get the best of you all in the business and I invite you to trade with me.' Then Mr. Keene began. . . . Ten thousand shares went out one day and were bought back the next day. He began moving it so many shares a day up and down, and kept swinging it back and forth—some days it was twenty thousand shares a day, again it was ten thousand shares a day. Then when the whole public was trading in whisky [stock] with a great big swing to the market, Keene gave them the whole business, possibly went short fifty thousand shares himself, and landed the entire stock of the pool on the public."

Other speculators operated with equal power and assurance. Barron quotes Herman Sielcken, the "coffee king," as saying early in 1904 of his manipulation of a commodity market, "I can put coffee down again just as easily as I put it down once before." And as for the operations of the most potent group of all speculators of those days, the "Standard Oil crowd" led by William Rockefeller and Henry H. Rogers, who made millions by promoting the Amalgamated Copper Company and by pushing the price of its stock up to 130 and down to 60 again, listen to the testimony of Henry Clews, who, far from being a radical critic, was an enraptured believer in Wall Street as a national institution.

Clews wrote in 1900: "At his best, Jay Gould was also compelled to face the chance of failure [in his stock-market manipulations]. Commodore Vanderbilt, though he often had the Street in the palm of his hand, was often driven into a corner where he had to do battle for his life; and so it had been with every great speculator, or combination of speculators, until the men who control the Standard Oil took hold. With them, manipulation has ceased to be speculation. Their resources are so vast that they need only concentrate on any given property in order to do with it what they please. . . . With them the process is gradual, thorough, and steady, with never a waver or break. How much money this group of men have made, it is impossible even to estimate . . . and there is an utter absence of chance that is terrible to contemplate."

So long had operators of this type enjoyed a field day that the supply of victims was bound ultimately to run short. By 1903 the crisis became acute. Syndicates which had been formed to launch new corporations found themselves with unsold securities piled upon their shelves. Market manipulators who had loaded up with stock in the hope of dumping it later into the laps of eager investors found the eagerness gone, stock-market prices sagging, and their loans from the banks frozen. So overgenerous had been the capitalization of most of the new giants of industry that a period of sustained prosperity would be necessary to squeeze the water out of them; and when the pace of business lagged a little and the strain on credit began to become oppressive, earnings declined, dividends were passed, some of the crazier of the new combinations went to the wall, and the stock market had a series of sinking spells.

Fortunately this crisis of 1903 was a "rich men's panic," and not to any large extent a poor men's panic too. The momentum of industry was still strong, and the speculative excesses and consequent financial indigestion were generally limited to the professional promoters and speculators. The little investor, the occasional speculator, had been singed, or at least scared, in the Northern Pacific panic, and had learned a measure of discretion; and after all he did not then constitute a very numerous species. It must be remembered that even at the height of the hysteria of 1901 the total of daily transactions on the New York Stock Exchange had barely exceeded three million shares, as against frequent daily totals of five or six or seven million shares in 1928 and after. The number of men who were staking their accumulated savings on the rise of the market was probably hardly a tenth of the number who were to do so in the bull market of the nineteen-twenties. Few newspapers printed daily tables of stock prices. Investing in common stock was still considered somewhat hazardous for all but astute business men, and outside of the Wall Street area, speculation on borrowed money was still generally considered a form of legitimized gambling rather than a form of prudent "participation in American prosperity." The rich men's panic caused some spectacular failures and annihilated many a Wall Street plunger; but it checked only briefly the onward march of American industry.

One thing which undoubtedly alleviated the troubles of the financiers was the cautious attitude of the government toward business. Theodore Roosevelt had boldly moved to dissolve the Northern Securities Company early in 1902, and after long delay the Supreme Court sustained him in 1904 and the biggest holding company in the railroad business was broken up; but Roosevelt, for all his vehement activity and his fighting display of teeth, was no headlong reformer. He preferred the middle of the road, and big business had so long had its way virtually unmolested that to stick to the middle of the political road meant to interfere very little with the going financial and industrial order. Furthermore Roosevelt, as a Republican, was the heir apparent to the financial support of the captains of industry, and could hardly afford to run the risk of being disinherited. As the election of 1904 slowly approached he became very wary. Business was none too good. It would not do for his party to risk making it worse. There were no more major forays in the direction of Wall Street. Roosevelt was elected over Alton B. Parker with the aid of contributions—made apparently without his specific knowledge, but clearly attributable to his amenable attitude at the time—of $150,000 from J. P. Morgan, $100,000 from Rogers and Archbold of the Standard Oil, $100,000 from George J. Gould, $50,000 from Harriman, $50,000 from Frick, and further large sums from other big bankers and insurance men and industrialists. Not until Roosevelt was safely President in his own right—"no longer a political accident," in his own words—did his zeal for reform find energetic expression again.

Furthermore, although the tide of public opposition to the financial empire was slowly rising, the inactivity of Roosevelt in economic reform was on the whole matched by the inactivity of Congress. The privileges of the banker, the promoter, and the speculator to have their way with corporate property—regardless of the wishes and the interests of unorganized stockholders and em-

ployees and consumers—had been multiplying rapidly,
but it was easier for a President or a Congressman to inveigh against "malefactors of great wealth" and "the conspirators of Wall Street" than to devise practical measures
to meet the situation. The venal politician—and his name
was legion—was not interested in solving the problem: he
knew on which side his bread was buttered. The disinterested politician, even if he watched the trend of economic affairs with concern, realized that so deeply were
banks and investment houses and innumerable corporations committed to the continuation of the going methods of incorporation and of distributing securities, and so
fully did these going methods depend upon an unques-
tioning public belief in their permanence, that to challenge them might bring widespread business troubles, at
least for the time being. In a real sense the whole economic system of the country was already locked into
acquiescence with the now established financial system.

Better not risk a major operation yet, a conscientious
Congressman would say to himself; better wait and see.
And of course there were public men who sincerely believed that any limitation upon the privileges of the capitalist constituted a blow at the "sacred rights of property," at "the pioneer spirit which had built up the country," and so on: who believed this, in fact, even when the
privilege under debate—like that of setting up a Northern Securities Company to keep a firm grip on several
railroads—was a new extension of a recent extension of a
privilege granted by public authority, the privilege of
incorporating to do business under limited liability.

So the challenge to the financial order was postponed.

Yet although the rich men's panic of 1903 was in a
sense a superficial phenomenon, to the men at the heart
of the financial world it brought troubles indeed. The
prevalence of indigestible securities hardly worried the

already aging Rockefeller, for his Standard Oil companies had never been overcapitalized and if his other investments shrank there were always new millions rolling in; yet his days of benevolent ease in the great house above Tarrytown were disturbed by a rising clamor of public resentment as *McClure's Magazine* published, month after month, Ida Tarbell's astonishing history of the Standard Oil Company, with its revelation of his merciless methods; and his associates found that for the time being their speculative operations were not certain of success.

Morgan was sorely beset. Filled with boundless confidence by his success in launching the Steel Corporation, he had tried to repeat the triumph by forming a gigantic holding company which would dominate transatlantic shipping. He had accordingly bought several British and American lines at extravagant prices. His International Mercantile Marine Company was a sad disappointment, however; violent British opposition to the threat of an American shipping monopoly prevented him from including the Cunard line in his group, the congestion in the securities market left his syndicate with quantities of unsold securities on its hands, and the new holding company never justified itself, at length sliding into receivership in 1915. It was clear that Morgan had guessed wrong, and his prestige suffered. Even his Steel Corporation languished during the rich men's panic and was forced for a time to suspend dividends upon its vast issue of common stock, the price of which sagged to eight dollars and seventy-five cents a share—a humiliating figure to the head of a syndicate which had distributed that stock to the public at forty or fifty dollars a share. That genial buccaneer, John W. Gates, furious at Morgan's having left him off the directorate of the Steel Corporation, now had his revenge; he got control of the Louisville & Nashville Railroad at a time when Morgan needed it, and Morgan had to send his partner Perkins to offer Gates ten million dollars more than he had paid for the road. Gates's relish at having "put one over on the old man" was brief, to be sure; shortly afterward the gambler retired in defeat to a little town in Texas to spend the rest of his days as a big frog in a very small pool. The Louisville & Nashville episode, however, was hardly agreeable to Morgan. And other blows fell upon him, including the Supreme Court decision in the Northern Securities Case. For a time his empire seemed almost to be tottering.

Harriman, too, had his reverses: during this period the "Rock Island crowd" of promoters, consisting of the Moore brothers and Leeds and Daniel G. Reid, took the Chicago and Alton Railroad away from him by the very method he had used in trying to capture the Northern Pacific—a surprise attack in the open market. (This Rock Island crowd, by the way, had just completed an experiment in corporate architecture which modestly anticipated a favorite design of the nineteen-twenties. In reorganizing the Rock Island road in 1902 they formed a holding company to control it, and so arranged the voting privileges of the stock of this company that they were able to dictate the use of a property capitalized at several hundred millions by keeping their hands on a block of preferred stock worth in the open market only some twenty millions.)

The rich men's panic was short-lived, as we have seen. By 1905 the financial digestion had been restored by enforced rest. The price-level was rising; Europe was prosperous and European financiers had money to invest in the future economic destiny of the young giant of the west; there were bumper crops on the prairies to gladden a farm population to whom bumper crops did not yet

mean disastrously low prices; corporation profits began
to climb with the price-level; there was a lively real-estate
boom; the dance of the stock-market speculators began
once more; and the sunshine of hope—which outside the
dark canyons of the financial district had merely been
dimmed during 1903 and 1904—flooded the whole country, Wall Street included. The captains of finance began
again to extend their spheres of influence. The day of
reckoning was not yet.

§ 2

The outlines of these spheres of influence were far
from clear. Indeed it may be remarked parenthetically
that even in 1913, when as a result of the Pujo inquiry
they were diligently mapped by economists and politicians and journalists, they were not as clear in fact as
they were on paper. To have representatives on a board
of directors is not always to dominate the policy of a
company; even to have a potentially controlling power
is not always to exercise it, or to know how boldly it
may prudently be exercised. The conception of a well
integrated empire of controlled corporations implies that
a thoroughly devised and generally understood and flexible policy can be imposed upon them, and this is too
much to expect of mortal men with limited foresight and
only occasional contact with one another. Even when the
influence is recognized, those who wield it or are subject
to it are not always sure to what extent it is based upon
financial control, and how much upon personal respect,
upon general harmony of ideas, or upon a mere desire to
avoid bringing up troublesome issues. A chart showing
lines of command running from a banking house down
through the interlocking directorates of banks and corporations to other banks and corporations can sometimes

be just as persuasively false to the truth as a spider's web chart of radical influences running from Moscow down through the interlocking directorates of radical organizations to liberal societies.

Nevertheless certain alignments were already pretty clearly defined by 1905 and 1906.

In the first place, as we have already noted, the tendency toward economic consolidation, especially through the medium of holding companies, was bringing more and more businesses under the influence of the men who sat in the counting-houses of Wall Street and State Street and Fourth and Chestnut Streets and LaSalle Street. The investment bankers who promoted the new combinations and sold their securities, the commercial bankers who financed their day-to-day operations, spoke with authority in countless directors' meetings.

Again, consolidation was slowly taking place in banking as well as in industry. Big banks were taking over smaller banks. The investment bankers were putting some of their rich profits from promotions into the purchase of stock in commercial banks and insurance companies, not without an eye to making them willing customers for future issues of securities. The biggest investment houses had eager allies in the lesser investment houses which wanted very much to share in the business of distributing Steel Corporation stock or Union Pacific bonds. And so the influence of these largest investment houses was immense and pervasive, although often vaguely defined.

The House of Morgan, for example, had the First National Bank as its unswerving ally. They owned stock in, or otherwise were influential in, a number of other New York banks such as the National Bank of Commerce, the young Bankers Trust Company, and the Liberty National. George W. Perkins, now a Morgan partner, still held his old position as vice-president of the New York Life Insurance Company. The House of Morgan was supreme in the financial counsels of the Steel Corporation, the International Mercantile Marine, the International Harvester, the General Electric, and many other sizeable corporations; among the railroads it and its like-minded associate, the First National Bank, dictated more or less positively to the directors of the Southern, the Reading, the Northern Pacific, the New Haven, the Erie, and others.

What such dictation sometimes implied was suggested by the fact that when President Roosevelt decided to settle the anthracite coal strike in 1902, and the coal operators were unwilling to negotiate, the man with whom he had to deal was Morgan—because Morgan was a powerful factor in the management of railroads which controlled most of the anthracite coal business. Banks and lesser investment houses took securities assigned to them by the House of Morgan for sale and did not waste time arguing about it. "You can stay out," Morgan would say with blasting finality if a lesser banker hesitated to market an issue of bonds, "but do not think you will share with us again."

When a representative of the House of Morgan appeared at a reorganization meeting, his word was usually law. A Boston manufacturer has told of having attended one of these meetings as a young man and of having naïvely refused to subordinate the claims of his company to those of the Morgan firm. "They looked at me as if I were a leper," said he. What Pierpont Morgan wanted to be done was usually done—because of his reputation among the financiers for fair dealing, because of the terrifying impact of his personality, but also because the whip which on rare occasions he deigned to crack could descend on a recalcitrant underling with cutting force. "Wherever

Morgan sits on a board is the the head of the table, even if he has but one share," said a railroad president to Clarence Barron in 1905.

During these years James Stillman's growing National City Bank was sometimes associated with the Morgan interests, but not so closely as after 1907. It was more often the instrument or the ally of the Standard Oil millionaires. The Standard Oil company was an empire in itself, impregnable and worldwide. The holdings of the men whom it had endowed with great fortunes ramified into another vast network of influence, less compact than that of the Morgans and less responsibly directed, but very rich.

The National City Bank and the Standard Oil men and George Gould (son of Jay Gould) and Kuhn, Loeb & Co. generally stood behind Harriman in his grandiose schemes of conquest; and the little man with the spectacles was now enlarging his sphere very rapidly. His influence in the Northern Pacific and the Great Northern and the Burlington, so dearly bought in the battle of 1901, waned after the Northern Securities decision of 1904, for the plan of dissolution which was adopted was a Morgan plan and left Morgan and Hill in the seats of power and Harriman protesting in the outer cold; yet he was supreme in the Union Pacific and Southern Pacific and their subsidiaries, he owned a half interest in the San Pedro route, and in 1906 and 1907 he sweetened the uses of adversity by putting his Northern Securities money into the purchase of a part ownership in no less than nine other roads. Harriman seemed on his way to become dictator of American railroading; and meanwhile he was negotiating in the Far East in the hope of building up, piece by piece, a transportation line that would circle the whole earth.

It is unnecessary to do more than mention the lesser

spheres of influence in the endlessly complex map of financial influence in 1905 and 1906—those which surrounded the investment houses of Kuhn, Loeb; of Speyer; of Lee, Higginson and of Kidder, Peabody in Boston; those which represented the power of the invested millions of the Vanderbilts and centered in the New York Central Railroad; those of the "Chicago crowd" and the "Rock Island crowd" and miscellaneous roving bands of capitalists and promoters and speculators; those of the traction magnates and the gas light magnates. One sphere, still relatively insignificant yet of future importance, may be noted in passing, however, as a reminder that in any period the seeds of the future are being sown: in 1905 the General Electric Company modestly organized the Electric Bond and Share Company, to manage its interest in various utilities which it had helped to finance or in which it had otherwise acquired a holding.

§ 3

What manner of men were these who so bestrode the American business world? How far did their influence reach beyond business? What was the effect of this influence upon the quality of American civilization? What did they think of America and their role in it?

A hundred such questions leap to the mind of any one who studies their lives and enterprises. It is not enough to say that they were neither the plaster saints depicted by dutiful official biographers, nor the black conspirators depicted by radical critics and Nebraska politicians; for to say merely this is to imply that they should be painted in shades of neutral gray, and neutral gray was surely not their color.

What may loosely be called the Wall Street influence was of course exercised by hundreds of men of varying character and talent and opinion; to attempt to generalize about so many men is to confront endless contradictions and confusions. Perhaps the easiest way of simplifying one's study of the men of Wall Street and their influence is to use as a sort of touchstone the study of a small group of the most powerful and vital of all. I have selected ten for this purpose—not necessarily the ten most important men of the Wall Street of the early years of our century, but among the most important. Their varied qualities may offer some clue to the qualities dominant in the financial world as a whole.

These ten are J. Pierpont Morgan; his fidus Achates, George F. Baker, president of the First National Bank, solid, tenacious, and silent; James Stillman, the brilliant and cold-blooded president of the National City Bank; Edward H. Harriman; John D. Rockefeller, who was already in retirement but was still a potent factor by reason of his huge and growing wealth; William Rockefeller and Henry Huddlestone Rogers, Standard Oil financiers, as to whose prowess in the world of promotion and speculation we have heard the awed testimony of Henry Clews; Jacob H. Schiff, the shrewd and kindly head of the banking house of Kuhn, Loeb & Co.; William K. Vanderbilt, the indolent chief representative of the influence of a family still powerful in the railroad and investment world; and James R. Keene, a stock exchange operator of commanding skill and prestige.

Other men might of course be chosen as substitutes for some of these ten. Perhaps Hill belongs in such a group, or Gary, or Andrew Mellon of Pittsburgh, or Yerkes of Chicago, or Frick, or Schwab, or Daniel G. Reid, or Thomas Fortune Ryan, or Elkins, or any one of a dozen others. One might include in it men of such contrasting qualities as Major Henry Lee Higginson, whom Barrett Wendell called "perhaps the most generous

and hearty benefactor of his time in New England," and
the gambler John W. Gates. However, the group is reasonably representative as it stands; it is convenient for
analysis because all ten men lived in New York; let us
narrow our focus for a moment and regard these ten
men.

Considering the authority which they wielded, they
were astonishingly little known to the nation at large.
This was partly due to the fact that most of them shrank
from the public gaze (by reason either of innate modesty,
or of a fear that their wealth would make them a target
for cranks and crooks and for the envious clamor of the
less fortunate: George F. Baker, for example, never permitted any of his possessions to be photographed if he
could help it.) Partly the public's ignorance of the big
financiers was due to deliberate concealment of their
operations, some of which could hardly stand the glare of
publicity. Partly it was due to laymen's difficulty in understanding the real meaning of complicated manoeuvres
described in the paralyzing language of finance. Partly it
was perhaps due to a certain lack of romantic appeal in a
career dedicated to the amassing of money. After all, there
are few things as dull as greed. When, for example, one
reads of the youthful Frick strolling up Fifth Avenue
with his friend Andrew Mellon, and looking at the Vanderbilt house with admiration, and figuring that a fortune of six million dollars would finance such an establishment, and saying to Mellon, "That is all I shall ever
want," one recognizes that the motive is human and
natural, but feels, perhaps, that a life ruled by such a
motive is not likely to be gallant.

Whatever the cause of the public's ignorance, it is
suggestive to note the number of lines in the *Reader's
Guide to Periodical Literature* given to listing magazine
articles about these ten men during the years 1900-1904,

compared with the number of inches given to listing articles about ten leading politicians of the time:

Number of Lines		Number of Lines	
Morgan	26	Theodore Roosevelt	379
Baker	2	McKinley	126
Stillman	8	Bryan	72
John D. Rockefeller	12	Taft	50
William Rockefeller	5	Alton B. Parker	44
Rogers	5	Mark Hanna	35
Harriman	7	John Hay	34
Schiff	6	Thomas B. Reed	24
W. K. Vanderbilt	8	La Follette	19
Keene	9	Joseph G. Cannon	16
Total	88	Total	799

Not one of these ten financiers had had a college education except Morgan, who spent two years in study in Göttingen in Germany. It must of course be recalled, by way of partial explanation of this fact, that by 1905 they were mostly elderly men: Morgan, the eldest, was sixty-eight; Stillman, the youngest, was fifty-five. The years when they might have been going to college fell in the eighteen-fifties and eighteen-sixties, when American colleges were comparatively small and few in number, and prepared men chiefly for the professions. (Incidentally, it may be remarked here that although six of the ten men were in their twenties during the Civil War, not one of them saw service in the army; for whatever reason, each was concentrating on business.)

Not that these ten men did not come in time to appreciate the advantages of higher education: with singular unanimity they sent their sons to college. Between them they had fifteen sons who lived to college age, and of these, eight went to Harvard, four to Yale, one to Brown, one to Amherst, one to Columbia. They showered benefactions upon the colleges, too: one needs only to recall Morgan's gift to the Medical School at Harvard; Baker's gift of a playing field to Columbia and of a chemical laboratory to Cornell, and his five millions to the Harvard Business School; the Stillman Infirmary and the Stillman professorship at Harvard; Schiff's founding of the Semitic Museum at Harvard; and John D. Rockefeller's vast gifts to the General Education Board and the University of Chicago.

They were mostly self-made men. Only two of them, Morgan and Vanderbilt, began their careers with the advantages of assured wealth. Morgan's father was a renowned international banker and a millionaire; the young Pierpont's first job was in his father's office in London. Vanderbilt inherited over fifty million dollars from his father, William H. Vanderbilt, son of the redoubtable Commodore, and other millions from other relatives. Schiff's upward progress was probably somewhat eased by his acquaintance with German-Jewish bankers in his native Frankfort-on-Main, and by his marriage to a Loeb within five months of his entering the young firm of Kuhn, Loeb & Co. in New York. Stillman's father was a man of means and had accumulated a million dollars by the time he died, and Harriman had well-to-do relatives and wealthy friends; but both Stillman and Harriman began their careers in small positions at an early age: Stillman went into the cotton business at sixteen, and Harriman's first job was as a five-dollar-a-week office boy for a broker. Other members of the group pushed their way up from the bottom or very near it. John D. Rockefeller began as a clerk in a forwarding and commission house in Cleveland; Baker, as a clerk in the New York State Banking Department at Albany. At the age of seventeen William Rockefeller was keeping books for a miller. Rogers's first salary was three dollars a week as a clerk in a store at Fairhaven, Massachusetts. Keene came to America from England at fourteen and began to earn money by selling milk, teaching school, caring for horses, working on newspapers, and engaging in other varied occupations in Shasta County, California; he got his real start speculating in silver mines.

When these men talked of working one's way up from the bottom, they knew what the words meant. They also knew the merits of frugality for a young man of financial ambition. Rockefeller began earning money at seven, and hoarding it in a blue bowl; at the age of ten he lent fifty dollars to a neighboring farmer at seven per cent interest. When Baker married, he was earning ten thousand a year and saving half of it.

§ 4

One of the most striking things about this group of men—and one of the things in which they were representative of their financial generation—was their piety. At least seven of them were churchgoers; six were actively interested in church affairs.

Morgan was perhaps the most prominent layman in the whole Protestant Episcopal Church—that affluent denomination in which (according to John T. Flynn) half of the seventy-five multi-millionaires in the New York of the nineteen-hundreds were communicants. He loved to attend the General Conventions of the Church as a lay delegate from New York; to convey a few well-chosen bishops thither in his private car and entertain them royally in the convention city at a house which he rented for the purpose, and which was always referred to as "Syndicate House." He gave nearly five million dollars to the Cathedral of St. John the Divine; he gave a new rectory and parish house to St. George's, his own church in New York. It was Morgan who in 1904 persuaded the Archbishop of Canterbury to come to America, and made a special trip from Wall Street to Bar Harbor to make arrangements with Bishop Lawrence for the English prelate's visit. During the summer of 1908, when three bishops visited Morgan at his splendid house in Prince's Gate, London, each day began with family prayers read by Bishop Doane in the Library. Every week the head of the House of Morgan breakfasted with Doctor Rainsford of St. George's Church; the meetings of the vestry were customarily held at his house, and there is a characteristic story to the effect that Morgan once objected to the election of a vestryman who he felt would not socially be quite suitable to such gentlemen's gatherings.

Patrician as he was in his conception of organized religion, Morgan nevertheless possessed a simple and genuine faith. When, after his death in 1913, his will was published, newspaper readers who turned to it in the expectation of finding a document concerned only with financial arrangements stood amazed at the mighty declaration of belief with which it began: "I commit my soul into the hands of my Saviour, in full confidence that having redeemed it and washed it in His most precious blood He will present it faultless before my Heavenly Father; and I entreat my children to maintain and defend, at all hazard and at any cost of personal sacrifice, the blessed doctrine of the complete atonement for sin through the blood of Jesus Christ, once offered, and through that alone."

The Rockefeller brothers were both prominent Baptists. William gave the church building in which he worshipped in Tarrytown. John was a Sunday School superintendent. His faith, like Morgan's, was simple and sincere; "I have *never* had occasion to doubt," he once said. His piety flowered in a series of munificent gifts. Even as a boy of sixteen he gave nearly a tenth of his tiny income to missions and kindred activities; and in his later years he was a fount of pecuniary blessings to the

Baptist denomination, as well as to education, public health, and other worthy causes. (Up to 1928 he had given away in all a little over half a billion dollars!)

Baker was a trustee of All Souls' Unitarian Church in New York, a regular churchgoer, and a generous donor (late in his life) to the Washington Cathedral. Stillman attended St. Bartholomew's Episcopal Church in New York, though not regularly. Schiff attended the synagogue with inflexible regularity, read his prayers every morning, said grace after meals, and refused to have anything to do with business on the Sabbath (a circumstance which, as we have seen, was awkward for Harriman on a certain Saturday in 1901). Schiff aided in the foundation of a Jewish theological seminary; he not only founded but served as chief executive officer of the Montefiore Home for Chronic Invalids, and on his visits to the Home he used sometimes to read the service himself and to preach. His abundant kindliness and generosity were of great aid to Lillian D. Wald from the earliest days of her Visiting Nurses' Service in Henry Street in the New York slums. On the afternoon of the Northern Pacific panic, Miss Wald had been reading the newspaper accounts of the disastrous struggle in Wall Street and was surprised to hear Schiff's voice over the telephone, asking her if this was not the evening when he and Mrs. Schiff were to take supper with her at Henry Street; and they came. After his death she wrote of him that "no interests of his business world were ever allowed to supplant his spiritual or altruistic interests."

Harriman went regularly to church at Arden, wrote letters to the men of the town urging church attendance upon them, used to walk home from the Sunday morning service with the clergyman and inquire about the mission work and about parishioners who might be in trouble, and established a boys' club in New York in which he maintained a continuing and lively interest. "He believed in God and he believed in worshipping God," wrote the clergyman at Arden.

Many people, aware of the yawning gulf between the prevalent conduct of business in Wall Street and the doctrines of the Sermon on the Mount, have leaped to the conclusion that the religion of such men as these must have been hypocritical: that they assumed an air of piety to curry favor with the righteous or to atone for their business practices. To assume this is to misunderstand completely the men, the atmosphere of the times, and the relation between business and the churches.

The contrast between faith and works is often striking: between Morgan and Harriman battling for the control of a railroad and thereby bringing on a panic, and Morgan and Harriman at worship; between Rockefeller receiving "drawbacks" and driving competitors remorselessly out of business, and Rockefeller picknicking and singing hymns under the trees of Forest Hill with the Sunday School children of the Euclid Avenue Baptist Church. It is perplexing to the student of financial history to note, on the one hand, the prevalence of huge slush-funds for the purchase of votes at Washington and at the state capitals, the hardness of heart shown to unprotected stockholders and bondholders in railroad reorganizations, the fleecing of the public on the exchanges, and the unconscionable profits made in stock-watering operations; and on the other hand to witness the frock-coated gentlemen who were responsible for such flagrant practices attending church and passing the plate and singing "For all the saints" or "When the roll is called up yonder, I'll be there"—and believing it, as Mr. Flynn says Rockefeller no doubt believed it.

It is anomalous to think of financiers worshipping Jesus of Nazareth, the simple carpenter of Galilee, and yet never coming into close human contact, in their mature years, with the workmen in the mines and factories subject to their control, and maintaining an uncompromising enmity against labor organizations. It is even stranger to find some of them assuming that the Lord was their ally in whatever they did, as when Rockefeller said, "God gave me my money," or as when George F. Baer, leader of the anthracite coal operators in the coal-strike dispute of 1902, sent to a critic of his stubborn attitude toward labor this sublime declaration: "The rights and interests of the laboring man will be protected and cared for—not by the labor agitators, but by the Christian men to whom God in his infinite wisdom has given the control of the property interests of this country." How can such paradoxes be explained?

Several things need to be borne in mind if one is to explain them—even after one has made due allowance for the normal frailities and backslidings of mankind, the difference between Sunday resolutions and week-day practicalities, and the disposition of clergy and laity alike to feel that the gift of a new parish house will atone for almost anything.

In the first place, the Christian religion, as practiced by most of these men, was only partially the religion of Jesus. The Old Testament had a large part in it, and the Old Testament contains plenty of passages which permit the exaction of an eye for an eye and a tooth for a tooth. Religions tend to take on the color of the communities in which they are practiced; and in the American community other philosophies than that of Christ had absorbed and diluted the Christian teachings. There was the Benjamin Franklin philosophy of frugality. There was the Puritan philosophy of sobriety, continence, and Sabbath observance. There was the laissez-faire tradition of business competition as a hard-fought battle without fear or favor. So completely had such philosophies and traditions been taken into the American blood-stream, as it were, that if an aggressive business man worked hard, saved his pennies, refrained from alcohol and adultery, wore a somber suit to church every Sunday, and put money in the plate, he was well on his way to be a model of Christian conduct. (In the Episcopal Church there was somewhat less emphasis upon a bleak sobriety than in the evangelical churches, but the rest of the formula remained virtually intact.) These were the accepted virtues, and the Bible was an arsenal from which one might select rhetorical ammunition with which to defend them.

The best of the church-goers of Wall Street probably felt very much as Clarence Day, in his delicious *God and My Father*, describes the elder Mr. Day as feeling:

"And nobody could tell him his duty—he knew it without that, it seemed. . . . It was a code, a tradition. It was to be upright and fearless and honorable, and to brush your clothes properly; and in general always to do the right thing in every department of life.

"The right thing to do for religion," continues Mr. Day, "was to go to some good church on Sundays." Even in the supposedly wicked metropolis of New York, church-going was in the early nineteen-hundreds a part of the expected duty of the respectable man. The church played so important a part in the community that a substantial citizen ran the risk of being thought a little queer if he did not participate in church activities. The prosperous naturally flocked together in churches where the clergymen—responding, perhaps, to the almost imperceptible pressure of their congregations—took on the color of their surroundings; and the teaching in such churches was not likely to have very embarrassing implications. Mr. Day says that his father liked St. Bartholomew's: "The church itself was comfortable, and the congregation were all of the right sort. . . . The place was like a good club. And the sermon was like a strong editorial in a conservative newspaper."

Yet even if we remember that the religion of Jesus had been subtly altered into something which would have been quite unrecognizable to the carpenter of Galilee, a large part of our paradox still remains. Even a code of simply "doing the right thing in every department of life" can hardly be reconciled with some of the practices freely engaged in by kindly and generous pillars of the church. Other explanations must be sought.

Bertrand Russell has said somewhere that any man of ordinary sensibility can sympathize with suffering that is visible to him, but only a man of exceptional imagination can be wrung by suffering at a great distance from him. It must be remembered that the damage done in the speculative campaigns of Wall Street, in the watering of stock, in outrageous reorganization plans, in the exploitation of labor, was usually remote from those who did it. When a man unloaded stock upon the public, for example, he did not see his victims face to face. The whole operation, performed in brokers' offices and reported upon a mechanical ticker-tape, was anonymous and impersonal. Often the damage was remote in time as well as in space: when one looted the credit of a railroad, for example, the result might not be felt for years; indeed, if times remained prosperous it might not be felt at all. In the endless complexity of economic events, how could one say upon whom the responsibility for a future disaster might rest?

Even more remote from the directors' conference table than the investor was the laboring man: if mills were closed or wages were cut or thugs were hired to break up a protest meeting in the mining camps, the families upon which the burden of such policies would fall were not as easily visualized as were the boys of one's little club in the slums. They were very far off, the figures on the profit-and-loss account were very near and very persuasive. When men in Wall Street spoke of Steel, what did they mean? An organization of over a hundred thousand human beings laboring at desks and in mills and in mines, with families to support, rent to pay, food and shoes to buy? Not at all: Steel was a symbol on the ticker tape, it was a counter in a speculative game: something one bought at 48 and sold at 56, something that the Chicago crowd were bulling and the Standard Oil crowd were gunning for. The movement of economic power toward the financial centers meant a movement toward absentee control, and absentee control always tends to be irresponsible, if only because of the weakness of men's imaginations.

Enormous allowances must also be made, too, for the sheer momentum of business competition: the fact that in the race for profits one was driven to do the same tricks which the other man did or be beaten. In competitive business, bad practices tend to drive out good. If I don't buy control of this company, Jones will, and he will milk it: therefore I'd better do it myself and do it quickly. The opposition are trying to bribe the legislators —we'd better get in there first. We can't afford to be squeamish. Business is business. In the memorable words of H. H. Rogers, "We are not in business for our health."

Another perplexing paradox lies in the apparent lack, even among the godly financiers, of a strong sense of public responsibility. Few of the financiers of Wall Street defied the officers of the law as flatly as Rogers, who in the Waters-Pierce case refused to admit knowing where the offices of the Standard Oil Company of Indiana were, and when the prosecutor asked him if he wished to say to the Supreme Court of Missouri that he as a director of the Company did not know where its offices were, replied coldly, "It is quite immaterial to me what the Supreme Court of Missouri desires me to say to them, other than what I have testified." A somewhat more polite hostility to the public authorities was nevertheless characteristic of the men of the Street.

Laws, to them, were obstacles to be got around. The corporation lawyer was the efficient pathfinder of circumvention. (Mr. Dooley once said that the corporation lawyer could transform a law which had been designed as a stone wall into a triumphal arch.) Governmental investigations were impertinent snooping-parties to be dodged. The contempt of the financiers for the general public was expressed forcibly in Baker's remark, "It is none of the public's business what I do," and in Morgan's angry retort to a newspaper man who intercepted him in Paris during the Northern Pacific panic and asked him if he did not owe the public an explanation in view of what had happened: "I owe the public nothing."

Here again, however, an explanation is in order. Such acts and statements are not always to be interpreted—though they have often been interpreted—as expressions of defiance to every interest but a selfish one. They must be interpreted in the light of the enduring laissez-faire tradition. The earliest Americans had fled from Europe to escape governmental pressure; the pioneer had been perforce a rugged individualist; the belief had almost inevitably grown up that government interference with private business was the beginning of tyranny, and that to resist the intrusions of government into economic operations was to play the part of a conserver of American liberties. The law of supply and demand offered all the regulation which an American would tolerate. One's business was one's private affair, like one's diet or one's underclothes. A strange idea, it may seem, in view of the fact that great concentrations of capital could take into their own hands the administration of the law of supply and demand, and that what these men considered their private business intimately affected the lives of millions of men and women. Yet emotionally it was a potent idea. (To some, it still is.)

Add to this idea the financier's scorn of politicians as purchasable commodities, as men ignorant of business who inflamed the envious and still more ignorant mob; add to it also a feeling that the man who had won out in the great game of competitive business had a right to the prize, and that those who wanted to change the rules were simply trying to win by cheating; add to it also the feeling that somebody had to rule in any community, and that if the "better classes" had their way, things would be managed with more wisdom and dignity and grace than if the "lower classes" took charge,—and we may understand why even high-minded citizens could quite sincerely view the government and the public as annoying meddlers in matters that were none of their business.

Yet when all these explanations are made and when due account is taken of the restraint often manifested by the more responsible financiers in the use of their power, one must add: All these were not enough. Through the story of these men's adventures and exploits there runs the thrill of conflict, of immense tasks boldly accomplished and emergencies boldly met, of a continent subdued to the needs of industry; yet the truly heroic note is missing. The note of self-forgetfulness is missing. The dollar is omnipresent, and its smell pervades every episode.

The men of Wall Street wanted money and got it. All the explanations and extenuations, however genuine, are but accessories after that fact. One wonders what might have been the destiny of America if men of the majestic force of Morgan, the brilliance of Harriman, the utter concentration of Rockefeller, the generosity of Schiff, had been ruled by the disinterestedness of the scientist in his laboratory.

§ 5

In one of the most opulent chapters of his monumental *Fifty Years in Wall Street,* Henry Clews, writing in the eighteen-eighties, described the process by which Western millionaires were drawn into the social life of New York. Their wives "have of course heard of Saratoga, the far-famed spa of America, and as the fortunes of their husbands mount higher and higher into the millions, they become more and more anxious to see this great summer resort of wealth and fashion. Their influence prevails, and at the height of the season they may be seen at the United States or the Grand Union. They are in practically a new world. There is the rustle and perfume, the pomp and circumstance of the more advanced civilization of the East, and the ladies, with innate keenness, are quick to perceive a marked difference between this gorgeous panorama and the more prosaic surroundings to which they have been accustomed. As people of wealth and social position, they are naturally presented to some of the society leaders of New York, . . . who extend an invitation to visit them in their splendid mansions in the metropolis. In New York the Western ladies go to the great emporiums of dry goods and fancy articles of all sorts, to the famous jewelry stores, and other retail establishments patronized by the wealthy. They form a taste for all the elegancies of metropolitan life. . . .

"New York . . . is really the great social center of the Republic. . . . Here are . . . mansions of which a Doge of Venice or a Lorenzo de Medici might have been proud.

Here are the most beautiful ladies in the world, as well as the most refined and cultivated; here are the finest theatres and art galleries, and the true home of opera is in this country; here is the glitter of peerless fashion, the ceaseless roll of splendid equipages, and the Bois de Boulogne of America, the Central Park; here there is a constant round of brilliant banquets, afternoon teas and receptions, the germans of the elite, the grand balls, with their more formal pomp and splendid circumstance; glowing pictures of beautiful women and brave men threading the mazes of the dance; scenes of revelry by night in an atmosphere loaded with the perfume of rare exotics, to the swell of sensuous music. It does not take much of this new kind of life to make enthusiastic New Yorkers of the wives of Western millionaires, and then nothing remains but to purchase a brownstone mansion, and swing into the tide of fashion with receptions, balls, and kettle-drums, elegant equipages with coachmen in bright-buttoned livery, footmen in top boots, maid-servants and man-servants, including a butler and all the other adjuncts of life in the great metropolis."

The invasion of society by the new rich, thus fulsomely described by Clews in New York in the eighties, was and is a perpetual process, though the methods and the details differ from period to period. Naturally, social prestige cannot be precisely measured; yet if we apply to our ten financiers such criteria as are available, we get at least a suggestion of the rate of its growth. Most of these ten men, it will be recalled, had begun life in humble circumstances (and only one had had a college education). Nevertheless in 1905 all but one of them were listed in the New York *Social Register*. (Schiff was the sole absentee, and his absence was presumably due to the fact that he was a Jew, and the Jews constituted socially a group somewhat apart; the fashionable clubs were almost exclusively Gentile, and the *Social Register* was virtually a Gentile Register.)

The nine men who were listed were recorded as belonging to an average of 9.4 clubs apiece. Though only two of them, Morgan and Vanderbilt, belonged to the Knickerbocker Club (the citadel of the patrician families), Stillman and Harriman joined these two in the membership of the almost equally fashionable Union Club; Baker joined these four in the membership of the Metropolitan Club (magnificent, but easier of access to new wealth); John D. Rockefeller, William Rockefeller, and Rogers, along with Morgan and Baker, were listed as members of the Union League Club (the stronghold of Republican respectability); seven of the group belonged to the New York Yacht Club. Morgan belonged to 19 clubs in all; Vanderbilt, to 15; Harriman, to 14. And on the opening night of the Metropolitan Opera season of 1905, the *New York Times* reporter, remarking correctly that this was "more of a social than a musical event," noted the presence of Mr. and Mrs. Vanderbilt in Box 6, of Mr. and Mrs. Harriman in Box 1, of Mr. and Mrs. Baker in Box 10, and of Mr. Morgan in Box 35. Mr. and Mrs. Schiff were in attendance on a later evening of the same week.

That was in 1905. By way of a footnote it may be added that although in that year only two of our ten financiers belonged to the Knickerbocker Club, in 1933 the sons or grandsons of six of them did. The following progress is characteristic: John D. Rockefeller, Union League Club; John D. Rockefeller, Jr., University Club; John D. Rockefeller, 3d, Knickerbocker Club. Thus is the American aristocracy recruited.

Nor is the process new. Let us glance backward as well as forward. In 1905 Mrs. William Astor—or Mrs. Astor, as she was generally called, with regal brevity—was nearing the end of her long reign as the acknowledged leader and arbiter of society. If anybody represented entrenched social prestige, it was she. Yet Mrs. Astor was the grand-daughter-in-law of a German immigrant who, though he made twenty million dollars in fur-trading and real-estate, was scarcely able to read and write.

Again, in the early years of the twentieth century, the Vanderbilts were the most glitteringly fashionable family in the United States. When Alfred Gwynne Vanderbilt was married to Miss Elsie French in 1901, the arrangements for their wedding were chronicled in the press almost as if it were a royal alliance. Yet not until 1883 had Mrs. Astor deigned to call upon Mrs. William K. Vanderbilt, thus bestowing social recognition upon the family. And William K. Vanderbilt was the grandson of a Staten Island yokel who began his career by rowing a little ferry-boat from Staten Island to Manhattan.

No further reminder is needed of the fact that in a democracy like the United States, in which there are no hereditary titles to provide a semblance of stability, the upper class is highly fluid. As a matter of fact, not only is it highly fluid, but it is composed of a number of over-lapping groups, themselves fluid and very vaguely de-fined. There are, for example, in any large American community, the old families, whose prestige is based principally upon their inherited position and inherited wealth (or what remains of it); they are usually the conservators of manners, and view with perennial dismay the rivalry of the new rich and the decay of the traditional standards of taste and conduct. Again, there are the lead-ers of fashion, whose preëminence is based upon wealth, style, and a zest for entertainment, with or without in-herited position. There are the new rich, many of them zealously seeking admission to the fashionable class by imitating fashionable manners and customs and by entertaining on the grandest scale of all. There are the substantial citizens who lead in the support of all manner of good works. The interplay of these and other groups forms a social drama which repeats itself in every large community and in every generation: the old families losing their money or sinking into inertia or dissipation; the fashionable people in their turn joining the ranks of the old families or wasting their substance; the new rich joining the company of the fashionable, and so on. But always the influence of money is commanding.

Nowhere had this drama been more exciting than in New York. Long before the days chronicled by Henry Clews, new wealth had migrated thither to exercise its social ambition. During the eighteen-nineties the aristocrats of that proud city, under the leadership of Mrs. Astor and her chief-of-staff, Ward McAllister, had attempted to circumscribe society and keep the invaders out of it. "Mrs. Astor," to quote Frank Crowninshield, "had very little use for newcomers. Only old families, old names, old lace, old operas, and old traditions appealed to her." To her, society was a sacred institution; and under her tutelage its rites were almost pontifical. Magnificent were the two-hour dinners, with eight or nine courses and five wines; the assemblies, the cotillions at Delmonico's, the stately teas, the massive evening receptions; magnificent, though sometimes a little dull.

But in attempting to keep society exclusive, Mrs. Astor only whetted the ambitions of prosperous men and women the country over. When Ward McAllister, finding that her ballroom would hold only four hundred people, remarked in 1892 that this did not greatly matter as there were only about four hundred people in society anyhow, the remark found its way into the newspapers; it promptly reverberated from coast to coast, and "The Four Hundred" became a national phrase. Stories of the conspicuous extravagance of the Bradley Martin ball in 1897 circulated everywhere, and although many good people regarded them with dismay or amusement, others lay awake wondering how admission to the Four Hundred might be achieved.

The walls of exclusion, so carefully guarded, held with some success until 1901, but with the formation of the Steel Corporation the pressure upon them became too great. The beneficiaries of Morgan's gigantic distribution of Steel stock arrived in the metropolis from Pittsburgh and points west; other beneficiaries of other distributions came with them or followed them; bankers and brokers grown rich through speculation in the bull market of those days built marble palaces in Fifth Avenue and sought admission to the circle of the elect. "The hordes waiting to be admitted to society, whether in New York, Newport, Long Island, Aiken, Tuxedo, or Lenox, were so numerous, so insistent, so rich, and, on the whole, so agreeable, that there was nothing to do but give up the struggle," says Frank Crowninshield. "And from that time on the men and women who were seen in general society multiplied like germs in a bouillon culture." The tempo of society was quickening, its tone was becoming gayer, its membership much larger and more heterogeneous. The new financial era was altering it in a thousand subtle ways.

Not all of the multi-millionaires, of course, cared for social conquest. Of the ten men in our group, for example, John D. Rockefeller did not care for it; his strict Baptist soul was content in the role of substantial citizen. Morgan, though he loved to play the grand seigneur on two continents, disdained the game of fashion. Keene was most at home in the company of horsemen: his only club was the Rockaway Hunt, his horses raced brilliantly at Belmont Park and Saratoga, his son Foxhall was the best polo player in the country and a dare-devil automobile-racer. Nevertheless the association between the financial empire of Wall Street and the fashionable society of Fifth Avenue was complex and intimate. The swallow-tailed gentlemen in attendance at Mrs. Astor's annual ball constituted a good-sized directory of directors. The C-spring barouches and electric victorias which rolled through the Park, the trotting horses which matched their form on the Speedway of a Sunday afternoon, the coaches-and-four which threaded the winding roads of Westchester, the champagne which flowed at an evening of *tableaux vivants*, the splendid luncheons at Sherry's, the new racing cars which tore along the sands of Ormond Beach, the diamonds which glittered in the great horseshoe of the Metropolitan, were paid for in considerable part from the proceeds of corporate flotations and successful bull or bear campaigns on the Exchange.

When prices sagged in Wall Street (wrote Edith Wharton in 1905 in *The House of Mirth*) "even fortunes supposed to be independent of the market either betrayed a secret dependence on it, or suffered from a sympathetic affection: fashion sulked in its country houses, or came to town incognito; general entertainments were discountenanced." When prices rose, society was buoyant. For example, the 20-point leap in Union Pacific stock which followed Harriman's raising of the dividend in the summer of 1906 caused intense excitement in Bellevue Avenue, Newport; every trader of note in the Newport set at least made his summer expenses, according to the gossip-monger of *Town Topics*; and although a tennis tournament was then in progress, "I noticed that from ten o'clock on Friday morning until the market closed none of the big operators went near the Casino."

For the sons of the fortunate, the path of least resistance led to a financial career. For example, of the 55 members of the Porcellian and A.D. clubs (the two most fashionable clubs at Harvard) in the classes of 1904, 1905, and 1906, no less than 25 were engaged in finance a few years after graduation, 2 more had been engaged in finance but had left it, and another 2 were in closely allied occupations. The social connections of well-groomed young men could be turned to good account in a banking or brokerage house. The chief ambition of most young Americans was to make money, and the best chance to make it on a large scale was to have a part in the handling of great capital funds.

And so it happened that while new men and new money from outside New York were constantly invading metropolitan society, this society was also determining in large degree the social atmosphere of Wall Street. If the market place was full of buccaneers insensitive to the public interest, it was also full of very agreeable men who after the day's work was over would ride uptown and change and go splendidly to a dinner for forty or fifty at the Gerrys' or the Goelets' or the Ogden Millses' or the John Jacob Astors'. And sometimes they were the same men.

§ 6

The American aristocracy was still a little unsure of itself. It was developing a social pattern, but still somewhat self-consciously, and with a frequent glance toward Europe—and especially toward England—to assure itself that the pattern was suitable. To entertain a visiting count or duchess from across the water was to score several points in the social game; to arrange a marriage between one's daughter and a foreign nobleman was to score a grand slam. Ever since Jennie Jerome, the daughter of a New York broker, had married Lord Randolph Churchill in the seventies, there had been an epidemic of international marriages. Gustavus Myers has estimated that by 1909 over five hundred American women had become the wives of titled foreigners and that the sum of about two hundred and twenty million dollars had gone abroad with them. William K. Vanderbilt's daughter Consuelo married the Duke of Marlborough in 1895, Cornelius Vanderbilt's daughter Gladys married Count László Széchényi in 1908, George J. Gould's daughter Vivien married Lord Decies in 1911—but the list would be interminable. English butlers opened the doors of the massive houses along Fifth Avenue; American gentlemen of fashion purchased English clothes, and their wives, Parisian clothes; the country life of the very affluent followed a fundamentally English pattern, with large week-end gatherings, hunting, shooting, and a plentiful supply of horses. And it was not simply spontaneous preference which determined such choices, but also a sense that they were correct because they bore the foreign cachet.

Yet if there was a trace of a national inferiority complex in the attitude of American society toward Europe, the complex was much more striking in the attitude of American millionaires toward European art. To be a patron of art was the correct thing for a successful banker or promoter or speculator. Among our ten leading financiers, three—Morgan, Baker, and Stillman—were notable collectors, and Schiff could almost be classed as one. Against the crimson velvet walls of the dining room of the house in Paris which Stillman occupied during the closing years of his life hung Rembrandts and Titians; over the library table hung an early Italian Holy Family; and in the private picture gallery were other masterpieces of assured merit, many of which his friend Mary Cassatt had helped him to select. Baker collected Chinese jade. Morgan's treasures of art were of enormous variety and value: he was one of the great collectors of all time. Yet it is curious to note how generally these and other millionaires regarded art as something outside the current of the American life of their time.

Although Schiff is said to have given commissions to living artists, and Harriman—a marked exception—insisted that everything in his huge country house at Arden, even to the tapestries and the marble bas-relief over the principal fireplace, should be of American workmanship, nevertheless the overwhelming preponderance of works of art collected by the millionaires of this period were Old Masters which, as Lewis Mumford remarks in *The Golden Day*, "had been on the market a long time, which had reached par, and could be certified by trusty advisers like the famous critic and appraiser, Mr. Bernard Berenson.

"This hunting for pictures, statues, tapestries, clothes, pieces of furniture, for the epidermis and entrails of palaces and cottages and churches," continues Mr. Mumford, "satisfied the two capital impulses of the Gilded Age: it gave full play to the acquisitive instinct, and, with the possible rise and fall in prices in even time-established securities, it had not a little of the cruder excitement of gambling in the stock market or in real estate. At the same time, it satisfied a starved desire for beauty and raised the pursuer an estimable step or two in the social scale. . . . The essential character of all these culture seekers was that their heart lay in one age, and their life in another. They were empty of the creative impulse themselves, and unwilling to nurture this impulse in the products of their own time. At best, they were connoisseurs, who could appreciate a good thing, if it were not too near: at worst, they were ragpickers and scavengers in the middens of earlier cultures. They wanted an outlet for their money: collection furnished it. They wanted beauty; they could appreciate it in the past, or in what was remote in space, the Orient or the Near East. They wanted, finally, to cover up the bleakness of their American heritage; and they did that, not by cultivating more intensely what they had, in fertile contact with present and past, but by looting from Europe the finished objects which they lacked."

The motives to which Mr. Mumford refers were not, of course, always conscious and deliberate. There is no question of the sincerity of the passion for beauty in men like Morgan and Stillman, whatever one may say of the motives which animated a man like Gates, who collected Corots yet was never seen by his secretary reading any book but *David Harum*.

The point is that the conception of art as a living thing which might flower out of the life about one and express the meaning and the beauty of that life, just as the great paintings of the Renaissance flowered out of the life of fifteenth-century Florence, would have been strange to these men, if not unintelligible. The life about them was crude, the scene about them was ugly—and had been made uglier by the industrial operations of men like themselves; there was no American art worth their attention; they turned to the art of the past and of Europe just as naturally as the patrons of the Metropolitan Opera turned to European operas and European singers, as the patrons of orchestral music turned to European composers and conductors, as American architects built railroad stations in the guise of Roman baths, and American country houses in the guise of French chateaux, English manor-houses, or Italian villas. What else was there to do? The foreign products were better. Therefore one bought them; or if this were not practicable, one had them imitated. Not yet was there in the Metropolitan Museum any American Wing. Financially the country had come of age; culturally it was still all too conscious of its awkward youth, and the attitude of the millionaires helped to keep it so.

It was natural for the men of an age of imperial finance to bring back trophies won abroad by their dollars, just as the emperors of an earlier time had brought back trophies won by the sword. It was natural for acquisitive men to think of beauty in terms of purchase and invest-ment. When Yerkes, the Chicago traction magnate, died, his canvas by Troyon, "Coming from the Market," had already appreciated forty thousand dollars in value since its purchase, according to the newspapers. This was a fact which any speculator could appreciate; perhaps there was something in art after all! At any rate, dozens of financiers were following the example of Morgan and Frick and Baker and Stillman—with Joseph Duveen as their broker and Berenson as their investment counselor. Almost as stimulating to self-assurance as an English valet or a stable of thoroughbreds or an imported Mercedes, was a genuine undisputed European masterpiece in the drawing room.

In Anna Robeson Burr's life of James Stillman there is a fleeting reference to Henry Clay Frick which hints at the cultural status of the new-made American million-aire during this lusty period. She reports that Frick was once seen "in his palace, seated on a Renaissance throne under a baldacchino, and holding in his little hand a copy of the *Saturday Evening Post*."

§ 7

They were prosperous years for Wall Street, the years 1905 and 1906. In those days the newspapers did not

print graphs indicating the rise and fall of the volume
of trade, but if they had, the curve of prosperity would
have been shown climbing somewhat above the highest
point which it had reached during the bull market of
1901, and lingering at that exalted level. And if for
millions of Americans life even in those years remained
an uncertain struggle for a drab and meagre existence,
few of the men and women in the great houses along
Fifth Avenue were deeply aware of the fact. Their little
world of magnificence was like an island set apart from
the common life of the country.

The news items of those years suggest, here and there,
the splendor of the life on this island, and some of its
characteristic contrasts. . . . Mrs. Astor, aged seventy-four
and in failing health, gave her annual ball at 840 Fifth
Avenue; she wore a magnificent Marie Antoinette cos-
tume of purple velvet, a massive tiara, a dog-collar of
pearls with diamond pendant attachments, a diamond
corsage ornament, and a stomacher of diamonds. . . .
Before this ball, Mr. and Mrs. Harry Lehr gave a dinner
for eighty-eight at the St. Regis; the table was fifty-eight
feet long and fourteen feet across, there were three thousand white roses upon it, and toward the close of the
meal the huge centerpiece was removed in order that the
host and hostess, fifty-eight feet apart, might signal to one
another when the time came to rise. . . . At James Hazen
Hyde's fancy-dress party at Sherry's, Madame Réjane
acted for his guests. The Armstrong Committee's investigation of the unsavory financial practices of the life-
insurance companies was shortly to cause Hyde's permanent departure for France, but meanwhile he was a gay
young host, costumed in his Coaching Club coat and
small clothes. . . . James Stillman gave a dinner dance:
his dining room was converted for the occasion into an
artificial forest in which, after the cotillion, a picnic sup-

per was served beside an artfully contrived waterfall. . . . John D. Rockefeller fled from his estate at Tarrytown to his estate at Lakewood, New Jersey, to dodge process servers from the Missouri courts. He also gave ten million dollars to the General Education Board. Shortly afterward John D. Rockefeller, Jr., spoke to his Bible Class on the topic, "Is it ever right to do wrong to achieve a right end?" . . . William G. Rockefeller, son of William Rockefeller and son-in-law of James Stillman, judged the beagles at the Fourth Annual Summer Dog Show at Mineola, Long Island. . . . Henry Clay Frick accumulated United States Steel stock; he also accumulated a Raeburn, an El Greco, a Van Dyck, a Titian, and a Ruysdael. . . .

At Newport, a journalist observed that the men and women of fashion were no longer content to drive in their stately carriages along Bellevue Avenue; instead, "people in goggles, veils, and dust coats tour all over this beautiful island." . . . One of the exciting events of the social year was the Vanderbilt Cup Race: at sunrise of an October morning the smart traps and foreign-built automobiles of society thronged about the scenes of action on Long Island—the start and finish at Westbury, the Hair Pin Turn, the road between Manhasset and Jericho. . . .

William K. Vanderbilt was said to be losing his grip on the New York Central, as he spent most of his time abroad; but his name led the list of winning stables on the French turf. . . . Alfred G. Vanderbilt was having a 250-horsepower car built to race at Ormond; the other entries in the Ormond races included a racer constructed by a less resplendent competitor named Henry Ford, whose little automobile company actually sold 1600 cars during the year 1906. . . . It was said that in the houses of Elbridge Gerry and Ogden Mills, dinner for one hundred guests could be served at an hour's notice. . . . In

Wall Street, speculation was booming. The interest rate for call money rose at one time to 125 per cent, but the big traders were willing to pay it to buy stocks on margin; for as a financial chronicler said in the New York *Tribune* at the end of 1905, "Never did a year close with better record—never did a new year dawn with prospect brighter. . . . Good times go marching on!"

Beyond the shores of this island of splendor, however, storms were rising. Not only a storm of popular resentment and distrust, which had long been brewing, but a storm directly resulting from the financial excesses in Wall Street itself. This storm was to break in 1907.

Chapter Four

PANIC

A NEW YORK business man, unfolding his copy of the morning *Tribune* at the breakfast table on Tuesday, October 15, 1907, and running through the day's news, would hardly have imagined that a five-inch item on page 15, carrying the headline, "UNITED COPPER BOOMING," would prove to be of momentous consequence to him and to millions of other Americans. The item reported a "sensation" of the previous day on the New York Curb—which in those days was a real curb exchange, the brokers jostling on the pavement of Broad Street, while boys with telephone receivers clamped to their ears hung on the window-ledges above and relayed orders to them by sign language through the uproar. From what the business man saw in the *Tribune*, he would have gathered merely that the stock of the United Copper Company, which was said to be under the control of a group of men headed by one F. Augustus Heinze, had leaped in price within a few hours from 37¼ to 60; and that the traders who had previously sold it short (knowing the depressed condition of the copper business) were unable to buy it back except at ruinous cost.

Surely, the business man would have said to himself (if indeed he had stopped at all to think about the significance of the news item), this is a wholly unimportant episode. What one man loses in a speculative bout like this, another man gains; and everybody knows that the fortunes of a few manipulators cannot affect the general prosperity of the country. Yet in fact the gamblers'

battle in United Copper stock was destined to be to the
financial panic of 1907 what the assassination at Serajevo
was to the World War of 1914: not the fundamental cause,
but the precipitating event. Even as the business man
sipped his coffee and turned the page, a relentless
sequence of events was preparing to drag him and his
fellows down into the whirlpool.

Not that business men were easy in their minds in those
mid-October days of 1907. It had been an ominous year.
During 1906 the strain of financial over-confidence and
of long-continued speculation had begun to tell severely
on the money market. The managers of several big railroads had entered upon campaigns of extension and
equipment as if the supply of capital to be drawn upon
was endless; the big speculators had borrowed money to
buy stocks as if the gambling mania would be endless.
Yet the drain on the world's supply of capital by the
Russo-Japanese War and by the San Francisco earthquake
and fire, though it had been hidden for a time, had been
real; and likewise the supply of new and eager stock-
market plungers was running out.

Conservative bankers began to be apprehensive. Altogether too much credit was tied up in Wall Street. Something like half a billion of it was of foreign origin, and
now the strain began to be felt abroad. In the autumn of
1906 the Bank of England warned the big joint-stock
banks of London against lending any more money whole-
sale to New York. The stock market faltered, sagged, and
in the middle of March, 1907, suddenly and disturbingly
collapsed.

"In Newport, Tuxedo, and Westchester County," as
Edwin Lefèvre wrote later, "were heard voices ordering
horses to be sold and stablemen to be dismissed; automobile repair bills were angrily sent back for revision and

itemized accounts were insisted upon and extensions of time asked for."

The apprehension of the financiers was increased by the fact that President Roosevelt, who in 1906 had driven through Congress the Hepburn Bill for the regulation of railway rates, was clearly not content with this restriction of the right of the grand moguls of business to do as they pleased. He was speechmaking vehemently about "malefactors of great wealth" and advocating further federal discipline of the corporations. Apparently the President of the United States was lost to sober reason. Say though he might to his intimates that "if trouble comes from having the light turned on, remember that it is not really due to the light but to the misconduct which is exposed," the men of Wall Street could not see things that way. To them the President was not only betraying his financial supporters in the 1904 campaign, he was a demagogue undermining public confidence and demoralizing business at the most dangerous moment. "I would hate to tell you," said Harriman to the reporters when his Union Pacific stock tumbled twenty-five points in the collapse of March 14, 1907, "to whom I think you ought to go for an explanation of all this."

Soon, however, a succession of foreign events bore witness that even far beyond the range of Roosevelt's insistent voice the world-wide speculative boom had undermined credit. In April and May there was a panic in Egypt. In May and June there was one in Japan. Early in October there was one in Chile. During the summer the stock market in Wall Street had another sinking spell. Commodity prices—some of which, like that of copper, had been artificially maintained by monopolistic control long after new contracts had ceased to be made—were sliding; the price of copper dropped from 26 cents to 22, to 18, to 13, and still buyers were scarce.

It began to be whispered that the supposedly invincible Standard Oil crowd of speculators, led by H. H. Rogers and William Rockefeller, were loaded down with stocks which they had bought for a seemingly inevitable rise in prices; and that instead of standing ready, as of old, to support the sagging market with new purchases, they were being forced to throw their holdings overboard for whatever they would bring. Corporations which could not continue in business without new money were becoming sorely embarrassed. The New York street railway combination failed. Now at last a crisis which had hitherto been acute only in the financial market-places of the country was beginning to throw out of work, by the thousand, men who knew nothing about the congestion in securities or the depletion of bank reserves, but felt their effect nevertheless: machines standing idle, factories closed down, foremen turning away workers.

With each new turn for the worse in the financial situation the bankers and the financial writers expressed a hope that the storm clouds had at last blown by; but however calm their faces, in the back of their minds grew a slow and restless fear. What next?

It was at this moment that Heinze and his friends pushed up the price of the stock of the United Copper Company.

§ 2

F. Augustus Heinze was one of the youngest and most picturesque of the buccaneers of finance. Only thirty-six years old, he had "the torso of a Yale halfback, muscles of steel, and a face of ivory whiteness, lighted up with a pair of large blue eyes." Part Irish, part German-Jewish, he had been born in Brooklyn but had gone out to Butte,

Montana, at the age of eighteen to seek his fortune, and had made it—none too scrupulously.

His first big exploit was to lease the Estrella copper mine, and to draw the lease so ingeniously that he was able to snatch all the profits from it and leave the owner none. In due course Heinze had a copper company of his own and was at war with the giant Amalgamated Copper Company, controlled by H. H. Rogers. Heinze's strategy was to claim that his veins of copper ore ran down under the Amalgamated's land and that he therefore had a right to them under the so-called "apex law," and then to bring injunctions against the Amalgamated. Since Montana judges as well as Montana legislators were often purchasable and were popularly elected, the copper war became a legal and political war waged with the aid of subsidized newspapers; and in this sort of contest young Heinze with his thirty-seven lawyers, his eloquence, his dashing good looks, his glamor in the eyes of the women, and his shrewd decision to pay high wages to his workmen was a formidable power. Clad in a loose black suit with flowing tie, his hands thrust into the old-fashioned waistband pockets of his trousers, he was the perfect swashbuckler of the mining camps—shrewd, reckless, popular, confident, and ready to use any and every weapon to annihilate the biggest and most overcapitalized copper company in the country. At last he sold out to Rogers, took his millions, came back to New York, and became—God save the mark—a bank president. Not that he was particularly interested in banking; but a bank president could command ready funds with which to play the market, and there wasn't a finer gambling game in the world.

In the United Copper pool with Heinze was a little barrel-shaped man named Charles W. Morse, who came from the sober state of Maine but possessed none of the scrupulous caution supposed to be characteristic of the New Englander. Morse had worked his way through Bowdoin in the grand manner by getting paid a salary as clerk in his father's company and hiring another man to do the work for less cash, while he himself divided his time between studying and journeying to New York to sell Kennebec River ice to a New York brewery and other concerns. By the time the big holding-company boom set in, Morse was promoting the American Ice Company and using his monopolistic power—with the aid of Tammany politicians—to push up the price of ice to the people of the metropolis. Presently he went into banking, for he too had discovered that it is convenient for a speculator and promoter to have access to depositors' funds. He borrowed large sums through "dummies" to finance his private operations; at one time, for example, his bank lent him a hundred thousand dollars in his stenographer's name. And he had made the further discovery that it was possible through a succession of borrowings to gain control of bank after bank. The Morse technic was simple: borrow money and buy the controlling shares in a bank; then put up these shares as collateral against another loan of money, with which you buy another bank, and so on. As soon as you control the bank it becomes quite simple to have such loans to yourself approved—and other loans, too, with which you may promote other companies and play the market.

Morse promoted a combination of most of the steamship companies plying along the Eastern seaboard. Financially as well as physically, his steamships, like his ice, floated on water, for he had learned well the peculiar advantages of overcapitalization. Morse was spoken of as the "admiral of the Atlantic coast." And now he, too, with only one eye on his banks, was toying with United Copper stock in company with F. Augustus Heinze, Edward

R. Thomas, and other like-minded spirits. They worked through the brokerage house of Otto Heinze & Co., in which were two of F. Augustus' brothers.

The flurry in United Copper on Monday, October 14, 1907, which as we have seen was inconspicuously reported in the next morning's *Tribune,* was part of a speculative campaign conducted by these plungers. They had made large purchases of United Copper stock through a number of brokers, who were supposedly holding the purchased shares for them; and so complete had been their control of the market that although the prices of other copper company stocks had been sliding, United Copper had stood firm until the preceding Saturday. On Saturday, however, there had been a sharp outbreak of selling and the price had gone down. The Heinze crowd suspected some of their allied brokers of selling—and also of having had to hock Heinze's stock certificates with the banks to get cash. On Monday various short-sellers bought stock to cover their commitments, and as we have seen these repurchases drove the price way up from 37¼ to 60. Thereupon Heinze and his cronies apparently guessed that they had the market cornered. If, they reasoned, we call upon our false allies to deliver the stock they have bought for us, they won't be able to do it, and we'll be able to dictate terms to them which will punish them for their treachery and make a round profit for ourselves. So they suddenly called for delivery of the certificates by 2:15 on Tuesday afternoon.

But they had guessed wrong. They did not have the shares cornered. Enough stockholders in United Copper, hitherto inactive, had seen in the newspapers just such items as our hypothetical business man read on that Tuesday morning, and had decided that this was the golden moment for selling out, to permit the allied brokers to cover their short purchases and comply with

the Heinze demand without running the price beyond
60. The stock was duly delivered—and the Heinze cash
ran out. In the last few minutes of Tuesday's trading
the Heinze crowd were selling United Copper frantically
to raise enough money to save themselves, and the price
dropped from 60 to 36. The next day—Wednesday the
16th—it plunged to 10. In the débâcle the firm of Otto
Heinze & Co. and one of its allies went to the wall. The
jig was nearly up for the young swashbuckler of the
mining camps.

Even so, the damage done by these failures would
probably have been limited had Heinze and his friends
not been bankers as well as gamblers. Heinze was president of the Mercantile National Bank; Morse and
Thomas were directors of it. When the Heinze failure
was headlined on the front pages of the papers, depositors naturally became suspicious and began to with-
draw their funds. Suspicion spread to the Morse chain
of banks, too. The Mercantile, finding its cash being
drained away by uneasy depositors, applied to the Clearing House for help. And the crisis of 1907 thereupon
went into its second stage.

§ 3

To understand the events of the second and third
stages of the crisis it is necessary to understand the nature
of the banking organization in New York at that time.

In the first place, there was then no Federal Reserve
System, able to mobilize money from scattered banks and
provide it wherever it might be needed in time of stress.
Each bank stood on its own feet, except for such aid as
the Clearing House might see fit to give it. In the second
place, the Clearing House—an association of banks which
took care of the daily exchange of checks between them

—was dominated by the more conservative and solidly entrenched institutions which were either within the Morgan sphere of influence or the National City Bank sphere of influence or were in substantial accord with those financial powers. In the third place, the big bankers who thus dominated the Clearing House management had long looked with disapproval upon the character of competition which the Heinze and Morse banks and others of similar nature had been giving them. In the fourth place, these Clearing House authorities possessed powers which enabled them to dictate terms to the lesser banks in time of crisis; for suddenly to deny Clearing House facilities to a bank at such a time would virtually condemn it to death.

Finally, during the preceding years there had been a tremendous uprush of trust companies in New York. Somebody had made the discovery that the trust company act was so worded that a trust company might legally do nearly everything which a national or state bank could do, accepting deposits just as if it were a bank, yet riding clear of the restrictions placed upon the banks in the interest of safety. Thus a trust company was not required to keep a 15 or 25 per cent cash reserve, and it might employ its funds freely in the purchase of stocks or of real estate; so it could pay ample interest on deposits, and could lure depositors away from the banks. Most of the trust companies were not members of the Clearing House, since they refused to meet what seemed to prudent bankers to be imperative standards of safety. Of these non-member trust companies, some cleared their checks through member banks, others got along without any facilities whatever for the exchange of checks. Like the banks controlled by Heinze and his kind, the trust companies as a rule did not enjoy the favor of the dominant banking powers of the city: the methods of many of them were considered dangerous—as they certainly were—and their success was uncomfortable. During the period between 1898 and 1906 their total deposits had swelled from a little less than two hundred million dollars to over eight hundred millions.   ·

When the Mercantile National Bank appealed to the Clearing House for help, and later when some of the trust companies did so, the conservative authorities of the Clearing House apparently realized that they had an opportunity to serve both the public interest (as they saw it) and their own interest. They had large disciplinary powers, and they were in a position to use these powers to eliminate noxious influences in the banking world—and noxious competitors. They swung into action at once, instituting what one of their number aptly referred to as "sanitary measures." They demanded the immediate resignation of Messrs. Heinze, Morse, and Thomas from all their banking connections. Day after day the front pages of the newspapers blared forth the tidings: on Saturday morning, October 19, MERCANTILE BANK DIRECTORS RESIGN; on Sunday morning, the 20th, C. W. MORSE FORCED OUT OF ALL BANKS; on Monday morning, October 21, THE THOMASES, TOO, QUIT THEIR BANKS.

It was also announced that the banks which had been under suspicion had been examined and found to be solvent, and that the Clearing House would come to their aid. But somehow this latter announcement did not ease the situation. The revelation that several banks were involved in one way or another in a speculative débâcle and were under suspicion was highly disturbing. Men and women, reading the headlines, began to worry about the safety of their balances, wherever deposited. Corporations prepared to withdraw their balances from any banks or trust companies which might possibly be subject to distrust. Fear was seeping like a fog throughout the city.

On Monday the situation looked a little easier and the turbulent stock market was quieter, but in reality it was the calm before the storm. Behind closed doors the fate of the big Knickerbocker Trust Company was being anxiously discussed. The president of the Knickerbocker, Charles T. Barney, had been close to Morse. The Knickerbocker had lent money to Morse. How far might it be involved in the unfortunate speculations of the admiral of the Atlantic coast? Better eliminate Barney, too, decided the Clearing House authorities, intent upon their energetic sanitary campaign. After the close of banking hours on Monday there came two more announcements —staggering announcements in view of the already widespread fear and the size and importance of the Knickerbocker Trust Company. First, the Clearing House committee had demanded the resignation of Barney. And second, the National Bank of Commerce, which had been clearing checks for the Knickerbocker, had decided to do so no longer.

That evening—Monday evening, October 21—the executive committee of the Knickerbocker Trust Company met to decide how to meet their desperate emergency. They met at—of all places—Sherry's restaurant on Fifth Avenue: "a fashionable restaurant on an autumn evening, filled with leisurely groups, laughing and talking, hearing beyond their laughter the familiar sound of the crowd that ceaselessly streams by along the glittering streets." Mrs. Burr, in her life of Stillman, has memorably suggested the fatal effect of holding such a meeting at Sherry's—the rumors running about as to what might be happening in that private room, "the words passing from one to another, without equal significance to all, but to all intensely interesting—that rumor, ignored by the puzzled, smiling women, yet laying a heavy shadow over the faces of the men . . . the waiters, alive to every whiff of gossip"; the failure to guard the doors of the conference room as time went on; the guests slipping into it from the supper-room, and hearing the talk within; and then the beginning of real panic: men slipping out of Sherry's through the windy night to the Night and Day Bank on Fifth Avenue, where checks might be cashed even before the Knickerbocker opened its doors for Tuesday's busi-, ness.

§ 4

It happened that for several weeks J. Pierpont Morgan, surrounded by bishops, had been enjoying the decorous deliberations of the General Convention of the Episcopal Church at Richmond, where the chief topic of debate had been the question whether ministers of other denominations might be permitted to make addresses to Episcopal congregations. During the last few days of the convention it had been noticed that Morgan received frequent telegrams from New York which presumably dealt with matters more mundane than the sanctity of the Episcopal pulpit. "If one came during a meal," writes Bishop Lawrence, "he tore it open, read it; then putting the palms of both hands on the table, a habit of his, he looked straight ahead with fixed eyes and deep thought for a few minutes. One day a member of the party said, 'Mr. Morgan, you seem to have some bad news.' He shot his eyes across the table at the speaker and said nothing. No question of that sort was asked again." By Saturday afternoon the 19th—the day when Charles W. Morse was being thrown to the lions by the Clearing House committee—the Convention had adjourned, and that night two special cars drew Morgan and the bishops back to New York.

"Sunday morning, as we ran into Jersey City," continues Bishop Lawrence, "we went into Mr. Morgan's car for some bread and coffee before arrival, and found him sitting at the table with a tumbler turned upside down in each hand, singing lustily some tune which no one could recognize. Arriving in New York, he put us into cabs. . . . As we parted, we asked him if we should see him at Saint George's, and he called out, 'Perhaps so.' He went to his library."

The old banker's first thought on returning from Richmond had doubtless been to defend his own interests against a possible storm. The fortunes of the Knickerbocker were no immediate concern of his, and it had been mixed up with the detestable Heinze and Morse. When three representatives of the Knickerbocker called upon him early Tuesday morning—a few hours after the meeting at Sherry's—and asked for help, he would do nothing.

In fighting panics, as in fighting forest fires, it is important to decide upon what line one shall make one's battle. Just where Morgan would set up his defenses was not yet certain. Nor, for that matter, was it yet clear that the panic would be really formidable. But one thing was already clear: so far as Morgan was concerned, the Knickerbocker lay beyond the line of battle. It was with heavy hearts that the representatives of the Knickerbocker repaired to their bank.

At nine o'clock that Tuesday morning a casual saunterer in Fifth Avenue might not have noticed anything amiss at the splendid marble-columned building which housed the main uptown branch of the Knickerbocker Trust Company at the northwest corner of Thirty-fourth Street, opposite the Waldorf-Astoria. But the checks which were being presented by messengers within the bank were for killing sums, and the lines at the paying tellers' windows were growing swiftly. By ten o'clock they reached far outside the building and up the Avenue. Carriages and automobiles were crowding to the curb to discharge depositors who had heard the rumors of disaster. A line of spectators had gathered on the opposite curb. Guests looking out of the windows of the Waldorf were asking one another what was amiss. All over the city —by word of mouth, by telephone, by those mysterious channels through which fear communicates itself from person to person—filtered the report: "There is a run on the Knickerbocker Trust Company."

Meanwhile within the bank, as within its downtown headquarters in lower Broadway, the cash was melting away rapidly. There had been eight million dollars or more when the doors were opened that morning. A little after noon they were gone. The Knickerbocker Trust Company was forced to suspend payment. The announcement of suspension to the men and women waiting in line at the Fifth Avenue branch was greeted by "groans, shouts, and catcalls."

The sudden closing of such a large institution immediately put a new and alarming face on the situation. The Secretary of the Treasury rushed posthaste from Washington to New York, after leaving instructions for the deposit of six million dollars in government funds in the leading national banks of the metropolis. That evening he and old Morgan and those two masks of silence, Baker and Stillman, gathered in conference with other high chiefs of the banking world in Cortelyou's rooms at the Manhattan Hotel. The Secretary agreed to throw additional currency into the breach. Not yet, however, was it clear just where the lines of defense would be drawn up, and the uncertainty was increased by something which happened at the close of that meeting at Cortelyou's rooms in the Manhattan on Tuesday evening.

George W. Perkins, a partner in the House of Morgan, talked with the reporters who were waiting for news of the conference; and the next morning there appeared in the New York *Times* and *Sun* an "official" statement which contained the scarcely diplomatic sentence, "The chief sore point is the Trust Company of America." Though the statement continued with reassurances that the conferees believed the company to be sound, that it had twelve million dollars in cash, and that as much more as might be needed had been pledged, the effect of that sentence was immediate. On Wednesday morning there was a terrific run upon the Trust Company of America.

As to the circumstances which led to this run there is unhappily a confusion of testimony. It is undeniable that while the Knickerbocker was collapsing, rumors were rife that the Trust Company of America would be the next to go. Barney, the president of the Knickerbocker, was a director of this other company and had borrowed from it $175,000, secured by Knickerbocker stock. This fact was a matter of common gossip in Wall Street—and the rumors which were flying about also charged that the funds of the Trust Company of America were invested in "cats and dogs" and that it was heavily involved with Heinze and Morse. A State bank examiner had visited it that very day to check up on these rumors. On the other hand, President Thorne of the Trust Company of America testified in the Stanley inquiry that the withdrawals on Monday and Tuesday, while large, had not been especially alarming: his net loss in deposits on Tuesday had been only a little over a million and a half dollars (as against thirteen and a half millions the very next day). Thorne testified that he had not sought aid for his bank on Tuesday, and in fact had not appreciated the gravity of the situation; that he had gone home that evening and then had been invited by telephone to come to the Union League Club to confer with Perkins of the House of Morgan and the young vice-president of the First National Bank, Harry Davison; that they had asked him about the condition of his bank, and he had told them, and they had "said they were very much pleased to know that it was in as good shape as it was"; and that he was not invited to go along with them to the conference at the Hotel Manhattan from which the "sore point" statement emanated. The whole burden of Thorne's testimony was that his bank was getting along pretty well until that statement focused the panic upon it.

Perkins, on the contrary, testified to the Stanley Committee that he distinctly remembered "Mr. Thorne coming to see us and saying that he had had heavy withdrawals and must have assistance and being very much alarmed that afternoon and evening over his condition." Perkins also denied having authorized any statement that evening, though he admitted that he gave the reporters "such information as I could that would be helpful."

The logical conclusion to be derived from this conflict of testimony would seem to be that the powers whom Perkins represented were distrustful of Thorne's bank (as the rumors gave them reason to be) ; that they were considerably less careful of their words than the situation warranted; and also, probably, that at this time they were not so much concerned with preventing the lightning from striking as with seeing that the stroke, if it came, did not damage the institutions in which they had full confidence.

Whatever the exact degree of alarm actually felt by Thorne on Tuesday evening and the exact significance of the "sore point" statement, early on Wednesday morning there were several hundred people standing in line in Wall Street to draw their money out of the Trust Company of America. In a vain effort to get rid

of that line of depositors, that all-too-visible advertisement of public distrust of the bank, President Thorne
put seven paying tellers at work disbursing cash; but
the line did not diminish. Thorne sent frequent messages to the Morgan offices to inform them of the rapid
shrinkage in his funds, and at half-past one or two
o'clock he walked up Wall Street to the Morgans', saw
Morgan, Stillman, and Perkins, and told them that if
help did not arrive very soon the bank would have to
close. The big bankers hesitated. They fully realized by
now the violence of the panic and the necessity for com-
bating it with all their power, but they were not yet sure
of the soundness of Thorne's bank, and apparently had
not yet decided whether it should be included within their
lines of defense or should be allowed to go under. Only at
the very last moment—a few minutes before three o'clock
—was Thorne supplied with a loan of a million dollars,
contributed by the House of Morgan, Baker's First National Bank, and Stillman's National City Bank. This
loan was just enough to see him through till the clock
struck three, for his cash was almost gone. Thirteen and
a half million dollars had been removed from his bank
that day.

It was a very narrow squeak. To the historian who en-
joys the comfortable advantage of hindsight, the hesitation of old Jupiter, coming on top of the drastic sanitary
measures of the Clearing House committee and the "sore
point" statement of the previous evening, might seem to
have been perilous. But it must be remembered that
everything was shrouded in a fog of uncertainty. Morgan
did not know how seriously the Trust Company of America might have been involved in dubious speculative enterprises; the Clearing House examiners were at work
within its walls, but had not yet reported; and the rumors

about it which flew through Wall Street were disquieting. Furthermore, Morgan had undertaken to bring together the presidents of the various trust companies and get them to organize and raise a fund for the support of their weaker brethren, and at that very moment these presidents were sitting in Morgan's front office and hesitating to come to the relief of the Trust Company of America or of the Lincoln Trust Company, which also was experiencing a run. Morgan, picturing the panic as a "trust company" panic—which it had now become—had told these gentlemen that the responsibility for saving Thorne's company rested upon their shoulders; and he was waiting for them to act. Only when it was clear that they were not ready to, did he step into the breach.

Late on Wednesday afternoon, Benjamin Strong, one of the men who had been examining the affairs of the Trust Company of America, came to Morgan with his report. Old Jupiter was sitting in a rear room of his banking house with Baker and Stillman, while the trust company presidents still squirmed and debated in the front room. Strong reported that he was satisfied that the Trust Company of America was solvent. "This, then, is the place to stop this trouble," said Morgan briefly.

From that moment on, there was no question where the lines of defense were to be drawn. Thorne's bank lay inside them and would be protected. Nor was there any further doubt as to the unified leadership of the forces of defense. Morgan was seventy years old, but in the days which followed he was completely the master of Wall Street.

Old rivalries and animosities were forgotten as Harriman and Rockefeller and other one-time foes of the Morgan empire put their forces at his disposal. The Secretary of the Treasury deposited in all thirty-six million dollars in the national banks of New York, specifying that ten millions of it was to be used for the benefit of the trust companies, but leaving the use of the rest of it virtually in Morgan's hands. The situation was ironical: President Roosevelt had spoken of malefactors of great wealth in terms which implied that Morgan might be included in their number, yet here was his Secretary of the Treasury accepting Morgan's judgment as to how these funds should be disposed. Cortelyou, however, was merely acknowledging, as did Harriman and Rockefeller, that circumstances alter cases. There was a panic raging, it must be stopped, Morgan knew better than anybody else what to do and how to do it, and people did what he told them to.

Always thereafter, so long as the panic lasted, the place where Morgan sat—whether in his office at Broad and Wall Streets or among the Peruginos and Pinturicchios in his gorgeous library uptown—was headquarters. Say what one will about Morgan's hard financial tactics in previous years or the ultimate advantages to his empire which accrued from the decisions of those troubled days, at least his dominance in the counsels of the bankers was the dominance of sheer personal power, utterly respected and obeyed. The crisis which had come was ideally suited to bring out the best in him. Corporate aggrandizement was not an issue, nor inflation of capital stock, nor the relations between owners and workers, rich and poor, Wall Street and Main Street. This was a crisis among bankers, and the interest of the general public was for the moment almost identical with that of the bankers themselves. The great need was for courage and leadership, and these Pierpont Morgan could provide. He was a rock to which frightened men might cling.

§ 5

The battle now had to be conducted on many fronts at once, for it seemed as if everything were going wrong. On the very Wednesday when Morgan said, "This, then, is the place to stop this trouble," there were runs on several other banks and trust companies, the Westinghouse electrical concern was tottering, the Pittsburgh Stock Exchange closed, the New York Stock Exchange was panicky, and the call-money rate for financing brokers' purchases of securities advanced to 125 per cent. That evening the trust company presidents were called into session again and subscribed ten million dollars for the relief of the Trust Company of America—but not until Perkins had secured for them from Cortelyou ten millions in government deposits.

Thursday came, October 24, and not only was there another long line of depositors waiting to draw this ten million dollars out of the Trust Company of America, but the trouble on the Stock Exchange reached a climax: there seemed to be no money at all for the purchase of securities, and prices were going down the chute. The Morgan forces were supporting United States Steel at 22, and it held fast, but Union Pacific dropped that morning from 108½ to 100, Northern Pacific from 110 to 100½, Reading from 78⅝ to 70½. Toward the end of the morning, sales almost stopped on account of the scarcity of cash. President Thomas of the Stock Exchange consulted Stillman. What could be done? Stillman told him to go to Morgan; and so, like everybody else who needed money in those days, Thomas proceeded to 23 Wall Street. Arriving there, he found the outer office full of excited men. He sent in his name and sat down to wait. Twenty minutes went by. Then old Morgan, who had been apprised of Thomas's need by Stillman, came out of his inner office.

"We are going to let you have twenty-five millions," said he shortly. "Go over to the Exchange and announce it."

Thomas did so, the panic was quieted for the moment, and the money rate dropped forthwith to six per cent; stocks rallied a bit. Morgan, acting on behalf of the bankers in whose institutions Cortelyou had made deposits, had thrown into the Stock Exchange panic an amount almost exactly equal to that of these deposits. Yet the relief even from this audacious stroke might prove to be merely temporary. How would the next turn of the panic be met?

As Friday dawned (October 25) there seemed, in the words of Perkins, to be "not a ray of hope in the situation." Here were millions of dollars being paid out right and left and there was no doubt what was becoming of them: they were being hoarded, they were being swallowed up in safe-deposit boxes, and still depositors and brokers called for more cash. How on earth could it be found? What would happen on the Stock Exchange today? Would the Trust Company of America survive another few hours of this madness? As early as six o'clock that morning Perkins and Cortelyou were sitting on the edge of the latter's bed at the Hotel Manhattan, debating what on earth could be done next. Perkins went on to Stillman's house; Stillman communicated with some of his wealthy allies, and among them Rockefeller is said to have put up ten millions for relief and to have pledged fifty more. Morgan stormed at the trust company presidents again, and when they showed further reluctance to support the Trust Company of America, he went to the Clearing House and labored with the Clearing House bankers to scour up another fifteen millions. It was barely enough to bridge over the situation in the call-money market; as Perkins later testified, "If twenty millions had been needed that day, the Stock Exchange and a hundred or more firms would have gone up, it was just that close. It was touch and go." And still the siege of the Trust Company of America continued; and that day a number of small banks failed.

On Saturday, October 26, the clouds lightened momentarily. The decision was made to issue Clearing House certificates to serve the banks temporarily for cash. On Sunday, however, the storm advanced from a new quarter. The authorities of the City of New York informed Morgan that they had thirty million dollars' worth of short-term obligations coming due which it would be impossible to meet in view of the disordered state of the money market, and that unless they were assured of a loan of thirty millions, the city would go bankrupt. For two days Morgan considered this new problem; then on Tuesday he called to his library the Mayor and other city officials, and seating himself at a big desk, wrote out with his own hand an agreement to organize a syndicate to float thirty million dollars' worth of six per cent City bonds. This act relieved the City's financial distress, and served notice on the community that Morgan was not afraid to go on doing business. Once more the skies seemed brighter.

Brighter, in fact, they remained during the rest of that week, despite a series of untoward events—the suspension of grain trading at Duluth, the declaration of banking holidays in several states, other indications that the panic had now spread throughout the country, and continued nervousness on the Stock Exchange.

Day after day Morgan sat in his office, a big black cigar in his mouth, and the princes of the financial world came in one by one and took his orders—delivered with gruff finality and sometimes with scorn, as when a bank president complained that his reserves were being gravely reduced, and Morgan withered him with "What! Do you realize what you are saying? Tomorrow you may have no reserves at all."

On more than one night the lights burned late in that graceful white building the notepaper of which was headed, with royal brevity, simply

The Library
Thirty-three East Thirty-sixth Street

while financiers who had been summoned by Morgan argued over the possible ways and means of meeting his demands upon them.

The west room of the Morgan Library was walled with red silk damask, patterned with the arms of the Chigi family of Rome; on the walls hung splendid Florentine masterpieces of the fifteenth and sixteenth centuries; upon the bookshelves stood a bust by Michelangelo and a rock-crystal bowl said to have been mounted for Queen Christina of Sweden; the mantelpiece and the gilded ceiling had been made for great Italian houses. Morgan sat in a red plush armchair by the fire in this great room, smoking his black cigar and playing solitaire, with a Madonna and Child by Pinturicchio looking down over his shoulder, and Fra Filippo Lippi's altar-piece of St. Lawrence and Saints Cosmo and Damian facing him from the opposite wall. It was not his way to wrangle over methods of financial relief; he left that to lesser men to do in another room, while he sat in the red plush chair with the card-table before him and slowly puffed on his cigar, and carefully placed the five of clubs on the two, and the eight on the five, and the jack on the eight.

From time to time the assembled bankers would send a delegate in to him with their conclusions, and he

would say curtly "Yes" or "No," and the delegate would
retire again to the east room, and the weary bankers
would resume their discussion of reserves and margins
and collateral, while the game of solitaire continued
under the watchful eyes of the Madonnas and the great
ladies of Florence, until at last the conclusion which
Morgan wished had been reached and the immediate
objective in his battle gained.

So the fight went on. But as the week drew to an end,
the hope that victory might be achieved by sheer dogged
endurance began once more to fade. A new crisis was
at hand, and the men who would have to face it were
almost worn out by the strain of the preceding ten days
and nights.

§ 6

The new crisis was of a double nature.

In the first place, the run on the Trust Company of
America was continuing relentlessly, and the cash already raised was petering out. Morgan figured that at
least twenty-five millions more would be required—if
indeed even this would save the day. The bank was
sound, but panic is unreasoning.

In the second place, a broker named Grant B. Schley—
he was George F. Baker's brother-in-law—was in difficulties. He was heavily in debt to his firm, the firm in turn
was in debt to various banks; and among the securities
which he had put up as collateral for his loan from the
firm, and which the firm in turn had used as collateral
for its loans from the banks, were a large number of
shares of the Tennessee Coal & Iron Company, a big
steel concern. These shares, while potentially of great
value, were not readily salable except at a great sacrifice
in price. Schley's failure might precipitate another agon-

izing crisis on the Stock Exchange, and that in turn might mean more trouble for the banks, so dependent was their whole structure of collateral loans upon the stability of security prices.

On Saturday evening, November 2, there was a great gathering of financiers at the Morgan library to consider these two new crises. It was as if the full cast of characters in the banking drama had assembled for their most critical scene. James Stillman was there, that eagle of the financial world, cold, astute, money-minded—a man whose fury at human errors filled his underlings in the National City Bank with terror, whose outbursts of kindliness to friends and children were like flashes of sunshine through the clouds on an overcast day. The bewhiskered George F. Baker was there, curt, absorbed, ready as always to suggest the strategy which Morgan's gruff authority would enforce. Perkins and Steele of the House of Morgan were there, worn by arduous days and nights of labor; and the correct and diplomatic Gary, with Filbert of the Steel Corporation at his side; and the lawyers Ledyard and O'Brien; and a host of bank presidents and trust company presidents and their young executives.

For the time being, Morgan had left the crimson-brocaded west room and had retired to a small room at the rear of the Library. In the west room sat the trust company presidents. In the high east room, hung with tapestries and surrounded by gallery upon gallery of bookshelves, sat the Clearing House bankers. Hour after hour dragged by, while in the rear room Morgan and his immediate advisers wrestled with the double emergency which now faced Wall Street.

A loan of cash, or of bonds on which cash might be raised, would probably save Schley and would thereby ease the situation for those banks which were nervous about the presence of so much Tennessee stock in the collateral which Schley's firm had put up. But Morgan had a better plan than making a loan to Schley. Somebody had suggested a way in which he might kill two birds with one stone—rescue Schley and do what might prove a good stroke of business for his Steel Corporation at the same time. If the Steel Corporation bought from Schley and others the control of the Tennessee Company, and paid for it with Steel Corporation bonds, Schley would be saved, the banks would rest more easily, and the Corporation would secure iron mines which might be of increasing value.

Of this ingenious scheme few of the men outside that small room were aware. Most of them knew only that Morgan was working out a plan and that they might be needed. Toward midnight, however, as Morgan debated the technicalities of his project with Gary and the lawyers, word was circulated among the waiting bankers that "a new situation" (which meant the Schley-Tennessee situation) had arisen, that it would require twenty-five million dollars, but that Morgan had decided to take care of it *if the trust company presidents would raise another twenty-five millions to take care of the Trust Company of America and other imperiled institutions.* That was Morgan's ultimatum.

The news created consternation among the bankers and most of all among the trust company presidents, who hung back in very natural trepidation at tying up further funds at such a time of panic. What would their directors think? How on earth could the president of an institution accept single-handed such a crushing responsibility? Was this the only way out? More hours dragged by, hours of consultation and indecision. The long suspense was telling upon these men. Benjamin Strong, who had been making another prolonged examination of the affairs of the Trust Company of America, has told how, as he sat waiting to make his report to Morgan, he dozed off to sleep; and James Stillman, sitting next to him on the lounge, asked him when he had last been to bed, and he said Thursday night. (It was then early Sunday morning.) There must have been other equally exhausted men among those who waited there and paced up and down the marble hall; these hours among the parchment-bound books and the Renaissance paintings must have been to some of them a gorgeous nightmare. But nobody could go home. Morgan had seen to that. If any banker had tried to walk out, he would have found the massive front door of the library securely locked. Morgan had the key in his pocket!

At last old Jupiter, knowing that it was now or never, walked out to the crimson west room and confronted the trust company presidents. He told them that the panic must be defeated. His lawyers had prepared a subscription blank providing for a subscription from each trust company (computed on the basis of its resources) to a loan fund totaling twenty-five millions. One of the lawyers read the document aloud.

"Then"—to quote from Lamont's life of Davison—"they laid it on the table. Mr. Morgan waved his hand invitingly towards the paper. 'There you are, gentlemen,' he said.

"The bankers shifted from one foot to another, but no one stepped forward. Mr. Morgan waited a few moments. Then he put his hand on the shoulder of his friend, Edward King, and gently urged him forward. 'There's the place, King,' he said kindly but firmly, 'and here's the pen,' placing a handsome gold pen in Mr. King's fingers. Mr. King signed. The ice was broken. They all signed."

Morgan had triumphed—and in that triumph had reached the pinnacle of his career.

Now the front door might be unlocked. The Trust Company of America was safe for the time being—and, as events were to prove, permanently. The Tennessee negotiations, too, were past their worst stages. At a quarter to five on Sunday morning the weary bankers walked out into the dark and empty streets.

More conferences followed on Sunday, and on Sunday evening Gary pointed out a hitherto unregarded obstacle which might wreck the whole Tennessee plan. The President—the stiff-necked President, with his prejudice against Wall Street and his hatred of monopolies—what would he say to the acquisition of the Tennessee Company by the monster of the steel trade? Roosevelt's consent must be secured, and this must be done at once—before the Stock Exchange opened for Monday's business, so that the announcement of the purchase might be made at the opening. A little telephoning secured a special train on the Pennsylvania Railroad, consisting of a locomotive and a single pullman, with a right-of-way over everything else to Washington. Gary and Frick, having wrung from the President's secretary an early morning appointment with Roosevelt, boarded the train.

On Monday morning they were at the White House. The President interrupted his breakfast to see them.

They told him that "a certain business firm" would undoubtedly fail unless help were given, that among its assets were a majority of the Tennessee stock, that the purchase of these assets would be of "little benefit" to the Steel Corporation but would be the "only means of avoiding failure." They thought the purchase ought to be made unless the President objected to it.

Roosevelt had to decide instantly. Naturally—the panic having reached the stage which it had—he told them he felt it "no public duty of his to interpose any objections." At five minutes before ten—just as the Stock

Exchange was about to open—Perkins, sitting in the Morgan office with a telephone at his ear connected with the White House, heard Gary's voice telling him that it was all right. The announcement was duly made, the stock market rallied with delight, and every banker heaved a sigh of relief.

From this moment on, the skies slowly cleared. The worst of the panic was over.

That Gary's explanation to Roosevelt was somewhat disingenuous is obvious. Roosevelt might not have been impressed had he been told that the immediate beneficiary of this transaction was a brokerage firm, that of George F. Baker's brother-in-law; that no single loan to the Schley firm was secured wholly by Tennessee stock; or that the development of the open-hearth process of steelmaking was increasing the potential value to the Steel Corporation of the Tennessee's properties. It is also equally obvious that Roosevelt preferred not to question Gary and Frick too closely lest he discover something which it would be inconvenient to know. He could have pressed them for the name of the concern which was threatened with failure, but he chose not to. It is also clear that the transaction was not precisely an act of open-handed generosity on Morgan's part. It was a piece of business which he hoped would in time yield the Steel Corporation a good profit.

Do these cold facts somewhat dim the glory of that all-night meeting in the Morgan library, at which Morgan induced the trust company presidents to sign the subscription blank on the ground that he too was putting up twenty-five million dollars in another way? Perhaps; but the answer to this question must be made in the light of certain other facts as well. The blank which Morgan induced the trust company presidents to sign did not, of course, involve a gift, but a loan with interest: their action, too, would be profitable if all went well. Further-more, the announcement that the Steel Corporation was taking advantage of the crisis to enlarge its holdings was just the sort of announcement which would cause the men of Wall Street to cease thinking of the panic as a time to hoard cash and would persuade them to think of it as a time to pick up bargains. Morgan's contribution lay simply in having nerve enough to go ahead and do business and dragoon other men into doing it too.

Some of his friends have implied that in such negotia-tions as these he was quixotic. One may reasonably doubt this; quixotism does not flourish in Wall Street, and Morgan had flourished there for nearly fifty years. The truth is that in those long vigils in the Library he simply showed more solid courage than any other man.

§ 7

Gradually the situation improved, and before long ob-servers were able to survey the field of battle and take stock of its results.

Let us set some of them down categorically:

1. Inevitably, the panic was followed by a depression. But the depression did not long remain severe. The eco-nomic structure of the country was still strong at bottom, weak as the top had proved itself to be.

2. As to the weakness at the top, the panic had taught at least one lesson. There ought to be some systematic method of mobilizing bank reserves, as Morgan had mobilized some of them by sheer force of will. The re-sult, after long and obstinate delay, was the creation of the Federal Reserve System. Other lessons of the panic, however—such as that the banks were insufficiently safe-guarded either by law or by tradition, and too easily fell a prey to stock-market-minded men, if not to predatory

gamblers—were not destined to be fully learned for at least another twenty-six years.

3. The struggle had not been without casualties. Morse was on his way to prison for misuse of the funds of his bank. Heinze was under indictment; and although the indictment was later dismissed, his bright career was tarnished. Barney committed suicide.

4. Financial power had become more nearly centralized than ever. There were fewer banks in New York now; the Clearing House's authority was greater (and was peremptorily if not needlessly used, during the aftermath of the disturbance, against other small institutions); the Morgan and Stillman banks were relatively stronger. Stillman himself had found that there were advantages in an alliance with Morgan; from this time on he played less of a lone hand, associated his National City Bank more frequently with Morgan enterprises. "Keep on good terms with J. P. Morgan," he wrote to his aide, Vanderlip, in 1915; it was a text the full virtue of which he had apprehended in 1907. Harriman, weakened by what was to prove a mortal illness, was no longer so fierce a Morgan antagonist as before. Rogers and William Rockefeller had suffered in the collapse of securities in the panic year; Rogers had been forced to sacrifice millions, and no longer commanded a worshipful following in the Street.

Where there had once been many principalities, there was now one kingdom, and it was Morgan's.

He was an old man now, and as the years went on he was seen less and less at Broad and Wall Streets; but even when he was at Prince's Gate in London, or at Aix, or in Egypt, his son and his other partners carried on in the reflection of his glory, merging banks, consolidating and extending their sphere of influence.

One rival power, however, had not yet learned deference. There were forces outside Wall Street which in the next few years were to cause frequent embarrassment and tribulation to the ruling powers. To appreciate how these forces developed and how their counter-offensive took shape we must go back a few years and examine their origins.

Chapter Five

COUNTER-OFFENSIVE

THE great reform movement which was destined to fill the air with clamor, the statute-books with new legislation, and the hearts of financiers and industrialists with trepidation during the years between the Panic of 1907 and the war boom of 1915-16 was not a thing of sudden origin. To understand it, in fact, one must go far back beyond the bland days of 1900 and take note of the ferments which had been working during the preceding quarter century.

Of these ferments, the most potent had been the perennial discontent of the Western farmers. Marching out into a wide land of supposedly free opportunity, these farmers had found themselves surrounded by hostile circumstances. The era of subsistence farming with hand implements was drawing to a close; the era of money-crop farming with the aid of expensive machinery was beginning; for countless farmers this meant going into debt, which in turn meant coming under the sway of the local banker. In the deflation of the eighteen-nineties they suffered as debtors always do in deflations. Farmers who raised money-crops had to buy many goods and supplies which in a more primitive economy they would have raised or made for themselves, and the prices of these goods and supplies were often outrageously high. To ship their crops to distant markets they had to rely upon the railroads, many of which were scandalously managed for the profit of Eastern owners and manipulators and set their freight rates arbitrarily high. Hence there arose in the West a widespread and confused agitation against bankers, the gold basis of the currency, industrial monopolists, and above all the railroads: an agitation which in the eighteen-eighties had been chiefly responsible for the passage of such regulatory laws as the Interstate Commerce Act.

These farmers, being mostly property-owners, were not in any true sense enemies of capitalism, but where big business seemed to stand in their way they fought it tooth and nail. During the depression of the eighteen-nineties, their Populist Party became a formidable power in American politics from South Carolina to the Dakotas and beyond—a strange and motley band, animated by a revivalist fury and organized by a curious assortment of leaders: hard-headed opponents of privilege, visionary intellectuals, and bewhiskered hayseed demagogues. Some of the measures proposed in the Populist platform of 1890 had looked toward fundamental changes in the control of economic processes: for example, public ownership of the railroads and of the telegraph and telephone systems. Before long, however, the Populists succumbed to a fate which has often overtaken radical groups: they pinned their chief hopes on a single measure which seemed a simple panacea for their ills, they attracted to the support of that measure a huge and unmanageable following, and when the measure was voted down their strength was dissipated. "Free silver," said Henry Demarest Lloyd, "is the cowbird of the reform movement." So persuasive was the silver argument when young William Jennings Bryan uttered it at the Democratic Convention in 1896 that the Democratic Party advocated it and thereby inherited most of the Populist strength. After the vociferous campaign of 1896 ended in a public repudiation of free silver, and after Bryan in 1900 chose imperialism as his major issue and was beaten once more, the conservative journals had good reason to gloat with triumph: the farmers' revolt was broken—for the time being.

Another element in the revolt against big business which preceded the reform movement of 1900-15 was the long uphill battle waged by organized labor to secure union recognition, better wages, and relief from vicious working conditions. At intervals the battle had been bloody, as during the days of the Haymarket bomb tragedy in Chicago in 1886, the Homestead strike of 1892, and the Pullman strike of 1894. Nearly always the odds were against labor. The vast majority of employers resisted unionism strenuously. Only a small percentage of the workers were organized. When they used their only effective weapon, the strike, they found the temptation to resort to violence (to prevent other men from taking their places) almost irresistible, and usually violence alienated the sympathies of the general public. The courts, reflecting the prevailing conservative opinion of the day, had come to the remarkable conclusion that the Sherman Anti-Trust Act and other almost moribund measures originally designed to curb the great industrial combinations might be invoked to curb organized labor; thus workmen on strike often found themselves facing injunctions, the police, and the militia. Furthermore, their bargaining power was constantly being undermined by the annual influx into America of hundreds of thousands of immigrants. So long as there was still an open Western frontier, the plight of the laborer was mitigated by the hope of moving on to a new land of promise; but as the twentieth century dawned this outlet was closing.

In 1900 the strongest labor alliance, the American Federation of Labor, had 550,000 members; these mostly represented skilled crafts from which newcomers could be excluded. The Federation leaders, headed by the bespectacled, square-faced Jewish cigar-maker, Samuel Gompers, were mostly men of limited vision, sharp bargainers for practical advantage for their organizations; some of the lesser union leaders used dynamite as a means of persuasion; some were in secret alliance with employers (as in many rackets of later date). In the nature of things the majority of their followers were ignorant and undisciplined men, incompetent to understand and cope with the processes by which corporate power was being extended. Yet within the Federation and without, there burned a fierce resentment against the inhuman conditions prevailing in most industries— ten- and twelve-hour days, squalid and degrading slums and company villages, meager pay, utter insecurity, devious schemes for exploiting the worker through high rents in employer-owned houses and high prices in employer-owned stores. Under the pall of smoke which overhung the industrial towns this resentment was forever smouldering, and with it was allied the compassion of sympathetic men and women who felt that such conditions were a blot upon the face of America.

A third, though minor, element in the gathering ferment was the gradual importation and domestication of radical economic ideas of European origin, especially Marxian socialism. A fourth element was the influence of a number of widely circulated books of home-grown protest and challenge, of which perhaps the most seminal were Henry George's *Progress and Poverty* (published in 1879), Edward Bellamy's *Looking Backward* (published in 1887), Henry Demarest Lloyd's *Wealth Against Commonwealth* (published in 1894), and William H. Harvey's paper-covered manual of plausible monetary theory, *Coin's Financial School*. Young Robert LaFollette, borrowing a worn copy of *Progress and Poverty* from a Wisconsin blacksmith and gaining from it new assurance for his fight against privilege, was one of scores of future reformers whose thought was fertilized by one or the other of these books.

Such were the chief precursors of the reform movement. Along with them, and stimulated by them, went a subtle change in the attitude of innumerable men and women toward the American economy. We have seen how industries and financial operations had expanded in scope as if responding to a blind urge toward development on a national scale. This expansion was accompanied by a laggard and uncertain expansion in the individual sense of social responsibility—as if the democratic and humanitarian impulses were reluctantly feeling their way into the wider fields toward which the acquisitive impulse had broken a path. Timid and halting as was this social conscience when confronted by the interests of entrenched property, and almost imperceptibly as it undermined the traditional American belief in unregulated competition, it was a power of great potential force.

§ 2

Of the men who did most to liberate this force in the early years of the twentieth century, some were governors or mayors, like LaFollette in Wisconsin, "Golden Rule" Jones of Toledo, and Tom Johnson of Cleveland; one of course, was President Theodore Roosevelt; and one, as it happened, was a magazine publisher.

Samuel S. McClure was not a reformer by nature; he was simply a shrewd editor looking for popular reading-matter in order to be able to apply to magazine publication the principle of mass-production. The respectable monthlies of the time were discreetly written, gorgeously illustrated, and far less interested in the sordid drama of economic survival than in the well-bred consideration of highways and byways of Old Provence and first folios of Shakespeare. The supremacy of these respectable monthlies had been challenged during the eighteen-nineties by Frank Munsey's cheap and easy magazines, which became hugely successful. McClure, agreeing with Munsey that in low prices and popular reading matter lay the best hope of success, but bringing to the editorship of his magazine an intelligence of a much higher order than Munsey's, looked about for subjects of lively consequence to ordinary men and women. With the instinct of a born journalist, he realized that there would be popular interest in unflinching accounts of contemporary business; and he set a young woman named Ida M. Tarbell to work on a history of the Standard Oil Company, and did not abandon the project even though her colossal research went on for five long years. As she was finishing her study of Rockefeller's business methods, Lincoln Steffens, another of McClure's writers, went to Missouri and unearthed the scandalous story of municipal graft in St. Louis. "Tweed Days in St. Louis" appeared in *McClure's* in October, 1902; the first installment of Miss Tarbell's chronicle appeared in November, 1902—roughly a year and a half after the formation of the Steel Corporation and the Northern Pacific Panic, and a little over a year after Theodore Roosevelt's arrival at the White House. The era of the muckrakers had begun.

Not that the reproof implied in the term muckraker—which was first used by Roosevelt in one of the moments when he was leaning to the right to keep his balance on the political tightrope—was deserved by McClure's writers. Miss Tarbell in her Standard Oil history and Steffens in his series of articles on "The Shame of the Cities" were thorough and conscientious reporters of fact, as were Ray Stannard Baker in his examination of railroad practices and labor-union corruption, and Samuel Hopkins Adams in his articles on patent-medicine frauds. It was not until the egregious Thomas W. Lawson, a copper-company promoter and stock-market plunger, feigned conversion to the ranks of the righteous and sold "Frenzied Finance" to *Everybody's Magazine*, and William Randolph Hearst turned a lurid light on Washington in David Graham Phillips's series in the *Cosmopolitan*, "The Treason of the Senate," that Roosevelt pinned his phrase to the journalists of exposure. By that time there was good reason for reproof. Already, however, the country had been astonished and shocked by a prodigious array of diligently reported financial and political scandals. One of the muckraking books, Upton Sinclair's *The Jungle*, actually had an immediate and practical legislative result: it caused the passage by Congress of a packing-house inspection bill and hastened the passage of a pure-food bill.

To these disclosures in books and magazines were added disclosures by investigating committees, such as that of the life-insurance scandals in New York by Charles Evans Hughes. It was in the autumn of 1905, when prosperity was fat in Wall Street and speculation was roaring, that Hughes—then almost unknown to the public—revealed some of the uses to which the life insurance companies had put their policyholders' funds. It appeared that officers of the companies and members of their families drew large salaries and expense-moneys and were able to rake in additional profits through the use of company funds in favored enterprises. It appeared that insurance companies kept inordinate deposits in banks in which their officers were financially interested, and that on the other hand they were much too closely allied with investment banking houses to find it easy to preserve the disinterested attitude of trustees. For instance, George W. Perkins was simultaneously a partner in J. P. Morgan & Co. and an officer of the New York Life; in his former capacity he had sold to himself in his latter capacity four hundred million dollars' worth of bonds of the struggling International Mercantile Marine—eighty million dollars' worth of which, oddly enough, had been taken back temporarily by the House of Morgan as the day approached when the books of the insurance company must be examined by the State. Hughes revealed the disbursement of huge sums for surreptitious lobbying purposes, as in the maintenance of a mysterious establishment in Albany jocularly known as the "House of Mirth"; he revealed also the payment of comfortably large retainers to Senators Chauncey Depew and David B. Hill.

Gasping with astonishment at what they read in books and magazines and in the newspaper reports of the Hughes inquiry and other investigations, a vast number of men and women who had hitherto known little and cared less about the methods of expanding industry and high finance and about the way in which political pressures were exerted, were driven to the conclusion that the American economy and American public affairs were due for a housecleaning on an Augean scale. Meanwhile in a number of cities and states the cleansing process was already under way: in Toledo, for instance, where Mayor "Golden Rule" Jones and his successor, Brand Whitlock, single-taxers and disciples of Henry George, had been fighting the street-railway and electric-light corporations; in Cleveland, where fat, smiling Tom Johnson, whom Lincoln Steffens called "the best mayor of the best-governed city in America," had battled for a three-cent fare and had got it; and above all in the state of Wisconsin, where little Governor Bob LaFollette, whose stormy pompadour crowned a very hard head, had been making an astonishing record for legislation to subject the railroads to regulation, to restore popular rule, and to improve the calibre of men in the public services of the state.

Labor was simultaneously gaining in strength. In the five years between 1900 and 1905 the American Federation nearly trebled in membership. Socialism was growing: *The Appeal to Reason,* a Mid-Western socialist paper, had half a million readers by 1904. Debs, the Socialist candidate, had received less than a hundred thousand votes for President in 1900; four years later he received over 400,000. Big Bill Haywood's Western Federation of Miners, as fierce and uncompromising a labor organization as the country had ever seen, was on the rise. Early in 1905 Haywood and others met in Chicago and formed the International Workers of the World with the ringing declaration, "There is but one bargain that the I.W.W. will make with the employing class— *complete surrender of all control of industry to the organized workers.*" And at the very end of the year 1905, just as the Hughes investigation was closing, the country had a terrifying glimpse of what uncompromising warfare on the part of a militant labor organization might involve. Frank Steunenberg, ex-governor of Idaho, who had once put down a miners' strike with the aid of colored soldiers, was blown to pieces by a bomb placed at his front gate.

Haywood and Moyer and Pettibone of the Western Federation of Miners were tried for the Steunenberg crime (and acquitted) in July, 1907. The trial—with William E. Borah serving as counsel for the prosecution and Clarence Darrow serving as counsel for the defense —was a national sensation. Even in New York, two thousand miles away, Fifth Avenue was jammed, one day in May, 1907, with thousands upon thousands of workmen marching to the thrilling music of the Marseillaise and carrying banners which announced their sympathy for Haywood. It was a sight to make financiers, looking down from the windows of their great houses and their comfortable clubs, more than a little uneasy. Not only reform appeared to be gathering headway, but proletarian revolt of the most aggressive and vindictive sort.

§ 3

Throughout the early years of the reform movement the evolution of President Theodore Roosevelt was very significant, for he was its chief spokesman and exhorter and also a fairly reliable barometer by which to gauge its strength. As Henry Pringle has justly remarked, "The significance of Roosevelt's corporation activities lay in what he said rather than in what he did." Roosevelt was not in fact very much of a "trust-buster." During his seven and a half years in the White House, only twenty-five proceedings leading to indictments under the Sherman Anti-Trust Law were brought by the federal government; during the four years of the supposed conservative, Taft, forty-five were brought. In Roosevelt's first term, as we have seen, his chief onslaughts against the right of business to do as it pleased were his action against the Northern Securities Company and his insistence upon settling the anthracite coal strike of 1902; during the rest of the term his tendency was to play safe. Even during his second term he pushed to enactment few important measures designed to curb business: the only really vital one was the Hepburn Act, which permitted the Interstate Commerce Commission to regulate railroad rates.

Roosevelt's utterances, however—as distinguished from his acts—became steadily bolder during his second term, and furnished the urgent leit-motif for the whole reform movement. He opposed the use of the injunction in labor disputes, he asked for restriction of stock-market gambling, he advocated full publicity for corporate earnings and capitalization, he suggested in 1905 and definitely urged in 1907 the supervision by the federal government of all corporations engaged in interstate commerce; and he constantly lectured the irresponsible rich with furious emphasis. No one can recapture the feeling of those days without hearing in his mind's ear the loud Rooseveltian phrases echoing throughout the land with all the volume which Roosevelt's huge personal popularity and the sounding-board of Presidential prestige could give them: "malefactors of great wealth," "the tyranny of a plutocracy," "the kind of business which has tended to make the very name 'high finance' a term of scandal," "the speculative folly and flagrant dishonesty of a few men of great wealth," the need for "moral regeneration of the business world."

It is difficult, even after the lapse of many years, to view such a man as Theodore Roosevelt objectively. His bounding personality, his physical daring, his enthusiastic appetite for human contacts, his impetuous speech, his extraordinary range of interests, defy neutrality. The man was so enormously alive: not merely carrying the great administrative burdens of the Presidency, but denouncing nature-fakers, proposing simplified spelling, writing deliciously absurd letters to his children, clambering up cliffs in Rock Creek Park, devouring Tacitus and the prose works of Milton and thousands of other assorted books, announcing gleefully to John Burroughs his discovery of a yellow-throated warbler at Oyster Bay, writing voluminous letters to Trevelyan about the tactics of the generals of 1780, and inveighing against race suicide. To attempt a cold-blooded dissection of the policies of such a colossus of energy is like trying to make a precise working blueprint of a locomotive in full career. Yet the analysis of his economic position must be made if we are to understand the man, his influence, and his period.

Roosevelt knew little about economics. On matters like the tariff he accepted and repeated almost without question the traditional Republican arguments. The problems of banking and the currency were beyond him, and he knew it. He never seems to have made a careful study of the mechanics of corporate aggrandizement. The chief motive forces behind his economic policies and proclamations were, first, his wish to maintain the prestige of the government as sovereign even over the princes of finance; second, a natural and growing indignation at the process by which the rich expanded their already great power, corrupted governmental bodies to win privileges and immunities, bore down upon the laboring poor, and endangered the economic stability of the whole country by their speculative exploits; third, the political instinct for the middle of the road which kept him from going over all the way to the radical left, —an instinct buttressed by his conviction that only by staying in the middle of the road could he retain enough power to get anything done; and, finally, his overwhelming ethical bias, which led him to approach almost every problem with the animus of the "preacher militant" (to borrow Owen Wister's phrase) .

When Roosevelt took action against the Northern Securities Company it was largely from the first of these motives: to serve notice that Washington was still lord over Wall Street. When after an indignant sally against the powers of finance he would compromise and dally and fail to translate rhetoric into action, it was partly because he was too furiously busy with a thousand things to follow one of them through to a conclusion, partly because he had never developed a thorough-going economic philosophy, partly because political reforms engaged his interest more than economic reforms, but largely also because he knew that he must not get too far out of step with a conservative (and lobby-infested) Congress, a conservative Republican party, and an almost equally conservative country. It was far easier for a man in such a situation to denounce Wall Street than to find out where lay the springs of its power and decide what to do about them. It was also more in accordance with his preacher's temperament. Predatory finance was wicked and must therefore be excoriated.

It is easy to criticize the man as a straddler, a big talker who backed away from a fight. Despite all his large talk about honesty and courage, it is true that Roosevelt was a master of the weasel word. It is not an elevating prospect to see him squirming out of an acknowledgment of his previous cordiality to Harriman in order to abuse Harriman in 1907 and maintain an appearance of consistency; or to see him dismissing LaFollette's policies as "a string of platitudes" and LaFollette himself as one who offered the public "the kind of pleasurable excitement" that would be derived from "the sight of a two-headed calf"—and then, later, adopting many of LaFollette's policies without adequate acknowledgment.

Nevertheless there was a practical hard sense behind much of Roosevelt's compromising which some latter-day critics may not have taken into sufficient account. Being a Republican President of the United States, he faced the necessity—as the more consistent LaFollette, for example, did not—of keeping in some sort of line the East as well as the West, the stockholding community as well as union labor. To have become the hard-and-fast enemy of the financial powers would have left him as helpless in dealing with Congress and the country as was Woodrow Wilson in 1920. And if Roosevelt took out most of his reforming impulses in talk, it is only fair to add that many of them could never have been carried through to action in that decade. The temper of the country, even in his second term, was such that measures which called for mild governmental restraints upon business were viewed by business men generally as violently destructive attacks upon American prosperity. Nor should it be forgotten that Roosevelt's sermonizing did much to relax that temper and open the way to legislation. If he kept in the middle of the road, he at least succeeded to a measurable degree in moving the road.

In many ways Roosevelt typified the whole reform movement: its insistence upon a rebirth of public spirit, its tendency to prescribe for symptoms, its preoccupation with political as distinguished from economic measures (its chief energies were thrown into the initiative and referendum, the direct election of Senators, the direct primary, and so forth). He typified it also in his wary attitude toward any fundamental economic change. For the reform movement was not, considered in the large, a fundamentally radical movement.

Most of the reformers did not wish to make any far-reaching alteration in the capitalist system. They saw that it had so grown and spread that the captain of industry had powers which he had never possessed before; they wished to limit these powers for the protection of his little competitor and his employee and his consumers. They saw that he had become a successful political wire-puller; they wished to take the wires out of his hands and restore them to the rest of the voters. They saw many cruel results of the unregulated power of acquisitive commerce; they wished to forbid by law the repetition of these results. To think of the reformers as wishing to set up a fundamentally new order in America is to see them in a false light. Most of them—LaFollette particularly—looked back with nostalgic longing to the old days of little business and free competition. What they wanted to do was to restore the supposed freedom of those days by shackling the big bullies who had spoiled it.

In a very true sense they were conservatives—old-fashioned individualists trying to preserve individual liberty by calling in the policeman to protect it. In this sense it was the financiers, the promoters, the corporation lawyers, who were the true radicals of the time: it was they—though they would have been the last to admit it—who were taking the initiative in revolutionizing the American economy.

It is a mistake to think of capitalism as a system, in the sense of something fixed: an ancient structure of laws and rules and technics and traditions. It is a living growth, watered by acquisitiveness and constantly putting out new branches as new devices for the accumulation of profits or of power are invented or as old devices are adapted to new uses. The reformers were engaged in pruning it, cutting it back, lopping off ugly and misshapen growths. That Roosevelt often thought of himself as a sort of tree-surgeon whose exploits with the saw (or, to be more accurate, whose strenuous sermons on the need for using the saw) would lengthen the tree's life, is clear from many of his statements; and there was much reason in this argument. The reformers as a group were tree-surgeons—and while they were hacking away, the tree was continuing to thrust out new shoots.

Conservative business men, however, did not see

things this way. What they saw was a group of men with axes and Roosevelt cheering them on, and they feared that a venerable tree was going to be demolished.

Roosevelt was not without friends in Wall Street, but as his term of office drew to a close and his voice became more and more strident they became more and more bewildered and resentful.

"Theodore talks nonsense about Wall Street," wrote Major Higginson, the Boston banker, "where most of the men are honest—far honester than the politicians, who promise this or t'other for votes. He talks about the corporations as wicked, which means that the directors are wicked. I have known the inside of corporations for a great many years, and I have yet to see a director who has taken advantage of his position as director." (This was quite sincere and probably quite true: such things were not done where men like Higginson could see them.) The men in Wall Street saw Roosevelt's proposals for increased federal power over business as blows at the American principle of local self-rule, as measures which would submit the country to the dictates of cheap, bribe-taking politicians. They felt that he was posturing and blustering. They regarded him as dishonest for having accepted contributions from capitalists in 1904 and having denounced them subsequently. Many of them were completely convinced that his championship of the Hepburn Bill and his talk about rich men had brought on the Panic of 1907. They watched and waited uneasily as his term in the White House drew to a close, hoping for the day when his reproving voice would no longer carry Presidential authority.

When at last he left Washington and the vast and jovial bulk of William Howard Taft settled itself into the Presidential chair, most of the men of Wall Street would have echoed the remark popularly attributed to

Pierpont Morgan as the Trust-buster sailed for his African hunting grounds: "I hope the first lion he meets does his duty!" Now at last there would be a chance for men to do business again, a chance for prosperity without governmental interference. (Things had been looking up since the dark days of 1907, but there was still uncertainty in the air.)

They were mistaken, however. The reform movement still had far to run.

§ 4

During the next four years the reformers' counter-offensive made remarkable headway.

To imagine it to have been in any sense a united movement would of course be highly erroneous. As Hacker and Kendrick have well pointed out, in its ranks were "the conservationists, the settlement-house workers, the suffragists, the advocates of direct as opposed to machine government, the budget experts, the municipal reformers, the commission-government supporters, the advocates of workmen's compensation laws, mothers' assistance, and liberal factory codes. . . . And the reformers, very often, expressed not the slightest interest in one another's programs." It was "as though a great horde of people had suddenly become inspired by the same objectives and had simultaneously hit upon the idea of taking to the road." The politics of reform made strange bedfellows even in the supposedly homogeneous groups; in the innermost councils of Roosevelt's Bull Moose party, for example, sat the very George W. Perkins who had been simultaneously a Morgan partner and an officer in the New York Life Insurance Company. What was taking place was a complex and pervasive change in the intellectual and emotional atmosphere of America: the spread of a contagious desire to purify politics, win justice for the poor, protect the helpless, and subdue wickedness in general by statutes, regulations, and moral conversions.

Organized labor continued to surge ahead, though its prestige suffered a staggering blow in 1911 when two union leaders, the McNamara brothers, confessed that they had so far extended the arts of persuasion as to dynamite the building of the anti-labor Los Angeles *Times*. The toughly militant I.W.W. invaded the big industrial centers, reaching the height of its power in 1912 when it led the strikers in the textile mills of Lawrence to partial victory over a particularly blind and reactionary group of employers. In that year a socialist rival to Gompers won a third of the votes cast for the presidency of the A. F. of L., and Debs' vote for the Presidency of the United States was more than double what it had been in 1904 and 1908, running close to 900,000.

The reform movement was also giving a new shape to the contest between the two dominant political parties. This is no place to tell the familiar story of Roosevelt's triumphant return from Africa (where the lions had failed to do their duty); of his increasing impatience with his old friend and disciple, the all-too-compliant Taft; of his decision to run against Taft for the Republican nomination, his capture of most of the support which would otherwise have gone to LaFollette, his defeat by Taft in the Republican convention of 1912 as a result of the crushing performance of the political steam-roller; of his formation of a third party of miscellaneous reformers, idealists, bandwagon-followers, and cranks; and of the inevitable result: the division of the Republican vote and the election of a Democrat, Governor Woodrow Wilson of New Jersey. Suffice it to remark that Wilson, too, was a reformer, though of another breed from either Roosevelt or LaFollette. The counter-offensive had won its way back to the White House, and with a mandate for action.

By the time of Wilson's inauguration in 1913, an extraordinary quantity of legislation, particularly state legislation, had already been enacted at the instance of the reforming spirit: political measures to bring about direct primaries, the popular election of United States senators, the initiative, and the referendum; measures for the protection of labor—such as workmen's compensation laws, laws regulating hours and conditions of work (especially for women and children), industrial safety laws, tenement-house laws, and the first state minimum-wage law; measures for the regulation of public-utility rates by state commissions; and measures for taxation on new principles—such as the income-tax amendment to the Constitution; to say nothing of the legislative progress from state to state of woman's suffrage—and of prohibition.

§ 5

Still, however, the question of what to do about the extension of corporate power remained unanswered.

On this problem, counsel was confused and baffled.

To begin with, the status and interpretation of the Sherman Anti-Trust Law gave great difficulty. It forbade combinations in restraint of trade—but what was a combination in restraint of trade? The number of business combinations—principally through the medium of holding companies—had multiplied enormously. By 1908, according to LaFollette, their total capitalization had reached the vast sum of 31 billion dollars—nearly nine times what it had been in 1900. Would these hundreds of combinations be allowed to stand, or would they not?

The Supreme Court, which had interpreted the word "restraint" very broadly where labor unions were concerned, also seemed disposed for a time to interpret it broadly where corporations were concerned (a logical disposition, it may be remarked, since after all the law had been originally designed to apply to corporations and not to unions). This tendency caused much quaking in Wall Street, as did the activity of Taft's Department of Justice in bringing actions against some of the biggest combinations. (The list of the companies against which the Taft Administration acted included such giants of the industrial world as the American Sugar Refining Company, the International Harvester Company, the National Cash Register Company, the General Electric Company, and even the United States Steel Corporation.) When business, after an upsurge in 1909, declined again in 1910, a common explanation was that business leaders feared a general upsetting of the economic apple-cart. In 1911, however, the Supreme Court changed its position: it enunciated its famous "rule of reason." In the process of consenting to the break-up of the Standard Oil Company of New Jersey (the holding company which had fallen heir to much of the one-time power of the famous Standard Oil Trust), the Court stated that only "unreasonable" restraint of trade would be considered punishable under the Sherman Act.

But what was "unreasonable"? The Court did not adequately define the term. All one could be sure of was that whatever a majority of the nine justices of the Court considered reasonable in any given case would be permitted; whatever they considered unreasonable would be punished. Obviously the "rule of reason" did not dispel the fog which hung about the interpretation of the Sherman Act. It made only two things clear: first, that the Court intended, in effect, to exercise what had hitherto been considered a legislative prerogative, by revising the trust law to suit itself; and second, that the Court was on the whole disposed to look more kindly than heretofore upon the principle of combination, not penalizing it unless it was accompanied by flagrant acts.

Another source of confusion was the fact that although a large number of combinations had already been broken up by the government, they continued in most cases to operate virtually as units. A holding company might be duly dissolved and its stock might be distributed to the original owners, but if the men who managed the component companies had learned to work in concert and had found it profitable to do so, they would keep right on doing so in various hidden ways. What the hope of profitable operation had joined, man apparently could not put asunder.

But should the government any longer even attempt to put big combinations asunder?

Some of the reformers, hoping to restore the heyday of the little business man, thought it should. LaFollette's temperament, for example, drew him in this direction. In his *Autobiography*, published in 1913, LaFollette denounced Roosevelt for not having attacked all the combinations as soon as he entered the White House in 1901; and in his speech before the Periodical Publishers' Association at Philadelphia in February, 1912, LaFollette spoke of the necessity for "pulling down the false structure of illegal overcapitalization of the trusts." No wonder the prosperous men who heard the weary La-Follette stumble through that Philadelphia speech thought that he had lost his reason, for not only was it a confused performance—he was over-tired, and talked interminably and harshly, and apparently lost his place in his manuscript—but the "pulling down" which he recommended would have been enough to bring about a great panic, so pervasive and so long-continued had been the process of watering stock. Yet even in that speech LaFollette's logic was relentless. He held bravely to his convictions; he was no compromiser.

Roosevelt's attitude in these later years was different from LaFollette's. In the 1912 campaign, Roosevelt made it quite clear that he considered it too late to unscramble the economic omelette. He acknowledged that big business had come to stay, that attempts to break it up were futile. He contended that sheer size was not a crime, that only unfair acts ought to be prevented. He proposed to regulate the big corporations by a federal trade commission, and he made no bones of the need of a strong federal government to maintain supervision.

To some extent Roosevelt's objection to unscrambling the eggs may have been strengthened by an odd circumstance. It will be recalled that at the crisis of the 1907 panic, Gary and Frick had visited Washington to ask if Roosevelt had any objection to the purchase of the Tennessee Coal & Iron Company by the Steel Corporation, and Roosevelt had approved the purchase. When the Taft Administration, several years later, brought action against the Steel Corporation under the Sherman Act, one of the principal bases of its action was this very Tennessee purchase. The implication was that Roosevelt had had his leg pulled. Roosevelt resented this implication furiously; according to Mark Sullivan, it was the thing which made his break with Taft complete. Roosevelt was very human, and his ego often played a part in forming his opinions; possibly the incident which separated him from Taft also drew him subconsciously closer to the Steel Corporation and other huge concerns. He had approved the Tennessee purchase, therefore it must be all right, and other purchases like it must be all right. The argument may seem naïve, but that was the way in which Roosevelt's mind sometimes worked.

Similarly, Roosevelt's attitude toward the big corporations in 1912 may have been somewhat influenced by his desire to retain the good will of important financiers like Perkins. Perkins was for Roosevelt, Perkins was a fine fellow and a valuable ally, therefore the sort of business in which Perkins had been engaged must be all right.

But all this is conjecture. The Roosevelt attitude was at least realistic; and his insistence upon a strong federal agency of control harmonized with his continuing preference for a national government which could speak to Wall Street, as to everybody else, with unquestioned authority.

Wilson arrived at much the same conclusion as Roosevelt, though the color of his philosophy was different. Wilson approached the problem of business concentration as an old-fashioned believer in the rights of the small business man and in the merits of competition. Being a Democratic candidate, Wilson also talked a good deal about states' rights, suggesting that the states ought to undertake much of the work of business regulation. As Governor of New Jersey, in fact, he gave a demonstration of what a state might do: he secured the passage of new corporation laws which withdrew—for a time—the special privileges which had made New Jersey the favorite spawning-ground for holding companies. This was a genuine move to control combination at its source. But in developing his federal program, Wilson found the pressure of facts stronger than either the theoretical undesirability of the big combination or the theoretical preferability of state action. He, too, was driven to acknowledge that "the old time of individual competition is probably gone by," that it was hopeless to make war against sheer bigness, that the thing to do was to make war against monopolistic practices, that the states were helpless to cope with the larger combinations, and that the answer was therefore a federal trade commission: in short, a stronger federal government, willy nilly.

In fact, one of the oddest things about the campaign of 1912, as one looks back upon it a generation later, is the close agreement between Wilson and Roosevelt on the subject of big business. A voter who heard the Colonel deride and denounce the Princeton professor's policies would have supposed that the two men were miles apart; but their programs were almost identical, as indeed were some of the key phrases in their economic addresses.

These programs gave striking testimony (as did the Supreme Court's rule of reason) to the amount of water which had flowed under the bridge since 1900. The reformers were able to curb business in scores of places remote from its great centers of authority—regulating rates charged for services, regulating conditions of employment and pay, methods of competition, and so forth; but their two chief leaders now virtually admitted that the process of combination was irresistible.

The odds, they had learned, were all with the big capitalists. If one state withdrew its license to organize holding companies, the promoters simply sought out another state; not unless all states acted in concert would the competition in laxity end. After a big combination was set up, the state governments could make only a poor botch at regulating it; and even the federal government could hardly keep up with the rapid advance of the legal technic of circumvention. The corporation lawyers were always two jumps ahead of the Department of Justice.

Again, to harass the big corporations after they were once organized and engaged in business was to fill the whole economic world with a sense of insecurity: all drastic reform is deflationary. The process of combination could only be hedged about with restrictions, it could not be stopped. And even to hedge it about, the government had to add new bureaus, new staffs, new costs of operation. Wall Street and higher taxes both had fate on their side.

Chapter Six

PUJO

IT IS one of the ironies of American history that during the very years when the reformers were trying most vigorously to curb big business, the corporate tree was actually putting forth new branches and blossoms.

Only fitfully did prosperity return after the Panic of 1907. During 1908 there were valiant attempts to restore it by wishful thinking—by the promotion of a "sunshine movement" and the formation of a "Prosperity League"; in short, by the same sort of incantation which was to be used in 1930 and 1931 to assure the country that "prosperity was just around the corner." Trade still lagged, however; synthetic optimism would not suffice. There was a revival in 1909 and another in 1912, but they were brief, and during the intervening years the general pace of business was slow and the prospects uncertain. In 1913 there followed another relapse. The financial seers of the day (eager, as usual, to find a political scapegoat for an economic condition) generally attributed this relapse to the uneasiness with which business men faced the reform program of President Wilson; Alexander Dana Noyes, however, attributes it in greater degree to the outbreak of the Balkan War, the widespread fear on the Continent of a general European conflict, and the resulting international financial tension. At any rate, never between 1907 and 1914 was there any such protracted period of intense business activity as had preceded the Panic.

Yet despite the fitfulness of the economic weather and

the alarums and excursions of the reformers, the process of combination and concentration continued. A glimpse of a few of the developments of those years will suffice to suggest the drift.

It was less than a year after the Panic, for example, that a promoter-minded automobile manufacturer named William C. Durant brought together under the uncertain shelter of a new holding company several of the numerous automobile concerns that were then battling for the favor of a meager public. This holding company he called the General Motors Company; it was destined in due course to grow to a lusty size.

Parenthetically we may note that Durant hoped to include Ford in the General Motors combination and came within an ace of doing so; the negotiations fell through only because Ford demanded his eight million dollars in cash and Durant's bankers ruled that the business was not worth so much money. The man whom the bankers rejected went on alone—went on, in fact, to offer during the next few years a remarkable demonstration of the economic logic of mass production. Ford was concentrating on one model now, instead of many—the awkward, efficient black "tin Lizzie"; his marvelous assembly-line technic of production was cutting his costs; and instead of charging all he thought he could get, he was boldly and systematically reducing the price of his car and thereby increasing enormously his volume of sales. Early in 1914 he carried his logic a step farther—apparently a wholly unnecessary and hazardous step: he announced that he would pay his workmen five dollars a day. Whatever may have been the motives behind this furiously discussed decision, it was prophetic; for it was a spectacular answer—perhaps in its essence the best answer which capitalism could give—to one of the most vexatious questions which were to beset the American economy: how improvements in the technic of production could be made to bring benefit instead of hardship to the masses of the working population. The answer which Ford gave was of course familiar in economic theory and in the oratory of men like Schwab, but not in practice. It was that the benefits of increased efficiency must be deliberately passed on to the consumers—and that the employer's own workmen are consumers.

Another example of the process of concentration at work was the way in which power companies were being assembled under the aegis of the General Electric Company. By 1913 the three young holding companies owned by General Electric—the Electric Bond and Share Company, the United Electric Securities Company, and the Electrical Securities Corporation—had already acquired a dominating interest in the local electric-light plants in 78 cities and towns, and in the local gas companies in 19 cities and towns—to the benefit, naturally, of the sale of General Electric equipment. The business of federating public utility companies was making headway.

In the railroad field the process of combination lagged, partly because of the discouraging attitude of the government and partly because Harriman's reign was drawing to a close. The Little Napoleon of the railroads—and of the stock market—died at Arden House late in 1909, and presently the empire which he had left was split apart by the government's decree that the Union Pacific and Southern Pacific systems must be divorced. By an ironical turn of fate it was Pierpont Morgan, once Harriman's scornful rival, who was to offer the most conspicuous—and in its effects the most flagrant—example of railroad concentration in the years which followed Harriman's brilliant rise.

Morgan's attempt, in his old age, to build up a transportation monopoly in New England through the medium of the New Haven Railroad illustrates almost perfectly the sort of pitfall into which a man with Morgan's method of accumulation and Morgan's imperious will was likely to stumble. It was Morgan's way to undertake vast projects, to pay round prices for the desirable properties without undue haggling, to finance these lavish purchases by loading down his parent company with debts or with quantities of stock, and to trust to a great expansion of business to provide profits with which to carry the debts and pay dividends on the stocks. Wherever the natural tendency of economic growth was favorable, Morgan could make this method work to his own satisfaction and that of the investors. But in some cases, of which the New Haven enterprise was one, the natural tendency was not sufficiently favorable. New England business was not growing rapidly, and the golden day of railroading had reached high noon. An aging and wilful man, Morgan refused to accept these facts.

His influence was commanding in the New Haven management. According to Clarence Barron's notes, Charles S. Mellen, the president of the road, acknowledged that he "wore the Morgan collar" and was proud of it. Said Mellen to Barron, "I took orders from J. P. Morgan, Sr. I did as I was told, and when Morgan, Sr., who always sat at my left hand in the meetings of the board, desired the approval of the directors, he got it, and don't you think he didn't! When he wanted their negative vote he got that just as quick! Once in a while William Rockefeller would interpose some objection, but even he was most of the time dominated by the force and power of 'the old man' Morgan." At the time when Mellen said this he was presumably over-anxious to emphasize Morgan's authority; yet clearly it was with Morgan's hearty backing that the New Haven embarked upon a great program of purchasing properties in New England. It acquired the Boston & Maine Railroad; the Maine Central; the New York, Ontario & Western; it acquired steamship companies, street-railway companies, electric-light and water and gas companies. It paid amazing prices: for instance, it paid thirty-six million dollars for a little suburban road outside of New York which had no terminal in Manhattan and lost money consistently.

As always when men are determined to buy regardless of price or of legal obstacles, the railroad's agents were surrounded by swarming birds of prey: how much of the New Haven's money was dissipated in graft and in speculative profits for insiders, one can only guess from a few disclosures here and there. As a result of the orgy of purchasing, the bonded indebtedness of the New Haven was multiplied nearly twentyfold in nine years. The dénouement came in 1913, when the company was obliged to pass its dividend, thereby beginning the impoverishment of many a New England family. For years thereafter the road teetered on the verge of bankruptcy. A government suit under the Sherman Act smashed its monopoly. Its directors were criminally indicted; all New England rocked with the scandal.

By this time Morgan was dead. But the grievous effects of his insistence upon consolidating where consolidation on such terms could not succeed long outlived him.

During these same years, new devices for the quiet extension of financial power were being conceived: for example, that choicest of blossoms watered by corporation lawyers, the banking affiliate. For a long time past, bankers who were restive under the legal limitations which safeguarded national banks had found ways of securing simultaneously the advantages of operating a national bank and the advantages of operating a state institution under different regulations. For example, in the year 1903 the First National Bank of Chicago had incorporated another institution, the First Trust and Savings Bank, to serve as a sort of Siamese twin; it was managed by the same directors as the First National and for the benefit of the same stockholders, but could engage in business which was denied by law to a national bank.

The idea of thus achieving for a bank a dual personality was fascinating, and in 1908 it took a different turn. George F. Baker's mighty First National Bank in New York had been informed by the Comptroller of the Treasury that it must not hold the stock of other banks. While the tremors of the Panic of 1907 were still agitating Wall Street, the First National set up its own Siamese twin, the First Security Company, for the purpose of holding bank stocks and other securities which the bank could not properly hold.

In 1911 Stillman's National City Bank likewise achieved a dual personality by setting up the National City Company. By 1913 twelve national banks in various parts of the country with capital of a million dollars or more were equipped with affiliates, while several hundred other banks enjoyed the benefits of affiliation in one way or another.

The way in which an affiliate was organized was a beautiful example of the legerdemain of the corporation lawyer. Suppose the national bank which found the legal limitations of national banking cumbersome was fortunate enough to have built up a huge surplus, as were Baker's First National and Stillman's National City Bank. Out of this surplus it now declared a huge dividend to its stockholders, proposing that the money (which now technically belonged to the stockholders) be straightway invested in a new company, the affiliate. This new company would have the same directors as the bank; it would have the same officers; it would occupy the same quarters; its stock would not be salable except along with the stock of the bank—and yet it would not be a national bank, but a corporation empowered by state charter to embark in almost any business it chose! It might hold the stock of other banks, it might speculate, and the Comptroller of the Treasury could not object. It was completely outside his jurisdiction.

Surely the invention of the security affiliate was a masterpiece of legal humor. And surely it was also a body-blow at the principle of disinterested commercial banking; for although of course the affiliate did not directly involve the funds of the depositors in its various ventures, inevitably its existence invited bank officials to serve two masters.

The years which followed 1907 witnessed further concentration at the center of the financial world: a quiet drawing-together of the great powers of Wall Street. Morgan and George F. Baker had long worked hand in glove, but Stillman, the head of the National City, had been largely independent of them, sometimes an associate, sometimes a rival. Now the cold and imperious Stillman drew closer to the other two giants of Wall Street.

To be sure, Stillman spent most of his time in the quiet of the Rue Rembrandt or touring the Continent; but always he kept his finger on the pulse of Wall Street through carefully coded cablegrams and letters to his associate, Frank Vanderlip, and more than once he urged collaboration with the House of Morgan. The collaboration was forthcoming. Very often, now, the names of J. P. Morgan & Co. and the National City Bank appeared together on the announcements of new security issues. Morgan bought a stock interest in the National City and his son became a director of it. Stillman joined forces with Morgan and Baker in the purchase of a block of the shares of the National Bank of Commerce. Morgan, too, was spending much time in Europe now, and he and Stillman hobnobbed as friends.

The Morgan-Baker sphere of influence was extending. For one thing, Morgan bought in 1910 a controlling interest in the Equitable Insurance Company from Thomas Fortune Ryan and Harriman's estate. Ryan did not want to sell, it appears, but Morgan told him he had better, and he did. The price at which Morgan acquired the Equitable shares was so large that the yield on the investment was almost microscopic, but Jupiter did not mind that: he wanted to get the funds of the Equitable into what he considered reliable hands. (With Baker already in a position of influence in the Mutual Life, and the New York Life already close to the House of Morgan, three of the four biggest insurance companies were now well within the Morgan-Baker sphere.)

For another thing, the sphere now included more banks than ever before. Baker had bought a majority of the stock of the Chase National Bank, and his First Security Company was a considerable stockholder in other banks as well as in railroad and industrial corporations. Two Morgan partners (Davison and Porter) bought in 1910 an interest in the Guaranty Trust Company, and they and Baker constituted the voting trust which dominated it. Both the Guaranty Trust and that other Morgan-Baker ally, the Bankers Trust, were busily engaged in swallowing other lesser trust companies; in the years 1908-1913 they swallowed no less than six, the Guaranty thus becoming the largest trust company in the United States, with the Bankers occupying second place. The Farmers Loan & Trust was already closely identified with Stillman's National City. It was therefore possible for the Pujo Committee in 1913 to list as under the influence of the Morgan-Baker-Stillman triumvirate no less than nine banks or trust companies—the First National, the National City, the Bankers Trust, the Guaranty Trust, the Astor Trust, the National Bank of Commerce, the Liberty, the Chase, and the Farmers Loan and Trust—with total resources (including their affiliates) of something like a billion and a half dollars.

In the railroad and industrial world as well, the Morgan and Baker and Stillman influences were spreading. They or their associates had a voice in the management of most of the big railroad systems of the country and of such leading industrial or public utility corporations as American Can, General Electric, International Harvester, Lackawanna Steel, Pullman, United States Steel, American Telephone & Telegraph, and Western Union.

When in 1912 the House of Representatives authorized its Committee on Banking and Currency to find out whether there was a "money trust" and to prepare new banking and currency legislation, this committee divided into two groups. One, under Carter Glass, worked on legislation (later producing the Federal Reserve Bill) ; the other, under Arsène Pujo of Louisiana, did the investigating. It engaged Samuel Untermyer of New York as counsel, and during the hearings which it held in the winter of 1912-13 it piled up a staggering array of statistics designed to show that a "money trust" indeed existed.

The Pujo Committee found, for example, that the firm members or directors of the House of Morgan, the First National Bank, the National City Bank, the Bankers Trust Company, and the Guaranty Trust Company —in other words, the men whom the Committee regarded as definitely representing the Morgan-Baker-Stillman community of interest—held, together, the following directorships:

118 directorships in 34 banks and trust companies having total
     resources of over two and a half billion dollars
30 directorships in 10 insurance companies having total assets
     of over two billion dollars
105 directorships in 32 transportation systems having a total
     capitalization of over eleven billion dollars
63 directorships in 24 producing and trading corporations
     having a total capitalization of over three billion dollars
25 directorships in 12 public utility corporations having a total
     capitalization of over two billion dollars

—all of which the Pujo Committee added together to
make up the overwhelming total of 341 directorships in
112 concerns having aggregate resources or capitalization
of over twenty-two billion dollars.

On the basis of these and other findings the Committee
came to the conclusion that "If, therefore, by a 'money
trust' is meant

An established and well-defined community of interest between
a few leaders of finance which has been created and is held together through stock holdings, interlocking directorates, and
other forms of dominion over banks, trust companies, railroads,
public-service and industrial corporations, and which has resulted
in a vast and growing concentration of control of money and
credit in the hands of a comparatively few men—

your committee . . . has no hesitation in asserting as a
result of its investigation up to this time that the condition thus described exists in this country today."

There can be little doubt that the figures so diligently
piled up by the Pujo Committee seemed to prove too
much. In the first place, they suggested to the unwary
a huge mass of mobile funds at the disposal of a few men,
whereas of course the vast majority of the wealth involved in these tabulations consisted of non-mobile properties and investments. In the second place, the statistics
as to directorates suggested a non-existent unity of policy
and purpose. The presence of a man on a board of direc-

tors might mean any one of a number of things: for example, that he was able, or that his name had prestige value, or that he was associated with a bank which wanted to make sure that its funds were not wasted or that the securities which it had launched did not become insecurities. A director might have only the vaguest knowledge of the specific operations of the company over which he was supposed to be exerting control. The presence of one man on two directorates did not necessarily imply any concert of interests between the two concerns. There were many directors of industrial companies who rubbed their eyes in astonishment to find that they were considered by the Pujo Committee to be connecting links in a chain of interlocking directorates which reached from 23 Wall Street out into the remotest hamlet. They knew that no orders had ever been transmitted through them, that they had never so much as shaken hands with a Morgan partner; and they found it hard to imagine what kind of an influence they were held to be exerting on behalf of Morgan and Baker and Stillman.

Likewise the men at the center of things regarded the findings of the Committee with mingled amusement and dismay; they knew little about and paid little attention to the operations of some of the companies which were alleged to be tributary to them, and they quite sincerely believed that the Pujo contentions were absurd; they felt, moreover, that they used very sparingly whatever power they had.

Nevertheless the fact remained that banking power in New York was more concentrated than ever before, and that the influence of these men at the center, even when not crystallized through the existence of voting trusts or majority ownership of stock, ramified very far. It was compounded of many elements: the element of patronage—in other words the tendency among lesser bankers to follow the lead of the Morgan-Baker-Stillman groups in the hope of being remembered in the apportionment of securities for distribution; the element of fear—an obscure fear that a concern whose policies the key men of Wall Street considered "unsafe" would in some way open itself to reprisals—perhaps in the form of difficulty in getting credit at the banks; the element of community of interest—intensified by the fact that there was a general and wholly natural disposition on the part of the key men to favor, for vital positions in banks or businesses in which they had a voice, men whose ideas ran along with theirs; and, of course, the element of respect —a pervasive respect for these men and their opinions because to conservative business men generally they seemed the embodiment of success, astuteness, and wisdom.

One need not agree that there existed a money trust— even in the guarded way in which the Pujo Committee defined the word—to recognize that both the direct and the indirect influence of Morgan, Baker, Stillman, and their aides was prodigious, and that in these very years of the reformers' counter-offensive it had been extended and strengthened.

§ 2

The hearings of the Pujo Committee in the winter of 1912-13 were dramatic and illuminating. Samuel Untermyer, counsel for the Committee, summoned a succession of notable financiers to the witness chair. The taciturn Stillman was conveniently absent from the country, but Baker testified, and so did Morgan.

The committee room in Washington was jammed with men and women when Morgan was called, for his personality and his power had become almost an American legend. He was an old man now, seventy-five years old, and his son and daughter and son-in-law came with him and watched him anxiously through the long hours of his testimony, fearing the strain upon him of such an ordeal. He was flanked also by several attorneys; but he did not wait upon the attorneys for answers to the carefully contrived questions which Untermyer fired at him. From the moment when he was sworn by the chairman and Untermyer began, "Where do you reside, Mr. Morgan?" he took his own part. The center of the stage was his.

At first he was brief, guarded; but as time went on he became more animated—now striking the table before him for emphasis, now chuckling as the crowd laughed at some quick rejoinder of his, now swinging half around in his revolving chair after he had made a reply and looking at the faces of his son and daughter and his attorneys as if to say, "There; how was that?" He was always cordial to his inquisitor, offering to secure whatever information would be needed. But he was overwhelmingly positive. There was in his testimony none of that air of injured innocence which makes some financiers, cornered on the witness stand, sound like guileless and misguided morons. Even when his evidence seemed most flatly to fly in the face of reason, he uttered it with flat-footed authority.

He absolutely denied that he had any power. Once when he was insisting that no one man could get a monopoly of money or of credit, Untermyer asked him, "That is your idea, is it? Your idea is that when a man has got a vast power, such as you have—you admit you have, do you not?"

The old man stoutly replied, "I do not know it, sir."

"You admit you have, do you not?"

"I do not think I have."

"You do not feel it at all?"

"No, I do not feel it at all."

He even denied obstinately that he controlled his own firm. "You are the final authority, are you not?" he was asked. "No, sir." "You are not?" "No, sir." Stolidly he held to this position.

Untermyer tried to get him to discuss the propriety of a relation such as that between the House of Morgan and the Southern Railway. Morgan and Baker controlled the Southern through a voting trust. Untermyer wanted to know this: When the directors of the Southern, who were chosen by this voting trust, agreed with the House of Morgan on the terms upon which securities should be issued by the House of Morgan, were not Morgan and Baker in a sense dealing with themselves?

MORGAN. I do not think so. We do not deal with ourselves.

UNTERMYER. Let us see if you do not.

MORGAN. The voting trustees ——

UNTERMYER. The voting trustees name the board, do they not?

MORGAN. But when you have elected the board, then the board is independent of the voting trustees.

UNTERMYER. That is only until the next election?

MORGAN. It is during that time they act independently.

UNTERMYER. You think, therefore, that where you name a board of directors to remain in existence only a year and you have the power to name another board next year, that this board so named is in an independent position to deal with your banking house, as would a board named by the stockholders themselves?

MORGAN. I think it would be better.

UNTERMYER. You think it is a great deal better?

MORGAN. Yes, sir.

UNTERMYER. More independent?

MORGAN. Better.

UNTERMYER. Will you tell us why?

MORGAN. Simply because we select the best people that we can find for the positions.

UNTERMYER. . . . do you not realize that a board thus selected
   is under the domination of the people who name it?
MORGAN. My experience is quite otherwise, sir.
UNTERMYER. It is?
MORGAN. Yes, sir.

And he could not be budged.

Phillips Brooks, the great preacher, once remarked
that he did not see why there was so much talk about the
churches losing their hold; wherever he went, he always
found the churches full. Even when one has made due
allowance for Morgan's probable feeling that he must
on no account say anything which would give ammunition to the opponents of Wall Street, there remains in
the old man's testimony something which reminds one
of Brooks's remark. His influence so pervaded everything
he touched that he was hardly more conscious of it than
of the air he breathed.

His firm contention was that the basis of financial
power and of credit was character. To people who remembered Morgan's battle with Harriman over the
Northern Pacific in the stock market, or his liking for
voting trusts, or his campaign for the expansion of the
New Haven, this contention had its humorous aspects;
Morgan had been quite ready to purchase power with
money. Yet there was truth in the argument too, as those
who had confronted Morgan's piercing eyes knew well.
The banker reverted to this argument several times.
When Untermyer was trying to make him acknowledge
that he possessed power, he asked Morgan, "Well, assuming that you had it, your idea is that when a man
abuses it, he loses it?"

"Yes," replied Morgan; "and he never gets it back
again, either. . . . The question of control, in this country
at least, is personal; that is, in money."

"How about credit?" pursued Untermyer.

"In credit, too."

"Personal to whom? To the man who controls?"

"No, no," said Morgan doggedly; "he never has it. He cannot buy it."

"No," began Untermyer, "but he gets ——"

Morgan interrupted him: "All the money in Christendom and all the banks in Christendom cannot control it."

Later the questioner approached the topic from another angle.

UNTERMYER. Is not commercial credit based primarily upon money or property?

MORGAN. No, sir; the first thing is character.

UNTERMYER. Before money or property?

MORGAN. Before money or anything else. Money cannot buy it.

Untermyer was quite sure that banks were accustomed to insist upon collateral when making loans, or upon the existence of a going business with a pretty sure cash income. He asked whether a borrower got credit on his face or on his character. Suppose he brought some bonds to the bank as collateral?

"Yes," insisted Morgan, unrelentingly, "he gets it on his character."

"I see," said Untermyer ironically; "then he might as well take the bonds home . . . ?"

Morgan went on, oblivious: "Because a man I do not trust could not get money from me on all the bonds in Christendom."

He argued that the members of his firm went on boards of directors only because they had a large interest to protect. He refused to admit any other reason for his purchase of Equitable stock from Ryan than that he "thought it was better there than where it was." The single word "better," uttered by the florid-faced old man by the committee table, stood like a mountain in the way of Untermyer's attempts to analyze the nature of the Morgan influence. Morgan thought his way of doing things was better; and that was that.

Untermyer went into the matter of the control of the Steel Corporation. Morgan agreed that nobody went on the board of directors over his objection. Then followed this characteristic colloquy:

UNTERMYER. Who decided that J. P. Morgan & Co. should be the depositary of the United States Steel Corporation?

MORGAN. That was rather ex-officio, I think, sir.

UNTERMYER. You mean you decided it both ways?

MORGAN. When the company was formed, J. P. Morgan & Co. had the whole company at that time, and I think that is the way it came.

UNTERMYER. You thought it was good business, and so you thought you would take it?

MORGAN. No; I did not know whether it was going to be good business or not at that time.

UNTERMYER. It proved pretty good?

MORGAN. It did; very good indeed, sir.

UNTERMYER. You did not think you were taking many chances on its being good business when you took it up, then?

MORGAN. No; but I began to have doubts when the stock went to eight dollars a share afterwards.

UNTERMYER. Your doubt did not interfere with your buying heavily?

MORGAN. No; I bought all I could.

UNTERMYER. You did not have any doubt, did you?

MORGAN. (*forgetting that a moment before he had confessed to doubts*). Never, not for one moment.

UNTERMYER. You were getting the advantage of other people's doubts at that time?

MORGAN (*quickly*). Nobody ever sold it at my suggestion, sir.

UNTERMYER. No; I did not mean to assume that.

MORGAN. I know.

UNTERMYER. My question does not imply that.

MORGAN. I know.

UNTERMYER. It only implies your confidence in the company at that time.

MORGAN. I always had it, sir.

Confidence—utter confidence in himself, his partners, his associates, his ideas and the onward march of American business; that was one of the secrets both of Morgan's mistakes (as in the case of the shipping combination and the New Haven program) and of his successes. Another secret of the successes, of course, was his immense force. Perhaps the best brief suggestion of both the confidence and the force in his whole illuminating testimony before the Pujo Committee was buried in his answer to a question of Untermyer's, when the latter was asking whether it was fair for a private bank such as the House of Morgan, which was not subject to governmental examination, to accept deposits which might otherwise go to banks which had to submit to such examination. Was it fair to have such an advantage in competing with these other banks for the deposits? Morgan said he did not compete for deposits. But, argued Untermyer, if your House gets the deposits which might go to other banks, you are really competing, are you not? Said Morgan, unmoved: "I do not compete for any deposits. I do not care whether they ever come. They come."

They come. Thus speaks authority.

What shall we say of this man? He was a Bourbon, contemptuous of democratic processes: a believer in the manifest destiny of aristocrats like himself to enjoy and distribute the fruits of industry. The financial methods which he sponsored did much—as we have seen—to widen the gulf between rich and poor; to levy, as it were, a heavy Wall Street tax upon the production of goods, a tax sometimes too heavy to be borne. Whether the gulf might not have been still wider and the tax heavier if he had not lived, whether the concentration of power and of wealth was not inevitable anyhow, whether indeed it did not bring with it advantages—in commercial development—which outweighed its disadvantages, will always be matters of sharp disagreement. Yet even those who look bitterly upon the privileges of concentrated capital which Morgan did so much to extend, cannot fairly deny that he possessed in high degree that quality to which he so often referred in the Pujo inquiry: character. Among those who knew him as a man and not simply as the generator and symbol of enormous power, he was trusted. If such power had to exist, the country was fortunate to have him wield it, and not a less scrupulous man.

§ 3

From Baker, who appeared on the witness stand a few weeks later, Untermyer was somewhat more successful in securing enlightenment upon the concentration of power in Wall Street. Baker was frequently vague in his testimony, and his words did not have the sledgehammer force of Morgan's, but he had an analytical mind, and the closing part of his testimony was of peculiar interest. Pressed by Untermyer, he admitted that he thought the control of credit had "gone about far enough." He would not admit that "if it got into bad hands, it would wreck the country," because he did not think it could get into bad hands. He did not think bad hands could manage it; they "could not retain the deposits."

Untermyer clearly realized the significance of this reply, with its implication that the only test of the desirability of a policy from the point of view of the country at large was its adequacy from the business point of view. "I am not speaking of incompetent hands," said he. "We are speaking of this concentration which has come about and the power it brings with it getting into

the hands of very ambitious men, perhaps not over-
scrupulous. You see a peril in that, do you not?"

"Yes," said Baker.

"So that the safety, if you think there is safety in the
situation, really lies in the personnel of the men?"

"Very much."

"Do you think that is a comfortable situation for a
great country to be in?"

Very slowly, Baker replied, "Not entirely."

The astute counsel for the committee knew when he
had a climax. "I think that is all," said he, and thanked
Baker for coming. The spectators, wrote the reporter for
the New York *Tribune*, "sat back with a sigh."

§ 4

On the fourth of March, 1913, Woodrow Wilson became President of the United States. As he stepped forward on the platform before the Capitol to read his
inaugural address, his first sentence was momentous. It
was a sentence of only seven words: "There has been a
change of government."

Now at last the forces of reform were securely in
power. To be sure, the conservative Southern Democrats were in power along with them; yet the President
left little room for doubt that he meant to show them
the way in which they should go. A firm believer in the
adaptation of some features of the British parliamentary
system to American use, Wilson had declared, years before this, his belief that a wise President could and should
lead Congress and the country. "The nation as a whole
has chosen him," he had written in his book on *Constitutional Government in the United States*, "and is conscious that it has no other political spokesman. His is
the only national voice in affairs. . . . He is the representa-

tive of no constituency, but of the whole people. If he rightly interprets the national thought and boldly insists upon it, he is irresistible." Wilson's inaugural address revealed in every measured and stately phrase his interpretation of the national thought. It was calling for reform: for a reduction of the tariff (that ancient device for the governmental subsidizing of private business), for a revision of the national banking and currency system, and for legislation to curb big business through the establishment of a federal commission with regulatory powers.

Whether Wilson's leadership would prove irresistible, no one yet could tell, but at least it was eloquent and determined. A new day seemed to be at hand.

There were other signs that the old day was ended. Not only were Taft and his Republican aides out of office; not only was Bryan, the one-time idol of the Populists, firmly settled in the State Department as the President's right-hand man; but the old order was passing in finance and in industry as well. Harriman was dead. Stillman was in semi-retirement. Rockefeller was in complete retirement, busying himself with the establishment of his vast Foundation and submitting himself to the discipline of a caddy who was instructed to chant, as Rockefeller took his stance for a stroke at golf, "Keep your head down! Keep your head down!" Of the other former titans of the "Standard Oil crowd," Rogers was dead and William Rockefeller was in failing health.

And now Morgan, too, was gone. In the weeks which followed his appearance before the Pujo Committee, the old man had definitely retired from his banking firm and had left for Europe to conserve his strained and ebbing strength; he died in Rome on the last day of March, 1913 —less than three and a half months after his verbal battle with Untermyer and less than a month after Wilson's inauguration. Not only the American political system but the American economic system, it seemed, was to face a change of government.

The professor in the White House managed his legislative campaign with vigor and with cool discretion. He drove his tariff act through both houses, and this act not only lowered customs rates, but also put into effect what seemed to the conservatives of those days an alarming method of raising revenue—the Federal income tax. He pushed to enactment a bill establishing the Federal Reserve System: an extremely important reform of which there will be more to say in the next chapter of this book. Within a year of his inauguration, both the new tariff act and the Federal Reserve Act having been triumphantly passed and signed, Wilson proposed to Congress the fulfillment of the Democratic pledge to regulate big business and to bring monopoly to an end.

The legislation which Wilson called for took due shape in two measures, the Federal Trade Commission Act and the Clayton Act. The Clayton Act tried to clear up some of the confusion which surrounded the interpretation of the Sherman Anti-Trust Law, first by definitely specifying that it was not to be applied to labor organizations, and second by specifying certain business practices as monopolistic and therefore illegal. For instance, it would be illegal to quote different prices to different people with whom one did business, if the discrimination in prices tended to lessen competition or create a monopoly; it would be illegal to make selling or leasing contracts which forbade the purchaser or dealer to do business with a competing concern. It would be illegal for a corporation to acquire stock in another concern if the acquisition would lessen competition; and it would be illegal for a man to serve as a director in two competing concerns with capital, surplus, and undivided profits of over a million dollars, or to serve as a director or officer of more than one bank with capital, surplus, and undivided profits of over five million dollars. (These latter provisions showed the influence of the Pujo Committee's inquiry.) The Federal Trade Commission Act set up a commission of five men, empowered, first, to investigate business concerns which did an interstate business, and second, to issue "cease and desist" orders, forbidding them to continue practices which were unfair or dishonest.

In general, these two acts may be said to have put into practice the policies advocated by both Wilson and Roosevelt in the 1912 campaign. The giants of industry were not to be destroyed, but they were to be prevented from destroying the little fellows; they were to be made to behave themselves, and they were given a clearer idea than before of what would be considered bad behavior. The principle was furthermore established that their actions were matters of public concern. The Federal Trade Commission became a sort of federal detective force and police force, to deal with the big corporations somewhat as an apprehensive mother once was said to have asked her husband to deal with the children: "Find out what they're doing and tell them not to do it." This detective and police force was provided only with lightish weapons —but there was always the Sherman Act, now clarified by the addition of the Clayton Act, to serve as a heavy club in case of need. And the new legislation gave the government a marked advantage: a chance, in theory at least, to deal with business abuses reasonably promptly —without waiting for years while Sherman Act cases dragged slowly through the courts.

By the summer of 1914 these measures were being hammered into shape in Congress. The Federal Reserve System was in slow process of organization. Many of the recommendations of the Pujo Committee had been lost sight of in the press of new legislation—including its recommendations for the elimination of security affiliates, for the incorporation of stock exchanges so that they might be regulated, for the setting of stiffer margin requirements for stock-market speculators, for the prevention of stock-market manipulation, and for the supervision of security issues by the federal government; they were destined, in fact, to remain half-forgotten for nineteen years. Even without them, however, Wall Street felt that it faced a period of uncertainty and of governmental restraint. Change was assuredly in the air.

Nobody, however, foresaw the change which was actually to take place: the great and appalling event which was to twist out of shape the whole fabric of American life during the years to come, thrusting new issues and new problems before the country, shifting men into new alignments, and completely altering the pattern which these years of the reformers' counter-offensive had set. It came without warning. During most of the month of July, 1914, the commodity and security and money markets, those sensitive indices of the hopes and fears of men, gave no indication of any great disturbance ahead; and the minds of Americans generally were as unprepared for what was to happen as were the traders whose purchases and sales determined the tranquil course of these markets. But at the end of July the fires of war burst forth in Europe, and within a few days they had leaped from country to country and had set the Continent aflame.

Chapter Seven

WAR

THE events of the war years were so convulsively abnormal that to narrate them in detail would be to overload and distort the story which this book aims to tell. I propose therefore to run through them very rapidly, leaving to the reader's imagination (or memory) the crowded excitements of the period, and concentrating rather on the effects of the war adventure upon the American economy, and particularly upon the processes of economic growth and concentration. These effects were prodigious. When the war and the brief boom and depression which succeeded it were at last over and the country had returned to what President Harding liked to call "normalcy," the scene was very different from what it had been in July, 1914. This chapter will attempt to suggest briefly how some of the major alterations came about.

One warning must be given at once. Drastic as were the effects of the war upon America from the moment when the armies first mobilized in Europe, the reader must not be deceived into supposing that the reform movement petered out at once. It did nothing of the sort.

In so far as it depended upon Theodore Roosevelt and the Progressive Party, to be sure, it did. The election of 1912 had virtually killed the Progressive Party. Woodrow Wilson proceeded to steal their best thunder, and by 1914 Roosevelt gloomily confessed to a friend that in making speeches for the Bull Moose cause he knew he was carrying a dead horse on his shoulders. Roosevelt himself tried to be contented with the inactive life of a man of letters, rushed off in despair to explore the sources of a South American river, returned in shaken health to further dismal inactivity—and then found the joy of battle once more in a cause quite different from that of social justice: the cause of "Americanism" and of preparedness for American participation in the war. The fierce campaign upon which he now entered satisfied his ego by giving him an opportunity to lead an attack upon the administration in power; it suited his temperament by pitting him against Wilson, whose cool caution was hateful to his headlong and belligerent spirit; it engaged his nationalistic zeal, his boyish enthusiasm for the manly arts of war, his moral ardor; but it did not engage the economic reformer in him. In fact, as a friend of the Allies and an apostle of the Plattsburg movement he found ranged beside him most of the men whom he had once decried as malefactors of great wealth. By 1916 Roosevelt was quite at home in Wall Street. The past was forgotten; these fellows were "good Americans."

Yet the reform movement went on without him. The Wilson Administration not only pushed through the Clayton Act and the Federal Trade Commission Act but went bravely ahead to enforce them, busily hacking away, year after year, at monopolistic practices and unscrupulous trade methods. It wrote on the statute books the LaFollette Seamen's Act to improve labor conditions for American sailors; in the Adamson Act it decreed an eight-hour day for railroad employees; after the United States had entered the war it threw its influence behind the principle of collective bargaining and behind liberal labor policies for plants making war materials; and it gave Gompers a place among the advisers of the Council of National Defense. Men like Newton Baker and Brand Whitlock and George Creel, who had been enemies of the political power of big business, now sat in the seats of power. What happened was not that the reformers lost heart or position or that the Wilson Administration lost its liberal complexion, but rather that the war dwarfed every other enterprise, submerged every other issue, distorted the organization of American life, colored every emotion; and that when the war was at last over and the demobilization of men and of enthusiasm had been effected, the national spiritual exhaustion was such that the wish to regulate and control business and finance was thoroughly played out.

§ 2

When the armies began to march in Europe at the end of July, 1914, the first effect upon the American economy ·was a stroke of almost complete financial paralysis. The New York Stock Exchange was closed at once, to remain closed for months; if it had not been, the rush of European investors to convert their American securities into money against the unpredictable emergencies of war financing would have knocked prices down to the bottom, undermined bank loans, and imperiled the whole financial structure. Frightened hoarding began at once, and a panic worse than that of 1907 might easily have followed if there had not been invoked a half-forgotten monetary measure (passed in 1908 as a result of the lessons of 1907 and known as the Aldrich-Vreeland Act) which permitted banks, in such an emergency, to issue notes based upon non-government securities and commercial paper as well as upon government bonds. The very real danger to American credit was averted only by the bold action of a group of New

York bankers, headed by the Morgan forces, in forming a gold pool to meet the requisitions of the outside world. Not for a long time did the disorganized processes of finance come back to anything like a normal equilibrium; for example, not until the first of April, 1915, a full eight months after the invasion of Belgium by the Germans, was it considered safe to open the New York Stock Exchange to unrestricted trading.

The second effect was a partial paralysis of business. Nobody knew how widely the war might spread or what forms it might take, whether exports would reach their destination safely, whether European buyers would be able to pay their bills; foreign trade was violently disrupted, the prices of wheat and cotton and other commodities dropped, citizens were implored to "buy a bale of cotton" to save the South from disaster, business as a whole shrank rapidly, and unemployment spread. The winter of 1914-15 was a very lean winter for America—even for those parts of it in which the war still seemed to most people a remote unreality. There is no more instructive example of the difficulty of business forecasting than the fact that for almost a year after the war broke out, few Americans had any notion of the vast prosperity which it would shortly bring to their country.

When the recovery came, however, toward the middle of 1915, it was sweeping. The largest cause of it, of course, was the discovery of the Allies, and particularly of the British, that they could not hope to win without buying war materials and supplies abroad in quantity. But there were other causes. The world was calling for food and for other products of which the belligerent nations could no longer produce enough to meet the demand. Neutral markets, once dominated by the British or the Germans, were now open to American invasion. The British fleet had virtually cleared the seas of German warships; commerce with the Allies could now be undertaken without much risk. By the autumn of 1915 American factories were roaring, American farmers were closing a profitable season, the tonic effects of prosperity were stimulating business from coast to coast, and in Wall Street there was already a frenzy of speculation in the "war stocks"; the front pages of the newspapers told the happy story of the broker who in 1914 had staked his all on fifty shares of Electric Boat and was now worth half a million, and of another happy creature who had bought 1,000 shares of Bethlehem Steel at 18 for his baby and now estimated that the baby was worth $364,-000; and the sober *Commercial and Financial Chronicle* felt it necessary to remind its readers that the boom in war stocks was not "based on an enduring condition."

The expansion of currency and of credit which the war boom invited was greatly facilitated by the Federal Reserve System, now at last in full operation. The creation of this system had come about through a curious combination of forces.

The panic of 1907 had spectacularly displayed the weakness of what was known by courtesy as the American banking system: a collection of national banks (independent of one another except as they were locally organized into clearing-house groups) superimposed upon forty-eight collections of state banks. Not only were the standards of safety imposed by law varied and inadequate (and destined long to remain so) but the individual banks were so independent of one another that there was no way of mobilizing their scattered reserves to meet emergencies in one part of the country or another. Each bank had to sink or swim by itself, aided only by such relief measures as a local clearing house could contrive or as some local leader could impose upon the local banks (as Morgan had done in New York in 1907). The first great need was thus for a practicable device for shifting a part of the scattered reserves here and there in accordance with changing conditions. The second great need was for a more flexible currency: there was no way of providing for a suitable yet controlled expansion of it in times of expanding requirements. The Aldrich-Vreeland Act of 1908, though it was to prove very useful when the war storm broke in 1914, was frankly a measure for panic use only—a stopgap measure to serve until a more elastic system of currency could be devised.

For years after 1907, Senator Aldrich of Rhode Island and various astute bankers such as Paul M. Warburg, impressed by this double need, had been working on plans for a central banking system which could mobilize and hold ready for use a part of the reserves of the individual banks and could also issue notes based on commercial paper (and thus provide a currency sensitive to the volume of going business). They had labored to convince the slow-moving bankers of the country that such an institution was necessary, and had made some headway. Senator Aldrich finally went so far as to introduce a bill in the Senate in 1912.

The character of the Aldrich Bill, however, may be suggested by the fact that it was written at a secret conclave held at the Jekyl Island Club on the Georgia coast —a favorite playtime haunt of the New York bankers— by a small group of men which included, along with Aldrich and Warburg, two representatives of the dominant financial powers: Harry Davison of the House of Morgan and Frank A. Vanderlip of the National City Bank. Genuine as the wish of these men undoubtedly was to provide a superbank which would truly serve the national need, and adroitly as their proposal was adapted to meeting the shortcomings of the national currency, one could hardly expect that any plan which they drew up would seriously disturb their influence. The plan evolved at Jekyl Island called for a central reserve bank with a board of directors in which the private bankers of the country would have an obvious majority.

At a time when the air was full of talk of a "money trust" such a scheme was obviously impossible. It would be opposed not merely by the adamant conservatism of the average private banker, who distrusted any device which would hamper his individual freedom of action, but also by the fear among Westerners and Southerners and men from the smaller cities generally that a central bank would turn out to be a bank under the control of the powers in Wall Street, and still more potently by the insistence of the reformers upon curbing the financial oligarchy. But when the Wilson Administration came into power in 1913 it made a surprising and very canny move. It took over the Aldrich-Warburg idea and altered it to make it a part of the reform program. The bill which Carter Glass sponsored in Congress and which Woodrow Wilson backed with his commanding influence provided indeed for a superbanking system, but a decentralized one (to meet the jealousy and suspicion of the small cities) which while operated by men chosen by the private bankers (to placate the banking community) would be supervised and regulated by a government board (to prevent Wall Street control). The bill, that is to say, provided for twelve separate regional reserve banks, the directors of which would be chosen by the bankers of these various regions; but also for a supervisory Federal Reserve Board consisting of the Secretary of the Treasury, the Comptroller of the Currency, and five other men to be appointed by the President.

This masterly compromise won the day. Despite much shaking of heads among the diehards of the financial world, the bill was passed at the end of 1913. The Federal Reserve System was ready to begin operations in November, 1914, only a few months after the outbreak of the war. By the time the war boom gathered headway, late in 1915, the value of the System was already apparent. It did not especially curb the power of Wall Street, but on the other hand it did not accentuate this power. It made such banks as flocked to join it safer, providing indeed as much safety as could be expected in view of the fact that membership was not compulsory and that the legal standards for commercial banking remained varied and lax. And it provided ample currency and credit to meet the growing needs of a nation which had suddenly found itself doing a roaring business.

§ 3

When old Pierpont Morgan died, men had wondered whether the supremacy of the banking house which he had built would come to an end. If character were the secret of financial influence, as the old man had argued at the Pujo inquiry, perhaps the great days of the Morgan house were over; for J. P. Morgan the younger, who now at the age of forty-five became the senior partner, had given no evidence of any such colossal personal force as his father had radiated. He was an attractive young man, by reputation solid and reliable; he inherited his father's patrician spirit and tastes, his father's scorn of the common herd, and his father's blinding temper; but his capacity for personal leadership had not been tested. He was surrounded by exceptionally able partners; Harry Davison in particular, a protegé of George F. Baker's who had had a leading part in the organization of the Bankers Trust Company, was looked to as a rising power in the Street. But the question of the future influence of the firm remained open, and all

the more so because the Clayton Act soon forced the
members to resign as directors of the commercial banks
on whose boards they sat, and in deference to public
opinion they resigned also from thirty of the directorships which they held in business concerns. These resig-
nations had but a slight effect upon their influence, for
as already noted in the previous chapter of this book the
number of directorships which a firm held was by no
means a measure of its power; nevertheless the move
added to the uncertainty with which the future of the
House was surrounded. This uncertainty was not completely dispelled for two years.

The war boom of 1915 and 1916 dispelled it, however, and conclusively.

The House of Morgan had always been closely tied
to England. Morgan the Elder had received his early
training in his father's American banking house in London. He had spent much time at his splendid house in
Prince's Gate. He had been accepted by the leading
financiers of England as a kindred if somewhat over-
mastering spirit. Morgan the Younger was likewise sympathetic with the English. The House had a branch in
Paris, too, and a long record of close association with
French as well as British bankers. These facts, together
with the enthusiasm of the partners for the Allied cause
—"Our firm had never for one moment been neutral,"
wrote Lamont later; "we didn't know how to be"—and
with the supreme position which the firm occupied in
American finance, bore rich fruit in 1915.

As a result of the diplomatic suggestions of the ever-
alert Davison, who spent weeks in conference with British officials in London, the British government made
J. P. Morgan & Co. its purchasing agent in the United
States. The French government also decided to co-
ordinate its American purchases through the Morgan

office. And both governments made the House of Morgan their fiscal agent in the United States, entrusting them at the outset with the staggering task of selling to American investors a half-billion issue of Anglo-French bonds, the largest issue of securities ever floated in the country.

The position which the firm came to occupy in the American economy as a result of its successful exercise of the double function of purchasing agent and money-raising agent was as extraordinary as it was unprecedented. The Allied purchases of munitions and war materials of all sorts were growing and soon became enormous: they were the chief stimulant of the new prosperity of 1915 and 1916. The only way in which trade between the United States on the one hand and England and France on the other hand could be balanced while such vast exports were going on was by a combination of three simultaneous processes: first, the importation into America of over a billion dollars' worth of gold; second, the gradual sale to American investors, through the stock exchanges, of foreign-owned American securities to the extent of a billion and a half dollars (the selling of which, incidentally, was also entrusted to the Morgan firm) ; and third, the borrowing by England and France of over a billion dollars more. I say borrowing—but the money was all spent in the United States. It was taken in from American investors under the name of the Allied governments, and it was handed out to American manufacturers, also under the name of the Allied governments, in payment for munitions and supplies. And both the taking in and the handing out were managed by the House of Morgan!

To be more specific: J. P. Morgan & Co. organized the syndicates which borrowed the money for the Allies— huge syndicates, the first one of which, to distribute the

Anglo-French bond issue of 1915, consisted of several hundred banks and investment houses, sixty of them in New York alone. And through a special department headed by Edward R. Stettinius (who soon became a Morgan partner) the firm also apportioned the British and French orders among steel mills and powder plants and tool works and the numerous other plants all over the country which darkened the sky with their smoke as they fed the slaughter in Europe. No such direct economic power had ever been exercised by a single group of men in all American history.

As to the effect of all this activity upon the neutral position of the United States, it might be mentioned here that on August 15, 1914, when the war was hardly a fortnight old, Secretary Bryan had written to the House of Morgan: "In the judgment of this Government, loans by American bankers to any foreign nation which is at war are inconsistent with the true spirit of neutrality"; but that this virtual prohibition was later permitted to lapse. The stimulating effect of war orders upon American business and the quickly rising sympathy of Americans—especially in the East—for the Allied cause, were too strong to permit it to stand. There is little question that the extent to which American economic fortunes were staked upon an Allied victory proved a strong factor in aligning the United States with the Allies.

As to the manner in which the men at the corner of Broad and Wall Streets exercised their power, Lamont's figures in his life of Davison are illuminating: "The final record as to the British contracts showed that, of the hundreds of different concerns dealt with, there were only eleven in which the Morgan partners held any interest; and the largest interest they held in any one of those eleven did not exceed three per cent of the shares. In the case of the French, the percentage was even more trifling." The British government, hearing rumors of favoritism in the letting of the contracts, sent over an investigator but could find no basis for criticism. The firm made a practice of notifying the British or French government, in advance, of their precise interest in any firm to which they considered giving an order. Some of the profits made by munition-makers were immense—but the House of Morgan believed in profits.

The prestige of the firm rose to new heights. Morgan the Senior was gone, but the institution that he had set up was now mightier than ever.

§ 4

The twenty months or so between the beginning of the war boom in 1915 and the entry of America into the war in early 1917 were a time of furious activity—business booming, credit expanding; prices rising, wage increases being granted—or, if not granted, being demanded and struck for by workmen; profits leaping; the farmers enjoying the best times they had ever known; the stock market making fortunes in Wall Street. It was also a time of furious emotions. From the day that the *Lusitania* was sunk till the day that Wilson read his war message to Congress—all through the long months when the celebrated Wilson correspondence with Germany was indeterminately proceeding, and Roosevelt and the patriots of the National Security League and the Plattsburgers were shouting for preparedness, and Hughes was running against Wilson for the Presidency—the one great question which hung over the country was "Will America go to war?" and the answers given to it were hot with passion. As the months went by, gradually the war thrust other issues and other interests into the background; and when, on the last day of January, 1917,

Germany announced her intention to engage in unrestricted submarine warfare, it became clear that America herself was to be sucked into the maelstrom and that the concentration of the country upon war-making activities was to become furious and transforming.

What happened during the succeeding twenty-one months need not be detailed here: the decision of an anxious and depressed Wilson to call for a declaration of war and for a policy of conscription; the raising of an army of over three and a half million men, two million of whom were sent to Europe; the lethal campaign of 1918, in which American troops fought in the blood and filth and anguish of the trenches and aided the French and British to turn back the German tide; the tumult and shouting at home, the tramp of soldiers' feet on American pavements, the flags hung along the streets, the Hoover food-saving campaign, the frenzy of Liberty Loan campaigns and Red Cross campaigns and United War Work campaigns, the converging upon Washington of the dollar-a-year men; the fury and rapture of the war spirit, the unworldly idealism of the Wilson war messages; the long, long casualty lists, with all that they meant to broken families; and at last, the wild rejoicing of the first Armistice Day. For the purposes of this narrative, all that concerns us is the effect of this strange interlude upon the American economy. It was an effect multifold and significant.

In the first place, industrial production was still further expanded. It had to be expanded because Washington was calling insistently not only for men but for guns, shells, uniforms, cantonments, airplanes, trucks, rolling stock, ships, and other supplies in endless variety, to be delivered in quantity and at the earliest conceivable moment. This huge demand was superimposed upon a continuing demand for munitions and supplies for the Allies. In view of the shortage of men and of raw materials and transportation facilities, this inevitably meant cutting down on the production of things not needed for the winning of the war. It meant converting plants from peace-time uses to those of the emergency. In view of the utter derangement of supply and demand (for demand was imperative and almost unlimited), it meant regulating prices. Hence the creation of the War Industries Board, with its almost dictatorial power to decide to what uses the industrial machinery of the country might be applied; hence the Railroad Administration, which took over the roads and operated them as one huge system, giving priority to troops and to necessary supplies; hence the Food Administration and the Fuel Administration and other sources of inevitable interference with rugged American individualism.

During those twenty-one months the center of economic control moved definitely from New York to Washington. Wall Street became almost an outlying province. The House of Morgan was busy with many things, among them the difficult stabilization of British exchange; but it was shorn of its previous power. Morgan himself was not called upon by the Administration for any war service. Stettinius became an Assistant Secretary of War. Vanderlip of the National City Bank managed a war-savings campaign for the Treasury Department. Other bankers were drawn into the huge Liberty Loan organization. In every bank and corporation office there were now vacant places as men went off to the training camps, to France, to dollar-a-year service in Washington. In the drama of economic concentration through financial control, these months were an intermission, strange and exciting.

Wealth was not conscripted though life was, and in some cases wealth made a good thing out of the disaster.

Despite the contempt with which the country regarded "profiteering" and despite the efforts of the government to set prices at fair levels, it must be admitted that the vast volume of war orders, the increasing efficiency of production, and the fallibility of governmental officials combined to permit some very high profits. The biggest concerns which made war materials did not, on the average, fare quite as richly as during the boom of 1915 and 1916 when they had been making munitions at the behest of the House of Morgan, but this was partly because of drastic charges for depreciation and heavy excess-profits taxes—and it must be recalled that 1915 and 1916 had been altogether extraordinary years for such concerns. All things considered, they fared very well even after the United States went into the war.

For example: the net income of the duPont powder concern (after amortization but before interest on bonds) had been only a little over 5½ millions in the dire year 1914. In 1915 it had jumped to 57 millions, in 1916 to 82 millions. In 1917 and 1918, when the United States itself was calling for duPont explosives, it dropped back —but only to 49 and 43 millions respectively. Bethlehem Steel was another great munition-maker. Its earnings (after depreciation and fixed charges) had been a little over 5½ millions in 1914, had risen in 1915 to 17 millions and in 1916 to 43 millions, and fell back in 1917 and 1918 only to 27 millions and 15 millions respectively.

As for the United States Steel Corporation, its changing fortunes may be expressed in earnings per share on the common stock. In 1913 these earnings had been $11.02. In the bad year, 1914, they had dropped below zero (the corporation not quite earning its preferred dividend). In 1915 they had recovered to $9.96. In 1916 they had gone up to the remarkable figure of $48.46. In 1917 the decline was only to $39.15; and in 1918, to

$22.09. An average war-time profit of somewhere in the neighborhood of thirty dollars a share on Steel Corporation common stock! (To see such a figure in its full perspective one must recall the origin of those common shares, as recounted in the first chapter of this book.)

It might be added that accountants reporting to the Director General of Railroads subsequently gave—rightly or wrongly—much larger figures for the Steel Corporation. Adding to the net earnings, as reported by the company, various items which, they claimed, were "improperly deducted in the corporation's statements: Interest on bonds, etc., of subsidiary companies; inventory profits, intercompany; sinking funds on subsidiary bonds; and excess depreciation," they arrived at "adjusted earnings" totaling over eleven hundred million dollars in two years (1917 and 1918). Amateur statisticians may be interested to figure how this two-year total would compare with the total pay of all the soldiers in the A.E.F.

Large profits permitted the payment of very large dividends. Let us glance for a moment at the record of these same three companies, all of them big makers of munitions or war supplies. Bethlehem Steel paid $22.50 per share in 1917 and also declared a 200 per cent stock dividend; in addition, it offered its shareholders an opportunity to subscribe for further new stock at par; in 1918 the company handed out $10 a share on both the old and the new stock, thus giving shareholders the equivalent of $30 a share on their original investment. (Bethlehem's president, Eugene G. Grace, received bonuses of over a million and a half for 1917 and over a million and a third for 1918!) The Steel Corporation paid $16.75 per share in 1917 (of which one dollar was intended to be passed on to the Red Cross) and $16 per share in 1918. And as for duPont, perhaps the most striking testimony as to this corporation's endurance of the hardships of war is to be found in a passage from its annual report for the year 1918, in which I take the liberty of italicizing one clause: ". . . 1915-1918, the total dividends on the common stock of E. I. duPont de Nemours Powder Company and on the exchanged securities of E. I. duPont de Nemours & Company have amounted to 458 per cent on the par value of the original stock. *It is difficult to imagine a more satisfactory result,* especially in view of the fact that the liquidation of the balance of the military powder investment as it stands today cannot materially alter the conditions above described."

There were companies whose rate of profit was even higher than this. For instance, according to figures published in the Nye report in 1935, the Calumet & Hecla Mining Company made 800 per cent on its capital stock in 1917; the Utah Copper Company, 200 per cent. Some other concerns, one must remember, did not make money on their war orders; some sustained heavy losses by reason of expanding their plants in 1918 and finding their contracts canceled at the close of the war and their new equipment useless. Nevertheless that passage from the duPont report has a peculiar significance. Perhaps it had best be forgotten by those who write inscriptions for soldiers' monuments.

Another result of the war—and this, of course, must be borne in mind in weighing the figures given above—was that prices rose rapidly. By the time of the Armistice the cost of living had climbed 61½ per cent above where it had been in July, 1914. The wage-level likewise climbed; in fact, in some vital war-time occupations the shortage of labor caused it to rise to remarkable heights—till the wearing of silk shirts by shipyard employees became a matter of common talk. The shortage of labor (combined with the halting of immigration) also made it easier for workmen to organize and impose demands; the government was conciliatory, partly because of its liberal sympathy with labor and partly because of the need for maintaining enthusiastic and uninterrupted production; therefore there was a rapid growth in the membership of labor organizations of all sorts, conservative and radical: the total union membership rose steadily toward its post-war peak of over five millions. Labor wanted a place in the sun: was not the war being fought for democracy? Not until the war was over did the government with-draw its protecting hand and permit this new offensive on the part of the workmen to meet an equally deter-mined offensive on the part of unreconstructed employ-ers who preferred what they ingeniously called the "American plan"—meaning no traffic whatever with labor organizers.

Another class whose rising fortunes during the war were to have significant after-effects was the farm popu-lation. The demand for food was huge. The cry of "Food will win the war" echoed through the country. Prices rose to unprecedented heights. In the spring of 1917, for instance, wheat leaped to $3.45 a bushel; and the price of $2.20 which was shortly afterward fixed by the govern-ment, though it looked low by comparison, was a very high figure beside the normal peace-time level. At this price of $2.20 the government offered to take all the wheat that could be grown. The demand for other staples was likewise intense. Hence a great increase in the acreage planted, an increase in the use of farm machin-ery, and the beginning of a boom in farm lands which was to collapse a few years later, with paralyzing effects upon an unhappy farming class.

The government's financial program for the prosecu-tion of the war also left its marks upon the American economy. To reduce to the simplest possible terms the immense problem to which this program was the answer, the situation was this:—

First, the Allies had to be financed—no longer, of course, through private operations conducted by the House of Morgan, but through direct extensions of government credit—to the extent of no less than eight billion dollars. And second, to pay and equip and supply the American forces and pay the other costs of American participation required another twenty-four billions. Thus the total cost of the war to the United States was over thirty-two billion dollars—a staggering sum. (As Noyes points out, it was more than ten times the cost of the Civil War to the Union!) How could such an incredible amount of money be raised?

Despite the insistence of a large group of representative economists that the country must pay as it went, in order to avoid inflation, only about a third of the sum was raised by taxation—chiefly by great increases in the income taxes (with surtaxes running up to 65 per cent for the wealthy) and by excess-profits taxes. In other words, some of the money was collected by diligently taking away a part of the winnings of the fortunate corporations and of those who were fattening upon their dividends.

The remaining two-thirds had to be raised by borrowing on an unprecedented scale in five war loan campaigns. Yes, one may say, but how did the American people have so much to lend? One answer is the profits above mentioned. Another is that corporations purchased bonds with their surplus earnings. Another is that men and women sold other securities: the stock-market, which had boomed during 1915 and 1916, showed strikingly the effects of such selling while America was in the war. A fourth answer lies in the extraordinary breadth of the Liberty Loan campaigns, which tapped the savings and surplus earnings of men and women who had never before invested in securities of any sort. A fifth answer is that people borrowed from the banks to buy bonds—in other words, that they bought them out of anticipated earnings: a process which added greatly to the already large volume of credit outstanding and sharply accentuated the generally inflationary effect of the war upon the American financial system.

The Liberty Loan campaigns—ingeniously contrived, intricately organized, and advertised with an altogether unprecedented patriotic ballyhoo—were successful. The war was financed to a finish. We emerged from it the strongest and by all odds the richest nation in the world. But we also emerged from it with our public debt not two or three or four times larger than it had been when Wilson called upon Congress to declare war, but *twenty times larger*. Furthermore, we emerged from it with the Allied governments owing us upwards of eight billion dollars—a debt which was to cause endless trouble. And although it was pleasant to reflect that we were now a creditor nation, this fact, too, was to cause us trouble, because we did not quite know how to play our new economic rôle.

One more word as to the significance of these figures. It might aptly be said that during 1915 and 1916 the House of Morgan had been engaged in conducting a huge public-works campaign—raising the money for it, placing the orders for it—and that in 1917 and 1918 the Government took over this task on a much enlarged scale. From the point of view of "scarcity economics" this campaign was devoid of one embarrassing result which conservatives discern in public-works campaigns in peace time: it did not "compete with private business" by producing useful goods which would remain to satisfy the population and limit their desire to buy. What it produced was conveniently useless except for purposes of destruction, and much was promptly blown sky-high. But inflation it did produce on a gigantic scale. Those who distrust governments which run into debt in order to feed the hungry should reflect that in less than two years the American government went over twenty billion dollars into debt and other governments went other billions into debt—with consequences which plague us to this day—not to feed the hungry, but to kill and maim and destroy. There is no surer engine of inflation than war.

§ 5

When the Armistice was signed and the guns ceased firing along the Western front—on November 11, 1918—there was wild jubilation everywhere. After the anxieties and horrors of war, the prospect of a return to the ways of peace seemed incredibly happy. But sober financiers and economists faced the future with some disquiet. War contracts were at an end; a powerful stimulant to prosperity was now suddenly to be removed. Three and a half million Americans were about to strip off their uniforms and look for jobs. The governments of the world were bowed down with debts. Many other wars had been followed by long periods of economic exhaustion, and surely Europe, if not America, must be exhausted now.

The events of 1919 and 1920, however, took a strange and unexpected turn. For a few months there was an anxious pause as business tried to adjust itself to altered and confusing circumstances; then there began, not a decline, but a furious boom.

So many cross-currents of economic tendency and of emotion were running during those years of demobilization that it is difficult, even at this late date, to present a clear interpretation of the forces that made this boom, gave it its peculiar qualities, and then destroyed it. Yet the attempt must be made, for here again the forces proved to have long-term consequences.

To begin with some of the economic factors: It was quite true that Europe was groaning with debt. But for a time she continued to live on borrowed money. For example, she went right on purchasing from America on credit—not materials of war, but materials of reconstruction. (In the year after the Armistice the Allied debts to America made a further growth from a little over eight billions to more than nine and a half billions.) In the second place, a considerable part of the world had gone for a long time without the necessities of normal life and was in a mood to buy them wherever they could be bought—for a time at least. It was these two factors which set the 1919 boom in motion; there was a sudden jump in American exports during the months when the peace commissioners were laboring at Paris, and this jump in exports sounded the note for an advance.

The emotional factors in the 1919 boom were complex. In the first place, the war had been conducted under a pressure of terrific enthusiasm; this enthusiasm did not disappear at once, but was at first transferred to other causes and enterprises, taking strangely varied forms. It brought about, for example, the ratification of the suffrage amendment—and the prohibition amendment. It sent Wilson to Paris to try to establish a League of Nations which would end war once and for all. It led thousands of Americans to dream of the establishment of a socialized economic order, to endorse the Plumb plan for permanent government ownership of the railroads, to back the demands of labor for a larger share in the fruits of industry. It led business men and financiers to entertain extravagant hopes of making the United States a nation pre-eminent in foreign trade. And it also led labor to feel that now its day had come. American workmen had had an unprecedented bargaining power during the war, they were better organized than ever before, having secured at last a toehold even in the steel industry; they saw labor parties rising to power in Europe and the proletariat even winning its way to dictatorship in Russia; and they forgot, perhaps, that when the troops were fully absorbed into the working population the bargaining power of labor would be diminished. Suffragists, drys, Wilsonian peace-lovers, radicals, exporters, labor leaders—all of them, in 1919, resolved in their varied ways to carry to a conclusion the "lessons taught by the war."

Another emotional factor—which likewise took various forms—was a very natural desire to be rid of the constraints and duties of war-time. Among many business men it took the form of an intense resolve to get away from government regulation and red tape, to throw off the burden of high taxes, to cease what they considered a dangerous and economically unsound truckling to labor. They wanted independence again. They wanted to be running things again. Some of them wanted to speculate again. Again, among many workmen this same revulsion against restraint took the form of a feeling that now they could strike and not be called unpatriotic—and that they would do it and get what was due them.

Finally, there was the growing mood of disillusionment—the gradual spread of a feeling that the high resolves of war time had been too high, that the Wilson program was a lovely pipe-dream, that Utopia was a long, long distance away, and that in the meantime you might as well decide what you wanted and grab it, for this was the way of the world. Slowly disillusionment began to tarnish the remnants of war-time enthusiasm, and to transmute the desire for independence into ruth-lessness and greed.

The result of these interworking forces in 1919 was a brief and utterly undisciplined boom in business, com-bined with a bitter conflict between labor and capital. When American foreign trade began to pick up in the spring of 1919, business men regained their confidence and proceeded to make the most of the new prosperity. There was wild speculation in commodities, which lifted prices sky-high; there was speculation in stocks, an in-temperate expansion of exports, and in general a sharp inflation. This boom was punctuated by a series of grim strikes: a great steel strike, a coal strike, even a police strike in Boston. The employers (particularly men like Gary, whose refusal to recognize labor unions had the full support of the masters of Wall Street) held fast, and fought the unions with the aid of company police, espio-nage, government injunctions, and a great deal of patri-otic flag-waving to convince the public that they were defending the American order—"American principles of liberty" was Morgan's phrase—against Bolshevism. Meanwhile the crazy purchasing of goods against a sup-posed world shortage continued apace—until the spring of 1920, when the inevitable and long-postponed collapse began. Even after it had begun, the speculators of Wall Street continued to sport with the shares of Baldwin Locomotive and Mexican Petroleum and Crucible Steel, and there was a spectacular corner in the shares of the Stutz automobile company.

The collapse which began in 1920 continued for con-siderably over a year, and the damage it did was wide-spread. South American and Cuban buyers of American goods canceled their contracts, and the export bubble was punctured. A widespread buyers' strike against high retail prices took effect, and down came prices, fast and far; there was a dismal writing-down of inventories for American business concerns in 1921. Down came farm prices in particular, bringing with them real estate values in the formerly rich farm lands and ruining a great number of little banks which had been formed during the war and the succeeding year or two. Down came steel operations to eighteen per cent of capacity. And down came the hopes of union labor too. Adverse economic conditions, combined with post-war disillusionment and with that curious distortion of patriotism into a frightened Toryism which I have described at length in *Only Yesterday*, broke up the labor offensive and restored to the managers of American industry their former independence.

§ 6

With the depression of 1921 the war period of American finance and economics may be said to have closed. As the recovery began, in 1922, the abnormal influences of the war had in some degree worked themselves out; things had begun to approach a normal balance. Let us pause for a moment and take stock of what these eight years had done to change the economic scene and prepare the way for a new era.

1. They had greatly stimulated industrial production and efficiency; had intensified the use of machinery; had developed new industries and had matured others (such as the automobile industry).

2. They had perhaps interrupted somewhat the process of concentration—but an increasing number of mergers of banks and industrial companies showed that the trend was still toward concentration and that the process was ready for thorough-going resumption. (For instance, the railroads were now back in private hands, and in the

Esch-Cummins Act Congress had actually given permission for their consolidation into large systems, if this could be managed to the satisfaction of the Interstate Commerce Commission.) Furthermore, the passage of the Webb-Pomerene Act in 1918, which permitted corporations to combine forces for foreign trade purposes, inevitably had opened the way toward combinations for domestic trade purposes. Not that this Act allowed companies to agree on domestic prices and other domestic policies. This was still forbidden. But if a group of managers are permitted to meet and fix prices on exports, it is very easy for them to discuss domestic prices too without anyone's being the wiser. Another breach had been made in the Sherman Act's wall of defense against monopoly.

3. The national debt had become enormously larger. Not only that, but the expansion of governmental functions which had begun during the pre-war reform period (under the impulse to regulate business and provide services to the public) had continued during and after the war, the result being that the yearly expenditures of the Federal government had jumped from about three-quarters of a billion dollars in 1915 to over six billion dollars (including interest on the national debt) in 1920, and that the expenditures of state and local governments had similarly multiplied. Apparently there was no escape from the principle that as the trend toward centralization continued, so must the trend toward growth of governmental functions and of taxes continue.

4. Meanwhile there still remained the Allied debts to the United States; and as Europe was still prostrated, there remained a tendency toward a lop-sided balance of trade. Since the United States did not see fit to lower its tariff and thus permit Europe to pay its debts (and balance its purchases from the United States) in goods, the

only way of achieving a balance was the dangerous method of lending the necessary money to Europe. This, in effect, was what we had done during the war, and the results had been very persuasive. Yet it was a strange method to adopt for permanent use, and there was some question how long it could be resorted to without trouble.

5. The inflationary effect of the war had geared American business to a new price level; even the collapse of 1920-21 did not bring prices down to anywhere near the level of 1914.

6. American agriculture was very sick, with little prospect of recovery. Its booming export business had gone, never to return on a large scale; for other countries were resuming production of wheat and other staples, and there was new competition from South America. The drop in farm prices had undermined permanently the values of farm property and farm mortgages, and thus had reduced a part of the country to comparative poverty.

7. American finance, however, was doing very well. New York had become the most powerful financial capital in the world. The Federal Reserve System had come through the war with flying colors; and its mobile reserves had been so effective in preventing a serious money crisis in 1921 that bankers began to believe that the System offered an automatic guaranty against another panic. This confidence in the System, coupled with a confidence born of America's new financial pre-eminence in the world, was tending to relax that eternal financial vigilance which is the price of security: to make men think that a good System of reserves could atone for loose and inadequate banking standards.

8. The Liberty Loan campaigns had done much to form among Americans the habit of investing. The big

war-time profits of many corporations and the stock market booms of 1915-16 and 1919-20 had played a supporting part in developing this habit. The result was a remarkable increase in the number of stockholders of American corporations: the total number of book stockholders in thirty-one large corporations more than doubled between 1913 and 1923; and according to the estimates of H. T. Warshow, the total number of book stockholders in all corporations must have almost doubled. The Liberty Loan campaigns had also taught business men that you could accomplish almost anything through a publicity campaign. Both facts were to prove important: the first, in pulling hundreds of thousands of people into the stock market and preparing the way for new methods of corporate control and aggrandizement; the second, in preparing the way for public-relations counsel and other masters of the art of whitewashing.

9. And finally—the war and its aftermath had left the American people in a state of spiritual exhaustion. The reform impulse was at last moribund. The fear of the trusts, and especially of a money trust, was almost forgotten—it seemed like last year's nightmare. The frenzy of war-time was gone; the millennial hopes of war-time had turned to dust and ashes. Trying to improve things seemed a wearisome and futile occupation. Let us go back to business and get rich and forget all that, said the American people in effect.

They repudiated Wilson and all the ideas for which he had stood, and in 1920 they elected Warren Gamaliel Harding, an amiable and second-rate man who could, they thought, be trusted not to cause business any trouble. Harding wore a McKinley carnation in his buttonhole; and business men, recalling vaguely the dear dead days of McKinley—when the promoters were making millions, and Mark Hanna kept the government at

Washington in its place, and the reformers had not begun their impertinent attacks upon American prosperity—felt that the "normalcy" which Harding promised was all that their hearts could desire.

Normalcy. Back to the good old days. Hands off business. Those were the mottoes which appealed to the tired business men of the post-war years.

But it was impossible to go back to the good old days. The world had changed. The industrial order had changed. The financiers and corporation lawyers had been developing new devices to perpetuate and extend their sphere of power. Now that the brakes were removed, the process of concentration was to proceed in strange new ways and to unforeseen ends—as we shall see.

Chapter Eight

THE SEVEN FAT YEARS

BETWEEN the autumn of 1922, when the ascent of American business out of the canyon of the post-war depression became swift and convincing, and the autumn of 1929, when it turned abruptly downward into the great abyss, lay a period of approximately seven years. When this period began, the amiable and indulgent Warren Harding was occupying the White House and the Ohio gang were collecting their dubious tribute from the public coffers. When it ended, Harding was long dead, Calvin Coolidge had spent his five-and-a-half unobtrusive years in the Presidency and had slipped away to Northampton, and Herbert Hoover was in his eighth month of authority. Times had changed: of all the men who had sat at the Cabinet table in 1922, only one still occupied the same chair in 1929, though Republican rule had been uninterrupted.

Yet this man typified in striking degree the unifying principle of those seven years. For he was Andrew Mellon, Secretary of the Treasury: banker, super-capitalist, multi-millionaire, suave and gracious exponent of the economic and political philosophy of Wall Street and of the great industrialists of the country. Throughout the seven fat years, business—and especially financial business—was king. The overwhelming majority of the American people believed with increasing certainty that business men knew better than anybody else what was good for the country, and that the government had better keep its hands off their affairs and thus permit economic nature to take its course.

This belief was not, of course, unanimous. There was a prolonged outcry in the farm belt for measures which might alter the course of nature to the extent of rescuing agriculture from the slough of despond, and in 1924 the LaFollette campaign, which to a considerable degree represented hopes for a new economic deal, won nearly five million votes—mostly from the farmers and from labor—out of a total of twenty-nine million.

Nor were all of the defenders of the principle of "hands off business" consistent in their views and actions. Most of them looked with complete equanimity upon government intervention in business affairs when this took the form of tariffs, subsidies, and other favors of the traditional American sort. Besides, even the ruggedest individualist would leap eagerly upon the train for Washington or for his state capital to support a bill which might increase his profits by restricting his competitors: witness, for example, the attempts of the independent grocers to defeat by law the advance of the chain stores. Washington and the state capitals were thick with lobbies; to a greater extent than ever before in American history, the process of legislation became a tug-of-war of lobbies, each pulling for special advantages for its own group and special disadvantages for other groups; and even though a hundred lobbyists may agree in devotion to the principle of laissez-faire, if each of them proposes an exception to the principle—just one exception—their combined impact upon Congress or upon a state legislature is likely to result in more laws rather than in less. One of the choicest ironies of this period was that many, if not most, of the new measures which interfered with business freedom were passed under the heavy pressure of groups of business men who professed to hate interference.

It must be admitted, furthermore, that the costs of government did not decrease as one might have expected under the circumstances. To be sure, the federal budget shrank, partly as a result of the liquidation of some of the indebtedness incurred during the war; but so rapidly did state and local budgets swell, that by 1929 the *combined* expenditures of federal, state, and local governments had grown to the vast total of nearly eleven and a half billion dollars, as against a little over three and a third billions in 1915—a very large growth even if one makes due allowance for the decline in the purchasing power of the dollar. The lessons of this growth were clear. A country cannot undergo the relentless processes of urbanization and of large-scale economic organization without increasing its need for public services and for public institutions for the defective and the helpless, even if most of its voters prefer, in principle, to keep governmental activity to a minimum. And a people possessed with a lust for ostentatious growth, a boom spirit such as pervaded most of the United States in the nineteen-twenties, cannot resist the temptation to appropriate public funds for magnificent brick school-buildings and four-lane concrete highways. Keeping up with the Joneses meant keeping up the public expenditures and the public debt.

Yet the "hands off business" sentiment had a very real effect upon the relation between government and private enterprise. Not only did some of the new laws which were passed—such as the amendments to the Delaware incorporation laws, for example—give new kinds of freedom to the masters of capital, but there was a subtle change in the spirit in which the old laws were interpreted and administered. Although most of the regulatory legislation of the two preceding decades remained on the books, the public zeal for enforcement had weakened. The officials responsible for enforcement were naturally not always selected for their vigilance. More often they were selected for their party regularity or their pliability. Some were exasperatingly ignorant of the industries which they were supposed to supervise; others, in the process of learning about them, had become so inoculated with the ideas of the men who ran them that they could hardly see the need for any supervision at all. And even truly vigilant officials found that the odds were heavily against the sort of administration which had been hoped for in the early Wilsonian days.

There is no lonelier man than a government official who finds himself confronting, month in and month out, year in and year out, plausible arguments for easy interpretation or lax administration of a statute—to say nothing of temptations to close his eyes for a price—and who hears from a forgetful and indifferent public no word of admonition or support. What was taking place was a very familiar phenomenon: St. George attacks the dragon valiantly and is furiously applauded; but there comes a time when St. George is dead, when the audience has dispersed, and when St. George's successor finds the dragon a very persuasive fellow and begins to wonder why such a to-do was ever made over dragon-slaying, whether times haven't changed, and whether there is any need for subjecting the dragon to anything more than the mildest restraint.

Let us see for a moment what became of some of the reform legislation passed in the days of the Counter-Offensive, now that the temper of the country had changed.

The Sherman Act—that venerable relic of the year 1890—stood fast; in fact, during the eight years of the Harding and Coolidge administrations no less than 138 prosecutions were undertaken by the Department of Justice for alleged infractions of it. But the Federal Trade Commission Act and the Clayton Act—the two chief instruments with which the Wilson administration, at the high tide of the reform era, had hoped to police industry and business and to forestall monopoly—fared somewhat differently. The orders issued by the Federal Trade Commission diminished in number. The Commission devoted most of its energies to the enforcement of that section of the Act which forbade unfair methods of competition: in other words, to acting as umpire in the struggle for commercial advantage. Against the sort of concentration of economic power which had so alarmed the Pujo Committee a few years earlier it played a much less active part. It issued no orders at all against interlocking directorates, it permitted the issue of non-voting stock, and it generally permitted the expansion of financial sovereignties through mergers and through the use of holding companies.

For a time the Federal Trade Commission even permitted, in specific orders, so-called "codes of practice" drawn up by the trade associations in various industries (when these had been approved by the Department of Justice, as over forty of them were). These "codes of practice" were agreements to eliminate objectionable methods of doing business. They were not, of course, approved by the government officials if they contained any clauses which seemed to look toward the fixing of prices or the elimination of competitors. Doubtless many of them were in fact quite innocent of any such intention. But just as the passage of the Webb-Pomerene Act, some years before, by allowing business men to agree on prices to be maintained in their foreign business, had made it easier for them to agree—secretly, this time—on prices to be maintained in their domestic business, just so the approval of the codes of practice facilitated the secret extension of these codes into what were really monopolistic agreements on prices or on the division of markets. And thus, despite the continued existence of the Sherman Act, the way was partly opened for what became a common though well-concealed practice in industry after industry: the fixing of prices by agreement among the most powerful concerns.

Still another example of the way in which the attitude of the government toward big business became relaxed was the gradual whittling down of the reform legislation on the statute books by the United States Supreme Court and other judicial tribunals. In a long series of decisions the Supreme Court gradually restored to business a good deal of the freedom which in the days of the Counter-Offensive had been taken away from it by popular mandate, and simultaneously took away from labor a good deal of the freedom which had been given to it by popular mandate.

§ 2

But these changes in the relation between business and government were a wholly inadequate measure of the change in the public attitude toward business. Legal institutions, legal interpretations, move slowly; ideas sometimes move very rapidly. There had been a striking turn in the intellectual weather.

The economic reformers who a decade or two earlier had fought so hotly for the principle of government regulation were tired, uncertain, disillusioned. The young intellectuals, who in other days might have been exercised over economic issues, were indifferent to them; they were debating about Freud, Jung, Watson, Proust, Hemingway, and Cézanne. They retreated in large numbers to Montparnasse to get away from George F. Babbitt's moral intolerance, his zeal for standardization of the private lives of Americans, or his crudity in matters intellectual and aesthetic; but they seldom bothered to question his financial practices or his labor policies. If anybody had told them that young men and women much like themselves would in another ten years be turning communist and becoming enamored of the proletariat, they would have been astonished and dismayed: economics and politics were such a bore and the proletariat were such morons!

No longer was organized labor militant and defiant. The American Federation of Labor was becoming an elderly organization, broad-waisted, slow-moving, set in its ways. Its membership declined. Strikes decreased in number. Some labor leaders were now working hand in hand with employers to increase efficiency, some were conducting themselves essentially as conservative bureaucrats or as politicians bargaining for commercial advantages for their constituents, others were managing their unions virtually as profitable rackets—in collusion, sometimes, with gangsters and gunmen. The heart was going out of the radical movement, both within the ranks of labor and without it.

Indeed, so great was the change of temper which these few years wrought that by 1928 the discontent represented by the big LaFollette vote of 1924 seemed to have melted away like snow in April. The sheer figures of the 1928 election are illuminating. The Socialist vote for President sank to a meagre 267,000 (compared with 897,000 in 1912, when the electorate had been less than half as large!) The Communist candidate had less than 50,000 votes to his credit. Hoover's only formidable opponent in that election of 1928, Governor Al Smith of New York, took care to suggest in various ways that if he were elected to the Presidency, business would be almost as untrammeled as if Coolidge and Mellon were in power; and even Al Smith was overwhelmed by the landslide of more than twenty-one million votes for Herbert Hoover. Big business and big business men basked in the sunshine of unprecedented public approval.

To some extent this sunshine of approval was an artificial product. In part it was due to the diligent work of publicity men—or, as they were styled in the exalted language of the new era, public relations counsel—who flooded the newspaper city-desks with ingeniously devised news-stories designed to present their clients and their clients' opinions in a favorable light; who prepared "ghost-written" interviews and magazine articles and brochures and books in which they set forth virtuous principles over these clients' signatures; and who on occasion directly or indirectly subsidized lecturers, textbook writers, and professors. To cite but a single example of newspaper publicity work, one organization in Oregon prepared "canned" editorials on the iniquity of public ownership of utilities and on similar topics, distributed them to local newspapers all over the country, got thousands of them published, ostensibly as spontaneous expressions of editorial opinion—and for this service was paid $84,000 in four years by interested corporations. It was a frequent experience for magazine editors to be offered an article on some economic topic with a choice of two or three alternative signatures of big industrialists or utility magnates ("Just tell me which man you'd rather have sign it.") Sometimes supposedly independent writers collected two payments for their work—one from the newspaper or magazine to which they contributed, and another from the company or trade association whose interests they were quietly furthering. The total amount of subsidized reading-matter which was consumed by the American public with hardly a suspicion that it was subsidized was undoubtedly enormous.

The chorus of acclaim for business was also due in part to a form of subsidization much less deliberate and direct but equally efficacious. The profit-seeking newspaper or magazine publisher whose fortunes were dependent upon advertising knew very well that a friendly attitude toward business executives and financiers and their policies would help in the sale of advertising space, and that a critical or skeptical attitude might have the opposite effect. It was good business, for example, to describe Samuel Insull as having got the utilities "out of politics and speculation and into the realm of service." It was good business to say that "captains of industry are strong, hard-working, modest, square men, who have the qualities common to all of us, but in just a little greater degree." It was good business to print success stories telling how these hard-working, modest men had risen from the ranks, or to set forth observations on the American economic system written for their signatures by still more hard-working and modest ghostwriters. It was such distinctly bad business to offend utility companies, Florida real-estate promoters, and investment banking houses, and thus to run the risk of losing highly remunerative advertising, that there was hardly any critical examination of, let us say, the Insull holding-company pyramid in the days when it was being built to the skies; there was hardly a voice raised against the excesses of the Florida real-estate boom in 1925 or of the stock-market boom in 1928 and 1929—until after they had crashed. So effective, in fact, was this subtle and unformulated censorship of the press and so numerous and loud were the paeans sung in praise of the business man and all his works, that the disinterested publisher or writer was likely, by contrast with the general tone of comment which appeared, to seem by contrast a caustic muck-raker, a destructive and radical fellow. I do not mean to imply that in most respects the press was not quite free, or that outright intimidation of the press by advertisers was common, or even that most publishers did not believe themselves to be independent of business pressure. I mean simply that publishers wanted to make money and found it easier to make money by publishing the sort of thing which their advertisers would like. Mutual back-scratching was the order of the day.

In part, the vast prestige of business was due to the vigorous pressure of majority opinion upon the heretical, a pressure most heavily felt in the small city or town. The orthodox thing to do was to boost the town, to follow the lead of the Rotary and the Chamber of Commerce, to accept without question the policies of the economic masters of the community; the heretic might retain his technical freedom of speech and of action, but there were a hundred ways in which he might be made uncomfortable. To question the soundness of a local real-estate development, to question the rates set by the local electric-light company, to believe in labor unions, was in many communities to be considered queer, or unreliable, or even "un-American,"—to have trouble, perhaps, in getting credit at the bank, or getting a job, or making sales; to meet opposition when one sought admission to clubs and other organizations; to be looked at askance at social gatherings; to be, in short, at a general disadvantage in the great race for success and prestige.

Yet even the flood of propaganda and the pressure of majority opinion could not have been effective unless most men and women had *wanted* to believe that the business man was the heir to the ages, that independent business was the great American cornucopia of plenty. In part, the chorus of acclaim which we have been analyzing was quite spontaneous. As prosperity advanced, a natural market was created for the flattery of big business. The reason why *The Man Nobody Knows*, which described Christ as "a startling example of executive success," was for two years the best-selling American book in the non-fiction class, was that ordinary men and women had become ready to listen to and to endorse such preposterous doctrine. The business propaganda of those days is not to be thought of as the dark device of a minority to convert or bamboozle a skeptical majority. It merely reflected and intensified the views of the crowd, merely added somewhat to the size and velocity of a snowball which was already rolling downhill.

For seven years the big business man enjoyed a golden age of power and public obeisance. For seven years the public distrust of Wall Street steadily diminished, until by 1928 and 1929 the big financiers, like the big industrialists, had become the objects of a general veneration. Rich men predominated in the Cabinet at Washington; cartoons which depicted the millionaire as a portly gentleman with a greedy face and a huge dollar-mark on his convex waistcoat became a rarity; the dissenting voices of the radicals and the skeptics were drowned in the hosannas of the faithful. It was the rulers of big business who held the golden keys to a golden American future.

§ 3

How is this extraordinary change to be explained? The explanations already given in these pages—such as the reaction from governmental regimentation during the war, the reaction against too strong a diet of idealism, the influence of business propaganda, the pressure which business could exert upon the community—are only partial explanations. There is another and very potent one. The system worked—or, if you prefer, it seemed to work. At the end of these seven years the economic condition of the American people was on the whole better—or again, if you prefer, seemed to be better—than ever before in the history of the country.

That such prosperity could have been achieved when the economic relations between the United States and other countries were highly abnormal was nothing less than astonishing. Europe owed America huge sums of money. She could make payments on these debts only in goods—for such is the nature of international trade. America refused to give up the idea of receiving such payments. And yet America also stubbornly refused to lower the high tariff barrier which prevented goods from coming into the country in quantity. The effect which any economist would have expected from this combination of circumstances—the seemingly inevitable effect— would have been a forced shrinkage in the exports from America, which would have been very bad for American business. But the shrinkage did not take place. What prevented it was partly the lavish expenditure of money in Europe by Americans traveling abroad in unprecedented numbers, and partly the purchase of vast amounts of foreign bonds by Americans. In other words, most of the money which Europe needed in order to make payments on her debts without ruining the foreign business of American corporations was obligingly lent to her by the American purchasers of European bonds; the rest was spent in the Rue de la Paix and on the Riviera and in London by Americans on vacation. Thus the reckoning was postponed, miraculously and precariously postponed.

That prosperity could have been achieved when agriculture was continuously depressed was no less astonishing. For generations past, the economic health of the farming community had been the foundation upon which the prosperity of the rest of the country was built. In 1879 and in 1897, the turn of the economic tide had been effected by bumper American crops and good prices for them in foreign markets. In 1922, on the other hand, there was no such stimulus to trade. All through the seven fat years, in fact, the growers of staple crops like wheat and corn remained in a very bad way. The foreign markets which they had won during the war had been lost—permanently, it seemed. Meanwhile farming had become more efficient. Production was therefore large, and prices were low. The farmers were burdened with mortgages and taxes based upon the inflated land values set during the war-time boom, and many of them were burdened also with expensive machinery which could justify its cost only if production were heavy and prices were high. The result was trouble for the farmer. Nothing but an extraordinary prosperity in the cities and towns could have enabled the country as a whole to withstand the depressing effect of prolonged hard times on the farms. Yet to a large extent this effect was successfully withstood. Industry and commerce were strong enough to redress the balance.

There were several reasons for their strength.

One was the emergence of several industries which offered irresistible temptations to spend money in quantity: for example, the automobile industry and the brand-new radio industry.

Another was a prolonged boom in the construction industry: the building of countless suburban developments (due largely to the new popularity of the automobile), big apartment houses, and skyscraper business buildings. All the way from Coral Gables to the Empire

State Building the masons and plasterers and riveters were at work, and the financial top-heaviness of many of the structures that they built was shored up by a faith which even the collapse of the Florida land-craze did not weaken for long.

Another reason was that on top of the inflation brought about by the war there was a further large inflation of credit, partly through the purchase of heavily mortgaged houses, partly through the purchase of automobiles and other expensive articles on the installment plan, and partly through the stock-market boom of 1928 and 1929. Of the way in which this stock-market boom was engineered and of its effects upon the country we shall have more to say in a later chapter; for the present it is enough to remark that if a hundred men each buy, let us say, American Can at 87 and sell it at 112, and each purchases a shiny new automobile with his profits, the money for these hundred automobiles goes into circulation and the factories hum—though this money may have come out of thin air and be destined one day to return to it. So long as the debts keep piling up and the stock-market prices climb the steep ascent of a speculator's heaven, just so long business will boom.

But there were also sounder reasons for the prosperity of the seven fat years. There was an astonishing gain in manufacturing efficiency. New and more ingenious machines were devised; industrial managers were learning the lessons of scientific efficiency which had been taught by Frederick W. Taylor, Henry Ford, and other pioneers in intelligent factory management; the use of scientific research, the employment of engineers and efficiency experts and economic consultants became widespread; the big executive's desk was littered with blue-prints and charts and scientific reports and graphs, and some of these proved useful. A further aid to quantity production was the growing use of steam power and particularly of electric power. In *Recent Economic Changes*, that encyclopaedia of economic facts produced in 1929 by a committee headed by Herbert Hoover, there is one statistic which presents clearly the result of this increase in efficiency: During the five years 1922-27, the output per man increased in manufacturing establishments by an average of 3.5 per cent *each year*. That adds up to nearly 19 per cent of increase in output per man in five years: it is a striking gain.

We have heard much in recent years about technological unemployment. A new and more complicated machine is put to work in a factory; as a result, the factory can produce with fewer workers the same amount of material which it produced before; the superfluous workers are thereupon thrown out of employment. What about technological unemployment during the seven fat years? The figures available give a fairly clear answer. The increase in the volume of goods produced was almost exactly equal to the increase in the productivity per worker; in other words, the number of workers employed in industry remained just about stationary. Just about as many were taken on—in new factories or in enlarging industries—as were thrown out, by the machine or otherwise. Meanwhile, of course, the country was growing in population, and also the number of women who had jobs was increasing. Industry could not take care of this increase in the working population. But the overflow did not go into bread-lines—it went into selling goods and into all manner of services: the ex-automobile-maker ran a gas station, the ex-textile-worker became a shopgirl, and quantities of young men whose fathers had "begun at the bottom" in the factory became teachers or brokers or insurance salesmen or government employees. In so far as these surplus workers became dependent upon the luxury trades, upon the prosperity of the well-to-do classes, and thus upon the credit inflation of which the well-to-do classes were the immediate beneficiaries, the choice of occupation which was thrust upon them probably increased the economic instability of the country; but for the time being the inroads of technological unemployment were counteracted by the gain in these other occupations, and few of the disastrous effects so dramatically set forth by the technocrats in 1932 were visible.

Meanwhile, also, those wage-earners who were able to hold their jobs were getting some of the advantage of this new efficiency. Just how much, it is difficult to say positively; on this point there is a conflict of statistics. If we accept the careful estimates in *Recent Economic Changes*, we may say that during the 1922-27 period, while the output of each factory worker was increasing by 3.5 per cent a year, his earnings were increasing by 2.4 per cent a year. A considerable increase; but not quite enough—if these estimates are accurate—to give him the full benefit of the improvements in technique, especially as the cost of living rose slightly in the interval. And it is interesting to note that during the 1923-27 period the profits of industrial corporations increased by as much as 9 per cent a year, which suggests that part of the benefit of these improvements was being drawn off at the top in enlarged dividends. Apparently, too, the drawing-off process was accentuated in 1928-29.

Nor should it be implied, when we speak of the seven fat years as prosperous, that the industrial wage-earner's standard of living, even at the end of this period, was any great credit to the country. According to the estimates in *America's Capacity to Consume*, published by the Brookings Institution, in the year 1929 the wealthy and well-to-do (families with income of over $10,000 a year and unattached individuals with incomes of over $5,000) constituted only 2.4 per cent of the American population; the comfortably and moderately circumstanced (families with incomes of between $3,000 and $10,000 and unattached individuals with incomes of between $1,500 and $5,000) constituted only 19.6 per cent; the remaining 78 per cent of the American population lived on family incomes of less than $3,000 or individual incomes of less than $1,500. And of these 78 per cent, *more . than half* had family incomes of less than $1,500 or individual incomes of less than $750 a year.

To talk of the saturation point having been reached in the American public's demand for goods when millions of Americans were living on such a meagre scale is preposterous; to use the word prosperity at all in connection with a period when the workingman remained in such a plight may seem almost equally preposterous. Yet all things are relative; and the fact remains that the workingman, by and large, was better off during the seven fat years than he had been before, and that he had sufficient hope of improving his condition to be in the main not keenly dissatisfied with the going economic order, so far as he could understand the nature of it. And in certain effectively unionized trades—in the building trades, for example—his wages were so high that many observers, seeing the lines of Fords and Chevrolets, yes, and Buicks, parked beside a construction job, could not believe that labor in general was not actually prosperous far beyond all precedent.

Meanwhile the gain in prosperity for those who were fortunate enough to be neither farmers nor industrial wage-earners was on the whole greater, and at some points was immense. Salaries, profits, and dividends rose. The total national income soared from a little less than

65 billions in 1922 to almost 90 billions in 1928. Unequally as this income was distributed and unstable as were some of its foundations, for the time being it seemed to justify everything that was shouted in the chorus of acclaim for big business. And apparently this new age of plenty was just in its infancy. The day was coming soon—so men and women cheerfully believed—when there would be two cars in every garage—even, perhaps, in the day laborer's garage. If business men were only given continued free rein, the future held the promise of boundless wealth.

§ 4

With the coming of the seven fat years, the movement for which old Pierpont Morgan's formation of the Steel Corporation had struck the keynote back in 1901 went into double-quick. These were conspicuously years of concentration of economic power, of big business becoming bigger business, of vast and dazzling financial operations, of the mighty aggrandizement of capital.

The extent to which business was becoming organized into larger and larger corporate units has been graphically sketched by Berle and Means in *The Modern Corporation and Private Property*. Let us first set down a few of the facts assembled by these students, in order to make the general outlines of the picture clear. (Berle and Means leave out of their analysis the banks, and other financial concerns such as insurance companies; the figures given here are for non-financial corporations only.)

1. In 1929 there were over three hundred thousand non-financial corporations in the country. That is a very large number; clearly, the average American business was still a small business.

2. But mark this contrasting fact. Among these three hundred thousand corporations there were giants; and the biggest two hundred of these giants controlled nearly half of all the corporate wealth and did over two-fifths of the business in the non-financial field. To put it in another way: for every one of these two hundred giants there were 1500 little corporations—and yet the giants did two-thirds as much business as all the little corporations put together!

3. Furthermore, the giants were growing much faster than their little rivals. In 1909, the assets of what were then the 200 biggest had amounted to 26 billion dollars. Ten years later, in 1919, the figure for the giants had risen to 43.7 billion dollars. In 1929, at the end of the seven fat years, it had almost doubled again, reaching 81 billion dollars. And this growth, according to the compilations of Berle and Means, was *two and a half times as fast, during those twenty years, as that of the smaller corporations. During the years 1924-28, in fact, it was three times as fast.* The giants were crowding out the rest.

Notice also that these giants whose growth was measured by Berle and Means were all non-financial corporations. In addition to them there were financial giants: banks, bank affiliates, insurance companies, and toward the end of the period, investment trusts. The trend toward larger units was marked in finance too. Consider, for example, the banks and the insurance companies.

Up to the depression of 1921, banks had been becoming more plentiful in the United States. Many of these were small-town banks whose business was largely dependent on farming. Many of them would never have been allowed to open, much less to continue in business, if the banking laws in many parts of the country had not been—as we have previously remarked—inexcusably lax. All through the seven fat years these small banks were dying: dying at the incredible rate of something like fifty a month. Meanwhile there was a great increase in bank mergers and in branch banking. (The number of branches in the United States had been only 1,280 in 1920; by 1930 it had risen to 3,516.) The result of these changes was that the number of banks in the country dwindled by over five thousand in the nine years 1920-1929; and that on the other hand the big urban banks, and particularly the metropolitan banks, grew much faster than the other survivors. At the beginning of 1930, therefore, this was the situation: There were something like 25,000 banks in all. And one per cent of these 25,000 —only 250 giant banks—controlled 46 per cent of the total resources.

Meanwhile the giant insurance companies were likewise growing at an astonishing rate: by 1930 there were three companies—the Metropolitan, the Prudential, and the New York Life—each of which had assets greater than all the life-insurance companies of the country combined had had in 1900. Here again, financial decisions involving billions of dollars in all were coming to be made by a few men.

Of the power represented by the investments of the big banks, the big insurance companies, and the big investment trusts there will be more to say later. At this point it need only be noted that, combined with the power exercised by the controlling forces in the 200 nonfinancial giants, it tended to bring into the hands of a few thousand men the immediate direction of something like half of the corporate business of the United States.

§ 5

How was this concentration, which we have been trying to measure, brought about?

One way in which it was brought about, of course,
was through the ancient process of the survival of the
fittest. The large concern—if efficiently managed and
properly decentralized in its operations—was able to
make the most of several advantages: it could buy its
materials at lower prices than its competitors, it could
cut prices and undersell its competitors at critical points,
it could spend more money on research, on advertising,
and on salaries to able executives.

Another way in which concentration was brought
about was by mergers of existing corporations. During
the seven fat years there was a positive mania for mergers:
it was a dull week that brought no marriage announcements in the financial pages. Over twelve hundred of
these weddings were solemnized in the years 1919-1928,
involving over four thousand concerns (for some of the
alliances were not monogamous). To some extent the
merger mania was due to a belief that a large concern
with a varied business would be more stable than a
smaller one, less subject to ups and downs of fortune.
To some extent it was due to a desire to bring about
more economical operation: if, for example, one salesman could sell two lines of goods instead of one, the cost
of selling dropped (along with the second salesman).
To some extent it was presumably due to a desire for the
power that comes with size—the chance of being in some
degree able to dictate prices, to approach monopoly.

Another less creditable but potent reason for merging
—especially during the feverish days of the big bull
market—was that a merger gave the men on the inside

a chance to make money in the stock market. Sometimes the terms of the alliance put an extravagant value upon one or the other of the companies, and thus enhanced the immediate value of its stock; and anyhow, speculators had got the idea into their heads that mergers meant prosperity for the concerns involved. Therefore to arrange one of these alliances was to have a beautiful opportunity to push up the prices of the stock of the contracting parties, with easy profits for those who bought early and avoided the rush. And perhaps still another reason for many mergers was sheer vainglory: the blind urge toward bigness, the very human wish to do what everybody else seemed to be doing and do it on a suitably impressive scale.

Two examples of concentration, familiar to everyone, will illustrate what mergers and the survival of the fittest did to the American scene during the seven fat years. The first of these is the rise of the chain stores. By 1930, chain stores were doing practically one-fifth of the retail business of the country; in town after town, the local merchants along Main Street were failing one by one under the competition of groceries, cigar stores, drug stores which owed allegiance not to any citizen of the town, but to an office in a city hundreds or even thousands of miles away. The other example is the concentration of the booming automobile business into fewer and fewer big concerns. In 1923, 85 per cent of the sales of cars had been divided among six companies. By 1930, 83.3 per cent—almost the same proportion—was divided among *only three* companies. Ford, General Motors, and Chrysler had taken the middle of the road, and gradually their competitors were being forced off it.

Another way of achieving concentration, perhaps the most effective way of all, was through the use of the holding company—that far-from-ancient device which, as we have seen, had first come into wide popularity during the latter eighteen-nineties. Holding companies were legion now; indeed, to a large extent the economic history of the nineteen-twenties is the history of the holding company.

According to Berle and Means, among the 573 corporations whose stock was active on the New York Stock Exchange during the year 1928—an array of corporations which included most of the biggest in the country—92 were holding companies pure and simple, 395 were holding companies as well as operating companies, and only 86 were definitely outside the holding-company class. If there was a mania for mergers, so also was there a mania for the use of the holding-company device. By 1930, twenty per cent of the total railway mileage of the country had come under the domination of holding companies. (Shades of the Northern Securities Company!) As for the public utilities of the country, holding companies were taking them over so rapidly that by 1930—to quote N. R. Danielian—"about three-quarters of the power resources of the United States were under the aegis of nine holding-company systems."

The most extraordinary device of all for achieving concentration was an extension of the holding-company device: what became known as "pyramiding"—namely, the organizing of holding companies to control holding companies which in turn controlled other holding companies—and so on almost *ad infinitum*. How pyramiding could be used to bring a whole flock of once independent businesses under the control of a single corporation, and could enable a financier to do this with a minimum investment of his own money, may be illustrated by the following simplified example. It offers clues to much of the recent economic history of the United States.

Suppose there are four corporations, known as A, B,

C, and D, engaged in independent businesses. They may be electric-light companies in four different localities, for example. Each of these four corporations represents an investment of a million dollars, so divided into bonds (which have no voting power), preferred stock (which has no voting power) and common stock (which alone has the right to vote, and thus to control the management of the corporation), that an investment of $250,000 will enable you to maintain control of the whole million-dollar concern. (All you require, to give you undisputed control, is fifty-one per cent of the common stock, and often much less will serve the purpose; thus it would ordinarily take less than $250,000 to get a firm grip on a million-dollar concern. But let us arbitrarily adopt $250,000 as our figure.)

Let us say that you would like to get control not merely of one of these companies but of all four of them—but this would require four times $250,000, or a million dollars, and unhappily you do not possess so much money, or you have other uses for it. All you wish to put up is $250,000—enough to buy control of only one of the four.

Confronted by this difficulty, you meet it as follows: You organize Holding Company X. You put your own $250,000 into the purchase of enough stock in X to control it. You sell to the public the bonds and preferred stock of X and the rest of its common stock, thus bringing the total investment in Holding Company X up to a million dollars, of which you yourself have contributed only a quarter, and the outside public has contributed the other three-quarters.

Then with this million dollars, the disposal of which you can now dictate, you can achieve your objective: Holding Company X buys the control of Companies A,

B, C, and D, paying $250,000 for each. You have got all four of them, and you have invested only your $250,000.

But this is not enough. You would like to get hold of other companies too. Corporations E, F, G, and H look tempting to you. Let us suppose they are of the same size as A, B, C, and D, which you now have in your domain.

You now organize a super-holding company, which we may call S, also with a capitalization of a million dollars, which an investment of $250,000 will control. You sell to the public the bonds and part of the stock of Super-holding Company S, thus getting $750,000 from the out-side. With this money, so cheerfully contributed, you ar-range for Super-holding Company S to take over your stock in Holding Company X, while you quickly substi-tute for this investment of yours in Company X an in-vestment in a controlling share in Super-holding Com-pany S—somewhat as a man doing up a package holds down with one finger the knot which he has just made while he ties another knot.

Now you have your own $250,000 invested in Super-holding Company S; S has $250,000 invested in Holding Company X, whose control of A, B, C, and D is still secure. And notice this. The $750,000 which the public put into Super-holding Company S is still free and clear, ready for investment.

With that $750,000, the disposition of which you can dictate (since you control S), you can easily organize Holding Company Y, which in like manner can take over Companies E, F, G, and H.

So presently you will find yourself in this enviable position: you sit at the top of a pyramid: you, with your $250,000 investment, control S, which in turn controls X and Y, which in turn control A, B, C, D, E, F, G, and H. You had only money enough to pay for a quarter of

the bonds and stock in a single company, yet you now
have eight operating companies, two holding companies,
and a super-holding company where you can do as you
like with them. And you have done nothing which the
business community considers in the least irregular. You
have merely carried out the holding company principle
to its logical conclusion. Or rather, part of the way; for
the process can be carried still farther if your confidence
and ambition hold out and the banks will favor you by
lending you money at the proper moments to hold your
knots securely in place while you tie new ones.

This is an arbitrary and over-simplified example, of
course. Nevertheless it illustrates the general principle
by which a little money could be made to go a long way
in building up an economic empire, once pyramiding
had been accepted as an orthodox financial device.

If you think it may possibly be an over-elaborate
example, consider the elaborateness of the actual device
by which the Tidewater Power Company in North
Carolina was controlled by the Insull interests. Accord-
ing to Professor Norman S. Buchanan, the Tidewater
Power Company was controlled by the Seaboard Service
Company, and the Seaboard by the National Public
Service Corporation, and the National by the National
Electric Power Company, and this National Electric
Power Company by Middle West Utilities; and Middle
West was controlled jointly by Corporation Securities
Company of Chicago and Insull Utility Investments, Inc.
—which in turn were controlled by the Insull family
and by the banking house of Halsey, Stuart & Co. It was
a very long distance from that little power company in
North Carolina to Samuel Insull; there were at least six
steps to this pyramid; but Insull dominated it nevertheless.

Pyramiding had many advantages to the pyramider,

besides that of making a little money go a long way. In another chapter we shall follow the adventures of some noteworthy pyramiders and discover what some of these advantages were. For the present it is enough to remark that if it had not been for the lavish use of this logical extension of the holding-company device, many of the giants of the economic world would never have got their growth.

§ 6

But we are by no means done with describing the concentration of economic power during the seven fat years when we have measured the growth of the business giants and have listed some of the ways in which they added to their stature. It is just as important to inquire how these giant corporations themselves were owned and controlled. Let us begin at the beginning. Who owned them?

The answer to this question does not suggest concentration of control at all. On the contrary, it suggests wide dispersion of control. The fact is that the ownership of these big concerns was becoming more widely distributed than ever before.

Let us take as familiar examples three of the very biggest of them, three super-giants. First, the United States Steel Corporation. In 1910 it had had about 28,000 stockholders; in 1920, it had had 95,000; by 1930, it had 145,000—a steady increase. Second, let us take the Pennsylvania Railroad. In 1910 it had had 65,000 stockholders; in 1920, it had had 117,000; by 1930, it had as many as 207,000. Third, let us take an even more conspicuous example, the American Telephone and Telegraph Company—the biggest monopoly in the United States. In 1910, its stockholders had numbered 41,000. In 1920, they had more than tripled: the figure was 139,000. By

1930, they had more than quadrupled again, reaching 567,000—over half a million. So rapidly, in fact, were the Telephone stockholders multiplying that the amateur statistician could amuse himself by calculating that at the 1920-1930 rate of multiplication, it would take less than fifty years more for every man, woman, and child in the country to become an owner of Telephone stock.

In corporation after corporation the same tendency was exhibited. As the company expanded, so did the number of its shareholders expand. Surely, thought many observers, here was the conclusive answer to those who talked about the concentration of economic power. Industry and business were being democratized. The school-teacher with her ten shares of Telephone, the shopkeeper's widow with her ten shares of Steel, the mechanic with his five shares of Pennsylvania Railroad —these were certainly not capitalists in the traditional sense, yet they were part owners of vast properties, they were voters in growing industrial republics. And there were millions of such little shareholders.

So huge had some of the corporate giants become that no longer was it possible for any individual to own a majority of the stock. Indeed, in the hugest of them no individual held more than a trifling percentage. In 1929 the twenty largest holders of Steel stock owned together only 5.1 per cent of the total number of shares; the twenty largest holders of American Telephone owned only 4 per cent; the twenty largest holders of Pennsylvania Railroad stock owned still less—a mere 2.7 per cent.

Yet the directors and officers of most of these companies remained securely in the saddle, small as were their collective holdings. How did this happen? Was it simply that their management of the properties was so capable that the numerous owners were continuously pleased?

Hardly that. But a large electorate is easily dictated to. Just as a city population is more easily controlled by political bosses than a village population which can gather in town meeting, so an army of stockholders is more amenable to the policies of the management than a corporal's guard. They cannot readily meet to discuss the affairs of the corporation. If some of them wish to propose a change, the sheer immensity of the task of consulting their thousands or even hundreds of thousands of widely separated fellow-stockholders—to say nothing of the expense—is virtually prohibitive. It is enormously easier to sell one's stock than to fight.

If one objects to the way in which this economic community is administered, one does not have to go on living in it, as one usually would have to go on living in a political community whose administration one disliked. One can move out, as it were, at a few hours' or a few minutes' notice. In nine hundred and ninety-nine cases out of a thousand, the disgruntled stockholder simply sells; and the management continues firmly in office, unless failing revenues or rivalries in the inner circle cause dissension there. The men of this inner circle— directors, executives, bankers—maintain their power by being entrenched at the center of things, somewhat like a political ring—except that political rings are from time to time thrown out by an enraged electorate, and it is not easy to recall a single case during the seven fat years when the electorate of one of the giants threw anybody out (although from time to time they took sides in battles between the big insiders, as in the contest between John D. Rockefeller, Jr., and Colonel Stewart for the control of the Standard Oil Company of Indiana) .

If the insiders remained in harmony, the stockholders dutifully and unquestioningly signed their proxies designating certain gentlemen of the management to vote on their behalf at the annual meeting. The votes of the school-teacher, the shopkeeper's widow, and the mechanic were thus cast exactly as the gentlemen of the management wished them cast. Dissensions there were, changes of control there were; but seldom if ever did the electorate bring them about.

Not that the electorate was not assiduously wooed and flattered by the management. There was always, of course, the distant possibility that it might discover its latent power. More vital to the management, however, was the fact that the men and women of the electorate were potential buyers of the company's products, potential allies of the company against political opposition or interference, and—if there were employees among them—potential defenders of its wage and dividend policies. Many big corporations made a point of selling stock to their workers to give them a practical interest in profits, to align them with the interests of capital. Many of the public utilities made a point of selling stock to those who used their electric light or their gas or water, to make these consumers less skeptical about rates, more amenable to large dividends, more enthusiastic about private operation as against public operation. In any case shrewd corporation executives considered it wise to do their best to secure the stockholders' good will as a prerequisite to securing the good will of the general public.

Thus the purchaser of a few shares of stock would perhaps receive a letter signed (in persuasive facsimile) by the president of the company, welcoming him as one of the "partners in the business," pointing out that if he patronized the company's products he would thereby "increase directly the sales and earnings," and suggesting that he must "feel at liberty to write me personally at any time." Or he might receive a pamphlet describing the company's business, with the president's card neatly attached to it with a clip. The annual reports which came to him were sometimes replete not only with figures but with graphs and attractive photographs of the company's products or properties. When he sold his stock, he might receive another letter expressing the president's personal regret at his departure and the hope that the company had not failed him in any way. Forms, all of these, of course; forms devised by ingenious experts in public relations, and distributed by the hundreds of thousands; yet sometimes they were so telling that the small stockholder who received them and then saw a Buick pass on the road or a General Electric fan whirring, would warm momentarily with the sense that he himself was one of the proprietors of this useful product.

Yet sober second thought must have convinced him that he was hardly that. Only in a very limited sense did he enjoy the prerogatives or responsibilities which usually accompany ownership, and which in the earlier days of corporations had actually accompanied the ownership of shares. The average stockholder realized that the administration of the company was far beyond his reach. If he found the company to be engaged in lawless or nefarious business practices, he did not regard himself as in any way responsible. If he believed that he was not getting his fair share of its profits, he almost never thought of fighting out the issue. He knew, in short, that for practical purposes what he had bought was not a certificate of part ownership, but a certificate of his right to receive such dividends as the directors saw fit to declare, and of his right to take a profit if the price of the stock went up on the market. Not that the average stockholder felt badly about this. What he wanted was the dividends (or the profits). If they failed to come, he could sell out; and of course in those days they usually came. He accepted implicitly the truth that in this supposed corporate democracy an oligarchy reigned securely.

§ 7

The power and responsibility of the stockholder who was not an insider were diminished not only by the sheer size and unwieldiness of the enterprise, but frequently by various specific devices through which the management could effectively shoulder him aside or disfranchise him. Some of these were old devices, some were new; but most of them came into wider and more confident use in the seven fat years than ever before.

Some of them, it must be said, were only incidentally useful in keeping the stockholder in his place; they were primarily invented for other purposes. For instance, some companies had established their nominal headquarters in small villages in order to avoid property taxes which would be levied in a city; but it also was presumably convenient to have to hold the annual meeting of the stockholders in a place so inaccessible that few of them would be likely to attend and ask questions. One chain-store organization, for instance, with over a million shares of stock outstanding, held its annual meeting in the post-office building in the village of Eddyville, New York. Here—in a small bare room furnished with a couple of wooden benches and a few chairs and a desk—a group of insiders, holding proxies for a million shares or more, could transact the necessary business of the day. Other devices were deliberately invented in order to permit power to be concentrated.

For example, there was the voting trust: an old device by which a small group of men were empowered, by the terms on which the stock was issued, to elect directors annually for a certain term of years. When first used, the voting-trust device had been much criticized as involving virtual disfranchisement of the stockholders. But Morgan the Elder had used it freely—and had defended it strenuously, as you may recall, before the Pujo Committee. It was still in use in the nineteen-twenties, though perhaps not as popular as in previous years.

Then there was the issuing of non-voting stock. For a considerable period the right of the promoters of a company to issue non-voting preferred stock had been generally recognized, but the frank disfranchisement of common stockholders was a comparative novelty. Yet it was widely resorted to in the seven fat years, though always it was under criticism. For example, when the Dodge Brothers automobile concern was reorganized in 1925, not only the preferred stock but four-fifths of the common was deprived of any vote; the result was that the New York banking house of Dillon Read & Co., which performed the reorganization, was able to control a company representing a total investment valued at 130 millions by taking 2½ million dollars' worth of Class B common stock.

There was the somewhat similar device of vesting a disproportionate voting power in one class of stock. For instance, in 1929 the Cities Service Company (the capstone of a pyramid of utility companies) issued a special class of preferred stock to H. L. Doherty & Company, and this preferred stock *had twenty times the voting power of the common stock*; a fact which enabled Mr. Doherty, as it were, to hold control of Cities Service and its subordinate companies with one hand, although the Doherty concern paid only one dollar a share for its twenty-vote stock, while new common stockholders were paying from twenty to sixty-eight dollars a share for their one-vote stock!

Another device was the outright extension of the legal

powers of the directors of a company, by the passage of
new incorporation laws which gave them the right to
do things which had hitherto been banned (as infring-
ing upon the rights of the owners of the corporation).
It was the State of Delaware, under the political
suzerainty of the wealthy duPonts, the powder and munitions manufacturers, which in the seven fat years took
a long lead in the race among the states to secure incorporation fees by accommodating their laws to the wishes
of company promoters. A generation earlier the rush of
promoters had been to New Jersey; it was in Hoboken
that the corporations which they formed had preferred
to hang their hats. In the latter nineteen twenties the
rush was to Delaware, and the corporate hats were hung
in Wilmington.

In a single building in Wilmington, the Industrial
Trust Building, some ten thousand corporations made
their legal homes. It was not a large building; it was
only ten stories high and ten windows wide on the front
—in New York or Chicago it would be considered rather
small. Nor did the ten thousand corporations occupy the
whole of it. On the contrary: they all had their headquarters on the tenth floor (though there were stenographers and clerks available for their use on two or three
lower floors).

The only readily visible sign of their legal tenancy of
these modest offices was in the entrance lobby downstairs,
where the visitor, expecting perhaps to see the usual
moderate-sized framed panel containing the directory of
tenants (with the names in white letters on a black background), saw, instead, panels on every side of him reaching almost from floor to ceiling and containing tier upon
tier of names in small print. And what names! The
Standard Oil Company of New Jersey, the Radio Corporation of America, the United Corporation, the

National Dairy Products Corporation, the Pullman Company, and so on. (Indeed, some of these tenants appeared on the list not singly but in squad formation, followed by their subsidiaries: a visitor to the building in 1934 noted the names of 30 different corporations in the McKesson squad, of 18 in the Warner Brothers squad, of 13 in the Publix squad. The vast General Motors Corporation had its technical residence across the street, in the duPont Building, but a squad of its subsidiaries were listed here.)

Why this eagerness to take up legal residence in Wilmington? Because, in the first place, it need be only a very casual residence. According to the Delaware laws, none of the directors of a Delaware corporation need live in the state; it was not necessary to hold the directors' meetings or even the stockholders' meetings in the state; and the corporation might do its actual business anywhere on the globe. But also because, in the second place, the Delaware laws gave to directors such privileges as these:

They need not own any stock whatever in the company which they directed.

They might issue stock, not only in return for cash or for property, but, if they preferred, in return for "services rendered"—the value of which they would of course fix.

They might arrange the voting rights of various classes of stock as they saw fit.

And, what was more, they might at any time dilute the stockholders' share in the ownership of the company by issuing new stock without offering it first to the existing stockholders or even getting these stockholders' permission; and to such new stock they might give such voting privileges as they saw fit.

In short, the stockholders of a Delaware corporation which took full advantage of its legal opportunities were shorn of many of the traditional prerogatives of owner-ship. (Strong to survive, however, are ancient ways of thought: if you had suggested to one of these stockholders that a Federal incorporation law might be to his ad-vantage, he probably would have opposed such an inno-vation as "threatening the rights of property." And of course he would have opposed it as undermining "states' rights"—that rugged principle of local self-rule which enables New Yorkers to do business in California under the laws of Delaware.)

Still another device was the banker-controlled re-organization. If a company went into receivership or was for some other reason to be reorganized, it had become the custom for bankers not only to put up the money necessary to finance the financial operations which were required, but to dictate the terms of the whole reorgani-zation. In theory such transactions were completely under the supervision of the courts, in order that the bondholders and other creditors and the stockholders and other interests involved might be fairly treated. What sometimes happened in practice has been clearly brought out by Max Lowenthal in his analysis of the reorganization of the St. Paul Railroad, the biggest of all such rearrangements of capital during the seven fat years.

This reorganization was managed by the Wall Street private banking firm of Kuhn, Loeb & Co. This banking firm, seeing that a receivership was inevitable, selected a "friendly" creditor and suggested that it ask for the re-ceivership. (Incidentally, this creditor was a coal com-pany—and one of the heads of this coal company, on its being selected, at once obeyed a natural impulse and sold a thousand shares of St. Paul short!) The banking firm selected the judge before whom the creditor was to ap-pear; consulted the judge in advance about whom to appoint receivers, and got a satisfactory group of three; selected the heads of the committees who were to represent the various classes of bonds and stock in the negotiations; and selected most of the members of the committees, including, as members, various eminent bankers who owned none of the securities whose interests they were supposed to represent. The banking firm further selected the trustees for the bondholders and the lawyers who were to represent various groups of security holders; and they secured the adoption by these committees of a complicated and lengthy agreement which maintained Kuhn, Loeb's hold on the situation. Not only did the fees allowed to the banks and trust companies and corporation lawyers and to the firm of Kuhn, Loeb & Co. itself, for their services in reorganizing the railroad, run into the millions—which had to be paid out of the resources of this bankrupt road before the regular creditors got a penny—but naturally the plan of reorganization which was adopted left the control of the road firmly within the sphere of influence of Kuhn, Loeb & Company.

Indeed it was very generally the custom, when reorganizations took place, not only to levy large fees but also to make up the new board of directors in such a way that the control rested wherever the bankers wished it to rest. Once more the investor who was not an insider found himself at the mercy of those who held the reins of power.

Sometimes the bankers and corporation lawyers at the center of things exercised this power of theirs scrupulously and beneficently, sometimes they exercised it scandalously; the point which I am making here is simply that the power was theirs to exercise as they pleased.

There were still other devices by which insiders could acquire or protect their control. For example pyramid-

ing, which we have already discussed, undoubtedly deserves mention here again.

It must be understood that often the men who put
these devices to use had no sense that they were wielding power to which they were not entitled. The custom
of taking such power had grown up through a long series
of corporation lawyers' inventions, and there were many
arguments in favor of these inventions. They made for
speed, for efficiency, for harmony; they did away with
red tape; and they put the affairs of the corporation in
question in what the insiders naturally considered to be
the most capable and deserving hands—to wit, their own
hands and those of their friends. Seldom did investors
protest audibly; as we have seen, the investor, loudly as
he might defend his rights of property in the abstract,
was quite reconciled to relinquishing many of them in
the concrete. And in the enthusiasm of Coolidge prosperity he was inclined to accept anything and everything
which the masters of capital chose to do as superlatively
wise and right.

One further fact should be made clear. Not all directors of corporations were necessarily insiders in any real
sense. A director might concern himself with only some
limited phase of the corporation's activities, or he might
be ornamentally inactive; he might actually know almost
as little as the outside stockholders about what was going
on in the enterprise which he was supposed to supervise.
When one man held 45 directorships, as did Albert H.
Wiggin, chairman of the Chase National Bank, in the
heyday of his career—or 52, as did Percy Rockefeller, or
even 66, as did Charles Hayden—what were the chances
that he would be able to devote time and care to a
study of each corporation's work? Many financiers, when
blamed in later years for scandals in the companies of
which they had been directors, testified quite truly that

they had been ignorant of what was happening. Often the real authority was lodged in one or two men. Decisions involving not only the fortunes of stockholders but the livelihood of employees, and affecting the whole economic destiny of an industry or a region, could be made by such men subject to only the flimsiest sort of check from either the ostensible owners of the property or their ostensible representatives.

§ 8

To be an insider could on occasion be very profitable. There were many ways—ranging all the way from the reasonably defensible to the utterly indefensible—of making money by reason of one's inside position. John T. Flynn has remarked that very few Americans have made as much as a million dollars merely by saving their salaries, even by saving hundred-thousand-dollar salaries. It is probable that most of the self-made millionaires and multi-millionaires—and there were thousands of them—won their fortunes by exercising the prerogatives of insidership: by being awarded stock for services (either with or without quotation marks), or by being awarded bonuses by their fellow-directors, or by using their inside knowledge to speculate in the stock market, or by engaging in personal transactions with their companies, or by investing in concerns to which they threw company business, or by siphoning the money of their companies into holding companies in which they held an interest, or otherwise.

As far back as 1904, Thorstein Veblen had called attention, in *The Theory of Business Enterprise*, to the divergence between the pecuniary interest of the insiders and that of the ordinary stockholders. He had noted, for example, that the easiest way for an insider to make money was to trade in the shares of his own company, buying these shares when he knew the company was doing better than the proxy-signers supposed, and selling them when he knew it was not doing so well; and that, once this insider's position at the center of things was secure, it was less to his pecuniary interest that the enterprise should prosper than that there should be a discrepancy, one way or the other, between the market value of its shares and their real value. As the corporate giants grew and their shares were more generally listed and more actively traded in, and the devices which we have been discussing came into common use, this divergence of interest became a much more widespread and more striking characteristic of American business than it had been in 1904.

The more dubious of the exploits by which insiders took their private profits seldom became widely known. Even if they became widely known they were usually regarded with considerable tolerance in the business world. Indeed, one of the most flagrant of all which came to light during this period—the Continental Trading Company deal, in which a group of officers of various oil companies drew off a profit of over three million dollars on an inter-company sale of oil (a profit which would otherwise have gone to one or more of their companies) —would hardly have caused the removal of Colonel Stewart from his position at the head of the Standard Oil Company of Indiana, if John D. Rockefeller, Jr., had not employed all the voting power of the large blocks of stock which he controlled, and all the great financial and moral influence which he possessed, to push Colonel Stewart out.

There were insiders of the most scrupulous integrity in big corporations, of course, but there were others to whom a position on the inside was a legitimate opportunity to draw off the gravy from the dish; and for these latter there were opportunities in plenty.

But far more important for our consideration than the profits made by insiders at the expense of other participants in business is the effect which the growing concentration of a large part of American business into the control of a few corporations, and of the power over these corporations into the hands of groups of insiders, had upon the economic organization of the country. It is difficult to escape these three conclusions:

1. Some of the devices which were now permitted and were used on a large scale made for general financial instability. This was conspicuously true of the holding-company pyramid, and to a lesser degree was true of holding-companies in general, of investment trusts, and of other financial superstructures of the new-era model. Companies at the top of holding-company pyramids, for example, could not even pay the interest on their debt—let alone pay dividends—unless the companies in which they held stock could pay common-stock dividends. These financial superstructures were built for fair weather. If a storm should come, they were in danger of outright bankruptcy. They would not be able to afford to let the companies which they controlled pass dividends; in fact, they were under the most severe temptation to milk these companies of funds in order to protect themselves, and the banks which were involved with them, from disaster. The maintenance of prices or of rates was essential to their life; the maintenance of employment was not essential, at least not immediately; thus the almost inevitable thing for them to do under the pressure of fear would be to save money on labor and to try to hold their wobbly financial structures intact. But almost nobody foresaw foul weather then. The skies were clear, confidence ran high, and so capital built its

superstructures high and handsome—and not nearly wide enough. The tumble was to come later.

2. The general process of concentration made for irresponsibility of management, because again and again the power which men wielded far outreached their personal stake in the enterprises which they controlled. It must be remembered that the right to form a corporation, with limited liability for those who conduct it, is not a natural right of man, or even a very ancient right of property. It is a privilege extended by the state, under restrictions which have traditionally been designed to assure a responsible exercise of this privilege. The utmost pains were taken, when the corporation was a comparative novelty, to make sure that those who put money into it were protected, that the directors whom they chose were subject to their control and could do nothing contrary to their wishes; and also, on the other hand, that owners and directors alike were under restrictions as to the sort of businesses in which they could engage and were otherwise limited in power and scope. By the nineteen-twenties, however, it was possible to organize a corporation whose charter permitted it to do almost anything; it was possible for the management to act without the stockholders' consent on vital matters, even to enjoy opportunities to make money at the stockholders' expense, and to do all this without the financial risk which attends ordinary ownership. So complex were these financial structures, furthermore, that nothing less than a battery of accountants and investigators could find out whether the insiders had or had not lived up to their trust. Power without responsibility is dangerous. The men who occupied such favored positions would have had to be extraordinarily disinterested never to take advantage of their opportunities to profit at the expense of others, and extraordinarily far-seeing as well as disinter-

ested not to engage in operations which would add to the instability of the national economy.

3. Finally, the concentration of so much power in a few hands had virtually the effect of setting apart a special economic class—a class of insiders, of economic rulers, almost as far removed, in opportunity and interest, from the ordinary stockholders—the proxy-signers—as the office executives were removed from the day laborers.

Here we must be very careful with our definitions. If we speak of the insiders as forming a class, we must not imply that it was a recognized class—consciously recognized either by itself or by most other people as possessing a well-marked identity of interest—or that it was a homogeneous or hereditary or exclusive class. Some of the members of it inherited their power, others rose from the ranks and seized it. They were scattered all over the country, though a large proportion of them—probably as many as half—were in Wall Street.

Nor must even Wall Street be thought of as representing anything like a united front. There were fierce divergencies of opinion there. There were men wielding large power in Wall Street who had never met one another. No man spoke to the financiers with such authority during the seven fat years as the elder Morgan had spoken to them a generation before; the voice of the House of Morgan, while it was listened to with deep respect not unmixed with fear, did not now call the tune so definitely as it once had. Indeed, so abundant were the opportunities now open to this class, so easy was it for men of inordinate ambition to carve out for themselves new principalities, that discipline was largely lost. Here was no firm hierarchy, no well-organized general staff for the forces of finance and industry, but rather a confusion of powers.

But enough of such generalizations and reflections.

Let us turn to drama. Let us watch some of these insiders as they use the privileges and devices which we have been analyzing. Only if we do this can we fully realize what an age of financial wonders was that span of years from 1922 to 1929.

Chapter Nine

BUILDING THE PYRAMIDS

IN THE year 1878, when Benjamin Disraeli was prime minister of England, there lived in London a humble young clerk named Samuel Insull. His father was an impecunious clergyman. His mother kept for a time "Insull's Temperance Hotel." Young Samuel himself was a stenographer in an auctioneer's office, where his wages had begun at five shillings a week.

Fifty-one years later, Samuel Insull had become the most powerful man in Chicago. His system of public-utility holding companies controlled several hundred electric light and power plants and gas plants and other properties scattered from Maine to Texas and Oklahoma. At his own (subsequent) estimate he was worth one hundred and seventy million dollars. Few men in the country wielded a mightier or more pervasive influence. He seemed to have reached the pinnacle of financial fortune.

Five more years passed, and Samuel Insull had become a fugitive from justice, rocking across the Mediterranean in a dingy little Greek steamboat in the futile hope of finding somewhere a refuge from the police.

It has been the fate of few men to rise so high from such simple beginnings, and then to fall again so sickeningly. But the career of Samuel Insull is interesting not merely because of its extraordinary contrasts, but also because of the way in which it illustrates the possible effects of an almost unrestrained use of some of the financial devices which had been developing in the

United States since the turn of the century and which flourished riotously in the nineteen-twenties.

The fact that Insull came to grief and was at last brought to trial on a charge of fraud has seemed to set him widely apart from other financiers of his time: has made him, in the public mind, one of the chief scape-goats for the financial follies of those days. It must be remembered, however, that the operations upon which the charge of fraud was based were not undertaken until his pyramid was already toppling about his ears; and that the structure of that pyramid was not essentially different in most respects from the structure of some other pyramids which fell less resoundingly or even re-mained intact. (Indeed, some of the devices which char-acterized the Insull financing were found in even more exaggerated form elsewhere.) The chief reason for citing the Insull empire as the prime example of the technic of pyramiding in the public-utility field is that it has been more thoroughly illuminated by the spotlight of pub-licity than any other, and that the sequence of events which led to its collapse reveals with singularly dramatic force the temptations to which pyramiders were subject and the results of succumbing to those temptations. There are no doubt other Americans who might have said, as they read of Insull's humiliating flight from the Piraeus in that dingy Greek boat in the early days of 1934, "There, but for the grace of God, go I."

Samuel Insull's early career seems to have been ready-made for the use of a modern Horatio Alger. To be sure, luck played a large part in its early phases. The nineteen-year-old English stenographer had read with admiration about the inventions of young Thomas Edison, and had even written a paper on Edison for a little literary so-ciety. Shortly afterward he lost his job in the auctioneer's office where he had been employed. Looking for another job, he answered a newspaper advertisement—and discovered to his rapture that the man who had inserted it was the London manager for Edison's fledgling enterprises! He got this job—as a stenographer—and showed so much more than mere stenographic ability that when Edison himself needed a secretary he cabled to England for young Insull, who thus found himself at the great inventor's very right hand and close to the center of what was to prove to be a vast industry.

Luck had thus far showered its favors upon him; during the next twenty or thirty years, however, it played a smaller part in his rise than sheer ability and knowledge combined with furious determination. While he was still in his twenties he became an important figure in the business management of the Edison companies. In his thirties he became the president of Edison's electric light company in Chicago. He managed it brilliantly and soundly, and it absorbed rival companies one by one, until in his forties he had achieved a monopoly of the electric-light business in the city.

He was coming on very fast, this young Anglo-American, and his progress was creditable. You might not have enjoyed his companionship particularly, for like other young men of his time whose overwhelming ambition was to get on in the world, he seemed to live for business; but he was sober, hard-working, and extraordinarily competent. Flynn describes him at this period as "a rugged, thick-set Briton, radiating self-assurance and power, with an iron jaw under a cushion of fresh, pink skin." He knew the business of producing and distributing electricity in every detail, he was almost a genius at organization, and the contributions which he made to the development of the electrical industry were undeniably very valuable. He realized the great advantages of mass-production. He realized that if the most were to be made of them, it was essential for local electric companies to be monopolies. And he also realized—as many men did not—how necessary it was, to the industry as well as to the public, that rates should be lowered as the consumption of electricity expanded and the production of it became more efficient. Indeed, he even welcomed governmental regulation. Said he once, "If there is anything wrong with my business, I want to know it. And the best way for me to know it is to have a public official who has the right to look into my affairs, in a position so he can employ the highest class of talent to help him." In fact, Insull once went so far as to say—at a time when the idea of government interference, as sponsored by Theodore Roosevelt and Robert LaFollette, was filling the business community with dismay—that if public regulation failed, public ownership would be necessary.

Insull's domain was soon to expand, and with it, his ideas. In 1905 he began to acquire electric light and power plants outside the Chicago area, making an investment in two small concerns on the Ohio River. In 1912—when he was still in his early fifties—he formed the Middle West Utilities Company to raise more capital for his acquisitions, and his career entered a new phase.

For he organized this Middle West company in such a way that when he had been fully reimbursed for the properties which he had turned over to it, he was fifty thousand common shares to the good. The operation was performed as follows: Insull sold his properties to the new-born Middle West for $330,000. The company then issued to him—or, if you prefer, he issued to himself, for he was president of the company—40,000 shares of preferred stock and 60,000 shares of common stock. For these he paid $3,600,000. This was such a good bargain with the company which he himself headed that he was able to sell the preferred shares and 10,000 of the com-

mon shares to the public for $3,600,000—enough to re-
pay him for his investment—and still have 50,000 shares
of common left, for which he thus had to pay nothing!
And he had control of the new company.

It was a perfectly characteristic job of stock-watering
—reminiscent in some ways of the formation of the Steel
Corporation and of other financing operations which
we have witnessed. It could be defended on the ground
that these common shares which Insull acquired would
be of no value unless by excellent management he increased profits, in which case his efficiency would be
largely rewarded. But it was perhaps too instructive a
lesson in how to make money in the utility business. The
big money was made in selling stock to the public for
more than you had had to pay for it (or, to put it another way, in selling the stock of your own company to
yourself for less than its potential market value.) To do
this, you had of course to put a high—if not actually
extravagant—valuation upon the property which the
stock represented, and to paint a rosy picture of possible
earnings. And to make good on this picture, you had to
provide the earnings. Ordinarily, the operation was one
which could not soon be repeated without disastrous results: even in a rapidly growing industry, it usually took
time for earnings to catch up with expectations. But
possibly ways of finding them—or seeming to find them—
could be discovered.

Wrote George Savile, first Marquis of Halifax, in the
seventeenth century: "A Cunning Minister will engage
his Master to begin with a small wrong step, which will
insensibly engage him in a great one. A man that hath
the Patience to go by steps, may deceive one much wiser
than himself." Samuel Insull was taking his first steps in
the new finance.

The early steps, however, were short ones. In the next

few years Insull acquired or formed many new companies in various parts of the Middle West, but his most impressive advance in power and prestige was in Chicago itself. The war came and Insull, as the biggest man in Chicago business, became chairman of Governor Lowden's State Council of Defense, which had charge of various war activities in Illinois. The local gas company was in difficulties, and he was asked to save it, and did. He combined the local traction companies and restored them to comparative economic health. By the beginning of the seven fat years his organizing ability had become a legend.

He was now in his early sixties. He still worked furiously; usually he reached his desk well before eight o'clock in the morning. If you had met him outside of business, you would probably have been charmed by the range of his knowledge, by his capacity for taking a personal interest in your affairs, no matter how busy he was, and by the disarming gentleness which his brown eyes could assume. He was generous with his millions. He did not forget his friends. As a knickerbockered country squire at Libertyville he could be mellow affability itself. Yet in business affairs he was dictatorial and ruthless.

His will seemed to dominate the affairs of the city of Chicago. Apparently he was quite complacent about the political corruption of the city; he and his henchmen aided both political parties. Among the beneficiaries of his generosity was the chairman of the commission which ruled upon utility rates and utility financing in the State of Illinois, and the contributions were made in cash—envelopes stuffed with bills. "When you want the money, come and get it," said Insull to the political agent who collected such largesse, according to the agent's subsequent testimony. Englishman though Insull was by birth and early loyalty, he did not seem to mind supporting Big Bill Thompson, whose expressed ambition was to "bust King George on the snoot." Business was business, and politicians could be useful. Insull was feared; by some who had felt his ruthlessness he was hated; yet he was also mightily respected for his actual prowess as an executive and his supposed prowess as a financier.

It was during the seven fat years that Insull's steps in the new finance became reckless. The lucrative possibilities of holding-company pyramiding had been discovered in many quarters, and several big systems of electric-light and power companies were growing with astonishing rapidity. The competition among them became furious. There was the Electric Bond and Share system, the biggest of all, built up by a brilliant financier, S. Z. Mitchell, as an offshoot of the General Electric Company. There were also the Byllesby system, the Cities Service system, the Associated Gas and Electric system, the American Waterworks and Electric system, and many others. These systems were engaged, seemingly, in a race to see which one of them could buy up the greatest number of local electric light companies. They were spawning new holding companies and super-holding companies to widen and consolidate their control. Securities were easy to sell, for to the investing public the prospects of the electric-light industry were incredibly dazzling. With confidence unbounded, Insull expanded his system. He sought to have the biggest empire of all.

We must pause now for a word of explanation. How could the electric light and power business be so lucrative? The local companies—being monopolies—were regulated by the states, were they not? They were supposed to lower their rates as business expanded and efficiency increased, rather than to pile up huge profits, were they not? What, then, was the great advantage in buying up these companies so lavishly?

There are several answers to this question. One was that a holding company which controlled a number of operating companies was able to provide them with good management, to command better engineering ability than they could afford individually, to save money by mass-purchasing, by consolidating income-tax returns, and otherwise, and to secure them new capital on better terms than they could command individually. Another reason was that the business was expanding so rapidly and gaining in efficiency so rapidly—partly as a result of the very competition of which we have been speaking —that often profits could grow even if rates were lowered. Another reason was that political pressure could sometimes succeed in keeping rates from being lowered; a legislator who wanted to lower them could be made to seem a destructive radical, an enemy of the business man; or else perhaps he could be bought.

Still another reason was that a holding company was something like a cream-separating machine, which skimmed off the richest of the profits when these were increasing. Ordinarily the holding company held only the common stock of the operating companies, or part of it, leaving the bonds and preferred stock in the hands of the general public. If we think of the earnings which went to pay interest on the bonds and dividends on the preferred stock as resembling the milk in a bottle, and the further earnings which went to pay dividends on the common stock as the cream at the top, we can see how advantageous it was to skim the cream from ten or twenty bottles: one inch more of cream in each bottle, and the cream-separators would find their haul growing out of all proportion. (Conversely, of course, the cream-separating business would languish if the cows gave a poorer quality of milk—but that is the sort of thing which does not occur to investors in boom times.)

By piling holding companies on top of one another, one could still further increase the richness of one's cream. For just as the bondholders and preferred stockholders of the operating companies got the milk of profits, and the common stockholders got the cream (if there was any) , so the bondholders and preferred stockholders of the holding companies (which we have likened to cream-separators) got the ordinary cream, and the common stockholders got the extra-heavy cream at the very top (if there was any) . To own the common stock of a super-holding company might be to get the best of the extra-heavy cream, skimmed, as it were, from forty or fifty bottles (again, if there was any) .

But there were other advantages still. One was that a holding company could siphon money out of its operating companies—and so adroitly that a regulating commission could not see it go. For instance, it could charge the operating companies very heavily for the management and engineering services which it undertook on their behalf. How could a state regulating commission tell whether the amounts of money which a local power company spent for management and engineering services were reasonable? It could not examine the books of the holding company which performed these services—for this latter corporation was in no way under its jurisdiction unless it actually sold power itself; in legal theory it was not engaged in the electric power business at all. The holding company was safely beyond the regulating commission's reach!

Let us watch this siphon at work. One of the Insull group of companies (the National Electric Power group) had such services performed for it by a concern called the Electric Management and Engineering Corporation.

During the period between July 15, 1925, and September 30, 1930, this Electric Management and Engineering Corporation performed services for the operating companies which cost it, in all, a little less than $2,100,000 —and it charged over $4,100,000 for them, collecting a profit of 98.8 per cent, neatly sucked out of the various operating companies.

And perhaps the choicest advantage of all was that a system of holding companies and operating companies could manufacture profits by marking up the values of properties and finding ways in which the mark-ups might appear on their books as profits. One way of doing this was to have the various companies in the system sell properties to each other at rising prices. It was somewhat as if Mr. Jones owned a piano for which he had paid a thousand dollars, and Mrs. Jones owned an Oriental rug for which she had paid a thousand dollars. Presently Mr. Jones sold the piano to his wife for $1500 and she sold the rug to him for $1500, and they declared that it had been a profitable year for them because each of them had made five hundred dollars on the sale of property— despite the fact that the piano and the rug were still right in their living-room and that not a nickel had come in from outside the family! Does this seem to you a curious way of keeping accounts? Perhaps; it is hardly more curious than the method employed from time to time in the Insull system.

For example, in January, 1928, the Middle West Utilities (one of the Insull holding companies) sold some securities to the National Electric Power (another Insull company, which incidentally it controlled) for over three million dollars more than it had paid for them; and simultaneously—indeed, by the very same agreement—the National Electric Power sold some other securities to the Middle West Utilities for over three million dollars more than it had paid for them. The securities were simply exchanged; they stayed within the family, just as did the Joneses' piano and rug, and no money had come in from the outside. Yet those two companies chalked up two profits of three million dollars each. And as the Middle West controlled the National Electric Power, and thus had cream-skimming rights over it, the Middle West got not merely its own three millions but the National Electric Power's three millions too, and chalked up a profit of six millions!

In defense of such remarkable accounting it could be argued, of course, that the rising prosperity of the electrical business was causing all values to increase, and that this was simply a way of taking due advantage of the swelling wealth of the utility systems. But as Professor W. Z. Ripley pointed out, such revaluations were "paper profits, not real ones at all." It was unwise to distribute them as dividends; it would be better to "salt them down against an evil day when something may happen to the other side of the ledger." Furthermore, it was largely because revaluations were constantly going on, in system after system of utilities, that the upward march of market values was so impressive, and that there was thus a shadow of an excuse for the practice. Indeed, the sequence of cause and effect in the operations of these utility systems was circular. Because the holding companies could be made to show big profits, it was easy to raise money to finance them. (It was also, incidentally, easy to persuade public-service commissions that rates could not be lowered; had not the Supreme Court declared it legitimate to claim a fair return, not merely on the original investment, but on what it would cost to reproduce the investment in these days of higher prices?) Because it was so easy to show profits, the stock could be watered and the magnates at the center of things could make much money through financing operations. Because so much money could be made, the systems became more and more ambitious and tried to get hold of more and more operating companies. Because they tried so hard, the market value of electric light plants increased. Therefore there was a plausible excuse for writing up the assets of existing companies. And therefore the systems could be made to show big profits. It was an endless sequence; and it was enough to turn the head of any but the coolest of financiers.

By 1926 or thereabouts—when Coolidge prosperity was coming richly into flower—Samuel Insull's head appears to have been pretty thoroughly turned. (His financial head, that is to say; he still remained a brilliant operator of utility plants.) The expansion and elaboration of his pyramid of corporations was now going on at a terrific rate. Already it was seven or eight stories high. In his reckless zeal for the acquisition of new operating companies and water power sites, he was striking some strange bargains—buying paper and textile mills and even a tire-fabric company and a shoe-factory in New England; buying real-estate development companies near Kansas City, and in Texas (one of which was designed to transform Port Isabel, Texas, into "the Venus of the South"). He was paying strange prices; said the president of an electric light company to N. R. Danielian, when asked why he had sold out to Insull: "What in hell would you do if some one came along and offered you three times as much as your company was ever worth?" So curious were some of the Insull investments at this time that it is doubtful if the mad adventure could have gone on long, had it not been possible to mark up values and shuffle investments about among the numerous corporations in the Insull family, and to sell more and more stock at more and more inflated values. Mr.

Danielian estimates that Middle West Utilities, which paid good dividends and the stock of which went to 570 in 1929 (that stock which Insull had got 40,000 shares of without charge, back in 1912), would have run at a loss during most of its career if it had had to depend upon the sort of profits which cold-blooded accountants permit to be shown as profits. But investors were greedy and stock-salesmen were operating under high pressure and high profits were being shown all along the line— and the speculative fever was in the air. So the adventure went on.

To look at a chart of the Insull pyramid as it appeared during those lush days is almost to be persuaded that one is dreaming. Certainly, one thinks, here is corporate capitalism gone mad.

At the top of the pyramid (as it existed in 1929) was a so-called investment trust known as Insull Utility Investments, Inc. This concern held stock, directly or indirectly, in four others of imposing size: The Public Service Company of Northern Illinois, the Commonwealth Edison Company, the Peoples Gas Light and Coke, and the Middle West Utilities. But the Middle West Utilities was itself the capstone of a lesser pyramid, controlling holding companies which controlled holding companies which in turn controlled other holding companies or operating companies. The system was not symmetrical, neither did it retain its shape for any long space of time; there was a constant shifting of investments going on, a constant passing of properties from hand to hand (often at rising prices); but some notion of its dimensions and complexity may be obtained by following up the lines of control from the bottom to the top in one or two places. For example, as we have already seen in Chapter 7, the Tidewater Power Company (in North Carolina) was controlled by the Seaboard Service Company, which was controlled by the National Public Service Corporation, which was controlled by the National Electric Power Company, which was controlled by the Middle West Utilities. For another example, let us move from North Carolina up into Maine. The little Androscoggin Electric Company in Maine was controlled by the Androscoggin Corporation, which was controlled by the Central Maine Power Company, which was controlled by the New England Public Service Company, which was controlled by the National Electric Power Company, which was controlled by the Middle West Utilities. These are only two instances of the relationships in a pyramid consisting of scores of corporations. And each of the corporations in this vast system had its board of directors, its officers, its investments, its ledgers, its complex system of accounting, its annual reports, its various classes of stock, and its army of minor investors.

Does this seem complicated enough? One more element of confusion must be noted. The lines of investment and control did not simply run from the top of the system to the bottom, as one might expect. They ran every which way. Sometimes they ran upward. For example:

When Samuel Insull formed the Corporation Securities Company of Chicago, late in 1929, to try to maintain his control over a system that was already getting out of hand, he arranged that this newest of all his concerns should hold a large block of the stock of Insull Utility Investments, Inc., which he had formed in the previous year to put at the top of his pyramid. At one time "Corps"—as Corporation Securities was known to its intimates—held 28.9 per cent of the stock of Insull Utility Investments. But Insull Utility Investments also owned 12.5 per cent of the stock of "Corps." Each of these two super-super-super-holding companies thus held a firm grip on the other. Again, at one time "Corps" held a little over ten per cent of the stock of Middle West Utilities, which was a story below it in the pyramid, so to speak; but Middle West also held 1.2 per cent of the stock of "Corps." In the face of facts like these, one is at a loss for figures of speech which can be applied to the system. A pyramid, was it? But what sort of a pyramid has a lower step partly resting upon the step above it? A family tree, was it? (Financiers often refer to "parent companies.") But in what sort of a family is the child a part-parent of the father?

Years afterward, Owen D. Young said that he had to confess to a "feeling of helplessness" when he attempted to understand the tangle of corporations which had grown up under Insull's sovereignty. "I say it is impossible," insisted Mr. Young, "for any man to grasp the situation of that vast structure . . . it was so set up that you could not possibly get an accounting system which would not mislead even the officers themselves." . . . He expressed the belief that the intricate relationships "got even beyond the power" of Samuel Insull, "competent as he was, to understand" them. Mr. Young was putting it mildly. When, in 1934, Insull was tried for fraud, the Federal Attorney struggled to find a formula by which he could show the jury that the real value of the stock of "Corps" was not what the Insulls had claimed it to be. On a blackboard in the courtroom he wrote two equations:

$$X = A + \left(\frac{a}{b}x' \right) - C$$

$$X' = A' + \left(\frac{c}{d}x \right) - C'$$

The bewilderment of the twelve good men and true when

they looked at those equations was hardly greater than would have been the bewilderment of any man who had tried to discover what Insull was really doing in his endlessly complex financial pyramid-building.

Yet few people had any doubts, in 1929, of Insull's ability to understand what he was doing. If there was some conservative questioning in the East, Chicagoans were tempted to ascribe it to jealousy. He seemed to be a miracle-worker. His prestige was colossal. He was chairman of the board of directors of 65 different concerns, and president of eleven others. His wealth was reputedly vast. John Flynn quotes a cynical reporter of those days as saying that it was worth a million dollars to any man to be seen talking to Sam Insull in front of the Continental Bank.

He had built a great opera building—popularly known, on account of its shape, as "Insull's Armchair"—in which the new Civic Opera Company which he financed was preparing for its first brilliant season. (Oh, yes, he was a patron of the arts: had he not, among other things, humored his wife's ambition to return to the stage by spending a quarter of a million or so that she might appear as Lady Teazle in "The School for Scandal"?) High up in this same opera building he had a magnificent apartment, in the central room of which there was a grand piano and also a directors' table, suggesting the union of finance and its tributary arts. Flynn tells a story of a man's coming to see Insull in this apartment and wanting to talk to him confidentially, and noting as they conversed that a group of men were talking in an adjoining room, the massive oak door of which stood open; and of his wondering uneasily whether the men were within earshot; and then of his seeing the oak door close as if of its own accord—slowly, noiselessly. And on Insull's vast estate at Libertyville, the villagers were said to have "built homes on Insull real estate, sent to an Insull school children born in an Insull hospital, used Insull light, cooked with Insull gas, traveled on an Insull road, saved in an Insull bank, and played golf on an Insull golf course." Great was Samuel Insull.

§ 2

Such, at least was the appearance. In reality, however, the monarch sat somewhat uneasily upon his throne, even in the confident year 1929. He had just formed his penultimate holding company, the Insull Utility Investments; and his purpose in so doing was to secure from investors the sinews not so much of conquest as of defense. His position was vulnerable: much of his system of control depended upon minority holdings of stock, and there was always the danger that someone might seize a part of his corporate domain, as Harriman had sought to seize a part of Hill's domain in 1901. Insull must not let this happen. He must call the investing public to his aid, to provide money with which he might strengthen his hold on his empire.

To Insull Utility Investments, this new holding company (or investment trust, as it was somewhat inappropriately called), he transferred nearly all the holdings of his family in Middle West and the other upper companies of his pyramid.

It is interesting to notice, however, the way in which this transfer was made; for it suggests that even at this moment of insecurity Insull and the men about him had the speculative virus in their veins. He and his family received, in return for the stocks which they transferred, not only a block of preferred stock in the new corporation, but also nearly three quarters of a million common shares valued at $7.54 a share; to say nothing of warrants which entitled him to buy further shares—half a million more of them—at $12 and $15 within the next two years. Presently the stock was listed on the Chicago Stock Exchange. The trading was to begin which would establish a market price for these new holdings of his.

At the moment when the trading began—on a January morning in 1929—the only shares in existence were those which had been issued to Insull and his family for $7.54 apiece. If any buying and selling were to be done, only the Insulls could do the selling.

At the opening of the market, that day, there were quantities of bids to buy Insull Utility Investments "at the market"—for speculators were extravagantly eager. Yet at first no stock was to be had. Then it began to come out—at a price, not of $7.54 a share or anything like it, but of $30 a share. Insull's brokers were taking advantage of the wild demand on the part of speculators to give the Insull family a paper profit of almost exactly 400 per cent. Nor did they let the price lag. They kept buying and selling "to maintain the market"—buying mostly, at first—and the price kept rising. By the end of February it was 46, by the end of July it was 126, and one day in August it actually touched 149¼. Insull salesmen were using these prices as a guide in determining the prices at which they should sell other shares to the public outside the Exchange. Thus the public was buying at prices ten or fifteen times the price at which Insull himself had bought—Insull, who as the head of the company was supposedly the chief representative in its councils of these very investors. As the price soared, the man's paper profits became enormous. It must have seemed to him as if the secret of wealth unlimited had been discovered.

Still, however, his grip on his empire was insecure. And if he sold permanently many of the hundreds of thousands of shares which he had acquired at low prices, and thus took his paper profits, it would become still more insecure. So he decided to form still another holding company (or investment trust), the Corporation Securities Company of Chicago—"Corps," as we have already called it. That would draw in still more investors to help him hold the bag from which flowed this mighty stream of potential gold. Were promoters trying to dislodge him from his throne? All he needed to do, it seemed, was to form a new corporation, mark up values again, declare more dividends, and sweep on to victory.

Then came the panic of October and November, 1929, in which marked-up values collapsed with a tremendous crash.

To tell the rest of the story of Samuel Insull is to carry ourselves far beyond the seven fat years. We need not do more than summarize very briefly what happened. The financing of his huge collection of corporations had reached the regions of complete unreality. Prices, values, even dividends, had become speculative rather than substantial. And now the ground began to fall away from under them. Company after company found its assets beginning to look more and more dubious; the excuse for handing stocks about at rising prices began to look thinner and thinner; and to make matters worse, as business slackened and the earning power of the operating companies was affected, there began to be, as it were, a deterioration in the quality of the cream on the top of the corporate bottles, that cream upon which the holding companies were vitally dependent for their revenue. Furthermore, a ramifying structure of bank loans and credit had been built upon the speculative values of 1928 and 1929, and as these values sank the Insull credit began to crumble. Yet the system had set for itself a pace of growth and of declared earnings and dividends which it would be very dangerous to slacken, lest public confidence be utterly lost.

Insull was caught in a speculator's trap. Retreat was impossible. He could only go on; and he went on—showing profits and paying dividends. Long after the panic, the salesmen of Insull securities were still selling stocks to the little investors who were considered more likely to hold them than the big investors. Wrote Frank R. Evers, secretary of the unit which distributed shares, "The success of our business has lain in our getting the small fellow to buy." And again, . . . "my experience with these big buyers has been that they sell out on the least turn of the market." There was a note of unintentional irony in a letter from Halsey, Stuart & Co., Insull's bankers, in 1931, to a woman investor, suggesting that she buy Corporation Securities shares in place of her United States Government bonds; they explained to her that on account of the demand for Government bonds on the part of banks, the market for them was "artificially stimulated to a great extent." All this time Insull's brokers were stimulating the market for the shares of Insull's corporations by buying and selling in the hope of holding up prices.

The hope was vain. The undertow of liquidation was too strong. The brokers bought more shares of Insull Utility Investments than they sold—but still the price sagged. Alas for Insull's mighty paper profit: it was of little use to him now. Eaton, a Cleveland financier, had accumulated a big block of Insull stock and said (so the story goes) that he would throw it on the market if Insull did not buy it at his lofty price. Insull bought; he did not dare risk the effect of a new torrent of selling upon his price structure.

Yet gradually that structure, rotten as it was with speculative values, succumbed. Insull did not desert it;

he believed in its validity. He and those about him borrowed frantically, putting up stock as collateral. As the margins of safety behind these loans diminished, the bankers called for more collateral, and the Insulls had to find it wherever they could. The credit of company after company suffered in this desperate defensive campaign. Nor did the slow processes of collapse bear down upon the Insull companies alone. Investors by the thousand were affected; banks were affected; other corporations were affected. These corporations were tied by a thousand strands to other parts of the American economy. Insull had not been building his pyramid in a vacuum. He did not, could not in the nature of things, go down to defeat alone.

At last the day of doom arrived: the day when Owen D. Young and a group of New York bankers confronted Insull in Young's office and told him that surrender was inevitable. The meeting took place on April 8, 1932— two and a half years after the panic.

"Does this mean a receivership?" asked Insull, when Young, after a private discussion with the bankers, crossed the room to explain that they regarded the situation as hopeless.

"Yes, Mr. Insull, I'm afraid it does."

A witness of that scene has testified that Insull seemed to be in a state of collapse. "I wish my time on earth had already come," he said.

But it had not. Investigation, flight, indictment, refuge in Greece, capture, and trial in Chicago were still to come—grimly underscoring the tragic conclusion of a financial adventure in which a brilliant career had been wrecked, and American investors had lost nearly three-quarters of a billion dollars, and the economic system of the whole country had been gravely shaken.

§ 3

None of the other public utility pyramids combined in such lavish measure as Insull's the qualities of immense size, immense complexity, reckless expansion, and speculative management. Yet some of the peculiarities of some of these other systems deserve a passing mention, if only to suggest that Insull was not in all respects unique.

Take, for example, the matter of complexity. Anybody who tries to study these public utility systems as they rose during the heydey of the pyramid-builders is constantly baffled, not merely by the intricate relationships between the holding companies, but by the similarity of their names. At this writing the Federal Trade Commission's investigations of American utilities are recorded in no less than seventy-one good-sized volumes. Pick up any one of these volumes, and you are in a jungle of confusion: there are so many dozens of corporations whose names sound much alike that even the best memory is baffled to recall which is which. And sometimes it almost seems as if the confusion must have been deliberate.

Suppose, for example, you wished to discover the exact status of an operating company, and traced its control to the Associated Electric Company, only to find that this was controlled by the Associated Gas and Electric Corporation, which was controlled by the Associated Gas & Electric Company, which was controlled by the Associated Securities Corporation, which was controlled by the Associated Gas & Electric Properties. Suppose you found, in this same system, both a Rochester Central Power Corporation (of New York) and a Rochester Central Power Corporation (of Delaware). Or two separate concerns which were known respectively as Mohawk Valley Company and The Mohawk Valley Company (only the definite article in the name of the latter concern distinguishing it from the former). Would you not wonder what legitimate purpose there could be behind such a bewildering method of nomenclature?

Suppose you found many corporations which were separate legal entities and had officers and directors, ledgers, minute-books, and stock outstanding, *but no employees.* A Federal Trade Commission examiner, Charles Nodder, said that this was true of most of the sub-holding companies in the Associated system. Suppose you found a company as large as the Standard Gas & Electric, with assets of one hundred and ninety million dollars at the end of 1929, getting along with no payroll at all and being managed by a subsidiary corporation. Would you not wonder what had become of corporate responsibility in a case like that?

Or let us consider the matter of personal responsibility for corporate affairs. Presumably one may expect that when a man's name is connected with a company, he is able to give it some substantial personal attention. With all due respect to E. P. Summerson, secretary of Electric Bond & Share, one may reasonably ask how much personal attention he could give to the companies with which he was associated. At one time there were 240 of them, according to a report made to the House Interstate and Foreign Commerce Committee by Walter M. W. Splawn in 1934. Nor was Mr. Summerson alone in his multiplicity of duties. Another man was connected with 212 companies; three other men were connected with between 175 and 200 each.

So many, many corporations—and so many species of securities! Here we run into another tangle of confusion. Prior preference stock, preferred stock, cumulative preferred stock, common stock, Class B common, common stock with warrants—and sometimes warrants with the most complicated conditions of exercise: even to understand the financial status of a single one of these corporations might tax the mind of a practiced accountant. To take one example only, the investor who in 1929 decided to put his money into the Associated Gas & Electric Company (not the Corporation, or the Properties, but the Company) had no less than twenty different classes of securities to choose between—including, if you please, an issue of bonds due to be retired on the first of January in the year 2875. (There's long term debt for you! One takes off one's hat to the assurance of men who borrow money with a solemn promise to pay it back at a date more distant in the future than the Norman Conquest is distant in the past—presumably on the assumption that even at that remote time their subsidiaries will still be operating electric-light plants in American towns.)

The Insull system was by no means alone in marking up values, though not often did companies in other systems resort to the over-simple practice of classing as income their profits on inter-company transactions. According to N. R. Danielian, the inflation in value of the assets in twenty holding-company systems amounted to a total of at least $839,000,000, and probably a good deal more.

And how about the imposition of service charges? We found, you may recall, a company in the Insull system which supervised operating companies and performed other services for it at a profit of 98.8 per cent. But we also find—according to Professor Buchanan's analysis—the Southeastern Power & Light Company supervising at a profit of 95 per cent on the cost of its services during the three years 1925-27 inclusive, and the American Gas & Electric Company supervising and performing other services at a profit of 73.3 per cent. Besides such hand-

some takings the 50.8 per cent service profit of Electric
Bond and Share from 1908 to 1929 looks moderate (although for the year 1927 the Federal Trade Commission
calculated its profit on cost to be at least 106 per cent);
and the failure of the North American Company to
impose any service charges at all seems positively
quixotic.

In most systems the services for which these goodly
fees were charged were of course substantial and valuable; but there was always the temptation to take the
payment and then slight the services. Here is a bit of
testimony before the New York Public Service Commission with regard to the management fees collected from
an operating company in the Associated Gas and Electric system:

Q. Did the J. G. White Management Corporation perform any services or do anything for the New York State
Railways to your knowledge, and if so what, during the
time this contract was in effect?

A. Nothing that was helpful. They did advance the
money, but it was not helpful, and a few other things,
but nothing helpful.

Q. What did they do outside of this advance of
money?

A. Called up on the telephone occasionally and asked
different information, and so forth.

Q. Did they ever send any one there to advise you or
assist in management or operation of the road?

A. No, sir.

It is not necessary here to dwell upon the wildly extravagant prices paid by some of these other systems for
properties when the competition in expansion was at its
height; or upon the opportunities which insiders had
to speculate in the stocks which represented these prop-

erties while negotiations were in progress; or upon the equally extravagant heights to which the stocks of the upper companies in pyramid after pyramid leaped in 1928 and 1929, often with the aid of persons close to the management who personally profited by this inflation.

Nor is it necessary to make more than a passing reference to the political pressure exerted by some utility systems and their friends to prevent the new status quo from being disturbed. (Do you recall the letter written by State Senator Warren T. Thayer of New York early in 1927 to a vice-president of the Associated Gas and Electric Company, in which he said, "I hope my work during the past session was satisfactory to your company, not so much for the new legislation enacted, but from the fact that many detrimental bills which were introduced we were able to kill in my committee"?) Nor do we need to waste time over the "educational" campaigns financed by utility magnates to assure the public that they were intent only upon service to the public, and that the widespread ownership of shares of their companies by consumers constituted a striking exhibit of local economic self-government in the best American tradition. (When Professor Ripley suggested that in view of the vanishing rights of stockholders, governmental supervision of corporate affairs might be necessary, a vice-president of the Empire State Gas and Electric Association charged him with uttering "the kind of propaganda on which demagoguery and communism feed.")

What does perhaps need emphasis is that the pyramiding of utility companies was essentially a new device, lavishly resorted to during the seven fat years, which bestowed upon a few aggressive insiders an immense and unseasoned power subject to grave abuses. These insiders did on the whole a splendid job with their physical properties: there is no denying that. They gave the public effective service, and their high-tension lines, marching over hill and dale, linked the individual properties together with fine engineering skill. But the price which they charged was heavy. The siphoning of money out of operating companies hurt the consumer, who had to pay more than he should on his electric-light bill or his gas bill because the monopoly which furnished him with these services, and which (because it was a monopoly) was supposedly regulated in his interest by a state commission, was vouching for "expenses" of operation which permitted large profits (invisible to the state commission) for those higher up. The optimistic bookkeeping and inflationary financing of some of these systems hurt the investor, who bought speculative securities often without the least notion that they were speculative. And —more important still—the whole process of inflating values and hopes put the general economic system of the country to a prodigious strain, since this process directly or indirectly committed not only individuals but corporations and banks and other institutions to the expectation of exaggerated if not actually indefensible revenues.

Inordinate profits do not come out of thin air. They come out of the consumer, or the worker, or the investor, or the future. It was the innocent delusion of the American public during the seven fat years that inordinate profits can come out of thin air. Pyramiding, and the financial expedients to which it almost irresistibly led in a time of overwhelming confidence, took inordinate profits out of the consumer, the investor, and the future —often including, of course, the insiders' own future, as Samuel Insull subsequently discovered.

§ 4

It is in young and rapidly expanding industries, like the electric light and power industry, that one expects to find daring financial devices flourishing. Not so in industries which have reached a comfortable middle age. The railroads had sown their financial wild oats long since, in the days of Gould and Fisk; they had reached their powerful maturity at the turn of the century, when Morgan and Harriman were in the saddle; by the nineteen-twenties they seemed to have accepted the limitations of circumstance and of advancing age, and they were living on a strict diet of regulation, subject to the doctor's orders of the Interstate Commerce Commission. It was anomalous, therefore, that one of the most remarkable financial pyramids of the seven fat years should have been built on a foundation of railroads.

Perhaps this anomaly may be partly explained by the fact that the two men who designed this pyramid were themselves young, and that they rose by way of real-estate promotion. The speculative sub-divider, after all, is a sort of belated and misplaced pioneer: the man who buys a tract of pasture land and turns it into a thriving suburb knows what it is to stake everything on a vision of the future, to take a long chance and subdue the earth. Let him turn to railroading and he may not be content with accepting the common lot.

These two young men were the Van Sweringen brothers of Cleveland, upon whom had been bestowed the singular names of Oris Paxton and Mantis James. They were not twins by birth, for O. P. Van Sweringen was two years older than M. J.; but they were twins by choice. They lived together, worked together, planned together; bachelors both, they were almost inseparable; they even slept in twin beds. Each knew everything the other did. They were almost like two halves of a single personality. And they had a joint and very remarkable career.

They began life in simple circumstances. (It is interesting, by the way, to note how many of the skyrockets of finance in the nineteen-twenties shot up from what might be called the lower-middle class.) Neither of the Van Sweringens went beyond the eighth grade in school. Oris got his start as an office boy, then as a clerk. But they were ambitious, and studied in the evenings. By the time Oris was twenty-one and Mantis was nineteen they were in the real-estate business.

Pretty soon they began to buy and lay out and sell land on a rural plateau east of the city of Cleveland. Their operating methods were novel, their plans were far-reaching and well-devised, and they were fortunate enough to anticipate that trend toward the suburbs which was to become such a significant factor in the expansion of American cities. When the Van Sweringens were still in their early thirties, Shaker Heights, the development which they had so skilfully and ambitiously engineered, was becoming a thriving suburb.

The brothers were doing extraordinarily well for themselves and for Cleveland, but still one would never have dreamed that they would become railroad magnates. The transformation was effected almost by blind chance. They needed better transportation service from the heart of Cleveland out to the suburb of Shaker Heights than the leisurely street-car lines would afford. They decided to build a high-speed electric line. Looking for a suitable place for a terminal in the city, they found themselves barred by the conflicting plans of the New York, Chicago and St. Louis Railroad—generally known as the Nickel Plate—for a freight terminal. The Nickel Plate was owned by the New York Central, but

—providentially for them—the Interstate Commerce Commission wanted the Central to sell it. The Van Sweringens decided to buy it themselves, and to use its property and its right of way in Cleveland both for their own original purposes and for its purposes.

But how to buy it? The price was eight and a half million dollars for the controlling shares, and the most that they themselves and their immediate associates could rake together was a million.

Perhaps you have already guessed the answer. They formed a holding company.

We need not go into the details of this transaction. All it is necessary to say is that the Van Sweringens sold enough preferred stock in their holding company to cover the first payment on their purchase, and thus to get control of the Nickel Plate without losing control of their Cleveland terminal properties. Of course they still had a lot of money to pay; everything depended upon whether they could get good earnings out of the Nickel Plate railroad line. But they were shrewd enough to select, as president of the road, one of the ablest operating men in the country, one J. J. Bernet. Soon Bernet was doing wonders with it—transforming it from a second-rate, run-down line into a successful one. In 1916 it had earned a little over six per cent on its common stock. In 1920 it earned over ten per cent; in 1921, over twenty-five per cent.

These earnings created such a cheerful prospect for the Nickel Plate Securities Corporation that the Van Sweringens were now able to issue more preferred stock, pay off most of their debt to the New York Central, and begin the purchase, on the installment plan, of three more small railroads. By this time they were no longer mere real-estate men of Cleveland; they were big railroad men too, and a new and exalted ambition was growing in their minds.

During the war the railroads had been under the direction of the Federal Government. The advantages of combining railroad resources and operating facilities had been so apparent that when the roads were returned to their private owners, the government had encouraged them to group themselves into a number of big systems, subject to the approval of the Interstate Commerce Commission. Just how this grouping was to be effected was a problem. In the East, for example, big systems would naturally be built up about strong roads like the New York Central, the Pennsylvania, and the Baltimore and Ohio, which might buy up other lines or merge with them. Such purchases and mergers, however, were easier to talk about than to accomplish; for rivalry was intense, railroad presidents and directors could be very obstinate in their independence, stock-market speculators were avid, and a small road which might be sought after by two or three big systems could become a tempting speculative prize in the Street. There were destined to be years of conferences and bickerings, while railroad presidents tried to come to agreement on the redrawing of the railroad map—with an uneasy or eager eye, meanwhile, upon the stock-market quotations. In the early years of these conferences, nobody seemed to think seriously of the possibilities of a major railroad system built up about the Nickel Plate, which ran only from Buffalo to Chicago and until recently had been a single-track, down-at-the-heels line. The Van Sweringens, however, were thinking of it very seriously. And they thought of it in terms of holding companies laid one upon another.

They were now in their early forties—two nice-looking, boyish young men; sturdy, round-headed, low-voiced, attractive; shy young men, who kept to themselves, seemed to care nothing for social life despite their growing wealth; who did not smoke or drink, did not believe that the road to success ran by way of the golf-links, took no vacations and seldom a day off, but were always working, whether in their adjoining offices or in their private suite at the Cleveland Hotel, or at their suburban farm, Daisy Hill, a few miles outside the city. To Clevelanders their names were already potent, seldom as they were recognized on the street; to the general American public they were completely unknown. But the seven fat years had begun—the great era of holding-company expansion—and they were soon to be heard from.

In 1925, the year when Coolidge succeeded Harding as President, the Van Sweringens bought the so-called Huntington interest in the Chesapeake and Ohio road— only a fifteen per cent interest, as it happened, but large enough to permit them to name the directors if the other owners were acquiescent. The Morgan partners had been watching them, liked their hard-working earnestness, raised no barrier to their purchase, and continued to watch them with approval. It took more than seven million dollars to make this purchase, but the brothers collected it by selling new bonds of the Nickel Plate road, and by borrowing. During the next two years they bought the Pere Marquette and also a large interest in the Erie, borrowing again to make the latter purchase. Old George F. Baker was the largest stockholder and the most powerful factor in the counsels of the Erie, and his opposition would have been fatal to their plans, but he too, like the Morgan partners, regarded them with a friendly eye. The story is that when they came to see him he asked them only two questions: did they work hard and did they sleep well? Satisfied with their answers, he let them buy the necessary stock to take over the direction of the Erie.

With such formidable allies in Wall Street as the House of Morgan and George F. Baker, the Van Sweringens saw the pathway to fortune lying clear before them. They went on buying railroads. But their purchases required money—lots of it—and they must have this money on terms which would not permit their sovereignty to be disputed. They got it by forming more and more holding companies: very big ones: layer upon layer of holding companies.

Incredible indeed, by 1929, seemed the achievement of these two young men. Thirteen years before, as a result of trying to build a rapid-transit line from Shaker Heights into Cleveland, they had put a million dollars into purchasing the control of the rickety Nickel Plate; and now, with the mighty House of Morgan as a potent ally, they were masters of a great system reaching from Chicago to the Atlantic Coast; a system with thousands of miles of track, over a hundred thousand employees, and assets in the neighborhood of two billion dollars. Until 1929, this great system had not spread beyond the Mississippi, but now the Alleghany Corporation—their biggest holding company—was purchasing stock in the Missouri Pacific, and thus was expanding the Van Sweringens' sphere of influence all the way to the Mexican border.

As a mere detail of their campaign of conquest and expansion they were rebuilding the whole central part of their native city. Their subsidiary corporations in Cleveland had been putting hundreds of millions of dollars into a vast and splendid urban real-estate project: railroad terminals, huge office buildings, a hotel, a seven-hundred-foot tower. They were multi-millionaires, too; for pyramiding could be very profitable if the pyramiders and their top holding companies transferred blocks of stock to new holding companies at rising prices. On some of their transactions their profits mounted into the tens of millions.

Not only in Cleveland but in Wall Street, too, the name Van Sweringen had now become magical. Yet the brothers themselves remained as modest and self-effacing as ever. They appeared in public as little as possible. When a great dinner was held to celebrate the opening of their new Union Terminal, they stayed away from it. They refused to have a New York office; when they visited New York, they had their papers bundled up and taken from their private car to a hotel. They preferred the quiet of their Cleveland offices or of their Daisy Hill farm, where a private telephone operator took care of the urgent long-distance calls which came in from all over the country as they spun their web of power.

The foundation of the Van Sweringens' glittering success, in railroading as in real-estate speculation, was undeniably sound. Their railroads were well run, as Shaker Heights had been well planned. Bernet, their best operating man, had followed the focus of their interest in efficient management from the Nickel Plate to the Erie, and from the Erie to the Chesapeake and Ohio, and each of these roads had responded to his magic touch. But on this solid foundation of operating skill they had raised an immense financial pyramid built of debt and of hope.

At the top of this pyramid sat O. P. and M. J. Van Sweringen themselves. On the step below them was the Vaness Company. The second step from the top consisted of the General Securities Corporation. On the step below the General Securities, and controlled by it, was the Alleghany Corporation, which in turn (another step down) controlled the Chesapeake Corporation and the Nickel Plate, and was acquiring control of the Missouri Pacific. We now descend to the fifth step from the top. The Nickel Plate controlled the Wheeling and Lake

Erie; the Chesapeake Corporation controlled the Chesapeake and Ohio; and this company in turn controlled (the sixth step from the top) the Hocking Valley and (with the assistance of the Alleghany Corporation) the Pere Marquette and the Erie.

There could be no more perfect example of the technic of remote control through pyramiding than this system. For example, according to the figures published by Berle and Means, the financial interest of the Van Sweringens themselves in the General Securities Corporation (as of April 30, 1930) was 51.8 per cent; in the Alleghany it was 8.6 per cent; in the Chesapeake Corporation it had dwindled to a mere 4.1 per cent; in the Chesapeake and Ohio, to less than one per cent; in the Hocking Valley to the ridiculous figure of one-quarter of one per cent—and yet with this minute personal financial stake in the Hocking Valley, the men at Daisy Hill were the arbiters of its destiny, so astutely had they managed to pile holding company on holding company, and to induce the public to join with them in investing in each.

A very persuasive structure, this pyramid; so persuasive that the Morgan partners, far from looking askance at it as they looked askance at the unwieldy Insull pyramid and some of the other financial structures of the day, were hopefully engaged in selling building-blocks in certain parts of it to all and sundry. Yet it had its peculiarities, and these peculiarities had their wide economic consequences.

For one thing, the Van Sweringens and their companies were always borrowing largely from the banks: each new offensive in their campaign involved them in new debts. For another thing, the formation of each new holding company meant the issue of bonds or preferred shares which were dependent upon common-stock earnings.

In short, here was the old cream-separating business all

over again; what you were buying, when you took an Alleghany Corporation·bond, was a first call on a cream-separating machine which in turn was partly dependent on another cream-separating machine. This fact was significant from your point of view as an investor; but it was even more significant from another point of view. It meant that the Van Sweringens had locked themselves into a situation where their railroads *had* to earn common-stock dividends—even on stock which had once been considered speculative—or the huge debt structure which had been built upon the hope of these dividends would come crashing down in bankruptcy.

Meanwhile, in the city of Cleveland, the Van Sweringens' spectacular real-estate operations had involved their local companies in debts to the banks, and had also encouraged a general boom in urban real-estate, thereby involving the Cleveland banks in all sorts of investments and loans based on speculative valuations. Though the shy, soft-spoken men from Daisy Hill were quite unlike Samuel Insull, their operations, and the operations which their dazzling career had suggested to others, had woven speculative values, as his had, deeply into the economic fabric.

Then came October and November, 1929, and—worse than that—the decline in values in the fall of 1930, and the slow avalanche of 1931 and 1932. An ugly time for borrowers; and for lenders too.

Not all the things which were done in those years of collapse make agreeable reading. Debt had hitherto weighed lightly upon the Van Sweringens; now its burden was terrific. They had to have money. One of their closest associates was the president of one of the Cleveland banks, the Union Trust. The Van Sweringens had borrowed so heavily from this bank that at last an unsecured loan to one of their companies was refused at the main office—but the president gave his oral approval and the loan was made. By 1930 they were so deeply obligated to the Cleveland banks that they could raise no more money there—in quantity, at least—and they had to borrow nearly forty million dollars from J. P. Morgan & Company. The Morgans required sound collateral, and it was vital to the Van Sweringens to remain in their good graces. Thereupon—to quote the words of the Senate Banking and Currency Committee—"substantially all of the collateral having any market value which was pledged with the Union Trust Company was released from the Cleveland loans and turned over to the Van Sweringens to hypothecate against the loans from J. P. Morgan & Company." New York must be served, even if others suffered.

Again, the Missouri Pacific Railroad, which the Van Sweringens now controlled, was under terrific compulsion to show good earnings, not only for its own sake but for the sake of the Alleghany Corporation, which as we have seen had a big stake in its fortunes. The Missouri Pacific reported as income the dividends which it received from a subsidiary to which it was lending money at the time—the money going to the subsidiary in the form of loans and returning in the form of dividends. And it also took profits on transactions in its own stock between two of its subsidiaries—an improvement company and a motor-bus company!—thereby reminding observers of the old grand-piano-and-Oriental-rug game which had worked so neatly in the Insull system.

But enough of such examples. The twistings and turnings of men in the grip of circumstance are not always pleasant to watch. It is enough to set down the facts of the situation as they stood in 1935.

The two biggest banks in Cleveland had crashed—ruined by their adventures in real estate and their other financial expeditions during the years of indiscretion, and by their frantic attempts to stave off failure during the years of reckoning. (It might almost be said that the Van Sweringen influence had found Cleveland a city of brick and wood, and had left it a city of marble—and of bad debts.) The Missouri Pacific road had gone into a trusteeship under the bankruptcy legislation of 1933. The Alleghany Corporation, unable to pay the interest on one of its issues of bonds, was negotiating a difficult capital readjustment. As for the Van Sweringens themselves, they still were in command of the railroads over which they had assumed dominion, but their stock was pledged as collateral against huge loans; if they were still afloat upon the sea of debt, it was because the life-lines of credit to which they clung were held at the other end by the strong hands of the Morgans and their banking allies. There were few people, any longer, who regarded the great Van Sweringen pyramid as one of the seven wonders of the financial world.

I have before me a photograph of the two brothers as they appeared when they came before the Senate Banking Committee for investigation in June of 1933. They are boys no longer, in that photograph, but elderly-looking men, solid and gray-haired, with old eyes.

Chapter Ten

BANKERS, SALESMEN, AND SPECULATORS

ONE day in 1915 or 1916 Charles Edwin Mitchell and Bruce Barton were standing together by a window in the Bankers' Club in New York, looking down upon the city. Said Mitchell:

"Every once in a while one of our bond men comes into my office and tells me he can't find any bond buyers. When that happens I don't argue with him. I say, 'Get your hat and come out to lunch.' Then I bring him up here and stand him in front of one of these windows. 'Look down there,' I say. 'There are six million people with incomes that aggregate thousands of millions of dollars. They are just waiting for someone to come and tell them what to do with their savings. Take a good look, eat a good lunch, and then go down and tell them.'"

Those remarks of Mitchell's—I quote them from a magazine article by Barton—were laden with implications of which Mitchell himself was then unaware. To be sure, they were made some time before he became one of the mightiest powers in American banking. They were made before his fortieth birthday; at just about the time when he was invited to leave his own investment-selling concern and become the president of the National City Company, the National City Bank's security affiliate: the Siamese twin by means of which it was able to trade in securities without incurring the displeasure of the law. Old James Stillman, though he was living mostly in Europe and was failing in health, was then the power behind the bank, and Frank Vanderlip was its active

304

head. The future still hid what was to come in the next few years: the death of Stillman in 1918; the falling-out between Vanderlip and the directors of the bank in 1919, which was to thrust young James A. Stillman into the presidency; and, after young Stillman in turn was thrust out in 1921, the selection of Mitchell as the new president.

The remarks were significant because they revealed the nature of Mitchell's indisputable talents, because the selection of a man of such talents as the chief executive of the richest bank in the United States foreshadowed a change in the spirit of American banking, and because the influence of Mitchell in the financial world of the nineteen-twenties was to give impetus to that change.

Mitchell was a salesman.

To understand clearly what it meant to have the spirit of salesmanship invade commercial banking, one must remind oneself of a few very elementary facts. In the first place, a bank—a commercial bank, that is to say, as distinguished from an investment banking house, which is quite a different thing—is a custodian of your money and mine, charged by law and still more by honor with the duty of lending or investing that money prudently, so that you and I will not suffer loss. In the second place, the bank, as lender and investor of our money, is a nourisher and stimulator of business. And in the third place, the bank is more than a custodian and lender of money: it is a manufacturer of money. Only a small proportion of the funds in use in the country—somewhere between a fifth and a tenth of them in normal times—are currency; the rest are check money, manufactured by the banks; and not by the banks as a group, but by individual banks wherever they may be from Maine to California.

The process of manufacture may be illustrated by the

following over-simplified example. Suppose you deposit a thousand dollars in the Middletown National Bank. This amount, minus what the bank holds as a reserve for safety—say ten per cent of it—is thereupon available for lending. Now suppose I come in and want to borrow from the bank. Nine hundred dollars of the thousand which you deposited is available to be lent to me. The bank lends it. But it does not hand it over to me in cash. The bank chalks up a credit of nine hundred dollars beside my name: those nine hundred dollars become a deposit to my account. Thus the total deposits in the bank are increased by nine hundred dollars; and thus, miraculously, the bank has more money available for lending—not the whole sum which was written opposite my name, for a part of this sum must be held as a reserve, but say eight hundred dollars of it. Now suppose our neighbor Mr. Jones comes in and wants to borrow. The bank can lend him eight hundred dollars, credit this sum to his account, and thus have, say, seven hundred dollars more to lend to Mr. Robinson. And so the process continues; not to the bitter end, of course, for each time you or I draw a check we thereby reduce the total amount of money which the bank can lend; but far enough to make the amount of check money in the country from five to ten times as great as the amount of currency. The example here given, it must be remembered, is over-simplified. In practice no single loan would go through the process outlined above. But it substantially dramatizes a development which actually would involve many banks and thousands of depositors.

To hear some people discuss inflation, one might suppose that the only possible kind of inflation were that which can be brought about by the government through the use of the printing press, printing greenbacks; but banking or credit inflation of the sort described above has been a normal financial process for a very long time and has come about as the joint result of innumerable acts of judgment on the part of thousands of individual bankers as they received deposits and made loans. The money thus manufactured is quite as legal as a dollar bill, as each of us is aware when he pays his bills by check.

Thus the commercial banker, although he is engaged in private business, is permitted to exercise a public function of high importance. The responsibility which rests upon him is thereby increased. For if he makes imprudent loans or investments he is not only imperiling your deposit and mine, he is also imperiling the quality and stability of a part of the national supply of money.

We have already noticed in previous chapters of this book how lax, during the early part of the century, were the standards of safety imposed upon the banks. Each state had its own legal requirements, and they were mostly low. The United States set higher requirements for national banks, but a bank was not required to enter the national system if it chose not to do so. Hence there were, in effect, forty-nine systems instead of one. The Federal Reserve System had been superimposed upon this chaotic situation, partly to mobilize reserves for use wherever and whenever they might be suddenly needed, as in a disaster or a panic, and partly to bring the supply of check money under a measure of control. It had been very valuable, during the war and the depression of 1921, as we have seen; so valuable, in fact, that there was a distinct impression in the public mind—and even, to a considerable extent, in the banking mind—that it offered a sure guarantee against disaster. But it did not. Its powers were limited. A vast number of the smaller banks were not Federal Reserve members and were thus beyond its reach, and even the member banks were to a very great degree free to lend and invest money according to their own best judgment.

It is very illuminating to notice what happened to this unsystematic combination of forty-nine banking systems during the years of boundless financial confidence.

To some readers who recall vividly the utter breakdown of American banking during the years 1930-1933 it may seem, in misleading retrospect, as if bank failures had been rare in the previous years of affluence. This is far from true; during the years 1923 to 1929, inclusive, bank failures occurred in the United States *at an average rate of nearly two a day*. During those seven years there were 4,787 failures; and they were well distributed throughout the period. Here are the figures. There were

648 in 1923
776 in 1924
612 in 1925
956 in 1926
662 in 1927
491 in 1928
and 642 in 1929

To be sure, during these years not a single big metropolitan bank went under. The victims were small banks, mostly in small towns. The direct cause of the destruction of most of them was the drop in the value of farm land after the agricultural boom which ended in 1920, leaving quantities of farmers with over-mortgaged acres and heavy debts for farm equipment, the payments on which could be met only by selling their crops at inadequate prices. Many other banks went down when the Florida real-estate boom and the widespread boomlets patterned upon it collapsed in 1926 and 1927. Yet they would hardly have perished in such numbers had most of them not been too small or too badly located to diversify their loans properly in the interests of safety, or too incompetently managed and complacently supervised to pursue sound banking policies. The record was disgraceful.

The city banks did far better. But they were changing character in a significant way. The chief traditional use for the funds deposited in a bank had been in the making of commercial loans: that is, loans to businesses to finance seasonal operations or specific ventures: loans which would be paid off when the goods which had been manufactured or bought with the borrowed money were sold. These short-term commercial loans were constantly being repaid; they did not tie up money over a long period of time, and were thus—if discriminatingly made —considered prudent. During the rising prosperity of the nineteen-twenties one might have expected an increase in the total amount of these commercial loans. Oddly enough, there was virtually none. There did not seem to be a growing demand for them, even when business was boiling. (It was easy to raise money for business by the sale of long-term securities such as bonds or stock; and furthermore, the giants of industry kept large cash reserves and maintained low inventories of goods and were thus able, as it were, to lend themselves most of the money which they needed from time to time.)

There was nevertheless a large banking inflation; so great was the increase in the amount of check-money manufactured by the banks that Dr. Lauchlin Currie has estimated that the total national supply of money climbed from about 21¾ billions in 1922 to over 26½ billions in 1929—a growth of nearly five billions. And there was also a very large increase in the total of loans and investments by the banks of the country—something like a fifty per cent increase; according to the figures for Federal Reserve member banks only, loans and investments moved upward from a little over 24 billions in 1922 to more than 35½ billions in 1929.

What accounted for this increase, if not commercial loans? The answer to this question is significant.

1. Investments in securities: there was a three-billion dollar increase in this item—from seven billions to ten billions.

2. Loans on securities: that is, loans which, if not paid back, could be made good only by selling the bonds or stock with which they were secured: there was a five-and-a-half-billion-dollar increase in this item—from four and a half billions to ten billions.

3. And, in minor degree, loans on city real estate (which during the latter part of this period was having a spectacular boom, and in any case could hardly be converted into cash on short notice) : this item increased from a little over one billion to over 2¾ billions.

The significance of these changes is clear. The commercial banks of the country were putting a smaller proportion of their funds than previously into the current financing of business—the traditional use for such funds, and the safest. They were putting a much larger proportion than previously into making—or backing—long-term investments in stocks, bonds, or real estate. Thus they were becoming more dependent, both for the safety of their deposits and for the quality of the money they manufactured, upon the condition of the investment and speculative markets—a fact which was to become distinctly and regrettably evident during the early nineteen-thirties.

They were also—a fact which was evident at once—becoming good customers for investment bankers who had securities to sell. This fact, coupled with the fact that insurance companies and other financial institutions were expanding rapidly, and the further fact that since the Liberty Loan campaigns more private individuals had become investment-minded than ever before, smoothed the pathway to success for men like Charles E. Mitchell. It is difficult, in matters like this, to distinguish clearly between cause and effect. The fact that the banking inflation was reflected in enlarged investments probably both encouraged Mitchellism and was encouraged by it. In any case it is fair to say that the rise and potency of such a man as Mitchell were characteristic signs of the times.

Mitchell was not born to the deep purple of the banking aristocracy. He came from the shabby and unfashionable Boston suburb of Chelsea; went to college at Amherst, but had to earn part of his expenses by teaching public speaking; began his business career as a clerk in the office of the Western Electric Company in Chicago, spent his evenings taking night courses in bookkeeping and commercial law, rose in a few years to the position of credit manager, developed a shrewd idea for the consolidation of a number of concerns which made telephone switchboards, took this idea to New York, to Oakleigh Thorne, president of the Trust Company of America, and made such an impression upon Thorne that he was asked to join the bank as Thorne's assistant. That was in 1907—on the eve of the great panic in which the Trust Company of America was to be a storm center. Through the exhausting days and nights of the panic young Mitchell, now barely thirty years old, was at Thorne's right hand; there were nights when he had to work so late that it was not worth while trying to go home, and he snatched a brief sleep curled up on the floor of the president's office. Four years later he formed his own investment house. Five years after that—in 1916 —he was chosen for the presidency of the National City Company.

What had brought him so far in such a brief span of years? Inexhaustible energy, a restless imagination, a powerful faculty for concentration; that talent for organizing and stimulating the efforts of other people which we call executive ability; that specialized and commercialized variety of the talent for persuasion which we call salesmanship. Mitchell was a big man physically, solid and broad-shouldered, with a strong face: bold jaw, blunt-ended nose, stern mouth, keen eyes: the face of a man, not of sensibility, but of gross power. He believed in keeping fit—for years he walked every morning the whole seven miles from his house in the east Seventies to the National City Bank. He worked mightily, studying, learning, and not forgetting that social contacts of the right sort can be very valuable to a rising financier. His confident energy galvanized other people. There flowed from him the sort of vital personal force which enables a military commander to rally his men for a successful assault—a force which the accidents of circumstance, in an acquisitive society, directed into rallying bond salesmen. When, like Napoleon upon a hilltop, Mitchell looked down from the windows of the Bankers' Club upon the field of campaign, he showed his lieutenants not an armed enemy but a host of sales prospects, millions of dollars strong.

When he took over the management of the National City Company, in 1916, it controlled millions of dollars but its staff consisted of only four people working in a single room. He saw a bright future for it, and began to build up a great sales force. Bruce Barton, than whom there was no more enthusiastic trumpeter of the glories of big business during the nineteen twenties, described the Mitchell method: "Instead of waiting for investors to come, he took young men and women, gave them a course of training in the sale of securities, and sent them out to *find* the investors. Such methods, pursued with such vigor and on such a scale, were revolutionary."

Still the National City Company was a mere appendage of the Bank. Yet there was no other man in the organization who equaled Mitchell in personal force. And so when James A. Stillman had to leave the presidency in 1921, Mitchell assumed direction of the whole vast concern: not merely of the expanding affiliate which sold and traded in securities, but also of the Bank itself, the custodian of other people's savings, the nourisher of business, the manufacturer of a part of the national supply of money.

All through the seven fat years Mitchell's salesmen— by 1929 there were 350 of them, with offices in fifty-eight cities connected with the New York headquarters by means of eleven thousand miles of private wire—were engaged in finding investors and telling them what to do with their savings. Behind these salesmen there was a relentless pressure to get results. Whether or not the sales letters quoted by Julian Sherrod in his *Scapegoats* were actually sales letters sent out from New York to Mitchell's men, at least they suggest the spirit in which these men and others like them were exhorted to dispose of their wares. "You cannot stand still in this business—you either go forwards or backwards." "The trouble with most Security Salesmen has been that in the past three or four years they have been order takers." "As I see it, you fellows are not Self-Starters." ". . . we do want to be absolutely sure that, with the exception of the cubs, we have no one in our sales force but producers." "I should hate to think there is any man in our sales crowd who would confess to his inability to sell at least some of any issue of either bonds or preferred stock that we think good enough to offer. In fact this would be an impossible situation and, in the interest of all concerned, one which we would not permit to continue. . . ."

There were sales contests for these salesmen of stocks

and bonds, just as there were sales contests in those days for men who sold vacuum-cleaners and novelties: in one contest which began in September, 1929, just as the prices of securities were about to go over the cliff's edge into the depression, the National City Company offered $25,000 in prize money and the scoring was done on an elaborate point system—one point for each share of General Mills common stock which they disposed of, 4 points for each share of Missouri-Kansas-Texas 7 per cent preferred stock, and so forth. Under the whip of such incentives, a salesman could hardly be expected to look with a coolly impartial eye upon the disposition of an investor's savings, or to recommend speculative investments only to business men in close and active touch with the course of the markets. What counted in such a business was results—"and results mean orders."

The Barton article on Mitchell from which I have already quoted bore a title which in retrospect seems ironical. It was called—after the hortatory style of the *American Magazine's* success stories in that era—"Is THERE ANYTHING HERE THAT OTHER MEN COULDN'T DO?" Apparently there was not. High-powered security salesmanship became widespread.

Buyers were so easily persuaded and the sale of securities was so lucrative that soon there was a furious competition among investment bankers and the investment affiliates of the big banks to find concerns which were willing to put out bonds or stocks for expansion. The manufacturer did not have to go hat in hand to the bankers to ask their assistance; the bankers came to him, eager to issue securities for him and feed them out to banks and private buyers. And among these bankers the representatives of the security affiliates of the commercial banks were becoming more and more numerous. Mitchellism was becoming contagious. In 1927 the affiliates originated less than one-sixth as much of the volume of security issues as did the private bankers; in 1928 they originated nearly one-third as much; in 1929, nearly four-fifths as much.

One sort of security which it was very easy to sell was the bonds of foreign states, and here the strenuousness of the competition approached the ridiculous. Young men representing big New York banks camped in Balkan and South American capitals in the frantic hope of inducing the local financial dignitaries to issue bonds. Sometimes these young men were not only ignorant of the language of the country but of its customs and traditions, and even of its political and financial record; and there might be three or four of them maneuvering for a single bond issue, each eager to get ahead of the others by whatever means could be contrived. Small wonder, under the circumstances, that some of this headlong financing did not redound to the credit of the banks which made the loans and sold the bonds, or that it led in due course to the shrinkage of assets of hundreds of American banks and to the impoverishment of thousands of embittered investors.

Before long some of the more experienced investment bankers became frankly apprehensive of the reckless way in which this foreign financing was being conducted. Said Thomas W. Lamont of the House of Morgan in 1927: "From the point of view of the American investor it is obviously necessary to scan the situation with increasing circumspection and to avoid rash or excessive lending. I have in mind the reports that I have recently heard of American bankers and firms competing on almost a violent scale for the purpose of obtaining loans in various foreign money markets overseas.

"Naturally it is a tempting thing for certain of the European governments to find a horde of American

bankers sitting on their doorsteps offering them money.
. . . That sort of competition tends to insecurity and unsound practice."

The House of Morgan had spoken—yet the business
went right on. For example, Mitchell's own National City
Company subsequently sold two issues of Peruvian bonds
—despite the fact that memoranda written from time to
time by officers of the Company and the Bank during the
previous five or six years had stated that "Peru has been
careless in the fulfillment of contractual obligations,"
and had referred to Peru's "bad-debt record" as an "adverse moral and political risk." The Company sold two
issues of bonds of the State of Minas Geraes, Brazil,
despite the fact that a member of the foreign department
of the bank had drawn attention to the "inefficiency
and ineptitude" of the officials of the state in connection
with previous loans to them, and "the complete ignorance,
carelessness, and negligence of the former State officials
in respect to external long-term borrowing." The Peruvian bonds went into default in 1931; the bonds of the
State of Minas Geraes, in 1932. Many other extreme
examples of foreign lending might be cited; and the
number of banking houses involved in them bears witness that "there was not anything here which other men
couldn't do." The business of selling foreign securities to
Americans assumed huge proportions—and by 1934 over
a third of the outstanding foreign securities were in
default.

In passing judgment upon such bond issues one must
make allowance for the fact that sincere opinions, even
within a single institution, may differ upon the merits
of any investment issue; and also for the fact that the
world depression dragged down into default many foreign bond issues which in the nineteen-twenties would
have seemed good risks even to the conservative banker.

It is difficult to escape the conclusion, however, that it was all too easy to decide in favor of an issue when other banking houses were also in the market for it and a staff of salesmen all over the country were ready and able to sell almost anything to small banks and private investors.

By 1927 Mitchell's men were selling not merely bonds and preferred stock but common stock also, thus definitely encouraging the speculative bull market. As the market boomed, the National City Company would accumulate stock by buying it on the market and would sell it all over the country through its salesmen. In 1929 it sold over a million shares of Anaconda Copper— a speculative common stock. It even sold over a million shares of the stock of the National City Bank itself, not only distributing them through its sales force, but trading in them on the market more heavily than any other firm or individual. (Banks were forbidden by law to deal in their own stock—but of course it was not the National City Bank which was doing the trading, but its affiliate.)

I know of no evidence that the lending or investment of the money deposited in the National City Bank itself was unfavorably affected by the aggressive selling campaigns carried on under Mitchell's inspiration by the Bank's *alter ego*. Yet the fact that the legal device of a technically separate investment affiliate enabled Mitchell and his associates to serve two masters bore interesting results.

For example, depositors in the National City Bank who wished the advice of the bank on investments would be referred to the City Company. Listen now to a bit of testimony in the Senate investigation:

MR. PECORA: And if that depositor or customer then followed up that suggestion by calling upon the National City Company for advice as to his investments, it was not an unusual thing for the National City Company to suggest investment in securities that the Company was sponsoring, was it?

Mr. Hugh Baker (President of the National City Company) : That is right.

Again, when a salesman from the National City Company called upon a small-town banker or investor, it can hardly be denied that he carried with him the prestige which grew out of the size and importance and sound financial reputation of the National City Bank itself. No wonder the small-town banker bought; anything which was good enough for the biggest bank in the country was good enough for him.

And one must also consider the effect of this double interest upon the officers of the Bank in their relation to the general economic situation. Early in 1929 Mitchell's bank lent millions of dollars in the call market to stockbrokers in defiance of the wishes of the Federal Reserve Board, which was trying to check the epidemic of speculation. Was his judgment in so doing completely unaffected by the fact that within the preceding four months he had been one of the managers of a joint-account operation in copper stocks; that his National City Company was selling common stocks, and had on hand at that time a large block of shares of Anaconda Copper common; and that his own financial fortunes were bound up with those of the National City Company through the existence of a "management fund," based on the profits of the Company, from which Mitchell had been given three-quarters of a million dollars as his share of the profits for 1928? Again, as the stock market began to collapse, in the latter months of 1929, Mitchell was one of the most vociferous of all defenders of the existing price-level. Was he motivated solely by his calm banking judgment as the head of a great institution sensible of its responsibility to depositors, to business, and to the country as a whole for the maintenance of economic stability?

Salesmanship in banking was having its inevitable effect.

§ 2

From Mitchell's National City Bank in Wall Street, New York, we now journey all the way across the continent to San Francisco. For the next tendency in American banking which calls for our consideration is the tendency toward concentration into a few hands of power over commercial banks, and the most picturesque and remarkable example of this was contributed by a San Franciscan: Amadeo Peter Giannini.

Giannini was a pyramid-builder. There were many striking parallels between his career and those of other pyramid-builders like Insull and the Van Sweringens. Like Insull, he was of foreign origin: though he was born in California, his father was an Italian immigrant. Like Oris Van Sweringen, he was aided throughout his career by a brother with a name as unusual as his: the younger Giannini was named Attilio. Like both Insull and the Van Sweringens, Amadeo Giannini was not born to wealth and his formal schooling was limited.

At the age of twelve this Italian boy was living on an incredible schedule: going to school by day, and getting up at one or two o'clock each morning to work in his step-father's produce firm until his school hours began. At the age of nineteen he became a member of the firm. At the age of thirty-one he retired from the produce business, having made enough money to bring him in an income of five thousand a year. But such energy could not long remain quiet: soon he was operating in real estate and serving on the board of directors of a bank, and in 1904—when he was only thirty-four years old—he established a bank of his own. It was in the Italian district of San Francisco, it was designed for the Italian-speaking population, and he called it the Bank of Italy.

Almost at the outset of his banking career Giannini showed his resourcefulness. In 1906 the city of San Francisco was rocked by earthquake and swept by fire. As the flames approached the little Bank of Italy, the young banker piled his cash and securities into a horse-drawn wagon and with a guard of two soldiers took them to his home at San Mateo, twenty miles from San Francisco, where he buried them in the garden; and then while the ruins of the city were still smoking he set up a desk in the open air down by the waterfront, put up a sign over the desk which read BANK OF ITALY, and began doing business again—the first San Francisco bank to resume.

His institution prospered and began to open branch offices. Before he had reached his fiftieth birthday there were twenty-five of them, mostly outside San Francisco. Then came the nineteen-twenties and the new era of financial ambition, and Giannini's banking system began to expand in earnest.

There is no need to trace in detail the steps by which this Italian ex-produce merchant advanced, but something should be said of the background and method of his expansion program. There had long been a prejudice in America against branch banking—in other words, against the operation of local branch offices by big banks. One reason for this was doubtless the small-town man's fierce distrust of the "city feller"; another was a very justifiable fear of reckless or unprincipled absentee ownership. It was good, thought the small-town merchant or the rancher or farmer of the neighboring countryside, to be able to call the president of the bank "Ed," and to know that it was run for the benefit of the community and not for the benefit of some metropolitan capitalist who might loot it for his own distant and devious purposes. There were, to be sure, two sides to this argument: the appalling record of failures among small-town banks in the nineteen-twenties is sufficient evidence that "Ed" was sometimes a fine fellow but an incompetent banker. The popular objection to branch banking, however, had crystallized into many laws and regulations restricting its development. And when a banker began to buy up other banks to convert them into branches, naturally rival bankers would oppose him by fanning the popular prejudice and, if necessary, by calling for new laws and restrictions.

In the early nineteen-twenties, this prejudice was slowly melting in the warm airs of financial confidence. Farm lands had not fallen in value so fast and so far in California as in other parts of the country, and thus the country banks in that state were mostly prospering well enough to appeal to an aggressive capitalist as investments. Giannini bought and bought—and presently the conservative bankers of the state realized that the little Bank of Italy, upon which they had hitherto looked with a condescending eye, had covered a good deal of the northern part of the state with branch offices and was becoming a menacing power in California finance.

They rose in opposition. Giannini, hot with zeal for expansion, sought to acquire banks in Los Angeles to serve as branches, and found that there seemed to be none for sale—his rivals had seen to that. Angrily he declared that he would open new branch offices in competition with the existing banks; he was said to have threatened to pepper the southern end of the state with branches so thickly that it would look like a target fired

upon at close range with a shotgun loaded with birdshot.
The state banking department stood in his way; Giannini
waged a political campaign against it and won. The
authorities somewhat relaxed their regulations, and he
went ahead faster than ever.

Ironically, even when the regulations which safe-
guarded branch banking in California were strictest,
they did not prevent Giannini from employing methods
of expansion which in the wrong hands could have become very dangerous. The ingenuity of corporation
lawyers is usually two or three steps ahead of that of legislators. His principal method was to form holding companies and use their funds to accumulate stock in local
banks, which he would then form into branches of the
Bank of Italy or of his big Los Angeles unit, the Bank
of America. He raised the money to form the holding
companies by selling stock to the public, through the
security affiliates of his banks as well as through other
investment concerns.

As time went on, he maintained his grip on the growing system by piling one holding company on top of another, Insull-fashion. Like Insull, he paid high prices
for what he bought: competition was sharp and he had
no choice unless he were to cease his campaign of conquest. As his reputation grew, the price of the stocks of
his holding companies shot up, offering a temptation to
speculators. His principal holding company during most
of this campaign was the Bancitaly Corporation. From
the first his loyal fellow-Italians had been eager to purchase Bancitaly stock; presently thousands of other California investors and speculators were attracted to it; soon
it was bought and sold in huge quantities on the New
York Curb Market as well as on the San Francisco Stock
Exchange, professional operators took it up, and little
plungers all over the country who hardly knew what

sort of business this Bancitaly was engaged in were staking their meager capital upon it. Giannini had become the center of a vast speculative boom, and there was grave danger that the nature of his operations would involve his banks and his whole corporate structure in sustaining this boom.

Despite this danger, Giannini drove ahead. He seemed to be putting his investors' money into the purchase of everything in sight. By 1929 the Giannini system included no less than 453 banking offices in California alone. His principal bank in San Francisco—no longer called the Bank of Italy, but naturalized, as it were, into the Bank of America National Trust and Savings Association—had become the fourth largest commercial banking institution in the country; it was bigger than any bank in Chicago, and only three of the giants of New York overshadowed it: Mitchell's National City, Wiggin's Chase National, and the Guaranty Trust Company.

Nor was Giannini content to operate in California alone. He had invaded New York itself, securing control of the old Bank of America, which by 1930 had 32 branches of its own. As if to show that it was not enough to have a banking empire, Giannini and his associates controlled a fire insurance company, a life insurance company, mortgage companies, and public utilities. They controlled a bank in Milan, Italy. And they even owned shares—under the spell of what imperial dream, who knows?—in the Bank of England, the Bank of France, and the Reichsbank. An extraordinary collection of properties for a man who twenty years before had been the head of but a single small bank used chiefly by Italian immigrants!

The endlessly changing pyramid of corporations through which Giannini ruled over this domain was topped, as you may have guessed, by a Delaware corporation: The Transamerica Corporation. Even a San Franciscan, when in the grip of financial ambition, would turn to that little state on the Atlantic seaboard for his instruments of conquest.

A strange and wonderful thing was this pyramid. Was there no better way, one asks oneself, of achieving the very real advantages of branch banking—the advantages of an opportunity for skillful management of little banks, for healthy diversification of loans and investments, and above all for the imposition of some sort of order upon a banking anarchy—than by thus piling together under one dominating management a vast number of banks, affiliates, holding companies, stock-selling concerns, real-estate companies, and public utilities, with all the invitations to unbridled irresponsibility and speculative management—in short, to the service of two masters—which such a structure offered?

Needless to say, when the speculative tide turned, thousands upon thousands of Giannini's investors suffered grave losses. Parts of the edifice were seriously affected. Giannini almost lost his control of the whole system to his Blair allies in New York. As it was, he lost his New York bank, the Bank of America; it was absorbed by Mitchell's National City. As the cream of earnings ran thin, the price of Transamerica stock slid from a 1929 high of 67⅜ down to a 1932 low of 2½. That the whole structure did not utterly go to pieces and that Giannini's California banking system did not collapse—except insofar as the entire banking system of the United States collapsed—was probably due to the fact that Giannini himself had not become thoroughly imbued with the speculative spirit, and that personal greed had not entered into his program as into the programs of some other pyramiders.

When the stock of his Bancitaly Corporation had gone

far too high in 1928, Giannini had not hesitated to protest that it was not worth so much. When he had given
a million and a half dollars to the University of California, it was reported that this sum constituted the
greater part of his personal fortune. Not caring over-
much for money for its own sake, he was able to resist
the invitations which his methods of conquest extended
to him, and in large degree to prevent his associates from
accepting them. With the aid of able assistants, including
some former Canadian bankers, he saw to it that his
bank's management remained within bounds. What
chiefly impelled Giannini was a sincere belief in branch
banking, coupled with a fervid ambition: a royal lust like
that of the Roman empire-builders—and of his com-
patriot Mussolini—for the glory of conquest. He loved
power, loved victory; and the way to power and victory,
for a modern Caesar of the financial world, lay in the
use of the corporate devices of the time, and above all
of the corporate pyramid.

The impulse to combine banks into systems and groups
and chains was not confined in the nineteen-twenties to
Amadeo Giannini. It was widespread. By the autumn of
1929 there were 273 chains or groups in operation in the
United States, involving 1,858 banks and over eighteen
per cent of the banking resources of the country. The
vicissitudes of some of these other chains and groups
show all too well the dangers inherent in holding-company control of banks. In Detroit, for example, two big
holding companies took charge of many of the leading
banks. Some of these banks had invested too large a
proportion of their depositors' funds in real estate, or
had otherwise succumbed to the lure of a bigger and
better speculative future. At the onset of the depression
in the nineteen-thirties, the profits of these banks naturally began to fall off, and the condition of many of their

investments became progressively worse. Yet they were compelled to go on paying dividends to the two holding companies—the Guardian Detroit Union Group, Inc., and the Detroit Bankers Company—in order that these holding companies might in turn continue to pay dividends. Had the dividends been earned? No matter: they must be paid. What happened later, everybody knows. It was the downfall of these Detroit banks, early in 1933, which precipitated the collapse of the entire banking system of the United States.

But during the seven fat years no such crises were putting the holding-company method of control—or any other method—to the test. Mergers or combinations of big banks were taking place not merely in California and in Michigan, but in Chicago and conspicuously in New York. The National City Bank took unto itself the Farmers Loan & Trust Company and thus became a two-billion dollar institution, to the accompaniment of enthusiastic applause. The Guaranty Trust Company took unto itself the Bank of Commerce, thus approaching the two-billion-dollar mark, if not quite reaching it. The Chase National absorbed the Equitable Trust Company, thrusting ahead of the others. The thrill of bigness had become as irresistible to banks as to the planners of twelve-hundred-foot skyscrapers. Bigness and power: they enthralled Mitchell of the National City and Wiggin of the Chase as they enthralled Amadeo Peter Giannini, the one-time produce-merchant's boy from the Italian district of San Francisco.

§ 3

As you approach almost any of our American cities by air, you see this city first as a large irregular brownish discoloration upon the landscape, overhung by a pall of smoke. But presently you notice at the center of the discoloration a protuberance: a jagged cluster of whitish pinnacles. That cluster of pinnacles—the towering office buildings, hotels, and apartment houses at the center of the city, where land is at a premium—is in large degree a surviving outward manifestation of one of the two great speculative manias of the nineteen-twenties. One of these manias, of course, was for speculation in stocks: a phenomenon to which we shall give due consideration shortly. The other was for real-estate speculation.

Someone has said that the history of the United States is the story of a gigantic land boom. By the nineteen-twenties the frontier had long been closed, but habits are slow to die and the boom continued. First it passed like a ravaging disease through the farm lands of the country, leaving behind it, after 1921, a trail of debt, wrecked banks, and distress. In 1924 and 1925 it descended upon the State of Florida; here the characteristic symptom of the epidemic was a delusion that there was an unlimited supply of millionaires and other idlers prepared to live for months of the year in Venetian luxury, playing golf and polo and rushing about expensive lagoons in speedboats. By the time the Florida boom collapsed—with the inevitable result of ruined speculators and dying banks—it had given impetus to a whole series of summer-resort, winter-resort, and suburban boomlets in other parts of the country, similar to it in frenzy, absurdity, and after-effects. But meanwhile the fever of real-estate speculation had entered the phase in which it was to do the greatest damage to the larger banks of the country. It had attacked the centers of American cities.

From Manhattan to Los Angeles there was a bull market in city lots and an aggressive building of skyscrapers. The logic of this movement was that the supply of desirable urban land was limited; few people seemed to realize that the possibility of pushing skyscrapers up to almost any height could pretty successfully defeat this limitation. Anyhow, each city thrust up its cluster of pinnacles at the center—pinnacles which, unlike the prices of common stocks, would not come down again when the impulse that had created them had been frustrated. They stand today where they were built, half-empty reminders of the fact that the speculative spirit of the nineteen-twenties saw its most dazzling future in raising the standard of living, not of the poor, but of the rich, by providing for them loftier and more luxurious offices and more lordly dwellings.

Possibly the most illuminating way of suggesting the effect upon the commercial banking system of this boom in city real estate, as well as of the boom in stocks, may be to look briefly at an extreme example, an exhibit of the pathology of banking. The failure of the Bank of United States, late in the year 1930, was the largest bank failure which had taken place up to that time in the whole history of the country. It was also the forerunner of further disasters to come. If we put the microscope to this egregious specimen we may see in aggravated form a few of the causes of some of those other disasters.

The Bank of United States, founded by a Jewish garment manufacturer named Marcus and managed in later years by his son and another garment manufacturer named Singer, had grown rapidly through a series of mergers, acquiring the stock of other banks or exchanging this stock for its own, sometimes at extravagant prices; by the spring of 1929 it had thus become a large institution, with deposits of over two hundred million dollars. Naturally, being an up-and-coming bank, it had a security affiliate; indeed, it had a whole series of affiliated or subsidiary corporations through which the men at the head of the bank might engage in various forms of investment or speculation, with the aid of money lent to these corporations by the legally separate bank: in other words, with the depositors' money. As M. R. Werner puts it in his account of the adventures of the Bank of United States: "Whenever they needed money for the enterprises in which they indulged, Marcus and Singer pulled corporations out of drawers and borrowed for them. The officers of these corporations were minor officials of the bank, and frequently the same three, Mr. Lipschutz, Mr. Duffy, and Mr. Rubenstein." Thus the bankers were ingeniously set free of the annoying restrictions which the laws had thrown about the use of depositors' money.

As 1927 gave way to 1928, and 1928 to 1929, these bankers became more and more urgently interested in the market price of the stock of their bank. One reason for this was that their affiliate, the Bankus Corporation, was actively engaged in buying and selling this stock as it rose along with other stocks in the bull market. Another reason was that Marcus and Singer had a syndicate of their own, through which they were personally engaged in pool operations in the stock. Still another reason was that when the Bank of United States absorbed other banks by exchanging its stock for theirs at goodly prices, the former stockholders of these other banks, finding blocks of Bank of United States stock in their hands and noting that the market quotations for it were invitingly high, were under a natural impulse to sell out; and this constant selling tended to depress those quotations, to the embarrassment of the Bankus Corporation and of Marcus and Singer's personal syndicate. Marcus and Singer therefore became actively interested in distributing the stock of the bank as widely as possible among people who would be unlikely to dump it on the market: in selling it to small depositors and other innocents. But still the price sagged. So the Bankus Corporation went on buying the stock to hold the price up. And it went on borrowing from the Bank to finance these purchases—borrowing the depositors' money.

Thus a desperate situation developed: to a greater and greater degree the Bank found itself financing a speculative campaign which could not be successful unless prices continued to rise.

But this was not all. The men who ran the Bank were not only stock-market minded, they were real-estate minded. Through the various dummy corporations at their disposal, they had been putting the depositors' money into the financing of ambitious apartment-house projects, mostly along the west side of Central Park, New York. The shining towers which they built adorned the rapidly changing skyline of Manhattan, but as investments they were declared by a bank examiner to have been "based exclusively on optimism instead of good business policies and sound judgment." Banks, of course, were not supposed to invest in real estate, but that fact did not trouble Marcus and Singer; banks could lend money to corporations, and these corporations could do it. Why lose such a chance to make big money?

The rest of the story can be very briefly told. After the panic of 1929, the price of Bank of United States stock fell. The money locked up in speculative real-estate ventures could not be extracted. The bank foundered.

Now it would be grossly unjust to suggest that such reckless adventures were typical of the course of American banking during the fat years. Most American bankers were men of probity, conscious of the gravity of their responsibilities to their depositors. Yet there is no denying that the tendencies shown in exaggerated form in the Bank of United States were sufficiently prevalent to affect the general banking structure.

Indeed, it may have occurred to the reader as he followed the story of this bank that there was something faintly familiar about some of the elements of it. Rapid expansion through purchases of other banks at high prices: did we not see this happening in California too, when Giannini was in full career? The bank's affiliate trading in the bank's own stock: was Mitchell's National City Company not doing this? Distributing this stock through a vigorous selling campaign: was not Mitchell doing that too?

Very well; but what about the element of injudicious investment in real estate? That this was a factor in the fortunes of other and less grossly mismanaged commercial banks than the Bank of United States, that there was some truth in the British remark that American bankers did not know the difference between a bill and a mortgage, is suggested, first, by the cold statistics of the increase in loans on city real estate by American banks from a little over one billion dollars in 1922 to over $2\frac{3}{4}$ billions in 1929. (One must bear in mind, too, the probability that the 1929 figure does not adequately represent the extent to which the commercial banks had become involved in the fortunes of skyscraper office buildings and big apartment houses: for real-estate ventures, as we have noticed, could readily be disguised as loans to construction companies.) The over-indulgence of bankers in real-estate financing is suggested, in the second place, by the experience of the men who examined the banks of the country after the grand smash of 1933: again and again they had to report that the greatest factor of weakness was the prevalence of real-estate paper in the portfolios of banks. And it is suggested, in the third place, by concrete instances such as that of two big banks in Cleveland.

These two big Cleveland banks were the Union Trust Company and the Guardian Trust Company. In January, 1929, the Union Trust Company had loans outstanding to a total of a little over two hundred and twenty million dollars; and of this total, over seventy-six millions—more than one-third—was in the form of loans on real estate. That was one of the effects of the building boom inspired by the glittering example of the brothers Van Sweringen. As for the Guardian Trust Company, let us turn to the report of the Senate Banking and Currency Committee which investigated the Cleveland collapse: "At the time of the closing of the bank the Guardian Trust Company and its subsidiaries were engaged, besides conducting a banking business, in the operation of an office building, a chain of hotels, a coal mine, and residential and business properties . . ." The Guardian, incidentally, had several subsidiary corporations which could take over its real-estate investments when these began to look a little questionable for the portfolio of a supposedly conservatively managed bank.

Speculation in the steel-and-masonry pinnacles of urban prosperity was not the exclusive concern of gentlemen like Messrs. Singer and Marcus.

Another form of speculation in which we have found these gentlemen engaged was personal speculation in the stock of their own bank. To find a parallel to this exploit we do not need to roam the country; we need only regard the exploits of the head of the bank which in 1930 passed the National City Bank in size and thus became the biggest in the country, indeed the biggest in the world: an institution of the most splendid importance, the Chase National Bank.

The Chairman of the Board of this bank was Albert H.

Wiggin. The bank had, of course, a subsidiary, the Chase Securities Corporation, which participated in many trading accounts (otherwise known as stock-market pool operations) in various stocks, including the stock of the Chase National Bank itself. But that is merely mentioned by the way. Albert H. Wiggin likewise participated in such trading accounts—not personally in his own name, but through the medium of one or the other of his private corporations.

There were few stranger blossoms in the corporate garden than the private corporation. It enabled one to engage in transactions with which one would not care to have one's personal connection generally known; and it also enabled one to put one's profits beyond the reach of the income-tax collector. Taxes on corporate profits were not as heavy as upon the upper brackets of personal income, and the profits of one's private corporation did not have to appear in one's personal accounts unless or until one chose that the corporation should pay dividends. A variant of this device, also in favor among the rich, was the use of a Canadian corporation. The Canadian income-tax laws happened to differ from those in the United States in that a Canadian corporation which acquired stock need not record this acquisition for tax purposes at the price which it paid for it; it could record it at the going market price. Thus if an American magnate who had a Canadian corporation in his financial stable had bought, say, a thousand shares of Steel for $150,000, and the market price for Steel had gone from 150 to 250, and he wanted to sell and realize a neat profit of $100,000, he could dodge the tax on this profit: by going through the appropriate legal motions he could transfer this stock to his Canadian corporation, record it on the books of the Canadian corporation at $250,000 rather than at the purchase price of $150,000, and let the Canadian corporation sell it for $250,000—showing no profit at all for tax purposes. Albert H. Wiggin had three American private corporations, officered and directed by officers and directors of the Chase National Bank and the Chase Securities Corporation; he also had three Canadian corporations.

His three American corporations, during the six years 1927-1932, inclusive, *made over ten million dollars in transactions in the stock of the Chase National Bank, of which he was the head.*

The man who through the medium of these private corporations, and with the aid of officers and directors of his bank, was engaged in serving his stockholders by buying stock from them cheap and selling it to them dear, and who was incidentally participating in stock-market pools in other stocks, with or without the assistance of officers and directors of the companies whose shares were thus taken in hand: this man was no ex-garment manufacturer from the East Side, no unseasoned novice at banking. He was a man of long financial experience, who had been with the Chase Bank itself for twenty-five years. He was a director of scores of corporations. His power was great. His influence was even greater. As the head of one of the mightiest commercial banks in the country, he bore a very heavy responsibility for the maintenance of sound banking conditions: for seeing that the speculative epidemic did not seriously involve the banking structure of the country to the detriment of depositors, business, and that structure of bank credits which served the country as money. And yet this man, wearing a disguise which might shield him from the tax collectors of the Treasury Department, was playing the market in the shares of his own bank.

Years afterwards, when the Senate Banking and Currency Committee had called Wiggin before them and had dragged from him these and other damaging admissions, Ferdinand Pecora, counsel to the Committee, asked him what had prompted the Chase Securities Corporation to engage in trading in stocks.

"I think the times," said Wiggin.

"I assume you mean the speculative atmosphere?" asked Pecora.

"I think perhaps that covers it," said Wiggin. "There was a great deal of atmosphere. There were a great many people who began to think you did a great injustice to everybody if you did not have equity stocks. It even got to be the custom to think that trust funds—it was a pity to limit them so that they could not invest in equity stocks; that we were doing a great injustice to them. In other words, it was the times."

"Did you yield to the temper of the times in that respect?" pursued Pecora.

"I am afraid so."

Let us leave it at that; realizing as we do so that we are setting down the only possible excuse for the speculative spirit which possessed many other men than Albert H. Wiggin, and which, along with the spirit of headlong salesmanship and the spirit of reckless expansion, pervaded the commercial banking system and prepared it for its downfall. "It was the times."

Chapter Eleven

INTO THE STRATOSPHERE

FOR the investment bankers—those midwives and attending physicians of the corporate world, whose function it was to provide, through the sale of securities to dealers and thus to the general public, the capital which governments and industrial and business concerns needed in order to carry on and to grow—the seven years 1922-1929 were fat indeed. The affiliates of commercial banks were taking some of the business which might otherwise have gone to them, yet there seemed to be enough for all, and the investment banking houses still enjoyed the cream of it.

They it was who, with the sleepless aid of their corporation lawyers, put into effect many if not most of the devices by which the promoters and organizers of corporations might do as they pleased without interference from the cohorts of the stockholders. During these years an endless stream of new issues of securities poured forth from their offices and were swallowed up by an eager investing public: foreign government bonds, foreign corporation bonds, railroad bonds, industrial bonds, utility bonds, preferred stocks, common stocks. And the stream grew in volume: between 1926 and 1929 the annual total rose from a mere seven billions to more than eleven and a half billions.

It was a very lucrative business. The profits of those investment bankers who had the prestige and the judgment to negotiate security issues successfully for the giants of industry were huge. Profits measured in terms of hundreds of thousands of dollars on a single issue were commonplace, and sometimes they rose well into the millions. For example, according to the report of the Senate Committee on Banking and Currency, the profits, commissions, and fees which went to Kuhn, Loeb & Co. for marketing securities for the Pennroad Corporation and for other services to this corporation during less than six months in 1929 amounted to about five million eight hundred thousand dollars. And the total profits of the House of Morgan for the year 1929 may be suggested by two recorded facts: first, that the partners paid in Federal taxes for that year a total of about eleven million dollars, and second, that during that year the net worth of J. P. Morgan & Co. and of its Philadelphia ally, Drexel & Co., increased by more than twenty-seven millions.

What made investment banking lucrative was not simply the opportunity to buy issues of bonds from corporations at, say, a price of ninety-five and sell them to the public at a price of ninety-eight or ninety-nine. (Although on a big issue a three-or-four-point spread could add up to a great deal of money, such a spread was ordinarily not unreasonable in view of the risk involved and the number of banks and bond houses among which the money was divided.) It was also the opportunity to be numbered, again and again, among the insiders who got common stock for very little money when corporations were formed or refinanced. In such operations the practice which Morgan the Elder had pursued when he formed the Steel Corporation had now for a long time been orthodox.

Most of the money which a company needed in order to begin business was raised by selling bonds or preferred stock, or both; sometimes all of it was thus raised. The common stock, on the other hand, was not usually distributed in quantity to the general public—at least, not directly. Most of it was issued to the insiders—the promoters, the investment bankers, and their allies—for little or no cash: either handed out along with the preferred stock which these favored gentlemen purchased; or issued to them for "services," or bought by them at very low prices. (When two or more companies were merged, the common stock of the big corporation which took their place was usually issued in exchange for their stock; but ordinarily this stock too, if one were to trace its previous history, would be found to have had a very inexpensive origin.) Thus these insiders found themselves in a delightfully favorable position: a sort of heads-I-win-a-lot, tails-I-can't-lose-much position. If the company did badly (which of course very frequently happened) their losses on their common stock were slight. If, on the other hand, it prospered, they were very well off indeed.

For the shares leaped in value; after being listed on a stock exchange, they were taken up by speculators, often by speculative pools; sooner or later they found their way into the hands of investors; and then such insiders as chose to sell might make handsome profits. (You may remember that when the Steel Corporation was organized, the Morgan syndicate had walked off with a profit of sixty-two and a half millions, of which considerably more than twelve and a half millions had gone to the House of Morgan itself.) It was very advantageous to be in on the ground floor in these operations.

During the nineteen-twenties the procedure was modified in many ways. For one thing, the eagerness of the general public to buy common stock made it often possible to sell such stock at round prices, even at the outset of a corporation's career. For another thing, the insiders now sometimes took their special advantage in the form of a new device, the option warrant which entitled them to buy more common stock in the future if they wished. For example, J. P. Morgan & Co., in 1929, were granted a million option warrants to buy United Corporation common stock at $27.50 per share at any time in the future. The amount of money allocated to the purchase of these warrants was one dollar per warrant. Heads-I-win-a-lot, tails-I-can't-lose-much again. If the stock did not gain in price, they need not exercise these option warrants; if it did, they could exercise them and at once sell the shares at a big profit, or they could sell the option warrants themselves. As a matter of fact, the Morgan firm sold 200,000 of their United Corporation option warrants during 1929 at a profit (based on the above allocated consideration) of over eight million dollars. The rest of the warrants were distributed among the partners of the firm.

Such practices—and they were widespread—were defended on the ground that they offered a logical opportunity for profit to the men whose imagination had foreseen new industrial opportunities and whose enterprise had transformed them into actualities. But they also constituted an almost ideal system for building up potential claims upon the future fruits of industry and preventing these fruits from being distributed in wages or lowered prices (or, if option warrants were issued, from being distributed in increased dividends). Let us see for a moment how this system operated.

Suppose the company whose common shares had been distributed to insiders for little or nothing began to do well. The stock was listed on an exchange; it was tossed about by speculators; it was bought by investors. An investor who paid one hundred dollars a share for such common stock usually imagined that he had put one hundred dollars a share into the business; that he was justly entitled to a return upon these shares from the business; that if it failed to give him such a return because it was lowering prices or raising wages, an outrage was being perpetrated upon him; the sacred rights of property were at stake. He did not realize that very little of the one hundred dollars a share which he had paid represented money which had ever gone into the business at all—had been used, let us say, for the building of factories; most if not all of it had gone into the pockets of the insiders and of the speculators and other investors who had preceded him in the ownership of this stock.

Nor was the investor in common stock without justification in feeling that a return upon what he had paid was due him. For as the stock passed from investor to investor, its curious origin seemed to have less and less to do with the merits of his claim. Common stock which had once been thought of simply as a bit of possible velvet for the insiders should their plans prove to have been well devised, became by gradual degrees something quite different in the public mind when it had passed through successive trades into the hands not only of the rich and powerful but of thrifty salary-earners, wage-earners, indigent gentlewomen, and the widows and orphans of orthodox financial apologetics. Its acquired value had been built into the economic and social structure so securely that to deny to this value a reasonable return in income would work real injustice to thousands.

A very remarkable system indeed, which could thus transform the slenderest into the stoutest of rights! How widespread it was—in other words, how large a proportion of the common stock outstanding represented money actually invested in industry or business, and how much represented merely insiders' and subsequent speculators' and investors' profits—no one apparently knows exactly. Yet if an exhaustive research were made into the origin of the common stocks listed on the New York Stock Exchange in 1929, it would probably show that the bulk of their value did not represent—as did the value of bonds and most preferred stocks—the bricks and mortar and steel and machines with which these corporations did business. Studies in the financing of the leading companies in certain industries are embodied in John T. Flynn's volume on *Security Speculation*: they confirm this hypothesis impressively.

As the public appetite for securities became keener and keener during the nineteen-twenties, it was not surprising that some investment bankers should have leaped at every opportunity, favorable or unfavorable, to form a new company, to merge two or three old ones, or to expand a company's business. The fruits of financial activity were so inviting that bankers began to operate with more and more regard for these fruits and with less and less regard for the effect of such activity upon the businesses involved. The feet of the gentlemen of Wall Street began to leave the hard ground upon which stood factories and shops; these gentlemen began to float higher and higher in a stratospheric region of sheer financial enterprise—a region of reorganizations and mergers and stock split-ups and trading syndicates and super-super-holding companies and investment trusts.

The perfect illustration of this stratospheric activity was the wild proliferation of investment trusts which took place during 1927, 1928, and 1929. Now the investment trust, in theory and sometimes in practice, was a valuable financial institution, especially for the small investor, enabling him to achieve well managed and diversified investment. But as soon as the public began to show an interest in the shares of investment trusts, innumerable men in Wall Street and other financial centers saw a great light. Here was the perfect opportunity to form a new corporation, with all the benefits to themselves attendant upon such activity, without ever having to bother about manufacturing and selling at all. Here was the Wall Street answer to prayer; a company which need have no business at all outside of Wall Street!

All it had to do was to invest in other companies—and to sell its own stock. And incidentally, if the trust were so capitalized that control remained with the insiders even though millions of dollars' worth of securities were distributed to the public, it might become an agency which would aid the investment bankers in gaining financial control of this concern or that, with further benefits.

We need examine only one conspicuous example from among innumerable trusts to show how the formation of such concerns could profit the bankers on the inside. In the year 1924, when the investment trust idea was still a novelty to Americans, the investment banking firm of Dillon, Read & Co. formed what was known as the United States and Foreign Securities Corporation. The first preferred stock and a quarter of the common stock were sold to the general public for twenty-five million dollars. The second preferred stock and another quarter of the common stock were sold to Dillon, Read & Co. for five million dollars—a considerably smaller sum than twenty-five millions, it will be noticed. And the other half of the common stock went (through somewhat complicated channels) to Clarence Dillon and his associates, for a mere one hundred thousand dollars—a very small sum indeed by comparison with the others. This small sum was equivalent to twenty cents a common share; and the number of shares which went to these men personally was half a million. Some years later, after the stock-market had been churning a long time, some of these men decided to sell some of this stock. So Dillon, Read & Co. made an arrangement with a firm of stockbrokers who in 1928 and 1929 churned the market some more, and disposed of 74,198 of these shares for approximately four million dollars; they also sold additional shares to the customers of Dillon, Read & Co., bringing their profits on this common stock which they had purchased (from themselves as the organizers of the trust) at twenty cents a share, to well over six million dollars.

(In fairness to Mr. Dillon and his associates it should be added that the figure of twenty cents a share was nominal; they considered their purchase of preferred and common shares as a single transaction. The point, however, is clear anyhow: men who had got their stock very cheap sold it for millions; and but little of the price paid by those to whom they sold it represented money originally invested in the Corporation.)

Needless to say, this is a somewhat extreme example; it suggests, nevertheless, one reason why investment bankers formed investment trusts by the score and why some of them could support racing stables, hunting preserves, and yachts.

With the investment banking business went power, too; the power that came from sitting on boards of directors, keeping a finger on what was being done, putting in a suggestion here and a word of warning there; the power that came from being able to hint that orders might well be placed with this or that other corporation within the charmed circle of one's influence; the power, sometimes, in foreign affairs that came from having huge commitments in foreign countries, which were supposed to be borne in mind by a State Department not always well-informed but usually anxious not to displease entrenched interests; and a further power—or rather, perhaps, an intangible influence—that could not be measured in terms of directorships or stock ownerships, but as we noted in an earlier chapter of this book was better measured in terms of the prestige which accompanies success.

The two most important of the private banking houses which dominated investment banking were Kuhn, Loeb & Co.—the firm which old Jacob Schiff had built up, and of which Otto Kahn was now the senior partner—and the House of Morgan. Jew and Gentile; the division between them was sharp. The Kuhn, Loeb business in securities was as large as that of the House of Morgan if not larger, but the Morgan influence was far more pervasive.

§ 2

No longer, of course, did Morgan the Younger and his partners stand in the strategic position which had been theirs in 1915 and 1916, when they were selling bonds for the British and French and acting as purchasing agents for the war materials for which the proceeds of these bonds were to go. Nor was there anybody now in that solid, fortress-like building at the corner of Broad and Wall Streets—that building so modest in size, so massive in effect—who wielded the colossal personal authority which had been in the mighty hand of Morgan the Elder. He was gone; yes, and Davison, who during the war years had been the most vital personality at 23 Wall Street, was gone too. Yet the tradition of the firm went on. A partnership in the House was as high a prize as a financier could hope for; it meant terrific work, arduous responsibility, yet it meant also great wealth and something more than that: it was a place on the general staff of what the business world considered the headquarters of financial power.

Morgan the Younger, the head of the firm, set the tone of the establishment; listened to the counsels of partners more brilliant than himself, and put in the last word.

A quiet and substantial gentleman, courteous and affable, he had the simplicity of assured position: seeing him, one thought of a constitutional monarch in mufti. In essence he was the good patrician: a little stiff, a little remote; contemptuous of democratic blunderings and vulgarities and proletarian clamor; quite unable to imagine what the world would look like to the eyes of a fifteen-dollar-a-week steel worker; yet straightforward, genuine, agreeable to those who were fortunate enough to penetrate his reserve, and far more conscious than most financiers of the imperial obligations which accompanied imperial power. At his right hand stood Thomas Lamont, the diplomat of the firm both abroad and at home—a man who could charm Chinese officials, Middle-Western bank presidents, and liberal editors into feeling that they saw eye to eye with him and that the power of the House of Morgan must be beneficent. About them were clustered veterans like Steele and Cochran and able juniors like George Whitney and Parker Gilbert.

The private offices on the second floor of 23 Wall Street were islands of modesty and quiet in the splendor and uproar of Wall Street. Their atmosphere was subtly British and old-fashioned. Wood fires burned in the fireplaces on chilly days; the well-worn easy chairs and couches were restful; a financial discussion there was like a chat in a gentleman's club. Whether or not the hand of the House of Morgan was a hand of iron, it wore a velvet glove of persuasiveness.

Was it a hand of iron? There were stories abroad to the effect that it was—stories of magnates to whom the law had been laid down in very positive terms: this is what you had better do. Yet the answer to the question was veiled in a becoming mystery. When directors of corporations were meeting in Wall Street and wished to refer to the influence or possible displeasure of the firm, they were often almost as hesitant to name it as an Italian would be to name Mussolini. In their euphemistic language, the House of Morgan became "the Corner." "How will the Corner like that?" one director would say to another. Minor officials of banks and corporations would sometimes be even more vague. "I don't know whether They'll like that," these men would say, as if the very walls had ears and might tell somebody who would tell a Morgan partner.

An influence so indefinable cannot be charted in a graph, to show its ups and downs. Yet there seems to have been a subtle change in it during these years. It was generally considered a conservative influence, skeptical of strange new financial devices and of the careers of young financial Napoleons. When, for example, Lamont spoke out about the preposterous competition in foreign financing in 1927, he was speaking in what had come to be regarded as the customary Morgan role. The House was thought of as a balance wheel. Yet as the financial Napoleons of the nineteen-twenties—the Mitchells, Dillons, Insulls, Van Sweringens, Gianninis, Wiggins—rose higher and higher in prestige and in confidence, and some of them began apparently to bother less about what might be said on the Corner, the weight of this balance wheel became a matter of some question. Presently the Morgan firm was flirting with the brothers Van Sweringen; then it was backing them; by 1929 it was floating their giant Alleghany Corporation; and in that same year it entered the competition for influence over the public utility systems by forming another giant of the new finance, the United Corporation, a superholding company for public utility stocks (with a little of the flavor of an investment trust too). Apparently the change in the atmosphere of Wall Street had had its effect. "It was the times."

Yes, the reader may say, but suppose the House of Morgan had really wanted to call a halt in the wild financial proceedings? Could it have done so?

The answer, I believe, must be no. The influence which was referred to with such bated breath in Wall Street was after all limited in scope. Over the financial policy of corporations within the Morgan orbit it was great; in contests with strictly business or financial rivals it could be great. But it was not so great that the firm could risk a pitched battle with an Insull, let us say, or a Mitchell, unless he were to tread on Morgan ground, and thus offend against the accepted principle of mutual tolerance among financiers. Only to a very moderate extent could it be exerted on behalf of a general principle of finance. It was by no means a police power. The House of Morgan was *primus inter pares* among the financial powers of the day: unquestionably *primus*, but not a dictator. There was no dictator.

A great deal has been said in these pages about the concentration of economic power into a few hands. But in essentials those few hands were mutually independent. Indeed, one of the strange things about the capitalist system in America was that, although it had undergone a revolutionary change as more and more devices were discovered and widely utilized by which the men at the top could acquire power and wealth, it was not really a system at all; not a hierarchy, but a free-for-all-insiders; not an order, but a disorder of irresponsible forces.

On certain things these men might agree and act together. They could unite, after a fashion, for the defense of their common prerogatives against radical assault. Yet broadly speaking they could not unite upon any positive economic program. Least of all could they have united upon a program which might interrupt or endanger the financial enterprises in which individuals

among them were engaged. Even had any one group of
men in Wall Street had the time to think steadily about
the possible economic and social effects of what was going
on, or the capacity to understand what these might mean
to ordinary men and women, this group would have
been virtually powerless to stop the mad rush toward
the edge of the abyss.

§ 3

In a vacant lot in the dreariest part of the dreary town
of Cambridgeport, Massachusetts, there used to stand,
many years ago, a huge bedraggled-looking signboard on
which was printed the single phrase, VOICI LE CENTRE
DU MONDE. What forgotten enterprise it had once advertised, few of those who saw it from the lumbering Boston-
bound trolley cars had any idea. It stood there, in a dust-
swept waste, as an ironical reminder of the vanity of some
promoters' dreams.

There have been times in recent years when such a
sign would have seemed almost as out of place in the
hall of the New York Stock Exchange. Yet during the
nineteen-twenties, and above all during the years 1928
and 1929, that great hall on the western side of Broad
Street, just below the corner of Wall Street and just
opposite the quiet Morgan fortress, was in a very real
sense the center of the world.

The trading in securities, and especially in common
stocks, which took place here had become the most powerful engine of American economic expansion. The enthusiasm generated here by an extravagant uprush in
prices was driving financiers and industrialists forward
into vast and perilous schemes for the development and
control of industry and trade. We have seen it shaping
the schemes of men like Insull and the Van Sweringens

and Mitchell and Dillon; what it did for them it did also for hundreds of others. The money which changed hands here was flowing out into the market-places of the country and providing one of the chief stimuli to business. The theories of American prosperity which were forced in this hot-house were finding their way into the thinking of men and women all over the country—even men and women who had never owned a share of stock—and were determining more and more surely the economic temper of the land. The roar which rose here from the throats of hundreds of jostling brokers as they made their purchases and sales, and the chatter of the tickers in innumerable scattered brokers' offices, had become the leit-motifs of American life.

Nor was America the only country to feel the power of this mighty engine of inflation. Money from abroad was tempted here; the prices established here influenced prices on the European bourses; profits made here found their way to foreign countries; and as in a hundred subtle ways the New York level of security prices affected the flow of international trade, the sales made by brokers on the paper-littered floor of this arena altered the fortunes of Zulu miners in the Rand and Malayan rubber-growers in the islands of the East.

The story of the last two feverish years of the big bull market on the Exchange—the years when it got quite out of hand—I have already told in some detail in *Only Yesterday*. But there are certain aspects of that story which deserve a passing mention here, in order that the mania for speculation in common stocks may assume its proper place in the larger story of American finance.

First let us attempt roughly to measure the astounding growth of this speculation. A reasonable measure is the number of shares of stock that changed hands year by year. Between 1910 and 1920 this number had never

been higher than 312 million. Nor was this figure soon
touched again, despite the fact that the Liberty Loan
campaigns had provoked a new interest in investments
and that the newspapers of the country were beginning
to give more and more space to stock-market price-tables.
During the next few years the annual trading fluctuated
as follows:

1920	223 million
1921	171 million
1922	260 million
1923	237 million
1924	282 million

But by 1925 Calvin Coolidge had been elected, the
Florida boom was reaching its climax, stock prices were
rising fast, and the momentum of trading in shares began
to quicken. (In this year the Van Sweringens already
had control of the Chesapeake and Ohio, the Erie, and
the Pere Marquette, and were looking for more worlds
to conquer; out in California, Giannini was battling with
opposing California bankers for the right to expand his
Bank of Italy all over the state; Insull's empire was beginning to grow by leaps and bounds.) In 1925 the number of shares which changed hands on the New York
Stock Exchange jumped from 282 million to 452 million.

In 1926 it lapsed a little—to 449 million. But in 1927
it shot up once more to 576 million. And then came the
years of the great madness.

It was in March, 1928, that the daily doings in that
great hall at the corner of Broad and Wall Streets began
to be a front-page sensation: that the rise of Radio and
General Motors became topics of furious discussion at
thousands of dinner-tables; and that the record for daily
trading which had been set during the Northern Pacific
panic was at last broken. It was in November of this same
year that Herbert Hoover defeated Al Smith for the

Presidency, thus assuring the speculative community that the United States would enjoy "four years more of prosperity." During 1928 the volume of trading climbed from 576 million to 920 million. And in 1929 it set an all-time record of 1,124 million—something like fifteen times the annual average for the war decade!

Or suppose we watch the rise in prices, another measure of the speculative boom. Here are the Standard Statistics common stock averages for the years from 1924 to 1929, expressed in terms of an index in which 100 represents the average for the year 1926:

                    June, 1924 .... 65.6
                    June, 1925 .... 85.1
                    June, 1926 .... 96.9
                    June, 1927 .... 114.

and then

                    June, 1928 .... 148.2
                    June, 1929 .... 191.

and at last

                    September, 1929 .... 216.1

The significance of these figures is clear. A well-diversified investment in the more substantial common stocks would have more than tripled in value in the space of scarcely more than five years. The total value of all listed stocks increased by many billions of dollars. These dollars were in a very real sense new money manufactured by the processes of the Stock Exchange. Some of them were being spent by lucky speculators, and thus were stimulating business. They were available as collateral for bank loans. To a considerable extent they were being recorded as profits by corporations, as we have seen. The whole American economy was becoming geared to the price-level which they represented. This is one reason why we may speak of the speculation on the Stock Exchange as a great engine of inflation.

But there was another reason. The bulk of these

millions of purchases of stocks at rising prices was made on margin—that is to say, mostly with borrowed money. The loans to brokers to carry customers' accounts also made a sensational rise. In the year 1922 these loans had not amounted to as much as two billion dollars. By the summer of 1926 they had risen to the very considerable total of almost three billion dollars. But that was nothing to what was to come. In 1927 they rose to nearly four and a half billion; in 1928, to nearly six and a half billions; and by September, 1929, to the incredible figure of over eight and a half billions.

Yes, but how many people were actually speculating? To Wall Street it seemed as if the whole American population were in the market, and this indeed has been the orthodox defense of the debauch of 1928 and 1929 submitted by some of the gentlemen of the Street. For example, when Richard Whitney, president of the Stock Exchange, was asked by counsel for the Senate Committee how it happened that stocks rose so high, he replied, "Ask the one hundred and twenty-three million people of the United States." The best available evidence would seem to indicate, however, that in this statement the president of the Exchange indulged in hyperbole. During the year 1929 the member firms of the Exchange had on their books a collective total of a little over half a million margin accounts. They had altogether a total of 1,371,920 customers, including those who bought stocks outright for cash. If we adopt John T. Flynn's method of arriving at an estimate, and double these figures to allow for those who did their business through non-member concerns and on other exchanges, we cannot be very far wrong. Let us say, then, that in 1929 there were probably well over a million people speculating on margin; that there were perhaps two or three million in all who were buying and selling stocks with an uneasy eye on the financial quotations, whether or not they gambled on margin; and that of course there were other investors—perhaps one or two millions of them—whose fortunes, large or small, were directly affected by what was going on in the Street, even if they had never learned to flip the evening paper open to the stock-market page. Unquestionably there were far more people speculating than ever before; unquestionably there were great numbers of clerks, stenographers, janitors, chauffeurs, and waiters in the market. Yet probably not much more than one person in a hundred in the American population was playing stocks on margin, and not much more than one person in twenty was directly affected through changes in the value of his or her possessions. The effect of the mania on the rest of the population was great, but it was indirect—brought about by the results of economic inflation and unbalance.

In another respect the orthodox Wall Street apology fails to conform to the facts. It suggests a picture of the big men of the Street standing helplessly by while Tom, Dick, and Harry put the prices of stocks up. The actuality was quite different.

Unfortunately no such exhaustive studies of the great speculation of 1928 and 1929 were ever made as it was possible for the Senate Committee's investigators to make of the lesser speculative outburst of the spring and summer of 1933, during the first few months of the New Deal. But the figures for that latter outburst—when the money-changers were supposedly somewhat chastened— are illuminating in many ways.

They show, for one thing, that during the month of July, 1933, the total trading on the New York Stock Exchange was about 120 million shares. The members of the Exchange and their partners bought or sold nearly 65 million shares *for their own account*. In short, they were on the buying or selling side of the market in over half the transactions; or, to put it another way, they did over a quarter of the total business for themselves.

In some of the stocks which rose most sensationally in value during that brief boom in 1933, and attracted most inevitably the little shoestring speculators who throng the brokers' board-rooms during a bull market, the part which the big speculators of the Street played in the trading was much greater. One of the wildest leaps of 1933 was made by the stock of the American Commercial Alcohol Corporation, the price of which rose in a little over two months from less than 25 to over 90—and then collapsed abruptly to less than 30. The Senate Committee's study of that egregious operation shows that fifty men were on one side or the other of three-quarters of the transactions during this period; and that *a mere five men were on one side or another of more than half of them. These five men did 27 per cent of the purchasing and 27 per cent of the selling.* What is more, if one examines carefully the records of the trading, day by day, in this stock—they are set forth in detail in John T. Flynn's *Security Speculation*—one will discover that the days when the volume of trading suddenly expanded, thus drawing the eyes of quantities of little speculators to American Commercial Alcohol as a promising speculative vehicle into which to put their meagre capital, were not days when these five big speculators stood by and idly watched. On these days they themselves were doing the bulk of the trading. And these five men were the specialist in the stock (the man who served as the Stock Exchange's referee, so to speak, between buyers and sellers) ; a market operator named Thomas Bragg, who was the manager of the pool; and three officers of the American Commercial Alcohol Corporation itself!

A glimpse of these five men in action—during a brief part of their sustained operation—may be instructive as showing how big operators could attract the public into the market and thus push prices up to their own profit. On June 26, 1933, the pool in American Commercial Alcohol had been at work for over six weeks. How it had obtained a supply of the stock to play with, by obtaining an option on shares which had fallen under the control of the insiders in the corporation, and how it had already pushed up the price considerably and then had sold a good deal of its stock while the price held steady, we need not recount in detail. Let us see what happened on June 26 and the succeeding days.

On June 26, 1933, the five speculators bought 14,200 shares and sold 12,800. (The total volume of trading in the stock that day was 31,900 shares.) This sudden burst of activity in American Commercial Alcohol, after a period of comparative quiet, brought the outside speculative public in with a rush. There always seem to be hundreds of traders at such times standing ready to buy a stock that is moving upward and appearing constantly on the ticker tape; speculative operators count upon such traders in their plans. And the fact that the five men on the inside bought more stock than they sold helped to put the price up: it went up two or three points. The next day these five men were a little less active, and they sold 800 more shares than they bought (purchases, 11,-100; sales, 11,900), but with the public swarming in, the price nevertheless went up again, several points. (The total volume of trading was larger than on the preceding day: 49,200 shares.) So far, so good. The little outsiders were now eager; wild expectations inflamed them; a lot more of them, anxious to get aboard the bandwagon before it was too late, decided to buy—and the five men on the inside were ready to sell to them. On the 28th of

June the volume of trading rose again to 52,300 shares, the biggest figure of this movement; the volume was so large, in fact, that it effectively masked the fact that although the five men bought 10,500 shares, they also sold many more, they sold 14,400 shares. And the price hardly sagged at all, so gladly did Tom, Dick, and Harry buy. During these three days the price of American Commercial Alcohol had risen several points, the outsiders had come in in large numbers to buy, and the five men at the center of things had actually succeeded in selling, at these rising prices, 3300 more shares than they had bought! That is how pools make money by coaxing in the general public.

This American Commercial Alcohol pool offers in some respects, it is true, a somewhat extreme example of manipulation of prices by insiders, including insiders who are officers of the companies whose stock is being taken for a ride; but it is not unreasonable to suppose that there must have been dozens of such pools during the wild years of 1928 and 1929. And it is certainly safe to say that a large proportion of the pools were carried on with the aid of corporation officers, directors, or other large stockholders.

A few scattered operations during these years have been investigated in detail sufficient to show us the corporate insiders at work. Let us look at one or two of them.

In 1928 there was a pool operation in the stock of the Sinclair Consolidated Oil Corporation. The manager of this operation was Arthur W. Cutten, one of the wiliest of the professional speculators. The participants included among others the Chase Securities Corporation (the affiliate of the Chase National Bank) ; one of Albert H. Wiggin's private corporations, the Shermar Corporation; Harry F. Sinclair of Teapot Dome fame, who was the head of the Sinclair Consolidated Oil Corporation itself; and several other officers and directors of this corporation. The total profits of the operation were nearly thirteen million dollars; in these profits, the share of the officers, directors, and large stockholders of the Sinclair concern amounted to more than two and a half millions. It is hardly necessary to remind the reader that these profits in large degree were made by buying stock from, and selling stock to, stockholders (old or new) of whom these insiders were ostensibly the servants.

Perhaps the most spectacular of all the advances made by individual stocks during the big bull market was that of the stock of the Radio Corporation of America. At the time when this market entered upon its final eighteen-month period of frenzy the quotation for Radio was $94 a share (this was on March 3, 1928); at one time during 1929 it got as high as $549 a share. This amazing advance did not come about without the active intervention of insiders. Of one phase of this advance we have precise knowledge. A syndicate which operated in the stock during a period of scarcely more than a week in March, 1929, made a net profit of over four million, nine hundred thousand dollars. This syndicate bought and sold most of its stock through the brokerage firm of M. J. Meehan & Company. The specialist in Radio stock was a member of that firm. And among the participants in the syndicate—along with Percy A. Rockefeller, Walter P. Chrysler, John J. Raskob, William C. Durant, and other men potent in the Wall Street of the day—was Mrs. David Sarnoff, wife of the president of this very Radio Corporation.

Among the participants in a pool in General Asphalt stock in 1929 was Horatio G. Lloyd, chairman of the executive committee of the company (and also a Morgan partner). Among the participants in a pool in Underwood-Elliott-Fisher stock in 1929 was one of the private corporations of Albert H. Wiggin, then a director or the company. When we add to these scattered examples those of which we have already caught a glimpse—Insull selling shares of Insull Utility Investments at thirty dollars a share which he had been assigned at $7.52 a share, at a time when he was the sole owner of the stock of this concern; Wiggin's private corporations making over ten million dollars in the shares of the bank of which he was the head; Mitchell joining with officers of the Anaconda Copper Company in a pool operation in copper stocks; and Dillon, Read & Co. arranging with a firm of brokers to distribute blocks of the shares of United States and Foreign Securities which men associated with the firm had so inexpensively acquired—we need be under no illusion that throughout this whole bull market there were not large numbers of insiders pumping up values, thereby adding to the speculative frenzy, and profiting hugely in the process. The public came in eagerly, it is true, but they came in at the urgent and adroitly contrived invitation of Wall Street. The Stock Exchange was a private association; during those years it might well have been called the Association for Improving the Condition of the Rich.

Nor should we overlook the part which leading American corporations played in the orgy by lending money from their surpluses to brokers to carry speculative loans. To give but a few examples: during the year 1929 the average amount which the Standard Oil Company of New Jersey had outstanding in call loans was about sixty-nine million dollars; the Electric Bond & Share Company and its subsidiaries, one hundred million dollars; the Sinclair Consolidated Oil Corporation, twelve and a half million dollars. At one time the outstanding loans by the Cities Service Company reached more than forty-nine million dollars. More than half of the colossal increase in loans to brokers consisted of loans like these from corporate treasuries. The interest rates were high and so the corporations took advantage of them—that was all. What was done with the money was apparently not their affair. The episode was an interesting example of self-rule by business.

If it is preposterous to regard a bull market so stimulated and so financed as the product of the spontaneous speculative madness of the entire American population, it is also, of course, almost equally preposterous to imagine, as some radical writers have done, that the big financiers and industrialists pocketed their profits and stood aside in the autumn of 1929, leaving the dear public to its doom. To suppose that this happened is to miss the crowning irony of the whole adventure. The truth is that for so many long months had pool operators unloaded their holdings and then shortly seen the stocks in which they had operated go roaring up again, either because new pools had stepped in or because the public had taken the bit in its teeth; so wild and unprecedented had the whole advance become, so persuasive was the doctrine that America was entering a new era in which none of the old rules for determining value were any longer applicable, and so thoroughly had the darlings of speculative fortune lost their heads, that when the month of October, 1929, arrived, most of them went over the edge of Niagara with their victims. They succumbed to the fate of propagandists who in the end come to believe all too fully their own propaganda.

During the boom there were, to be sure, voices raised in protest and warning—voices like Paul Warburg's, or that of Alexander Dana Noyes of the *New York Times*, or that of the staid *Commercial and Financial Chronicle*, which on January 5, 1929, said flatly that the huge increase in brokers' loans constituted a "menace to the entire community" and added that it was "a public duty for anyone in authority, or having influence and weight, to speak in unsparing terms in denunciation of what was going on." The Federal Reserve Banks tried to stem the flood in 1928 by making three successive increases in the rediscount rate; early in 1929 the Federal Reserve Board tried by direct pressure upon the member banks to prevent them from using Federal Reserve credit for loans for speculative purposes; and subsequently the Federal Reserve Bank of New York sought repeatedly to raise its rediscount rate still higher, though it was prevented from doing so by the Board in Washington, which preferred to rely upon the method of direct pressure and was moreover divided in opinion as to what to do. But these somewhat spasmodic efforts on the part of the various Reserve authorities were of little avail; the weapons at their disposal were ill-adapted for dealing with such a situation. As for those who had most "influence and weight" in the Street, the House of Morgan appeared to be otherwise occupied—in planning to launch the Alleghany Corporation and United Corporation. As for "those in authority" in the Administration at Washington (aside from the Reserve Board), President Coolidge and his multimillionaire Secretary of the Treasury had for some years past been giving intermittent aid and comfort to the bull party in the market by uttering soothing words when stocks showed signs of sagging; the President had once, in the early days of 1928, gone so far as to state publicly that he did not consider brokers' loans too high; and the nearest that Andrew W. Mellon ever came to that "unsparing denunciation" which had been urged by the editor of the *Commercial and Financial Chronicle* was to say very mildly that it was an opportune time for the prudent investor to buy bonds.

Meanwhile a host of prophets of the new economic era were shouting their fatuous proclamations of hope. They upbraided the Reserve Board for its attempts to interfere with the constructive forces of business. They defended speculation on the ground that the great men of all time had been adventurous, that Columbus, the American Revolutionists, and the pioneers of the West had been in heavy bondage to speculative fortune, and even that "Christ himself took a chance." So altered, indeed, was the whole economic atmosphere, that many distinguished and hitherto conservative economists were persuaded that a New Era had indeed begun.

And so the tickers chattered throughout the land, and the prices leaped and fell back and leaped yet higher, and the big manipulators pushed up this stock and that, and the little speculators ventured in and got something for almost nothing and bought new radios and new cars with a part of their winnings and staked the rest on new ventures, bigger and bigger ventures, and wherever there were men and women with invested capital the talk was of stocks, stocks, stocks, and the summer of 1929 came and went with prices soaring higher and higher, and it seemed as if the great advance had only just begun.

What shall we say of this wild bull market?

First, that for most of those engaged in it, it was a gamble pure and simple—if not, indeed, something much less pure and simple: a gamble in which some of the players had the inside knowledge and the financial power to determine the immediate outcome.

Second, that the economic justification offered for it by some of the apostles of the new era was fantastic. The current argument was that as the shares of successful companies became more and more widely distributed, the country would approach a condition in which everybody would prosper by holding stock, receiving dividends from it, and enjoying its appreciation in value. In so far as this argument dealt with income from dividends, it implied that the population could become prosperous by living on a sum of money which represented the difference between what they paid for goods and what they were paid for making them. In so far as it dealt with income from appreciation, it implied that during these years the population would live upon money which represented the expectation of such a difference in the nineteen-thirties: that, in effect, they would borrow and spend at once what they hoped that the nineteen-thirties would produce.

In the third place, the boom was not by any means an isolated phenomenon, apart from the general financial tendencies of the day. It was merely the most spectacular manifestation of those tendencies; of the spirit of something-for-nothing with which innumerable financiers and business men had become imbued.

Finally, this gamble drew into the stock market over eight and a half billion dollars of credit, introduced inflated values everywhere into bank portfolios and corporate financing, built up preposterous claims upon the profit-making powers of business concerns, invited unsound industrial expansion, and in these and other ways added to the increasing instability of the American economy. Harshly as one may justly comment upon the treachery of corporation officers who gambled in their own stocks at the expense of their stockholders, and upon the timidity or irresponsibility of supposed business and financial leaders who let the madness go on without lifting a hand to stop it, the morals of the big bull market were unimportant compared with its economic effects. The sublimest folly of those days was the often-expressed belief that the speculative gamble was after all an unimportant affair—that if it were to end in a shakeout, a few speculators would lose their shirts and this would be the sum of the damage. Never were words spoken which betrayed a more tragic incompetence to understand what such collective frenzy must precipitate.

Chapter Twelve

THE OVERLORDS, 1929

LET us pause for a moment, while the big bull market is still sweeping the prices of stocks irresistibly upward, and look briefly at the men involved in the financial drama now approaching its climax. It is the summer of 1929, that golden noon of the great age of American capitalism. We stand in the narrow canyon of Wall Street, half deafened by the uproar of riveters fashioning yet taller and more confident palaces of fortune, and watch the men surging past us on their varied errands. This is the capital of the American economy; these men are the insiders, who wield such far-reaching and expanding powers, and their allies and associates and emulators and underlings. What sort of people are they? Do they form a distinct ruling caste? In what sort of society do they move? What are their interests and preoccupations outside business, their standards of ethical conduct in business, their influence upon the quality of American civilization?

The difficulties of generalization are immense. One does not easily find common denominators for the personalities of, say, Thomas W. Lamont and Amadeo P. Giannini, or of John D. Rockefeller, Jr., and John J. Raskob. Yet the attempt must be made if we are to understand what happened to the American economy. It may be somewhat facilitated if, as in the third chapter of this book—when we glanced at the careers and influence of some of the colossi of American finance as of the year

1905—we analyze a few samples in the process of arriving at our conclusions.

It is interesting to note, by way of preliminary observation, that the leaders of American finance and industry in the latter nineteen-twenties were hardly better known to the public at large than their predecessors of twenty-odd years before, despite the diligent ministrations of public-relations experts and the swollen popular respect for financial and industrial success.

You may recall that in Chapter III we compared the number of lines in the *Reader's Guide to Periodical Literature* for 1900-04 which were given to listing magazine articles about ten leading financiers and also about ten leading politicians of that day; and that the tabulation gave us a total of only 88 lines for the financiers as against 799 lines for the politicians. Suppose we make a similar comparison between the number of lines given to listing magazine articles about ten leaders of finance and industry and ten politicians in the *Reader's Guide* for 1925-28 (a considerably larger volume). Such a tabulation may give us a rough suggestion of the extent to which the general public knew about these men as individuals and were interested in their careers and personalities.

NUMBER OF LINES		NUMBER OF LINES	
J. P. Morgan (the younger)...	6	Calvin Coolidge	427
Thomas W. Lamont..........	6	Herbert Hoover	353
Otto Kahn	7	Alfred E. Smith..............	312
Owen D. Young..............	29	William E. Borah.............	98
Charles E. Mitchell...........	6	Charles E. Hughes...........	71
Albert H. Wiggin.............	0	Charles G. Dawes.............	69
The Van Sweringens*........	8	Andrew W. Mellon...........	52
Samuel Insull	7	George W. Norris.............	46
Henry Ford	150	Robert LaFollette (senior).....	41
Pierre duPont	7	Albert C. Ritchie.............	34
Total......	226	Total......1503	
(Total without Henry Ford, 76)			

* We may perhaps be forgiven if we combine the two Van Sweringens and regard them as if they were a single man.

Clearly the road to financial and industrial power was not a road to wide personal renown—at least of the sort that is reflected in magazine articles—even in the nineteen-twenties. Ford, of course, was a shining exception to this rule; but Ford was clearly exceptional in other ways too. A financial maverick, he did not distribute the shares of his company, did not collaborate with the banking powers, eschewed Wall Street and all its ways; and he had a peculiar gift for dramatizing himself and his achievement. Some of the other men listed in the left-hand column of our table have been much publicized since 1929 —but that goes only to show that a banker's name does not become a household word in America until he is investigated.

§ 2

The men whom we see about us as we stand in the Wall Street of 1929 and survey the passing crowd are mostly well groomed, conservatively and impeccably tailored, pleasant-voiced, easy and courteous in address. There are, of course, rough diamonds among them, particularly among the playboys of the stock market, but it is doubtful if there are so many in 1929 as there were in 1905, and the dominant type is smoothly polished; even the go-getting Babbitt tends to straighten his necktie and lower his voice and adopt a more gracious demeanor in these patrician precincts. Wall Street is a school of manners. Go into one of the luncheon clubs where the men of the Street gather and you will note with half an eye that most of them have the air of gentlemen. How does this happen, in a nation whose business men, according to the observations of generations of foreign commentators and to the strictures of the contemporary Menckens, have been among the most strident—if also the most kindly—members of the human race?

One explanation, of course, would be that the Wall Street standard, in dress and in deportment, is set by men of assured wealth and the social and cultural advantages which wealth can bring, and that the others imitate them. But there is perhaps another explanation. There are fewer farmers' sons, laborers' sons, and ex-grocers' boys in the Wall Street of 1929 than in that of 1905. As the population of the United States slackens its growth and frontier opportunities are cut off and the increasing size of the big corporations sets directors and executives farther apart from their armies of workers, it is becoming harder for young men to climb, as Rockefeller and Carnegie and Baker did, from the lower levels of fortune to the upper. The roaring stock market is making new fortunes every day—but only for those who have at least a little capital to begin with or a favorable position close to the insiders. The American people are slowly settling into economic strata; and the upper stratum of all—or at least that part of it which is represented in Wall Street—is tending in some degree to become self-perpetuating.

You may recall that in the third chapter of this book we found that of the ten financial leaders of 1905 whose careers we examined, only one had been to college. Of the ten financial and industrial leaders of 1929 whom we listed a moment ago, six had been to college. But suppose we examine a list, not of ten men of 1929 but of fifty (in order to secure a broader basis for generalization, not merely on this but on other points) ; that we limit it to New York men (in order to facilitate various later comparisons) ; and that we make it up chiefly of bankers and other financial leaders rather than of industrialists such as predominated in James W. Gerard's list of "sixty-four rulers of America" (drawn up in 1930) . This list of ours

—including the ten senior Morgan partners in New York, six other private and investment bankers, eleven commercial bankers, and a scattering of insurance company heads, powerful private investors, brokers, market operators, industrialists, utility executives, etc., as indicated in the footnote on this page*—would make, of course, no pretence to include the fifty *most* powerful or influential men in the Wall Street of 1929, but it would be at least reasonably representative of the much-abused and much-feared influence of the Street, the tem-

* J. P. Morgan, Charles Steele, Thomas W. Lamont, Thomas Cochran, Junius S. Morgan, George Whitney, Russell C. Leffingwell, Francis D. Bartow, Arthur M. Anderson, William Ewing; Otto Kahn, Frederick Strauss, Clarence Dillon, Charles Hayden, Arthur Lehman, Mortimer L. Schiff; George F. Baker (senior), George F. Baker, Jr., Albert H. Wiggin, Charles E. Mitchell, Paul M. Warburg, Seward Prosser, William C. Potter, George W. Davison, William Woodward, Harvey D. Gibson, Jackson E. Reynolds; John D. Rockefeller, Jr., Vincent Astor, Frederick H. Ecker, Darwin P. Kingsley, David F. Houston, E. H. H. Simmons, Bernard M. Baruch, John J. Raskob, Percy A. Rockefeller, Matthew C. Brush, Owen D. Young, Alfred P. Sloan, Jr., Pierre S. duPont, Myron C. Taylor, Walter C. Teagle, Jesse I. Straus, Walter S. Gifford, Sidney Z. Mitchell, Floyd L. Carlisle, George H. Howard, Matthew S. Sloan, Arthur Curtiss James, Leonor F. Loree.

(Here, for comparison, is the Gerard list, with asterisks marking the names of men included also in the other: *Finance*—Andrew W. Mellon, J. P. Morgan,* William H. Crocker, George F. Baker,* Charles Hayden,* John J. Raskob,* Thomas W. Lamont,* Albert H. Wiggin,* Charles E. Mitchell,* Walter Edwin Frew, Amadeo P. Giannini. *Mining and finance*—Daniel Guggenheim, William Loeb. *Oil*—John D. Rockefeller, Jr.,* Walter C. Teagle,* R. C. Holmes. *Automobiles*—Henry Ford, Fred J. Fisher, Charles T. Fisher, Lawrence P. Fisher, William A. Fisher, Edward F. Fisher, Albert J. Fisher, Howard Fisher. *Steel*—Myron C. Taylor,* James A. Farrell, Charles M. Schwab, Eugene G. Grace. *Explosives and Manufacturing*—Pierre S. duPont,* Irénée duPont, Lammot duPont, H. F. duPont, Eugene duPont, A. Felix duPont, Eugene E. duPont. *Railroads*—O. P. Van Sweringen, M. J. Van Sweringen, W. W. Atterbury, Arthur Curtiss James,* Daniel Willard. *Utilities*—P. G. Gossler, Sosthenes Behn, Walter S. Gifford,* Samuel Insull, Sidney Z. Mitchell.* *Electrical equipment*—Owen D. Young,* Gerard Swope. *Copper*—John D. Ryan, Daniel C. Jackling. *Aluminum*—Arthur V. Davis. *Coal*—Edward J. Berwind. *Lumber*—Frederick K. Weyerhaeuser. *Motion Pictures*—H. M. Warner, Adolph Zukor. *Tobacco*—George W. Hill. *Mail-Order Retailing*—Julius Rosenwald. *Publishing*—Adolph S. Ochs, W. R. Hearst, Robert R. McCormick, Joseph Medill Patterson, Cyrus H. K. Curtis, Roy W. Howard. *Labor*—William Green, Matthew Woll.)

per of the financial leadership at the heart of the American system.

We find that of these fifty men, no less than forty had been to college or had had equivalent training. (Eleven of them had been to Harvard, five to the Massachusetts Institute of Technology, four to Yale, three to Amherst, three to Cornell, and the rest to scattered institutions—not, as it happened, including Princeton.) A very distinct change had taken place since 1905.

Incidentally, it is interesting to note that when, in 1932, Taussig and Joslyn published a study of the origins of 7351 "business leaders" of America—men who occupied important business positions throughout the country—they found that 45.3 per cent of these men had been to college. They also found that among the men in this big group who were connected with very large business concerns—the men who might be said to represent "big business"—the proportion who had been to college was considerably above 45.3 per cent; it was 53.8 per cent. If among our fifty representative Wall Street leaders the proportion ran as high as 80 per cent, the conclusion would seem to be inescapable: the higher one went in the scale of economic influence in the nineteen-twenties, the fewer graduates did one find of that traditional alma mater of the successful American business man, the school of hard knocks. For this fact the increasing prestige of the colleges was no doubt partly responsible. Yet presumably the sequence of cause and effect sometimes went the other way. Many a self-made man sent his sons to college not primarily to get an education but to "meet the right people."

Many of the fifty men in our list had won their way to financial preëminence from beginnings which would hardly have suggested the promise of future Wall Street success. Owen D. Young, for example, had been brought up in the simple frugality of a farm in upper New York State. John J. Raskob was the son of a struggling cigar-maker in Lockport, New York, and began his business career at the age of nineteen as a five-dollar-a-week stenographer. (Just as Insull started on the road to success by becoming Edison's secretary, so young Raskob profited by the lucky chance of becoming secretary to Pierre S. duPont.) Albert H. Wiggin's father was a Unitarian clergyman in a Massachusetts town, and young Wiggin went to work as a bank clerk in Boston at the age of seventeen. Clarence Dillon's father, born Samuel Lapowski, was a clothing merchant and small banker of San Antonio.

Yet there were other men in the group who might fairly be said to have been born to the financial deep purple: men like the Morgans, George F. Baker, Jr., John D. Rockefeller, Jr., Percy Rockefeller, Vincent Astor, or William Woodward. And as the sons of the privileged swarmed each year into downtown New York from the older universities, it was difficult to escape the conclusion that the number of those who owed their favorable positions at least partly to inherited advantage was growing. There was pretty surely a tendency toward the formation of a ruling financial caste.

§ 3

But this tendency had not as yet gone very far, as the instances of Owen Young and Raskob suggest, to say nothing of Insull and the Van Sweringens and Giannini. And the complexity of the economic class structure of America was accompanied and perhaps accentuated by a marked social complexity, nowhere more striking than in New York City itself, the metropolis whose centripetal force attracted financial talent and financial ambition from other cities and towns throughout the country.

New York had changed greatly since those early days of the twentieth century when there were no fifty-story skyscrapers, and automobiles were still playthings of the rich, and traffic policemen and traffic lights were unknown, and Central Park was gay of a spring afternoon with the victorias and barouches of the well-to-do, and the outlying clusters of population in Westchester and the New Jersey hills and on Long Island were still country villages. The social world in which prominent metropolitan financiers now found themselves had changed likewise. Society as Mrs. Astor had hopefully visioned it —a strict, self-contained group of men and women whose members all knew one another and took their aristocratic position seriously—had less of a semblance of reality than ever before; even the leadership of Mrs. Stuyvesant Fish, after Mrs. Astor's death, had failed to maintain the precarious prestige of the inner group. The battle for social recognition still went on, of course; it will continue to go on so long as men and women still know envy and vanity and pride; in various other cities of the country there were still fairly definite barriers of caste which controlled admission to the Assemblies or the Cotillions of the fashionably assured, and there were large numbers of people to whom these barriers were important, reluctant though they might be to admit it; but in New York, the outlines of Society had become so faint as to be almost invisible except to those who insisted upon seeing them. It became a truism for members of the passing generation to say that Society no longer possessed accepted authority.

For this change there were many reasons. One was that the city had become too huge for its society to remain under the domination of any one group of mutual acquaintances. Not only had the population of New York increased from a scant four million in 1905 to a full six million in 1929, with an even sharper increase in the outlying suburbs of the metropolitan area; there had also been a vast growth in the number of New Yorkers of great wealth. According to the income tax returns for 1928, there were as many as 243 people in New York State with incomes of a million dollars a year or more; presumably the great majority of these people lived in the city or its environs. New York had become the new frontier, the land of promise which beckoned to rich and poor the country over. It is a characteristic fact that of our fifty financiers, not more than sixteen had been born in New York City or its immediate environs. (Of the others, twenty-one were born in the Eastern States; eleven came from the Middle West, West, or South; two were born in Germany.) Rare was a dinner-party of the prosperous at which a majority of the guests were native New Yorkers. Society was swamped by sheer numbers.

Another reason for the change in the social texture, perhaps, was the fashion—led by those who in the early nineteen-twenties had attracted the shocked attention of the country as the "younger generation"—for carefree disregard of social conventions, for the cultivation of "amusing" people outside the almost-invisible social boundaries, for speakeasy life with its attendant social promiscuity.

Whatever the reasons may have been, prosperous New York in the latter nineteen-twenties consisted of a great confusion of loosely connected social groups. Indeed, one might with some plausibility argue that just as there were enormous opportunities for economic privilege and great wealth, but there was little accepted leadership or control among the insiders who seized these opportunities, just so there was an enormously enlarged plutocracy, without that cohesion or that firmness of tradition which characterizes an aristocracy.

In this confused social scene the financial powers of the day played varying but in the main substantial parts. Let us glance for a moment at our fifty representative men.

The great majority of them lived in what might loosely be called the Park Avenue district—reaching roughly from Fifty-ninth Street to Eighty-sixth Street and from Fifth Avenue to Lexington Avenue, Manhattan. Four of them maintained their winter headquarters in the suburbs; two of them had gone eastward in the migration of many of the well-to-do to the shores of the East River; the Morgans and George F. Baker clung conservatively to their old strongholds in the Murray Hill section, a mile or two to the south; a few others had taken up their abode in the apartment houses just north of the Grand Central Station. But most of the fifty lived farther north in Park Avenue—that monotonous street of huge packing-box apartment houses—or in Fifth Avenue, overlooking Central Park, or in the narrow side streets between Fifty-ninth and Eighty-sixth: if one marks their town houses upon a map, one finds the center of concentration to have been not far from Park Avenue and Seventy-second Street. It had moved a mile or so northward—and a little to the east—since 1905.

These fifty men were well represented in the fashionable and dignified clubs of the city. Six belonged to the Knickerbocker (three of them being Morgan partners). Fifteen belonged to the Racquet and Tennis, three to the Union, five to the Brook, eleven to the Creek, eight to the more intellectual and less fashionable Century, at least twenty-one to the New York Yacht Club, and no less than twenty-six to the Metropolitan—thereby enhancing its long-standing claim to the nickname of "millionaires' club."

Furthermore, nineteen of them belonged to the Piping Rock Club on the north shore of Long Island—a circumstance which introduces us to another characteristic fact about metropolitan men of wealth in the nineteen twenties: the extent to which this Long Island shore had become the out-of-town capital of the financiers. Naturally these fifty men had country houses as well as town houses (or apartments) ; some of them, indeed, had three or four. If one dots these out-of-town residences on a map, as many as eighteen of them will be found clustered near the northern edge of Long Island. The rest were widely scattered: there were a few in Greenwich or thereabouts, a few in northern Westchester County, or in Englewood or Morristown or Far Hills, New Jersey; or at Southampton, or at Tuxedo, or at Newport (still the headquarters of the old guard of formal metropolitan fashion) ; and there were summer homes on the Maine coast, "camps" in the Adirondacks, winter places in the South; but Long Island was definitely the favorite place for out-of-town living, especially for the bankers of the group and above all for the bankers within the Morgan sphere of influence.

Newport was very far from New York, for men whose fingers must constantly be on the financial pulse, and its social ritual was too solemnly punctilious to appeal to a free-and-easy generation. Tuxedo had no inviting waterfront. The Berkshire hills had long since ceased to attract the rich, and many of the grand estates of Lenox, with "For Sale" signs at their splendid entrances, were now growing up to weeds. On Long Island one was close to business; here were the sheltered waters of Long Island Sound for yachtsmen, here was Piping Rock—along with a dozen other clubs—for golf, here were gentle hills and pleasant valleys for riding.

The favorite sport of these fifty men, if we consider them collectively as a group, was perhaps golf, but there were many horsemen among them (and proprietors of racing stables, like William Woodward, owner of Gallant Fox) and hunters and duck-shooters and grouse-shooters; and collectively they owned twenty-eight yachts, ranging in size from little racing sailboats to Arthur Curtiss James's *Aloha* (165 feet long), George F. Baker, Jr.'s *Viking* (217 feet), J. P. Morgan's famous black *Corsair* (254 feet), and Vincent Astor's *Nourmahal* (260 feet). And as the year 1929 drew to its close, Morgan was building a new *Corsair*, 343 feet long: it was to be the largest private yacht in the world.

§ 4

"I do not scruple," wrote Anthony Trollope in his Autobiography, "to say that I prefer the society of distinguished people, and that even the distinction of wealth confers many advantages. The best education is to be had at a price as well as the best broadcloth. The son of a peer is more likely to rub his shoulders against well-informed men than the son of a tradesman. . . . The discerning man will recognize the information and the graces when they are achieved without such assistance, and will honor the owners of them the more because of the difficulties they have overcome;—but the fact remains that the society of the well-born and of the wealthy will as a rule be worth seeking."

The financial leaders of America unquestionably enjoyed the sort of cultural opportunities which Trollope described—though some had not acquired these until they had reached mature years and the patterns of their intellectual life had been set beyond the possibility of fundamental change. What sort of use did they make of these opportunities?

Here we venture upon very treacherous ground for generalizations. Certainly there were in Wall Street—particularly among the speculative plungers and their throng of eager imitators, a throng larger and more reckless in 1929 than ever before—a great many callous, money-minded vulgarians, who for all their superficial polish and their *bonhomie* were essentially thick of skin, limited in outlook, and vulgar in taste. There were also, in greater if not in predominating number, men of finer grain who yet wore the blinders of Wall Street conventionality. Of this type were hundreds of the correct young men who drifted almost inevitably into bond-selling from the approved universities, where as a matter of course they had not "cracked a book" except under the pressure of dire necessity and had been quite content with the bare passing-marks expected of privileged indolence. Pleasant of aspect—though some of them, with the passing of the years, began to look as if a season of asceticism would do them good—these men possessed that ease which is the product of social experience; they possessed also a well-trained sense of what a conventionally fastidious taste would approve in books and plays and etchings and furniture; yet in most cases they were mentally unadventurous, incurious, bound by the intellectual fetters of their class, slaves to the economic and political and social orthodoxy of the moment. Culturally they were willing followers, seldom contributors. Yet among them and among the diversity of other types which so large a collection of individuals must inevitably include, one found other men, especially in the higher ranks of the banking class, who had made full use of those advantages for "information and graces" to which Anthony Trollope referred. Some of these men, it might be added, were more sensitive of perception, more catholic and elastic of mind, than the majority of the radical critics who imagine all bankers to have resembled the gross, dollar-marked millionaire of the popular cartoons.

One thinks offhand of a powerful banker (a member, as it happens, of our group of fifty) who knew most of Gilbert and Sullivan by heart—and a good deal of Shakespeare as well; of another who, though he worked nine or ten hours a day under full steam of energy, yet found time to read voluminously, and could outmatch most professional publishers in first-hand knowledge and critical understanding of the current literary output; of at least two men who from time to time served as publishers' readers without pay, criticising not books on finance but fiction and memoirs; of another whose collection of modern paintings was known wherever artists and connoisseurs are found; and of other collectors—whether of paintings or books or of *objets d'art*—who combined with zeal in accumulating treasures a laboriously acquired knowledge of their significance and a genuine love of their beauties. One thinks of Morgan the Younger, to whom the enhancement of the huge collections built up by his father was not merely a duty but a pleasure. And of course one thinks of Otto Kahn, who not only was the heart and soul of the Metropolitan Opera but aided the Theatre Guild, the Provincetown Playhouse, Eva LeGallienne's Civic Repertory Theatre, and heaven only knows how many other artistic enterprises and how many individual artists and writers.

It would be grossly unfair not to recognize that men such as the best of these—men who were at home in the society of people of other nationalities and other vocations, familiar with the finest products of many cultures, and intent upon nourishing as well as enjoying that of their own country—lived up to a high tradition of the cultural function of the man of wealth and thereby helped to leaven our business man's civilization. If America was slowly coming of age culturally, if the man of means thought a little less instinctively in 1929 than in 1905 of art as something which you go to Europe to buy, if there had been real progress toward the development of native rather than derivative arts, and if there had been a little—a very little—mitigation of the common ugliness of the general American scene, to such men must go at least a share of the credit.

The pity was that there were so few of them (though there were more, perhaps, in Wall Street than in any other place where business men congregated), and that to the majority of successful American business men the stuff of which civilization is made was a mere decoration for a life dominated by the clatter of the adding-machine and the ticker.

§ 5

Another change which strikes the eye of anybody who compares the record of the financial leaders of 1905 with that of the leaders of 1929 is in religious affiliations and activities. Of the ten men in our 1905 list, at least seven were churchgoers and at least six were active in church affairs. Among the fifty men in the 1929 list, only about half either mentioned any church affiliations in *Who's Who* or were otherwise publicly known to have a part in church affairs, and the available evidence would seem to suggest that some of these affiliations were nominal. Although at least eight were actively engaged in church organizations—as wardens, vestrymen, or trustees of churches, or otherwise—it is pretty clear that the tradition that a man prominent in finance should also be prominent in the church was breaking down. This, of course, is not surprising: the churches no longer occupied so vital a place in the community as in earlier days.

That the tradition of good works had not broken down, but had simply become secularized, is however equally apparent. These fifty men made an impressive record in the holding of college trusteeships, and trusteeships or other offices in charitable institutions, settlements, hospitals, and institutions dedicated to science or to art. For example, they held, between them, no less than eighteen university or college trusteeships or directorships in educational foundations or associations. There were also, in this group of fifty men, five trustees of the Metropolitan Museum, five of the New York Public Library, three of the American Museum of Natural History, and three of the New York Zoological Society; five officers or directors of the various organizations responsible for the Metropolitan Opera, and one officer of the Philharmonic Orchestra Society.

Naturally, one reason why such men were invited to hold such positions was that they were rich. No director of a struggling charity—and nearly all charities are struggling—but yearns to have a millionaire on his board who at an opportune moment might say, "I'll take care of that." College officials, too, have been known to succumb to the temptation to woo wealth in the hope of new scholarships or a new chemical laboratory. It may be pertinent that the fifty financiers on our list had been awarded, up to 1930, a total of forty-six honorary degrees—nearly one apiece on the average! (Owen D. Young was high man, with 15; David F. Houston was second, with 8, mostly awarded while he was a member of President Wilson's cabinet; J. P. Morgan was third, with 5.) It is likely that some of these degrees were awarded in the remembrance or the hope of gifts. Yet to say this and no more, would be to misinterpret the position which these men held in the community.

They were eagerly sought after as trustees—and were awarded honorary degrees—because they were held in genuine admiration. By the great rank and file of business and professional men of what might be called the middle class, their judgment of policies and of men was considered the best that could be got. Their mere names had a great prestige value, standing as they did in the opinion of the well-to-do classes for success, power, hard sense, and reliability; and never before had this prestige value risen so high as it rose in 1929.

These men undertook their service as trustees of colleges and charities and civic institutions as their tribute— sometimes but by no means always perfunctory—to the principle of *noblesse oblige*. To this principle hundreds of men in Wall Street paid scant attention, but in the banking sector, at least, it was deeply rooted; in fact, there were so many prominent men of affairs on the boards of some of the local charities that many a young man with a shrewd eye for advancement would accept a gruelling assistant secretaryship or assistant treasurership in a local charity in the hope of falling under the appreciative eye of a grand panjandrum of the Street.

To the objective observer, the benefactions and public services of the wealthy might appear as attempts at partial reparation for the cruelties and uglinesses brought about by the order which made them rich. The objective observer might be reminded of Carnegie's giving to the cause of peace the millions which he had made manufacturing armaments. But to the men themselves such a parallel would have seemed grossly unfair. They did not regard themselves as responsible for the defects of the social order; and many of them conscientiously felt that their responsibilities to this order were being fully discharged by their services to educational and charitable and cultural enterprises.

§ 6

What of the ethical standards of the men of Wall Street in their daily work?

Here we must take leave of our list of fifty men, for we enter a realm of motive which objective facts and statistics will do little to illuminate.

At the outset of the discussion we shall do well to remind ourselves that we are dealing with thousands of men who ranged all the way from the incorruptible to the predatory; and also that this body of men was made up of various groups with different sorts of obligations and hence with different codes. The best we can do is to arrive at very tentative approximations of the prevailing standards—not of the exceptionally scrupulous or exceptionally unscrupulous, but of the rank and file of the financially powerful.

We shall do well to remind ourselves, also, of the background against which any such discussion must be carried on: the general standard of conduct of American business as a whole. So flagrant have been some of the financial operations uncovered during the past few years by the receding tide of business that many excellent people have come to believe that Wall Street was a haunt of natural villains, of men of lower principle than elsewhere. To believe this is to forget how widespread in the business world as a whole was and is the doctrine of anything for profit.

This doctrine perverts selling into an effort to unload goods by hook or by crook, regardless of the real advantage of the purchaser. It perverts advertising into a blast of half-truths and soothsayers' myths such as the radio pours daily into millions of ears. It perverts business-getting into a contest in the offering of favors and inducements; indeed, so instinctively does the average American male take for granted the inevitability of such offers that when a business man is caught giving a bribe to a public official, the recipient may be condemned but the giver seldom is: the implicit verdict of public opinion is that he was only doing what other business men would do in his place. The doctrine of anything for profit perverts the labor policies of companies large and small into an effort to get the utmost in production with the least in concessions. It perverts legislation into a compromise between the objectives of paid lobbyists working for the advantage of various business groups without the slightest concern for the general public interest. Few are the American corporations, large or small, which could submit all their transactions to the examination of Ferdinand Pecora's accountants, and all their policies to the glaring light of a congressional investigation, without a tremor of uneasiness. The generally prevailing standard of ethics of American business is perhaps not much higher than that succinctly expressed by Mayor Jimmy Walker of New York when Governor Franklin Roosevelt was examining him on the witness stand at Albany: "I don't think it is ethical for anybody to do anything illegal."

Never, perhaps, has the distinction between disinterested service and profit-hunting greed been so obscured by the haze of sentimental adulation for business success as in the nineteen-twenties; but the profit imperative was nothing new in our life. Look at the image of Uncle Sam —a smart trader indeed, if his appearance does not belie his character—and you will realize how long it has been accepted as characteristically American.

It is probable that the general average of character and

scruple was as high in the financial world as elsewhere in American business during the period which we are discussing; that, man for man, the financiers had at least as keen a sense of honor as one would be likely to find among the business men of the average small city. The only question is whether their principles were commensurate with their great opportunities and powers.

Another fact must be borne in mind. In almost every occupation one will notice that the relations among those who are engaged in it are on a higher standard than their relations with their customers or clients. The code of medical ethics, for example, is in effect largely a code of fair practice between physicians, for their mutual benefit; the protection of the patient is a secondary consideration. So with the elaborate codes of ethics drawn up by many trade associations: the primary purpose is to prevent men within the trade from damaging the business of their fellows. Just so in the financial world. There are many matters in which the standards are very high because they have to be, or everybody in the Street would suffer. For example, all transactions on the Stock Exchange are oral. When one man on the crowded floor of the Exchange offers a hundred shares of Steel at 42 and another man says "Take it," no documents are exchanged, yet there is no question in the mind of either man that this sale is as valid as if it were embodied in a written contract. Millions of dollars' worth of securities thus change hands every day at Broad and Wall Streets. Or consider the way in which orders involving hundreds of thousands of dollars are casually negotiated by telephone; or, if you prefer, how completely any depositor may take for granted that his bank will keep the tally of his balance honestly. The standard of integrity in such matters has long been very high, and naturally so; for otherwise it would be impossible for the bulk of financial business to be carried on.

Also it can hardly be denied that in certain of the established relationships between those inside the financial world and those outside it, the standard of decency had on the whole risen. For example, the attitude of men powerful in industrial management toward their employees was on the whole somewhat more civilized in the nineteen-twenties than a generation earlier. This, to be sure, is not to say much: the story of American industrial relations is one of the blackest chapters of American history. Nor had the advance, such as it was, come about without much pressure of outside opinion—without bitter labor warfare, long agitation, and the passage of humane laws opposed and defied by numerous employers. Yet there had developed, on the whole, a somewhat more decent regard for the safety and health of employees and for the provision of tolerable living conditions for their families. Enlightened men like William Cooper Procter, Henry S. Dennison, and Henry B. Endicott and George F. Johnson had done much to offset the disgraceful record of coal and steel companies which still regarded the laborer as a serf, to be fenced within his slatternly company town and terrorized into acquiescence by hired guards. There was even, during the nineteen-twenties, considerable lip-service paid to the idea that the worker was after all a consumer and that the payment to him of adequate wages might be advantageous in the long run to industries dedicated to the principle of mass production and therefore dependent upon wide markets.

Again, there were certain distinct improvements in the relations between the insiders of the big corporations and their stockholders. The managers of concerns like the General Motors Corporation were publishing more adequate and comprehensible financial statements than had been offered to stockholders of the preceding generation, and their example was being more and more generally followed; the New York Stock Exchange itself was working to make the publication of quarterly reports the accepted practice among the larger companies, to the advantage of the proxy-signers.

Yet the new corporate devices which now flourished opened up whole new areas for irresponsibility and rascality on the part of insiders. Just as the corporation lawyer is usually two jumps ahead of the legislator, so is he often two jumps ahead of his own conscience and that of the banker or corporation executive whom he serves—to say nothing of the public conscience, which generally is not heard from at all until the dubious practices in question have been exhumed in the ruins of a disaster, at which moment the public flies into a brief and indiscriminate fury. These new areas for irresponsibility and rascality—some of which have been surveyed in previous chapters of this book—were very inviting; and as yet there were few exhibits of the possible dire results of invading them, to serve as warnings to men who stood at their borders. The visibility was not so good in 1928 and 1929 as in 1932 and 1933.

Furthermore, the long-sustained rise in the value of securities and the generally rising trend of profits were enough to dull any but the keenest conscience. For example, the insider who speculated in the shares of his own company—unloading stock upon men and women to whom, as a director or an officer of the company, he stood in a responsible position—could easily excuse such a performance to himself with the argument that before long the stock would look dirt cheap at the price. Or the insider who did a little juggling with the accounts of corporate subsidiaries could argue to himself that earnings would be bound to go up next year and that all he was doing was anticipating the future. Or the banker who lent his depositors' money to the bank's affiliated investment company and then speculated with it could argue that all he was doing was putting the depositors' money to its most fruitful use. Specious arguments, all of them, yet they go far to explain the general relaxation of the financial conscience in the warm airs of prosperity. No Pied Piper of Hamelin ever made more tempting music than the stock tickers of 1929.

As for the effect of these temptations upon the conduct of even the better sort of men in the financial world, we need only to listen to the restrained words of Justice Harlan F. Stone of the United States Supreme Court, speaking at the dedication of the Law Quadrangle at the University of Michigan in June, 1934:

"I venture to assert that when the history of the financial era which has just drawn to a close comes to be written, most of its mistakes and its major faults will be ascribed to the failure to observe the fiduciary principle. . . . No thinking man can believe that an economy built upon a business foundation can permanently endure without some loyalty to that principle. The separation of ownership from management, the development of the corporate structure so as to vest in small groups control over the resources of a great number of small and uninformed investors, make imperative a fresh and active devotion to that principle if the modern world of business is to perform its proper function. Yet those who serve nominally as trustees, but relieved, by clever legal devices, from the obligation to protect those whose interests they purport to represent; corporate officers and directors who award themselves huge bonuses from corporate funds without the assent or even the knowledge of their stockholders; reorganization committees created to serve interests of others than those whose securities they control; financial institutions which, in the infinite variety of their operations, consider only last, if at all, the interests of those whose funds they command, suggest how far we have ignored the necessary implications of that principle. The loss and suffering inflicted on individuals, the harm done to a social order founded upon business and dependent upon its integrity, are incalculable."

§7

Another source of mischief in the financial world, and indeed the larger business world—even among men of probity—was the very prevalent reliance upon what might be called laissez-faire ethics, under circumstances which rendered such a code inadequate.

According to the accepted rules of free competitive business in a laissez-faire economy, each man serves his own interest, and the law of supply and demand takes care of the results. Business is a game, and to let slip an opportunity to score a point in this game is as needless—indeed, as foolish—as for a tennis player soft-heartedly to let slip an opportunity for a smash at the net. I make the best bargain I can for myself; it's up to the other fellow to do the same for himself. My corporation is out to clean up big profits, and the way to do this is to buy as cheap as possible—whether goods or services—and sell as dear as possible. If my margin of profit is large, that is something which the law of supply and demand will ultimately take care of in the public interest: competitors will come in and force prices down. Meanwhile I naturally take advantage of every opportunity that comes my way. Likewise the stock market is a game. Unless everybody takes every opportunity to buy low and sell high, speculation will not perform its traditional function of stabilizing prices. If I buy at a hundred and sell at a hundred and fifty, the fortunes of the man who buys from me at the higher price are no affair of mine. He may suffer, but that's all a part of the game: the smartest man wins; he ought to win. After all, I do not force anybody to buy that stock from me at a hundred and fifty. The buyer takes it of his own free will. And if, as it happens, I have knowledge or power which gives me the edge over him—well, isn't that the way life is?

This code was a very comfortable one to do business by. It made self-interest almost identical with the public interest.

The trouble with it was that there were considerable areas of the national economy in which it was no longer valid. It depended for its validity upon the free play of supply and demand, and in these areas the law of supply and demand had been at least partially nullified. Here are some of the things which had worked to nullify it:

1. The control of prices by big corporations, through monopolies, secret pools, or other arrangements, so that the going price was not a competitive price.

2. The fact that large-scale production not merely deprived the worker of ownership of the tools of his trade (the ancient lament of the unionist) but collected him and his fellows in huge groups, often isolated from other factories or businesses which might employ him, and powerless to reach them. The law of supply and demand, as applied to labor, naturally presupposes that the laborer, if offered an inadequate wage or laid off, can go elsewhere to seek employment. But suppose he is a penniless miner in a West Virginia mining town, in debt to his company (which may not necessarily mean that he has been improvident) and with a family on his hands? Or suppose he is a steel worker in a town hundreds of miles from the nearest other mill? In such circumstances the

law of supply and demand is a mockery, no matter how pretty it may sound in the mouths of academic lecturers.

3. The power of propaganda: a very great power which, as we noted in Chapter VIII, was available to those who had plenty of money to spend on advertising and on what were known as "educational campaigns."

4. The power of political influence, going in some cases so far as to put the police under corporation control. (This, if we regard business competition as a game, was tantamount to bribing the umpire.)

5. The stimulation of speculative markets by groups of manipulators so strategically situated and so well equipped with funds that for a time, at least, they exercised a controlling influence. What becomes of the law of supply and demand in a market of which it is commonly said, "Stocks don't go up—they're put up"?

These and other forces—such as we have seen at work in earlier chapters of this book—were undermining the validity of laissez-faire economics, the economics of free competition. Naturally they undermined also the validity of laissez-faire ethics. Increase the size and power of a corporation sufficiently, or combine under one management a whole hierarchy of corporations—such, for example, as Insull's—and you have a force at large which, if its managers live by the code of *sauve qui peut* and their urge for profits does not happen to coincide with the public interest, may be as dangerous to the citizenry as a ten-ton truck at large on a crowded city street. The law of supply and demand may not be able to stop it until the damage has long been done.

Though there was much sheer rascality in the Wall Street of the nineteen-twenties, much sheer greed roaming at large, and a widespread betrayal of the fiduciary principle, it may be that none of these things did as much damage to the country, in the sum total, as the sheer irresponsibility of men who, possessing vast powers, played the game of profit and loss without regard for the general public interest. To say that such men were not deliberate plunderers, that they were—as a jury has said of Samuel Insull—not guilty of fraud, is not to say the last word about them. They were living by a code no longer adequate for men whose decisions swung such collossal weight.

They were able men, nearly all of them; wise men, many of them. They were not quite wise enough to realize what they and their like had done to revolutionize American life, and what new responsibilities to their fellow countrymen now rested upon their shoulders.

§ 8

The golden summer of 1929 drew toward its close. Stock-market prices roared higher and ever higher. Investment trusts were being born every minute: a Wall Street broker estimated that sixty per cent of the financing done in the month of August was for these trusts. Sober citizens were becoming persuaded that a panicless, depressionless era had begun. Never had the well-groomed men of Wall Street trod their narrow canyon among the skyscrapers with mightier assurance.

Labor Day, 1929, came on the second of September. It was a very hot day in the East. The congestion of holiday-makers returning to New York City that evening was unprecedented. Fifty thousand automobiles clogged the highways of New Jersey, inching their way toward the bottle-neck of the Holland Tunnel; at midnight, sweltering men and women by the scores were abandoning the attempt to drive home and were parking their cars in Jersey City and Newark and riding to Manhattan through the stifling Tube. The congestion had broken a

record, announced the newspapers. This was prosperity. . . .

But the next day—an even hotter day, with the tem-
perature edging up to 94.2—a rather more important
record was broken. It was on that third of September
that the Stock Exchange price averages reached their
highest point of all time.

There were no big headlines to mark the event; what
were new highs to the headline-writers then? It was only
long afterwards that the significance of that torrid September day became clear. It was the moment when the
wave of prosperity, Coolidge-Hoover prosperity, specu-
lation-driven prosperity, insiders' prosperity, reached its
towering peak.

Chapter Thirteen

DOWNFALL AND CONFUSION

WHEN a wave breaks, it is the top that crashes first. Watch a great roller surging in upon a shelving shoal. It may seem to be about to break several times before it really does; several times its crest may gleam with white, and yet the wall of water will maintain its balance and sweep on undiminished. But at last the wall becomes precariously narrow. The shoal trips it. The crest, crumbling over once more, topples down, and what was a serenely moving mass of water becomes a thundering welter of foam.

When the American economic system broke, it was likewise the top that broke first: the crazily inflated structure of common-stock values which had been built up in the speculative madness of the Bull Market. Several times this structure had toppled—just as the crest of a roller curls over—in the successive stock-market breaks of June, 1928, of December, 1928, and of March, 1929; prices had cascaded down and thousands of speculators had been caught in the spate; yet each time the structure had recovered its balance and had lifted itself higher and yet higher. When, in the early autumn of 1929, another cascade of prices began, most observers supposed that, at the worst, these earlier episodes would once more be repeated. There would be a brief storm of selling, prices would drop thirty or forty or fifty points, a few thousand insecurely margined traders would lose everything, but the wave of values and of stock-market credit would catch its balance again and move forward. That the whole wave would go crashing down seemed almost inconceivable.

For a brief interval these observers seemed to be right. Prices broke early in September—very soon after that sweltering day when the pinnacle of prices had been reached—and recovered. They broke again, later in the month. The cascade continued in October, with added volume because the collapse of Hatry's speculative schemes in England had prompted European selling. It grew more and more torrential. And at last on Wednesday, October 23, the volume of liquidation became genuinely disturbing. Over six million shares changed hands, the ticker fell 104 minutes behind in its attempt to record immediately all the transactions on the floor of the Exchange, and the decline in prices was very severe.

Even then, however, there were few observers who anticipated what was to follow. The brokers' offices all over the country were crowded with worried traders, but among them there were many who were saying to themselves that this would be the very moment to buy—if one had the money; that this was the culmination of the worst break since the Bull Market had begun, and that presently the march of speculative prosperity would begin once more.

They did not realize how completely the whole structure of stock-market values had become honeycombed with brokers' loans. Still less did they realize that the wave of stock-market prosperity was running upon a shoal. The construction industry had been weakening since 1928, for in the Florida boom and the various winter-resort and summer-resort and suburban booms which had followed it, more houses had been built than could be paid for, and even the craze for putting up higher and higher skyscrapers in the great cities could not maintain the industry at its former pace of operations. The automobile industry had begun to slow up in the early summer of 1929, and with it the steel industry. The furious drive for bigger and bigger profits, and the financial inflation which was predicated upon the continuance of such profits, had prevented the distribution of the fruits of prosperity in the form of higher wages or lower prices, and thus the general purchasing power had become overstrained. In fact, so topheavy had the American economy become that only the lavish expenditures of the fortunate and the extravagant resort of the somewhat less fortunate to installment buying and other forms of personal credit were maintaining business at its full volume. But the speculators were unaware of the full meaning of the slight downturn in the business indices. And still less, of course, did they or anybody else realize to what far-reaching destruction any serious collapse in the stock-market might ultimately lead.

It was the very next day—Thursday, October 24, 1929 —at a little after ten o'clock in the morning, that the wave broke.

What happened that day is highly instructive as we view it in retrospect. In the first place, it seems well established that what brought down the avalanche was no attack of concerted short-selling; the amount of short-selling was small. What brought it down was the inexorable working of the very machinery of gambling which had facilitated the previous advance. When a margin speculator pays, let us say, only thirty dollars to buy a hundred-dollar share of stock, and his broker borrows the other seventy dollars to complete the purchase, the broker shares neither the speculator's gains nor his losses. If the price of the stock goes up to one hundred and thirty, the speculator has a nice hundred-per-cent profit. If it goes down to seventy, he has a not-so-nice hundred-per-cent loss. And more than that—if the stock goes down to seventy and the speculator is unable to put up any more cash, the broker inevitably sells the stock to rescue his own seventy dollars. The process is virtually automatic. When in a crowded market the prices of speculative common stocks slide down simultaneously, the money put up by thousands of speculators is exhausted and their brokers rush to sell. Unless there are other thousands of people standing ready to buy—and these other men are not frightened by the torrent of selling—a panic (large or small) almost automatically develops.

That is what happened on a huge scale on the morning of that doomsday of Wall Street prosperity, October 24, 1929. There was a vast flood of simultaneous selling orders. There were not enough people standing ready to buy. Prices did not merely decline—they fell hard and fast. Anxious traders took fright and sold in sheer alarm. Whereupon prices plunged downward as if bound for a bottomless abyss.

America was beginning to pay the inevitable price for a long chain of events: the general acceptance of the theory that the way to prosperity was through having as many people as possible buy securities which could be converted into cash at short notice; the acceptance of the theory that the way to make such instant conversion possible was through encouraging margin speculation; the widespread craze for common stocks as the cream of investments—and of vehicles for margin speculation; and the consequent conversion of the market for common stocks into a great gambling casino.

Some of the losses on that morning of October 24 were staggering. Though United States Steel, which a few weeks before had been selling for more than $260 a share and had opened today at 205½, slid down only to 193½, there were other more abrupt nose-dives. Radio, for example, opened at 68¾ and within three frenzied hours was selling at 44½. Montgomery Ward, which had opened at 83, coasted to 50. The volume of trading was terrific. The ticker fell so far behind that its report became almost useless to board-room traders. The telephone system of the Exchange was hopelessly clogged with frantic inquiries. This was panic indeed, sudden, bewildering, appalling.

But another instructive thing happened that day. Shortly after noon a group of Wall Street bankers met at the House of Morgan to form a pool for the support of the market. Thomas W. Lamont was there, representing the Morgan firm; the others were William C. Potter of the Guaranty Trust Company, Seward Prosser of the Bankers Trust Company, and two other gentlemen whose exploits we have specifically noted in a previous chapter of this book—Albert H. Wiggin of the Chase National Bank and Charles E. Mitchell of the National City Bank. The moment that the word got about that these men were on their way to the rescue, the rout stopped and a quick rally took its place. Wall Street—and with it the great company of the prosperous—still believed in the omnipotence of its gods.

The illusion was brief. For the rest of that day and the two succeeding days the market almost held its own, but not quite; on the following Monday the avalanche began again with such fury that all the bankers' pool could do was to try, by intervening now and then where there were no purchasers at all, to prevent utter demoralization. On Tuesday, October 29, the avalanche reached its maximum force; more than sixteen million shares were sold and the losses in value were enormous. Nor was that catastrophic day the last one of the panic. A rally was followed by further liquidation, and this liquidation continued until November 13.

By that time some thirty billion dollars in capital values had vanished into thin air. If you find such an immense sum almost meaningless, reflect that it was almost as great as the entire cost to the United States of the war against Germany; that it was about ten times as great as the cost to the Union of the Civil War; and that it was considerably greater than the national debt. An overwhelming loss—and the irony of it was that a good deal of it represented money which had already been spent as income by fortunate speculators as the market went up: spent on automobiles and radios, and part payments on houses, and innumerable other purchases which had helped to keep the wheels of industry rolling.

It must clearly be borne in mind that it was the prosperous upon whom fell the brunt of this body blow at the American economy. To be sure there were thousands of stenographers, clerks, janitors, and even day laborers whose painfully acquired savings had gone over the dam; but broadly speaking it was the rich who were soaked—directly. It was stock-brokers and promoters who were committing suicide in October and November of 1929, not unemployed clerks and laborers. Indeed, there were millionaires in those days who looked through the windows of their Rolls Royces with a new envy at the crowds of wage-earners in the streets—the lucky poor who were losing nothing in this catastrophe! The fact that the rich were the immediate victims of the panic helps, perhaps, to explain some of the lavish dividend disbursements of American corporations in 1930. Directors who voted for higher dividends in a season when their companies were dismissing workmen were not simply adhering to the philosophy of prosperity through big profits, not simply trying to re-establish the prestige of their companies among investors; they also, one suspects, felt that they were recompensing the chief losers in the débâcle of 1929.

Yet it must also be borne in mind that the indirect effects of the crash were far-reaching. Luxury businesses were hard hit. The fashionable dress-shops were suddenly almost empty. Chauffeurs, maids, gardeners were dismissed. The demand for automobiles and radios and furniture and other expensive goods fell off, and with it, the demand for materials which went into them. Frightened lest their goods pile up on their shelves and uncertain of the future, manufacturers cut down on their production. Thus unemployment rapidly increased; from Maine to California, factories began letting men go.

And of course the panic had a further effect: the whole precarious edifice of values which had been built into the financial system was shaken. The ubiquitous investment trusts were shaken. The pyramided holding companies which had written up their holdings were shaken. Flimsily financed real-estate and building developments were shaken. Every bank which had an up-to-date investment affiliate or had lent money in quantity against stock collateral was shaken. Every other company which was dependent upon the business of such concerns felt the shock. People still talked as if a speculative stock market were something apart from the rest of the national economy; a loud and wishful chorus of financiers and public men, led by the president of the United States, chanted in unison that no matter what happened in Wall Street, business conditions were "fundamentally sound"; yet when an earthquake took place in Wall Street its tremors inevitably ran far and wide.

§ 2

President Hoover now swung into action.

What he did, if we judge it by the prevailing economic philosophy of the time, was on the whole highly reasonable. He called to the White House a large group of insiders—bankers and industrialists—and labor leaders as well. He urged these men to continue business as usual. The industrialists were not to cut wages, not to abandon construction programs. The labor leaders were to refrain from rocking the boat. Wide publicity was given to the agreement of these men to go along as if nothing had happened. In order to encourage the rich to scatter prosperity about once more, Hoover asked Congress to cut the income tax. He also advocated a public-works campaign to take up any possible slack in employment, thus taking a leaf out of a different book of economics. And he continued, as did everybody else, to assert that conditions were fundamentally sound and becoming sounder. Under his baton, the chorus of insistence that everything was all right, that business was going ahead, that prosperity—in the well-worn phrase of the day—was "just around the corner," became almost deafening. If loudly expressed wishes had been horses, the American people would have ridden to wealth at a full gallop.

And what happened? The pool managers in Wall Street scrambled to their feet and began to push stocks up again. During the late winter and the early spring of 1930 there was a bull market of considerable dimensions; the volume of trading actually became for a time as great as in the summer of 1929.

It was piously believed in those days that the American public had "learned a great lesson" in the disaster of the preceding autumn, yet apparently to hundreds of thousands of people the lesson of the disaster was that the bright thing to do was to buy early and sell at the top. The prices of some of the favored securities mounted fast and far. By April, 1930, for example, Steel was once more nudging the 200 mark and American Telephone and General Electric had almost reached their preposterous pre-panic heights.

Though unemployment remained severe and the bread-lines in the streets were longer than at the worst of the post-war depression of 1921, stock-market-minded business men hoped and half believed that this was but a temporary trouble: did not the graphs of security prices on the financial pages show an encouraging up-trend? Many corporations, as we have already noted, increased their dividend rates; the total amount of money paid out in dividends was only three per cent less in 1930 than in 1929. New investment trusts were coming to birth, and the pattern which prevailed among them hardly suggested any widespread doubt in the resumption of old-style prosperity; for most of them were "fixed trusts," the managers of which were to invest in the stocks of the leading corporations of the country (as of 1930) and were not to be permitted to change these investments unless the corporations in question passed their dividends. Tom, Dick, and Harry were cheerfully buying participations in these curiously rigid trusts. Why shouldn't they? They knew enough economics to know that business ebbed and flowed in cycles; if you knew economics, you knew that the time to buy was after a panic, and that it was the leading corporations of the country that were likely to prosper most in the bull market of the nineteen-thirties.

Something was wrong, however. Business was not actually gaining; it was barely holding its own at a volume considerably less than that of 1929. Presently it began definitely to lose ground. The speculators who had learned the great lesson of the panic hastened to sell. In May, 1930, the stock market collapsed again. And presently the depression entered a new phase—the long, grinding, inexorable, almost uninterrupted disintegration of late 1930 and 1931 and early 1932.

§ 3

Let us try to analyze what was happening in those dolorous years of 1930 and 1931 and 1932.

The analysis cannot be simple, clear cut, dogmatic; for the sequence of cause and effect in our world of endlessly involved mutual relationships is exceedingly complex.

We must remember, in the first place, the continued existence of various distortions in the American economy which had made the recovery and prosperity of the country during the nineteen-twenties an astonishing achievement against odds. We must remember how curiously our foreign trade was balanced—that the only way in which we had been able to permit Europe to buy our goods was by lending her huge amounts of capital, and that obviously this could not keep up indefinitely. We must remember that the farmers who grew our staple crops had never fully recovered from the distress into which the collapse of their overseas markets had plunged them shortly after the war; and that as soon as industry languished, the country as a whole was likely to feel the dragging weight of a comparatively impoverished farming population.

Nor must we overlook the fact that the economic breakdown of the early nineteen-thirties was not simply an American phenomenon, but was world-wide. Europe in particular, staggering under a terrific burden of debts incurred during the war, and hampered by trade barriers built up by bitter national rivalries, had never enjoyed any such boom in the nineteen-twenties as had the United States, and was now drifting into a fresh economic crisis. This was bound to prolong and intensify the American crisis.

But it is doubtful if any of these factors—or all of them together—quite explain a breakdown as cumulative and appalling as that which actually took place. Let us look for other clues.

One of these clues is the increase in efficiency which was being brought about by improved methods of manufacture and of business, and especially by the machine—above all by the power-driven machine. As we have already noted (in Chapter VIII) machines were constantly replacing men. A given number of people were becoming able to produce and distribute more and more goods. There is no need to present specific illustrations of this fact; the Technocrats of 1932 deluged the country with them. But it may not be amiss to remark that the tendency toward technological unemployment about which the Technocrats talked so furiously was not confined to industry; consider, for example, how the output of American farms had been increased by the use of huge reapers and combines and also by the spread of knowledge about better farming methods; or consider how machinery and improved organization had likewise speeded up work in business offices. That the machine was an instrument for the production of plenty is undeniable—but that its increasing use was attended by economic strain is also undeniable. During the seven fat years the men whom it had thrown out of work had been absorbed in other occupations: the man who had lost his job in a textile mill became an apartment-house janitor, the man who had been fired from the automobile factory ran a filling station, and so on. But the strain was there—and it was just barely met.

To meet it, the American economy had to expand. There had to be constant growth—new factories, new construction, new industries, new occupations, new expenditures. The moment this expansion stopped for any reason, the American economy would begin, so to speak, to die at the roots—to suffer from an increasing technological unemployment. Prosperity had to go ahead very fast to stay in the same place.

For years past, this expansion had been achieved with the aid of a huge inflation of credit, and in particular with the aid of the speculative boom in real estate and then of the boom in the stock market. It was as if a huge bellows were blowing upon the industrial system of the country, making the fires burn brightly. Meanwhile, however, this expansion had had other effects—and they, too, are clues to what happened when the bellows ceased to blow.

For one thing, it had helped to bring about an immense increase in the internal debt of the country. One needs only to glance at the tabulations in Evans Clark's study of *The Internal Debts of the United States* to realize what a change had been brought about by the "investment consciousness" of the American people, plus the urgent salesmanship of the dispensers of securities and of life-insurance policies, plus the new financial gadgets of the time, plus the reckless optimism of the boom years. During these years, to quote Mr. Clark's book, we had "piled up our debts almost three times as fast as our wealth and income increased." While our wealth was growing only by an estimated 20 per cent, and our income by an estimated 29 per cent, the total amount of our long-term debt had been growing by an estimated 68 per cent—from 76 billion dollars to 126 billion dollars. A large increase? Yes, and it had come on top of another large increase during the war years. If we compare the long-term debt of the United States in 1929 with that in 1913-14, we find the increase in fifteen or sixteen years to have been no less than 232 per cent!

Part of this huge accretion was due to the same factor which had placed such a heavy burden of indebtedness upon Europe—the war. The Federal Government's debt was 1154 per cent larger in 1929 than in 1913-14. But the states and the smaller governmental units had also increased their obligations—by 248 per cent. And business, too, had succeeded in cumbering itself with fixed claims of unprecedented magnitude. The debt of the railroads had not increased very much, if only because they had been notoriously over-bonded in 1913-14; here the gain amounted to a mere 26 per cent. But meanwhile the total debt of the public utilities had grown by 181 per cent; the debt of industrial concerns, by 172 per cent; the debt of financial concerns (including especially investment trusts and insurance companies) by 389 per cent; and a series of real-estate booms had lifted the total amount of urban mortgages by no less than 436 per cent.

Now it is obvious that no man can say with certainty how large a burden of debt an economic system can carry. No man can say with assurance that this vastly enlarged debt was enough to break the American system. For one thing, one man's debt is another man's wealth. Yet here was at least a potential source of strain: a rigid structure of claims—many of them imprudent—in an otherwise highly flexible economy.

Nor was this mass of outright debt the only source of strain. There was also the huge body of claims upon future earning-power represented by issues of stock. The wild financial expansion during the nineteen-twenties had multiplied these claims. Many of them, as we noted in Chapter XI, did not represent any substantial investment of money in the companies against whose earnings they were a charge, but represented stock bonuses to insiders or the issue of stocks for "services." Again and again, in this book, we have noted the extent to which dividend claims—as well as debt claims—set up in the boom years were based upon hopes of steady fair weather in the future. Investment trusts and holding companies, for example, were largely dependent upon the cream which could be skimmed off the milk of corporate earnings. Write-ups and stock-watering operations necessitated fair-weather earnings to give them the appearance of validity. The stock-market boom had built up a general expectation of high earnings which corporate managers were bound to justify if they possibly could.

The burden of claims represented by issues of stocks was not, of course, rigid; it was not outright debt; yet it was very real. Not without a bitter struggle did corporations cut—or stop altogether—their dividends. Sometimes the dividends were continued even at the risk of disaster, as for instance in the Insull public-utility system. Even in the terrific year of 1932, when the corporations of the country were collectively more than five and a half billion dollars in the red, they were still paying dividends to the extent of more than four billion dollars; and of these four billions, over a billion and a half was paid by companies which were actually losing money.

Here, then, we have two circumstances appearing in conjunction. We have an economy that must grow in order to provide jobs for Americans. And we have this growth brought about by building up a vast load of fixed debt (and of dividend claims) which the economy must carry if it can.

Now according to the old-fashioned economics of rugged individualism, there was no reason why the country could not in due course adjust itself to the ups and downs of trade. From time to time deflation might be necessary—but this deflation would shortly bring about a cure. For one thing, as purchasing power fell off, the prices of goods would drop until latent buying-power was tempted into the markets and shops and the process would reverse itself. For another thing, during any serious depression enough companies would go into bankruptcy to reduce the burden of debt until it could easily be carried. Automatic adjustments of this sort had taken place during previous depressions; business men under the domination of the respected ideas of laissez-faire economics expected them to take place again and bring early and automatic recovery. Why did this not happen?

One reason was that there were now a great many big corporations—more than in any previous depression—with heavy administrative overhead expenses and heavy investments in plant and machinery. It was hard for these concerns to reduce their administrative expenses very much, or to reduce the fixed charges on their plant or machinery at all. The wages of machinery cannot be reduced. If these companies allowed prices to slide, they could not make enough money to meet their fixed charges, to say nothing of paying dividends. They were under an overwhelming compulsion to keep prices up if they possibly could, even if this meant making and selling less goods.

Some companies could hold prices up because they possessed monopolistic power, directly or through secret agreements with their rivals (ranging all the way from gentlemen's understandings to racketeering combinations); but the same pressure of circumstances was felt by monopolies and non-monopolies alike. The easiest item of expenditure on which to save was the wage bill. They actually were better off—for a time—if they ran their factories or mills on an abbreviated schedule, or shut some of them down altogether, than if they let prices slide. The result—particularly in the capital-goods industries—was that the prices of goods did not fall so fast as did the wage bill.

Gardiner C. Means, in his pamphlet on *Industrial Prices and Their Relative Inflexibility*, throws light on what happened. Between 1929 and the spring of 1933, while the prices of agricultural commodities (responding in the orthodox way to the law of supply and demand) fell 63 per cent and the production of these commodities fell only 6 per cent, a very different sort of change was taking place in other departments of the national economy. For example:

Prices of textile products	fell 45 per cent;	production, 30 per cent
" " automobile tires	" 33 " " ;	" 70 " "
" " iron and steel	" 20 " " ;	" 83 " "
" " cement	" 18 " " ;	" 65 " "
" " motor vehicles	" 16 " " ;	" 80 " "
" " agricultural implements	" 6 " " ;	" 80 " "

According to the computations of Frederick Mills, between 1929 and 1932 the average price of capital goods as a whole fell only 20 per cent; yet production in the capital-goods industries fell 76 per cent.

The causes of this phenomenon are not wholly clear, but it seems reasonably accurate to say that in the effort to carry a load of irreducible charges, these corporations were throwing off workers—and thus were killing the goose that laid the golden egg of revival. A new burden of unemployment was being added to that which would naturally have come about anyhow as soon as the national economy ceased expanding.

But why did not the situation cure itself speedily through a succession of bankruptcies? The answer is that the financial superstructure of debt and of dividend claims had become so enormous—and so pervasive in its influence upon the whole economic structure—that the country could hardly have stood the shock of such bank-ruptcies. Here we come upon still another possible clue to the situation.

To a much greater extent than ever before in the history of the country, the investments of the country were now in liquid form—in other words, in such a form that they could quickly be turned into money. Securities were listed upon stock exchanges to a greater extent than ever before. Banks, as we have seen, had less of their funds in commercial loans and more in bonds and in loans on securities than ever before. According to the estimates of Berle and Pederson, the total of liquid claims in the United States had never amounted to more than 20 per cent of the national wealth until 1912; between 1912 and 1922 it had gone up to about 25 per cent; by 1930 it had shot up to 40 per cent. A liquid invest-ment had its advantages for the individual: he felt safer if at any moment he could turn his holdings into money. But the existence of a large proportion of liquid invest-ments enormously increased the chances of panic. When a large number of banks and of businesses were trying to unload simultaneously in the same market-place, a panicky market quickly developed. Not merely the bonds and stocks of companies which were in difficulties dropped in price, but nearly all bonds and stocks. Furi-ously as corporations were attempting to meet their fixed obligations and their unfixed dividend obligations by throwing men into unemployment, the prices of these obligations cascaded as a result of fear and of forced sales. When there was a big failure—like that of the Bank of United States at the end of 1930, or those of Insull and Kreuger in early 1932—the shock to these markets was immediately visible and for this reason all the more staggering. If the process had gone on. . . .

But it did not go on. President Hoover prevented it

from going on by calling for the formation of the Reconstruction Finance Corporation to bring first aid to harassed banks and corporations and to stop the epidemic of bankruptcies. Thus another traditional cure for a business depression was withheld. Rightly or wrongly, the property interests of the country felt that the financial system could not stand such strong medicine. The debt structure—now supported by government intervention—remained almost intact. Many long-term debts—especially mortgages—were in default, but new ones had taken their places. The cold figures show what was happening: according to the computations of Dr. Simon Kuznets for the National Bureau of Economic Research, the amount of money paid out in interest in the year 1932 was only 3.3 per cent less than in 1929—though meanwhile salaries had dropped 40 per cent, dividends had dropped 56.6 per cent, and wages had dropped 60 per cent.

Thus the American economy went into a vicious downward spiral. The cutting of wage bills meant a decrease in purchasing power; the decrease in purchasing power meant a decrease in sales; the decrease in sales made the burden of capital obligations heavier and heavier and led to further cutting of production and of wages, and so on. Nor did the owners of debt claims and of stock prosper; for as the crisis was intensified, claims which they owned were becoming less and less valuable. The capital markets were demoralized, the demoralization of the capital markets demoralized the banks, and so on through another spiral of cause and effect.

Add to this chain of circumstances the unbalanced foreign-trade situation, the depression and financial panic in Europe, the weakened economic position of the American farmers, the inherent weakness of our collection of forty-nine banking systems, the direct though belated effects of the financial abuses and excesses and frauds of the nineteen-twenties, and the stubborn belief of American business men that a turn of the business cycle would inevitably bring back prosperity if wages were permitted to drop and capitalists waited hopefully for the dawn, and you have, perhaps, a reasonably adequate explanation of the great toboggan-slide of 1930 and 1931 and 1932. The era of high finance had so swollen the mass of claims upon the future that only roaring prosperity could sustain it; and the effort to sustain it even at the cost of purchasing power undermined the foundations of that prosperity.

§ 4

It was a bitter time in which to be President of the United States. No presidential reputation can withstand an economic depression; even those people who are most insistent that the government should keep its hands off business will blame the government when business goes wrong. It was a particularly bitter time for a President who had proclaimed in his speech of acceptance that "given a chance to go forward with the policies of the last eight years, we shall soon, with the help of God, be in sight of the day when poverty will be banished from this nation." Hoover had gone forward with the Coolidge policies; Andrew Mellon, the idol of the conservative business world, was still Secretary of the Treasury; and yet disaster was descending upon the nation with cumulative force.

By the autumn of 1930, the Hoover recovery moves of late 1929 and early 1930 were clearly failing. The cut in the income tax was accentuating a mounting governmental deficit. The public works program had not gone

far—the deficit stood in its way. The President's insistence that wages must not be reduced was being widely
disregarded, and even where the wage *rate* still stood
firm, the amount of money paid out in wages was becoming smaller and smaller as factories went on part time
or shut down entirely. The Federal Farm Board's effort
to sustain the price of wheat was a dismal failure, involving the government in huge losses. And as for the campaign of synthetic optimism, by the autumn of 1930 it
was already becoming a sour jest, and by the end of 1931
a compilation of the cheerful prophecies made by Hoover
and his aides and by the leaders of business and finance,
published under the scornful title of *Oh Yeah?* was
greeted everywhere with derisive laughter.

What should the President do next?

From the middle of 1930 to the middle of 1931, he
did virtually nothing. "This was the period," George
Soule justly reminds us, "which gave rise most of all
to the legend that the depression President was a spine-
less mass of jelly in the face of the nation's difficulty,
that he was incapable of action. Yet he was pursuing a
definite policy, a policy endorsed in theory both by the
financially powerful and by the conservative economists.
It was a slightly different one from that which he had
attempted to practise at the beginning, to be sure, and
yet the two were related. The first theory had assumed
that there was nothing much the matter, and that if
everyone could be induced to believe this, there would be
no danger. The second theory had to admit that there was
something the matter: in some mysterious manner, the
system had got out of kilter. But the way to remedy the
disease was to let it run its course without interference.
The economic order was a self-compensating one, and
if left alone would get into balance." Accepting, then,

the traditional laissez-faire theory that nature must take its course, Hoover stood aside.

The expected self-compensation, however, did not take effect. All through the autumn of 1930 and the winter and the spring of 1931 the decline continued, with but a momentary flare-up of hope in midwinter as the indices of production turned briefly upward.

Then in the early summer of 1931 the débâcle went into a new phase. The debt structure in Europe cracked. The Credit Anstalt, the largest and most powerful bank in Austria, was in difficulties; the Austrian Government was trying frantically to borrow enough money to shore it up; and throughout the Continent there was spreading a wild fear that the whole fiscal system of Central Europe would go to pieces. Here, felt Hoover, was an opportunity for constructive action by an American President. He proposed a year's moratorium on governmental war debts and reparation payments. The essence of his plan was that the groaning weight of the mass of international private debt would be eased by postponing for a year all payments on the inter-governmental debt, so far as this grew out of the war and the peace settlement.

His proposal was accepted—with modifications insisted upon by the French. But although the announcement of it had provoked another outburst of hope—and of speculation for the rise on the Stock Exchange—the Hoover scheme was not enough to stop the spread of financial panic. The Austrian crisis was followed by a German crisis, and the German crisis by a British crisis; in September, 1931, England was driven off the gold standard; and by this time the panic had leaped the ocean and was raging in America too. On the New York Stock Exchange, the prices of foreign bonds of all sorts

fell hard and fast. Other bonds followed their example
as thousands of American banks and corporations and
individual investors were forced to liquidate to save
themselves. A crack in the structure of debt was proving
to be a very serious matter indeed.

In American towns where not one person in a hundred had ever heard of the Credit Anstalt, disquieting
whispers were soon running about: that the local bank
was in difficulties, that its money was tied up in bad
mortgages and depreciated bonds, that the local tire factory owed it a quarter of a million dollars and could not
pay; that the only safe thing to do was to draw your
money out and keep it in your mattress, in bills if not
in gold. Panicky millionaires were transferring their
funds to France, to Holland, to Switzerland, or were
packing their safe-deposit boxes with gold. The Federal
Reserve figures during the autumn of 1931 showed that
something like a billion dollars was being hoarded in
currency. Ever since the onset of the depression the rate
of American bank failures—a rate scandalously high even
in the nineteen-twenties—had been dismaying; but now
all previous records were broken. In September, the
month in which England left the gold standard, 305
American banks were suspended; in October, no less
than 522.

The officers of thousands of other banks, miserable
with worry lest the lines of men and women at the paying tellers' windows should suddenly grow to panic
length, were deciding to call a few more loans, to sell a
few more bonds, to make sure they had plenty of cash—
and as their selling orders converged upon the market,
the demoralization was intensified. Not only did the
pressure of liquidation play havoc with bond prices; it
also drastically reduced the amount of money in the

country. The process through which banks create money by making loans and setting up checking-accounts—the process of bankers' inflation—was now working in reverse, automatically and rapidly. In the space of eight months, the amount of money in the country was reduced by as much as twenty per cent. Some ten billions of dollars evaporated.

As fear spread—the fear of a total banking collapse, the fear that America would follow England off the gold standard, and that vague fear of the incalculable future which expressed itself in the frequently heard phrase, "If everything goes . . ."—business shrank still more. Wage-cutting was general and unashamed. Unemployment was now going from bad to worse; it was now estimated that eight or ten million men were out of work.

It was during this panic of the autumn of 1931 that Hoover decided that the American debt structure must not be permitted to fall to pieces. He called a group of financiers to Washington to form a pool of credit for the rescue of distressed capital; and presently he asked Congress to take over the task by setting up the Reconstruction Finance Corporation.

The situation which thus arose contained, perhaps, a certain element of ironic humor. Now financial magnates who still cried out for "less government in business" and inveighed against "the dole" could go, hat in hand, to Washington and get the government to put itself into business by giving a dole of credit to their banks or their railroads. The apostle of rugged individualism had taken the longest step in American history toward state socialism—though it was state socialism of a very special sort.

Yet the situation had also a graver significance. Hoover and his advisers were acknowledging that the possible consequences of letting nature take its course were too terrific to contemplate. It was not simply that they feared that the rich would be impoverished—though this fear undoubtedly colored their thoughts. It was that they feared that the debt structure was so built into the economic fabric of the country that its disintegration would result in general chaos. Banks, insurance companies, and corporations large and small would alike be paralyzed, and in the catastrophe the poor would be ruined along with the rich. And so—to borrow George Soule's phrasing once more—the government increased the rigidity of the most rigid element of the American economic system, while doing nothing to stop the decline of its most flexible element.

Hoover also made or encouraged other moves to stop the spread of destruction. He fought hard to balance the Federal budget, believing that a return of confidence in the ability of the government to pay its bills would lead to a return of general confidence in the system which was collapsing; and in the spring of 1932 the Federal Reserve Board, having successfully protected the bulk of American banks from collapse until the Reconstruction Finance Corporation could aid in the work of rescue, did its best to inflate bank credit once more by open-market purchases of securities, hoping thus to prepare the way for a resumption of investments. But the budget could not be surely balanced without heavier taxes than Congress was willing to levy; meanwhile the general distress of the country was intensified by the fact that private charity and state relief could no longer pay the mounting cost of caring for the jobless unless the Federal government would help; and as for the Reserve Board's open-market policy, though it eased the situation somewhat for the stronger banks, it failed utterly to bring about a resumption of investment. The financial system of the country was still too shaken.

For Hoover, the struggle was a prolonged nightmare. He was being utterly defeated—not because he was stupid or indecisive or pig-headed so much as because the best devices of orthodox economics were helpless to meet the turn of events.

§ 5

By the first day of July, 1932—the day when the Democratic delegates at Chicago, "stupefied," as Walter Lippmann put it, "by oratory, brass bands, bad air, perspiration, sleeplessness, and soft drinks," nominated Governor Franklin Delano Roosevelt of New York for the Presidency—the economic condition of the nation had become truly appalling.

American business as a whole was deep in the red, despite its furious efforts to save itself. The *New York Times* Index of Business Activity stood at almost exactly 50 per cent of its 1929 high. And the number of people unemployed was variously estimated at 13, 14, or 15 millions. (Cold, impersonal figures, those unemployment estimates; what they represented in frustration, demoralization, hunger, and suffering no statistics could even suggest.)

Three and a half years before, when the wave of stock-market prosperity had first curled over and broken, it had seemed to the bankers and brokers of Wall Street that—in the phrase of the day—"stocks had fallen all the way to the bottom." Now it seemed to them, by contrast, as if the avalanche of 1929 had been halted on a plateau far up the mountainside. A few specific quotations will point the contrast.

	High price on Sept. 3, 1929—before the Panic	Low price on Nov. 13, 1929—after the Panic	Low price for the year 1932
American Can	181⅞	86	29⅝
American Telephone & Telegraph	304	197¼	70¼
General Electric	396¼	168½	34 *
General Motors	72¾	36	7⅝
New York Central..................	256⅜	160	8¾
Radio Corporation	101	26	2½
United States Steel..................	261¾	150	21¼

* Adjusted to put the price on the same basis as the previous figures. The actual low price for 1932 was 8½, but meanwhile the shares had been split 4 for 1.

Nor was the bond market in better shape. Forced liquidation and panic had reduced the prices of 40 leading bonds listed on the Stock Exchange to an average of 41.39 per cent of par. The newspapers had been accustomed to print graphs to show the trend of bond prices; now these graphs had to be elongated at the bottom to allow the line which represented prices to pursue its jaggedly precipitous downward path.

The mighty corporate structures of the super-finance of the nineteen-twenties were wobbling. Insull's pyramid had already fallen. The Van Sweringens were deeply in debt to the House of Morgan, and their Alleghany Corporation was in such shape that the price of its common stock had sunk to thirty-seven and a half cents a share. The Transamerica Corporation, representing the Giannini pyramid of banks and other enterprises, was quoted at a low for the year of 1932 of 2⅛. Most of the investment trusts into which investors had crowded to put their money in 1929 now showed staggering losses. So many banks were in straits that sober bankers were arguing that bank examiners ought to delay their tours of inspection; and the president of Hoover's Reconstruction Finance Corporation, Charles G. Dawes, had had to resign his position in order that the R.F.C. might authorize the lending of ninety million dollars to prop up his bank.

Public confidence in the men of the financial world was obviously falling fast, as the values of securities which had been distributed among investors during the boom years approached the vanishing point. The receding tide of business was uncovering corruption in the management of bank after bank, and even banking firms of unquestioned honor were losing their reputation for sagacity: had not Kreuger, the Swedish match king, twisted a group of conservative men round his finger and made them innocent partners in his gigantic frauds?

The men of Wall Street themselves were bewildered. They did not know whom or what to rely upon. When Andrew Mellon left the Secretaryship of the Treasury early in 1932 to become Ambassador to England, his departure caused hardly a flurry on the troubled waters of the stock-market. A few years before it would have caused a near-panic, but Wall Street was now losing faith even in its own gods. Fear was everywhere: once there had been no more rapturous optimist in the business world than Charles M. Schwab, but now—in April, 1932—he was quoted as saying, "I'm afraid, every man is afraid. I don't know, we don't know, whether values we have are going to be real next month or not."

One by one, the pet economic theories of the Street had been annihilated. The theory of the business cycle (as most financiers had interpreted it)—the theory that business ebbed and flowed in such a way that the business man who watched the statistical indices carefully could buy at the bottom and prosper—had betrayed its faithful adherents again and again; indeed, one of the things which had helped to defeat this theory was perhaps the very fact that it was so widely believed in. The theory that forecasters could forecast was a wreck. The theory that common stocks were a satisfactory medium for long-term investment was a wreck. Indeed, so general was the intellectual wreckage in the world of conservative economics that it was hardly surprising to hear one of the ablest leaders in the banking world confess, in a newsreel talk, "As for the cause of the depression, or the way out, you know as much as I do." Thus had the mighty fallen.

Looking for a scapegoat to blame for what was happening, Wall Street found it in Congress. Every time a Congressman proposed an inflationary program, Wall Street shivered and prices took another tumble. One might have supposed that the prospect of inflation would tend to lift the prices of equities; but no, the fear which possessed the men of property had become wild and unreasoning.

The rest of the country was bewildered too. Here and there one saw signs of revolt. During the summer of 1932 a bedraggled Bonus Army of war veterans descended upon Washington demanding funds—and were dispersed by the Army in a lamentably misplaced show of firmness. Farmers' strikes in Iowa bore witness that even staid and conservative citizens might be driven to violence by long-continued and unrelieved deflation. Yet the opposition to the ruling powers of the country was as yet incoherent and scattered. Hundreds of schemes for economic improvement were being advanced by business men, by economists of every school, by laymen, students, and cranks; magazine editors in those days had to spend half their time reading economic plans, most of them quite impossible of practical realization; yet the most striking thing about these plans, perhaps, was the multiplicity of divergent ideas which they represented. (The only radical economic plan which was to gain any large popular following prior to Roosevelt's inauguration had not yet caught the public attention: it was Howard Scott's Technocracy, a curious mixture of valid economic theory and exaggerated statistics and utopian proposals.) The Communists were making a great noise and converting many of the intellectuals of the country, but the rank and file of Americans—even among the unemployed —had no use for them. Discontent there was, and no wonder; a vague feeling there was that the government ought to pay more attention to the people at the bottom of the economic scale, and less to those at the top; but on the whole this sentiment was still formless and unorganized.

It was symptomatic of the temper of the time that when the Democrats met in Chicago to select a candidate to oppose Herbert Hoover, they wrote a platform which could hardly—considering the condition of the country —have been called radical. They called for the "protection of the investing public by requiring to be filed with the government and carried in advertisements of all offerings of foreign and domestic stocks and bonds, true information as to bonuses, commissions, principal invested, and interests of sellers"; they called for federal regulation of holding companies and of stock exchanges; they called for federal aid to the states for unemployment relief, and for expansion of public works; but they also called for a 25 per cent cut in the costs of the federal government, for a balanced budget, and for "a sound currency to be maintained at all costs."

The man whom they nominated, furthermore, was certainly no radical. Roosevelt was widely regarded in the West as a foe of Wall Street and a friend of the farmers and little business men and workers upon whom had descended the full weight of economic trouble; but there was nothing revolutionary about his program. It was an indistinctly liberal program, patterned generally after the progressivism of his late cousin and of the late Robert LaFollette. And as for the man himself, what Walter Lippmann had written about him a few months before his nomination expressed the opinion of a great many observers in the East who had watched closely his career as Governor of New York: "Franklin D. Roosevelt is an amiable man with many philanthropic influences, but he is not the dangerous enemy of anything. He is too eager to please. The notion, which seems to prevail in the West and the South, that Wall Street fears him, is preposterous. . . . Wall Street does not like his vagueness, and the uncertainty as to what he does think, but if any Western progressive thinks that the Governor has challenged directly or indirectly the wealth concentrated in New York City, he is mightily mistaken."

Behind Roosevelt, as the campaign of 1932 progressed, was concentrated a great mass of resentment at Hoover, of distrust of the financial chieftains whom Hoover had so often called into consultation, and of blind desire for change. But neither Roosevelt nor the majority of his followers proposed any major alteration in the economic organization of America. So completely had the American people accepted the financial and business order under which the country had grown and prospered that its downfall left them astonished, dazed, and unprepared with rational alternatives.

Indeed, their very bewilderment brought about a strange apathy, a downhearted quietness of mood. When one reflected that some fourteen million men and women were out of work; that many of them were in desperate want, and most of them faced a future empty of any definite promise of self-respecting self-support; that young people were coming out of school and college into a land which seemed to have no further use for their talents, and which no longer offered them a frontier to exploit; and that the crisis had been steadily becoming more grave for two and a half years, one could only conclude that the American people as a whole were behaving with extraordinary docility. Like a sick man who realizes that his illness may be mortal yet who distrusts strong medicine, the country waited, desperately patient, for recovery or for the end.

During the summer of 1932, recovery seemed once more to be beginning. Wall Street began to realize that some of its fears had been exaggerated: that Congress had not legislated the country into immediate bankruptcy, that the Reconstruction Finance Corporation was propping up the weaker banks (though at great cost), and that the European financial system had not utterly gone up in smoke. There were signs of decided financial improvement. The gold which had drained out of the country during the latter months of 1931 and the beginning of 1932 was returning in part; by the end of August, 40 per cent of it had come back. Cash was beginning to come out of hoarding. The big banks, especially in New York and Chicago, were in definitely improved condition. The formation of a new banking pool under the leadership of the House of Morgan had helped to bring about a belated upturn in bond prices. Signs of life appeared in the stock market, and prices made a brief but rapid recovery. And business, for a brief interval, definitely improved.

Had the American economy at last turned that momentous corner?

For a little while it seemed so. Yet while the political campaign was still in full cry, with Roosevelt promising to come to the aid of the Forgotten Man, and Hoover prophesying that a Democratic triumph would cause the grass to grow in the streets of America—the indices turned down again; not far down, but enough to check the country's half-despairing hope. The resiliency of the financial markets—even of the commodity markets—had not communicated itself to the general business structure. During the last months of the year 1932 business just about held its own. Roosevelt was overwhelmingly elected; the year 1933 began. And then suddenly, while the President-elect was engaged in chosing the members of his Cabinet, the economic system broke utterly at its weakest point.

§ 6

It was the banks which gave way.

The final abrupt collapse might have begun in any one of a score of places. But there was perhaps a certain poetic justice in the fact that it actually began in Detroit, where the skyscraper-building boom in the nineteen-twenties had been especially grandiose and the subsequent difficulties of the banks had been correspondingly severe; that the specific bank which was in trouble in February, 1933—the Union Guardian Trust Company—was dominated by a holding company, a characteristic flower of the financial exuberance of 1929; that this holding company controlled also not only nineteen other banks but also seven security companies and a variety of other financial enterprises, and had thus been tempted, as had innumerable other financial institutions, to serve more than one master; and that one of the things which now made the weakness of the Union Guardian Trust Company a matter of general concern was the very existence of this holding company: the fear that if the Union Guardian Trust Company went under, there would at once be a run upon the other banks under the same management, and that such a run would precipitate a general panic.

The Union Guardian had been sorely pressed for some time. It had already borrowed again and again from the Reconstruction Finance Corporation, its net borrowings amounting to some twelve and a half million dollars. Now, in February, 1933, it was slipping once more. It wanted more aid from the taxpayers' funds—much more, and quickly. There were frantic negotiations with the Federal officials. These negotiations—involving the Detroit bankers, the R.F.C., the Treasury Department, Henry Ford, and Senator Couzens of Michigan—have been the subject of much angry dispute, but they need not be discussed here. The significant fact was that the negotiations failed, and that in the early hours of February 14 Governor Comstock of Michigan, after conferring at length in Detroit with bankers and State and Federal officials, motored through the night to Lansing and issued a proclamation closing all the banks in Michigan for a "holiday" period of eight days.

This proclamation not merely paralyzed the financial machinery of Michigan; it also immediately set in motion the forces of panic elsewhere. Already the banks of the country had begun preparations to meet the probable storm. These preparations were now redoubled. Banks withdrew reserves from the Reserve Banks, and also withdrew money which they had on deposit in other banks: during February more than a billion dollars which had been deposited in New York by out-of-town banks left the city. They sold bonds; the bond market suffered fresh attacks of liquidation. Meanwhile corporations and individuals, all over the country, uneasy lest the panic spread, began withdrawing their deposits from the banks, and thus hastened the storm. In places hundreds and thousands of miles apart, there were bank runs of increasing seriousness. Hoarding began anew, to the extent of hundreds of millions of dollars. Gold began once more to leave the country in quantity.

For some ten days these phenomena were largely hidden from the eye of the casual observer. Newspapers gave them as little publicity as possible; indeed, even as late as March 2, when the panic had acquired terrific momentum, the *New York Times* still kept it off the front page, and its chronicle of bank holidays on page eight was topped by the gentle headline, BANKS PROTECTED IN 5 MORE STATES. But on February 24 Governor Ritchie had to declare a three-day holiday in Maryland, and from that moment onward the progress of the collapse was very rapid. The Federal Reserve System, admirably as it had been devised to meet localized emergencies, could not withstand the simultaneous onslaught of panics on every front. State after state was driven to pass emergency laws permitting banks to limit withdrawals if not to close their doors entirely.

By March 3, the ability of even the big financial citadels of New York and Chicago to hold out was becoming hourly more doubtful. In Washington, President Hoover's financial advisers were urging him to declare a national banking holiday and to put an embargo upon gold, but he could not be induced to act unless the incoming president would join with him, and Roosevelt refused to take administrative responsibility until he entered the White House; so nothing was done.

At last, at 4:30 in the morning of March 4, Governor Lehman issued a proclamation closing the New York banks, and almost simultaneously Governor Horner of Illinois took similar action for his state. With the issuing of these two proclamations, the financial paralysis of the country became virtually complete.

History does not often time its climaxes with precision. But in this instance the timing was diabolically perfect. No drama written to throw into bold relief the defeat of the financiers and the failure of Hoover's measures for recovery could have hurried to a more effective curtain. During the days when the bank-holiday epidemic was spreading, Charles E. Mitchell and his colleagues of the National City Bank had been on the witness stand before a Senate investigating committee in Washington; their shocking testimony—which had forced Mitchell to resign on February 26—seemed to point the moral of the events that were taking place. And now on the very morning when the doors of the great New York and Chicago banks at last stood closed to the public, Herbert Hoover was preparing to ride to the Capitol to relinquish the Presidency of the United States. His term of office had come to an end, and with it the financial order which he had labored so long to sustain.

Chapter Fourteen

ALL CHANGE

IF THE stroke of chance which closed the banks on Inauguration Day was bitterly tragic for Herbert Hoover, it was also staggering for Franklin Roosevelt. The country over which he was to govern was prostrate. The financial machinery had stopped. Most financial institutions were teetering on the edge of insolvency. Business was slumping fast to the low levels reached during the panicky spring of 1932. The farm population and the industrial population were in dire straits; unemployment and destitution were widespread. And who could be sure that the demoralization of the national economy had not only just begun?

Furthermore, Roosevelt's plans, formulated at leisure, had not contemplated the meeting of any such extraordinary crisis as the collapse of the whole banking system; at the very outset of his administration he must improvise. He and his cabinet officers were new to their jobs, to their staffs, even to each other. At a moment of the gravest danger the command of the Ship of State was being turned over to a group of passengers none of whom had ever been on the bridge before.

Yet in another respect the stroke of chance favored the new President. It gave him, for the moment at least, an almost united country. The closing of the banks had thrown rich and poor, employer and employee, banker and depositor, Republican and Democrat, into a common predicament; and this predicament was so sudden and unprecedented that divergent opinions as to the way out had not had time to crystallize. There was even, for millions of Americans, a curious thrill in the completeness of the breakdown after so many months and years of foreboding: a feeling of *Now it has happened: now for action.* When Franklin Roosevelt stepped forward on the platform before the Capitol and began his Inaugural Address, not only the throng below him but a vastly greater throng of listeners at millions of radios were ready to listen hopefully, to follow eagerly, to welcome a New Deal.

He did not disappoint those first hopes. Whether or not events make men, certainly the Franklin Roosevelt who assumed the Presidency on that eventful day seemed a wholly different man from the all-things-to-all-men candidate of 1932.

His Inaugural—delivered in a ringing voice—was clear, strong, confident; and citizens innumerable who had longed for action in the days when Hoover seemed to be doing nothing were thrilled as by the note of the fife when the new President pledged himself to ask Congress, if the need arose, for "broad executive power to wage a war against the emergency, as great as the power that would be given to me if we were in fact invaded by a foreign foe."

His promise of action was immediately made good. He met the banking crisis boldly and with a wholly contagious confidence. He at once called Congress to meet in emergency session. He at once issued—with a few changes—the national bank-holiday proclamation which had been prepared for Hoover's use a few days before. His smiling little Secretary of the Treasury, William H. Woodin, plunged into arduous preparations for the reopening of the banks—providing for a possible expansion of the currency based on the sound assets of the banks, and arranging to consider the condition of every bank and to decide which institutions could be opened, which must be placed under the direction of governmental "conservators," and which must remain closed. When Congress assembled, Roosevelt asked it for virtually dictatorial power over transactions in credit, currency, gold, and silver. This power was granted him the very day he asked for it. Nine days after the Inauguration the first banks were ready to be opened. And on the evening before the opening, Roosevelt sat before a radio microphone in the White House and talked to the American people as one would talk to a group of friendly neighbors, explaining with admirable clarity and persuasiveness just what he had been doing and what he expected them to do. The address was a triumph of democratic statesmanship. The banks were opened without panic, and stayed open.

To be sure, not all the banks were permitted to resume business. At least a fifth of the deposits of the country were still tied up, and the purchasing power of the country was correspondingly reduced. But Franklin Roosevelt had done his first great task brilliantly—and he still had the whole nation with him.

Even the men of Wall Street, shaken by the experiences of the past few weeks and by the obvious anger and distrust of the general public, had little choice but to go along with the new President who moved through the crisis with so sure a step, and who so obviously held their future fortunes in his hands. They were the more disposed to go along with him when he asked Congress —before the banks were opened—for authority to cut Federal expenses to the bone (yes, even to cut the veterans' allowances) in order to maintain the national credit. Even when Roosevelt, in April, issued an executive order prohibiting the export of gold, and Woodin formally admitted that the United States was off the gold standard (as in reality it had been ever since March 4) the financiers did not seem unduly dismayed; J. P. Morgan himself smilingly faced a group of reporters at 23 Wall Street and gave his approval to the move.

The country wanted action? Roosevelt gave it action. Throughout the spring of 1933 he showered recommendations and drafts of bills upon an astonished Congress which followed his requests as if in a trance. Bills to bring about financial reforms, bills to stimulate business in one way or another, bills to set up new governmental agencies: Congress passed them all—some of them before the members had even had a chance to read them, much less to ponder over them. There was every reason for the men on the Hill not to balk but to follow blindly. The Democratic majority was huge, the patronage was still undistributed; the country was in the mood for headlong change and was enchanted with Roosevelt; telegrams and letters urging Senators and Representatives to "support the President" were flooding in from all over the country.

The executive departments were in a fury of activity. Conferences were going on at all hours, bills were being drafted and revised and redrafted at breakneck speed, and in the mammoth new government buildings the lights burned late; the very atmosphere of the once placid city of Washington was electric with excitement. Officials and advisers representing the widest divergence of views were being pressed, helter-skelter, into the planning of the recovery program—hard-boiled business men, hard-boiled politicians, deserving Democrats, professors of economics, labor leaders, socialists, sentimental theorists of every hue. What would come of their furious labors was far from clear; but the country liked action, liked its smiling President, and liked to feel once more the sense of hope.

And it liked most of all the fact that a really definite improvement in the condition of the country was taking place.

As we look back upon the events of that spring of 1933, it is clear that to a considerable extent the improvement was due to the expectation of inflation. It did not really begin until after the Administration formally forsook the gold standard in April. It was given a distinct fillip by the action of Congress, in May, in giving the President permission to bring about inflation in any one of four ways. The fall of the dollar in foreign exchange was providing a temporary stimulus to exports; the prospect of higher prices (coupled with the prospect of governmental regulation through the N.R.A.) was causing business men all over the country to stock up with goods.

Nevertheless there was a new feeling in the air. Investors who in 1932 had rushed to sell because they thought there might be inflation now rushed to buy for the same reason. The rise in the price of wheat and other crops was restoring a measure of hope to the men and women of the farm belt. The wheels of industry were actually beginning to turn faster, the unemployed were actually beginning to be put back to work.

The rally had its disquieting features, and perhaps the most disquieting was the terrific outburst of speculation which accompanied it. Despite the public distrust of Wall Street, despite the widespread belief that prosperity on the 1929 pattern was false and dangerous, despite the grim experiences of 1930 and 1931 and 1932, the shorn lambs swarmed into the brokerage houses once more in incredible numbers. Where some of them got the money to speculate with was a mystery. More than a few of them, indeed, were shabbily clad; one had the feeling, as one watched the customers in a broker's office, hanging over the chattering ticker or following with eager eyes the moving figures on the trans-lux screen, that perhaps some among them were desperately staking their last savings on the turn of the Wall Street wheel. The behavior of the market as it skyrocketed upward gave plenty of indication that even if the bankers were somewhat humbled by recent events, the pool managers on the Exchange were not. Some of the manipulative operations in which the alcohol stocks (which were supposed to be about to profit by the coming repeal of the Eighteenth Amendment) were pushed up to extravagant prices—and into the hands of the suckers—were as outrageous as the worst pool exploits of 1929.

As for the volume of trading on the Stock Exchange, the amazing fact was that during the two successive months of June and July 1933, *this was greater than it had been in any month of 1929 except the panic month of October.* On no less than nineteen days during 1933 the daily volume of trading was more than six million shares—a strange phenomenon when one considers that there never had been even a single four-million share day until the bull-market frenzy of 1928. Speculation in the commodity markets was similarly feverish and unashamed.

It is true, of course, that the Administration, by dangling the idea of inflation before the public, was partly to blame for this debauch. Nevertheless the exaggerated form which the speculative campaign took was an ominous sign. The national economy seemed like an engine with a loose part: speed it up just a little, and it began to wrack itself to pieces.

Yet elsewhere the prospect was heartening. Even if the United States was not going back to work so fast as it was going back to speculation, the gain in economic activity in the brief interval since March was remarkable. By July, the index of industrial production had regained about half the ground it had lost since 1929; and while the rise in employment and in payrolls was decidedly less spectacular, it was sharp.

There had taken place, too, another significant change. No one could fail to realize that the economic initiative was now in the hands of Franklin Roosevelt. At scores of points in the economic system of the country the government—with public opinion still overwhelmingly behind it—was intervening or promising to intervene. The economic capital of America had moved from Wall Street to Washington.

§ 2

It is not easy to write down briefly the Roosevelt Administration's prescription for restoring the United States to economic health, for there were many physicians involved in the work of diagnosis and treatment, the clinical procedure was somewhat erratic, and sometimes the medicines which were administered had conflicting effects. President Roosevelt once likened himself to the quarterback of a football team, always ready to try a new play; adopting his figure of speech, one might remark that there were moments when various members of his team appeared to be simultaneously engaged in a line play, an end run, a forward pass, and a fake kick. But at least the recovery plan which was taking shape in Washington may be sketched in rough outline.

1. In the first place, the government was hoping to bring about a certain degree of controlled inflation in order to lessen the weight of debt. The theory was that since the debt burden was intolerably heavy and could not rapidly be lightened through bankruptcies without new damage to banks and other institutions, the best

thing to do would be to raise the general level of prices and incomes in order that debts might become relatively lighter. The government also hoped that the prospect of higher prices would cause business men to put in orders and that these orders would act like the push which one gives to a stalled automobile: presently business would proceed under its own power. That the effect of inflation would be only temporary unless the engine began to fire again was clear; that tinkering with the currency was a dangerous business at best was also clear, except to the unduly credulous. But the situation of the country was so very grave that even dangerous medicines seemed worth trying.

It is doubtful if Roosevelt had any settled opinion as to whether or how to inflate, and it is probable that he was dragged from position to position by changing circumstances and by popular pressure. At first, perhaps, he was sure only that the government could not go back on the gold standard on the old basis without a great danger of a new deflation; then he saw that Congress might force mandatory inflationary legislation upon him, and preferred to have it give him the power to inflate— which he might or might not use; then he was delighted to see the fall of the dollar giving business a push, and feared that if the dollar were stabilized before his other recovery measures could take effect, business might lose its momentum and all the benefit of the push might be lost, and so he dismayed the London economic conference by suddenly deciding that there must be no stabilization agreement; and then, when business did indeed slow up in the autumn of 1933, he thought that another little push might help, and thereupon embarked upon Professor Warren's gold-buying program—the so-called "rubber-dollar" program, which reduced the value of the dollar in terms of gold to a little less than sixty cents, and yet hardly affected the price-level at all. (This curious program was likened by a New York banker to an attempt to bring about warmer weather by lighting a fire under the thermometer.)

Yet despite the vagaries of Roosevelt's action, the general philosophy of it is fairly clear. He wanted to lighten the debt burden and also to give the American economy a shot in the arm. Meanwhile his Administration also made direct efforts to relieve the debt burden here and there, by government aid to farmers and householders who were oppressed by mortgages, and by legislation designed to make the processes of bankruptcy less slow and painful.

2. In the second place, the Administration realized that although industrialists, in hard times, managed to sustain prices to some extent by cutting down on production, the farmers had been unable to do so—and thus had suffered grievously. Why not make it possible for the farmers to take a leaf out of the industrialists' book? If the government were to offer them an inducement to produce less—the money for this inducement to be contributed by the rest of the country, in the form of a slight tax on the farm products which they consumed—farm prices ought to go up. This was the essence of the celebrated AAA program. There has been much ridicule of the principle of paying farmers not to produce—and for the long run the principle is of course preposterous —but no industrialist who has ever shut down a mill or run it three days a week in the hope of keeping the price of his goods from collapsing is in a position to join in the ridicule. The AAA was simply giving the farmers a homeopathic dose of the medicine which industry had consistently taken as a matter of course.

The administration of this agricultural program involved endless difficulties and led to many absurdities, but it seems on the whole to have made things temporarily somewhat easier for the farm population—until nature took over the business of crop limitation in 1934 and 1935 by blowing a good deal of the excess acreage away in dust.

3. Obviously the agricultural program would be futile unless industry and business meanwhile expanded. How, then, to expand industry? One way by which the Administration hoped to do this was by public works—in other words, by spending money (which would put cash into circulation and thus supposedly stimulate private business) and getting, in return for this money, things which would be of future economic benefit to the country. This program had its awkward aspects. One was that it would knock into a cocked hat the Administration's attempt to balance the budget. Another was that projects valuable enough to be defended as capital expenditures, and agencies solvent enough to undertake the projects, were hard to find. Another was that the chances for graft were terrific if the government did not proceed with great care; yet speed was also necessary—and speed and care do not naturally go together. For these and other reasons the Administration moved slowly with its public works program; so slowly, in fact, that although the total amount of money spent was very large, the push at any given moment was not. A patient can take a considerable amount of medicine in diluted quantities over a period of time without visible effect—except, perhaps, the effect of becoming dependent upon the medicine.

4. It was the NRA, however, upon which Roosevelt chiefly relied for industrial and business recovery. Here we confront one of the most curious confusions in the New Deal.

One theory behind the NRA was that since a dismaying phenomenon of the depression had been the tendency of industry and business, by reducing the wage bill, to kill the goose that laid the golden egg, the way out of the depression would therefore be to fatten the goose by raising wages; and that since no concern would do this unless other concerns also did it and thus added to the general buying power, the proper procedure would be to bring the business heads together, industry by industry, and get them to raise wages by agreement, the agreement to have the force of law. (A very difficult policy to put into effect: it ran head on, not only into the historic if unedifying habit of the business man to outwit the government if he could, but also into the cold fact that a wage-raising schedule which a prosperous company could afford might push other companies into bankruptcy—and men do not enjoy going into the red, and least of all at the instance of their government.)

The second theory behind the NRA was that unemployment would be relieved if the working week were shortened by agreement, and the available work were thus spread out among more people. (Wage rates being generally low, this might be described as a share-the-poverty plan.)

The third theory was that much of the trouble in business was caused by drastic cutting of prices (as from the business man's point of view it was) and that therefore price-cutting ought to be prevented in the agreements; prices ought to be "stabilized."

It happened that the men who were chiefly responsible for the establishment and guidance of the NRA were not the liberal "brain trusters" of conservative legend but a group of industrialists and business men, some of whom had long hoped to persuade the government to mitigate the Sherman Act; and thus it was this third theory that in practise had the best of things—especially as General Hugh Johnson, for all the picturesque fury with which he threatened to "crack down" on those who did not comply with the NRA codes, was quite unsuccessful in forcing general compliance with the wage-raising agreements, and in fact made only scattered attempts to do so. Thus although in some industries the increase in the wage bill was impressive, in others it was ridiculously small; and meanwhile the business men who had swarmed to Washington and perspired over the drafting of codes during the hot summer of 1933 found the opportunity to "stabilize" prices a godsend. Here, thought some of them, was a lovely chance for combination to run prices up. Hence there were some industries in which prices actually rose much faster than did the wage bill.

To say categorically that the NRA was a failure is, of course, to dodge the question of what would have happened during 1933 and 1934 if it had not been created. Certainly it diminished child labor and some of the worst sweating of workers. When most business was losing money there was at least a plausible excuse for stabilizing prices to enable companies to regain their feet. Yet as a scheme for distributing purchasing power the NRA proved uncertain at best. And surely it was anomalous that after the hullabaloo and the flag-waving and the patriotic speeches were over, and the Blue Eagle labels had been distributed, and General Johnson had stormed about the country as the herald of a new industrial order, and governmental board after board had been appointed to coördinate what refused to be coördinated,—that after all this, the NRA gradually stood revealed as a governmental arm which protected groups of business men in organizing to maintain themselves against new competition and against the reduction of prices to the consumer: as an agency which accelerated and only partially controlled that process of concentration which the government in earlier reform periods had so earnestly opposed!

While the Administration was trying to stimulate business, it was also trying to reform finance.

That it should be doing so appeared to many observers paradoxical and perverse. Wasn't reform always deflationary? If the people at Washington wanted men to do business, why pester and frighten them with investigations, regulations, and prohibitions? The principal reason, of course, was that the people at Washington knew that reform was long overdue (indeed, it is interesting to note that some of the changes brought about in 1933 and 1934 had been recommended by the Pujo committee twenty years earlier!) ; that if it were not undertaken at once it would probably not be undertaken at all, the public memory being short; and that without it, any recovery would probably be unsound and short-lived. (Another wild boom, more speculation, more debt-formation, more exaggerated prosperity for the rich, another break; and once again contraction, stubborn maintenance of prices to save the debt-structure, unemployment, misery.) There could be no enduring prosperity unless the structure of financial privilege which had come to grief in 1929 was altered.

And they knew also that from the point of view of the business world, it never is "the right time" to undertake reform. The voices which were raised in protest now were echoes of those voices which had charged Theodore Roosevelt with bringing on the Panic of 1907, which had assailed Wilson as an enemy of prosperity, had cried out in alarm at the establishment of the Federal Reserve System, and had inveighed against the Reserve authorities in 1928 and 1929 for their ineffectual attempts to halt the great stock-market boom.

(That there were also other motives behind the reform campaign than that which I have just given goes almost without saying. While, for example, one man might want to regulate the Stock Exchange because after witnessing the speculative debauch of the summer of 1933 he felt that the economic processes of the country should not be subject to such violent distortions, another man might want to regulate it because he wanted to be able to speculate on more nearly equal terms with the Cuttens and the Brushes, or because he thought Wall Street men were wicked and ought to be punished, or because he knew that a "vote against Wall Street" would be good politics on the prairie.)

The reforms which went into effect included the following:

1. To prevent bankers from serving two masters, it was provided in the Glass-Steagall Act of 1933 that national banks and banks with Federal Reserve privileges must not have security affiliates. (This change was so inevitable that some of the biggest banks had already anticipated it; even before the banking crisis was over, the National City and the Chase National had hurriedly decided to divorce their affiliates.)

2. With the same purpose in view, investment bankers were forbidden to act also as commercial bankers, or to serve on the directorates of commercial banks—a provision which required the House of Morgan and other big private banks which had previously exercised both the function of distributing securities and the function of accepting deposits to decide which one they wished to exercise and to give up the other.

3. To protect the investor from misrepresentation, the Securities Act of 1933 required those who issued securities to register them with a government commission and to disclose complete information about them; and also provided that any promoter, banker, or corporation executive who misrepresented the facts about an issue of securities might be held liable for losses sustained by purchasers of it.

4. To put the spotlight of publicity on the activities of insiders, the National Securities and Exchange Act of 1934 required every corporation whose stock was to be listed on any exchange to make public the stockholdings and salaries of directors, officers, and large stockholders, as well as any bonus, profit-sharing, or option arrangements or other material contracts which these men might have made with the company; and to report from month to month any change in these relationships.

5. To enable manipulation of the stock market to be checked and undue speculation to be prevented, the National Securities and Exchange Act also put the stock exchanges under government supervision, empowered the Federal Reserve Board to limit speculative margins, and empowered the Securities and Exchange Commission to make rules of various sorts intended to stop pool operations.

In an effort to reduce the financial superstructures of the public utilities to a rational basis, legislation was being considered in the spring of 1935 to put holding companies in the public utility field under Federal regulation, and to empower the government to insist upon the break-up of any holding-company system which did not seem defensible—by reason of the close geographical grouping of its properties—as an operating unit.

Some of these reform measures were so drawn that they involved bankers and brokers and corporation officials in a vast amount of paper work, red tape, confusion, and delay; for example, the Securities Act of 1933 required the filing of so much detailed information that an application for registration of an issue of securities might require the preparation—at heavy expense—of a mountainous stack of documents. And to some extent the reform measures might be described as laborious attempts to lock the barn after the horse was stolen (if not, indeed, to burn the barn down). History, alas, is a one-way street; you cannot legislate things back into the shape they held before the abuses at which you are aiming were invented, and if you attempt to do so, your legislation will sometimes have unforeseen results. But certainly the abuses at which these reform measures were aimed had done grave harm and the reforms themselves in their general outlines were logical.

Indeed, in some respects they were singularly moderate. For example, up to the spring of 1935, the new legislation failed to bring every bank in the country into a single system, and thus failed to rectify an ancient and glaring defect. It did not outlaw holding-company banking, and thus left at least one way open to the service of two masters. It put no limitation upon pyramiding, except in so far as the 1935 legislation might curb it in the public-utility field. It did not touch the personal holding company, and thus left a door wide open to those who would evade tax laws and other statutes. And there was no attempt to require large corporations doing an interstate business to submit to Federal incorporation; they still remained free to incorporate under the laws of whatever state might make things easiest for the promoters—and some of the states still made things very easy indeed. (Indeed, the government added to the irony of the situation by forming its own New Deal corporations in Wilmington!)

As to the New Deal program as a whole, two things remain to be said. In the first place, Roosevelt's point of view was clearly quite different from Hoover's. To say that Hoover thought of business in terms of corporations and profits, and Roosevelt thought of it in terms of people, is perhaps not quite accurate. But I think it is fair to say that Hoover thought first of the owners and managers: if they prospered, he felt, their prosperity would filter down to the less fortunate. Roosevelt thought first of the less fortunate: if they prospered, he felt, their prosperity would seep up to the owners— even if the owners meanwhile had to be subjected to a little restraint. The Roosevelt legislation, to be sure, was far from consistent in this respect; nevertheless the change of emphasis was significant.

In the second place, the Roosevelt program involved a deliberate recognition of the end of laissez-faire. For the first time in American history, the government definitely assumed responsibility for the functioning of the American economy. The measures which Roosevelt put into effect were not by any means revolutionary; this assumption was.

§ 3

Franklin Roosevelt had been in the White House only a little more than four months when two things happened simultaneously. First, the New Deal program which we have been reviewing began clearly to pass from the stage of feverish preparation to that of execution: it was on July 20, 1933, that the President issued the NRA's "blanket code," which was intended to bring about immediate raising of wages and shortening of hours in all industries and businesses throughout the country, pending the adoption of the various special codes. (At this time only one of the special codes had been put into effect.) And, second, the wild speculative boom broke with a resounding crash.

The coincidence was striking. On the very day when Roosevelt announced the terms of the blanket code drawn up by the NRA, the price of wheat was falling, the alcohol stocks in Wall Street were collapsing, and the prices of many other stocks were being abruptly cut in half. (One stock, American Commercial Alcohol, took one of the longest and fastest roller-coaster rides in speculative history, dropping in the space of only four days from a price of 89⅞ to 29⅛!) There could hardly have been a more effective—and disconcerting—advertisement of the difference between joyful promise and sober performance.

There followed a considerable setback in trade; and then—as the New Deal program gradually was converted from dream into reality—there began a long period of virtual economic stalemate.

Month after month, season after season, the business indices moved up and down within moderate limits, never falling so low as in the terrible days of mid-1932 and early 1933, but on the other hand never rising as high as during the early summer of 1933. Busily the Administration developed and expanded and revised its recovery program—and yet the stalemate continued. Bankers and business men alternately cried havoc and predicted a new boom—and yet neither havoc nor boom eventuated.

Not that this long period was uneventful. On the contrary: it was lively with alarums and excursions. First there was the vociferous campaign to put NRA codes into effect in innumerable industries and trades, ranging all the way from the huge steel and automobile and textile industries to such pillars of the American economy as the dog food industry, the vegetable ivory button manufacturing industry, and the shoulder-pad manufacturing industry; all through the autumn of 1933 and the following winter, the voice of General Johnson was loud in the land. Then there was the Treasury's brief gold-buying experiment—a bewildering adventure which formally came to an end on the last day of January, 1934, when Roosevelt stabilized the dollar (temporarily at least) at 59.08 cents in terms of gold. There was the long procession of bankers to Washington to face the Senate Committee on Banking and Currency and its courteous but indefatigable counsel, Ferdinand Pecora; already the members of the House of Morgan had come before the Committee—in a series of sessions curiously reminiscent of the Pujo inquiry, twenty-one years earlier—and in the autumn of 1933 it was Wiggin's turn and the turn of the Detroit bankers. There was a long series of bitter strikes, rising to a brief climax in the angry general strike at San Francisco in the summer of 1934. All through that same summer there was a devastating drought in the wheat belt, followed by the most destructive dust storms ever known on the plains. There were intermittent war scares in Europe, preventing international economic barriers from being lowered and disturbing the American equilibrium. In the spring of 1935 there was the exciting campaign for the payment of a cash bonus by the printing of greenbacks—a campaign stopped by Roosevelt's magnificent veto message. And only a few days later there came the Supreme Court's decision that the NRA codes were unconstitutional—a staggering decision that brought the second phase of the New Deal to a confusing end.

All through this period there was a torrent of news from Washington of the government's new programs— the Civil Works program, the home renovation program, the silver-buying program, the social security program, and dozens of others; new alphabetical agencies, new administrative commissions and coördinating committees and boards of review appeared in bewildering succession, and authority was shifted and re-shifted among them until the Roosevelt economic offensive became as difficult to chart as the Insull utility empire. Busily the Presidential quarterback called new plays; now the team appeared to gain a little ground, now to be thrown for a short loss—but still the goal line was very far away.

Before me is a graph showing the rise and fall, month by month, of the *Annalist's* Index of Business Activity—a fairly accurate measure of the rate at which business is moving at any given time. On the graph the long collapse of 1929-32 is represented by a line running jaggedly downhill from a high point of 116.7 in the middle of 1929 to a low point of 59.7 in the middle of 1932. The line runs up a few points, then drops again, still farther, to 58.4. That still lower point indicates the paralysis of business caused by the banking collapse of March, 1933. Roosevelt comes into office, the banks are re-opened, the New Deal is formulated, and the line leaps upward from 58.4 almost perpendicularly to 89.3—the high point of July, 1933. But notice what happens now. In the autumn of 1933 it sags from 89.3 all the way to 68.4, losing more than half of the gain made during Roosevelt's first four months in the White House. In the winter and spring of 1934 it climbs slowly back to 80.2; in the summer of 1934 it slides down to 66.5; in the autumn of 1934 and the early months of 1935 it inches up again to 83.3; then it begins to decline once more.

Was this a jagged progress upward or a jagged progress downward? The answer which one gave to this question depended partly upon the moment at which one looked at the graph and partly upon one's preconceptions. But surely the significant thing about the period between the late summer of 1933 and the spring of 1935 was the stubborn duration of stalemate. The economic machine did not slide into the ditch, it did not roar away to prosperity; it limped along uncertainly at half-speed.

§ 4

That public opinion should remain static during such a prolonged period of suspended economic animation was manifestly impossible. Enthusiasm for the New Deal waned. Millions of Americans, unable to understand the economic situation and almost unaware of it except as some small part of it disturbed their daily lives, lapsed into indifference again; it is hard to remain excited about a semi-permanent emergency. And the New Deal also lost support through defections both to the Left and to the Right.

The defections to the Left are properly outside the scope of this book; yet they must at least be mentioned, for they were considerable and significant.

The Communist Party was still too small, too dogmatic in creed, and too devoted to the terminology (as well as the philosophy) of European radicalism to be a vital political influence; but the communist idea had gained strength. In many of the strikes of 1934, communist leaders forced the hands of the A. F. of L. leaders; and it was characteristic of the times, too, that among many of the younger urban intellectuals, Marx and Moscow now commanded the sort of homage that Proust and the Left Bank had commanded a decade earlier.

To most of the intellectuals of the Left, the irresistible meaning of what had been happening for five years was that capitalism was in its death-throes. The New Deal was merely a superficial and wrongheaded attempt to shore up a vicious and doomed system. When the New Deal failed—as fail it must, since it insisted upon trying to "organize scarcity" instead of "organizing abundance" —the alternatives would be fascist revolution and communist revolution, for "the overwhelming fact of our epoch" was "the irreconcilable conflict between capital and labor." The only tolerable conclusion of this conflict would be the final victory of the proletariat. Liberals who wished to mediate between these two opposing forces were simply tender-minded sentimentalists (if not fascists in lambs' clothing). The prospect of revolution was not cheerful, but one must face it realistically. Capitalism must go, said the intellectuals of the Left, and the sooner the better.

What gave this doctrine its very considerable strength as an influence in American thought was the striking extent to which its diagnosis of the situation was borne out by many of the facts of the economic breakdown. Its weakness lay in the treatment it proposed. So steeped were the American people in the tradition of the acquisitive life that a good many bayonets would probably be required to induce them to give up private profit entirely; and so steeped were they—despite their occasional outbursts of violence and bitterness—in the tradition of democratic friendliness, of neighborly tolerance, that to most of them the idea that class hatred was necessary and right was bound to be deeply repugnant. In 1935 there seemed to be little likelihood that the Marxians would win any such immediate popular support as would the siren-singers of easy palliatives.

One of the significant events of 1934 was Upton Sinclair's almost-successful campaign for the Governorship of California, with a program which aimed to set up a socialist order for the impoverished side by side with the going capitalist order. Yet even this curious proposal was not, perhaps, so significant of the temper of the country as was Dr. Townsend's ingenuous scheme for bringing back prosperity by paying to every old person in the country an old-age pension of two thousand dollars a year; or as Senator Huey Long's vague proposals for "sharing the wealth" of the country (apparently without remaking the complex wealth-producing machinery so that re-concentration of economic power in new hands would not follow upon confiscation); or as the extraordinary influence of that latter-day Bryan of the radio, Father Coughlin of Detroit, with his bitterly eloquent attacks upon the bankers and the Federal Reserve System and his pleas for inflation.

Just as in 1896 the Populists had followed Bryan into the free-silver campaign, so in 1935 enormous numbers of Americans, battered and discouraged by a far worse crisis yet by no means temperamentally radical, looked for magic formulae which would conjure prosperity out of a hat—or out of the government printing-presses. They did not want the profit system to be abandoned. Anger and despair might sometimes drive them to riot against the seizure of their farms for debt, against the sale of their milk at starvation prices, against employers who threw them out into the streets, against scabs who took the jobs which were all they had to bargain with; but what the vast majority of them wanted was not revolution but jobs and money and hope, with as little change in the going system as possible. That they groped with pathetic eagerness for short and easy ways out of the wilderness followed inevitably from the ugly fact that the years were crawling by and still the American economy was partly paralyzed and jobs and money were cruelly scarce.

§ 5

There was thunder on the Right, too.

At first it was barely audible above the echoes of the banking crash, the shouts of acclaim for Roosevelt the deliverer, and the tumult and confusion at Washington. The big bankers and insiders were licking their wounds, thankful for the moment to follow any leader who might salvage the economic wreck; they distrusted Roosevelt's ideas, but felt that there was no possibility of stopping him; and besides, the stock market was going up, and life is seldom altogether intolerable for the financial and business community when it sees plus signs after the names of its favorite securities in the afternoon papers. When, however, the Roosevelt bull market of 1933 broke, the conservatives began to recover their voices; and from that moment on, their cries of irritation and disapproval and fear became louder and louder.

The attack from the Right came in a series of overlapping waves of protest and panic; and it is interesting to notice that the usual sequence of events was somewhat as follows: each wave was met by the Administration with a conciliatory move—whereupon there was a momentary return of conservative hope that now the worst was over and business could go ahead again; but business failed to go ahead, and a new wave of adverse opinion rose.

1. The first wave (in the early autumn of 1933) was of dismay at the "regimentation" under the NRA, at the idea of raising wages before profits were assured, and at the attempt of the framers of the National Industrial Recovery Act (who were represented in the conservative press as radical professorial "brain-trusters") to balance their permission to employers to organize by permitting labor to organize too. A considerable section of the business community and most of the financial community agreed with Hearst that the letters NRA stood for "No Recovery Allowed" and said so emphatically. Other conservatives, perhaps more astute, had meanwhile discovered that there were distinct advantages in climbing aboard the NRA bandwagon and helping to steer it, that General Johnson's bark was worse than his bite, that

there were ways of getting round the labor provisions of Section 7a, and that even if most employers had to raise wages, it was possible for them also to raise prices.

2. Already, however, the second wave was mounting high. This was a wave of fury and fear at the Warren gold-buying scheme in the last months of 1933 and the beginning of 1934—a scheme which, according to Wall Street, led straight to printing-press inflation. The inflation panic was eased somewhat when Roosevelt stabilized the currency in terms of gold at the end of January, 1934, and the conservatives breathed again—briefly.

3. The third wave was of protest at the Administration's reform plans. These lamentations and prophecies of disaster reached a temporary climax during the spring of 1934, when Congress was debating the stock-exchange bill and considering the modification of the Securities Act of 1933. Richard Whitney, President of the New York Stock Exchange, declared that the stock-exchange bill, as first drafted, would "mean the end of liquidity in our markets." Bankers declared that recovery was impossible unless the Securities Act were modified. Financial writers in the newspapers declared that Washington was engaged in senseless persecution of Wall Street. Indignant financiers declared that the Administration which professed to want to protect the investor was proceeding to abolish him altogether. So heavy was the barrage of adverse criticism that both the stock-exchange bill and the Securities Act were somewhat modified,—and the President appointed, as head of the agency which was to administer them, a former stock-market-pool operator! By the end of June, 1934, the financial columns of the New York *Herald-Tribune* were remarking that "Wall Street is perking up with regard to Federal control; the brokers, giving increased study to the Act, are beginning to voice the opinion that the

measure may well serve as the needed impetus to a revival in trading"; and soon the opinion was freely expressed in the Street that now money would begin again to pour into the capital market.

4. As the summer of 1934 wore on, however, this did not happen—and a new outcry arose. What business needed, it seemed, was a clear indication from the government that it was not opposed to the profit system. Business men were afraid to go ahead because they thought the Administration was bent on ending or taking away all profits. This wave ebbed somewhat when the President duly said a good word for profits ("Not clear enough!" cried the intransigeants), and it ebbed still more when he appeared in a friendly mood before the members of the American Bankers Association, and Jackson Reynolds of the First National Bank, in an admirably diplomatic speech, prepared the way for what was hopefully referred to in the press as a "reconciliation" between the President and the financiers.

5. During the winter of 1934-35 and the spring of 1935, however, there were two more waves of protest. One was directed against the Administration's proposed bill to regulate holding companies in the public utility field; and the other, prompted by new fears of inflation, was directed against governmental extravagance.

To write as if these various waves of protest were separate and distinct is of course to over-simplify the story. The objections to the government's unorthodox financial operations, to the heavy governmental expenditures and the unbalanced budget, to heavy taxes, to "interference" with business, to the government's going into business itself via the Tennessee Valley Authority and other agencies, and to the campaign for financial reform, were continuous and simultaneous. The dominant note in the whole long chorus of conservative lamentation and attack was that what the country was suffering from was mainly "lack of confidence," and that confidence would not return until the government ceased experimenting and reforming. ("Confidence"—that ever-potent word: have we not met it before in this chronicle?) As Silas H. Strawn put the argument in an address to the United States Chamber of Commerce in May, 1934 (when there were still ten million men out of work), Roosevelt ought to issue a clear-cut statement "that the emergency is over and that there will be no more requests for emergency legislation." As General Johnson put it in the *Saturday Evening Post* the following winter, "It is trite to say that the single missing element is confidence. . . . Men can't go back to work until money goes back to work, and money won't go back to work until those who have or are responsible for money to invest in creating work know that, once it is out of their hands, no magic is going to frisk it away." . . .

This general view of the crisis—accompanied by distrust of Roosevelt's impulsiveness—gained such headway that by the spring of 1935, according to such a well-informed observer as the writer of *Kiplinger's Washington Letter*, some eighty per cent of the business men in the country, large and small, were opposed to the New Deal, and some thirty per cent of them were bitter in their opposition.

One reason why the thunder on the Right was so loud was that most of the press was under the control of men who represented the insiders' point of view. The average well-to-do American, encountering these arguments constantly in his newspapers and magazines, absorbed them almost through his pores, until by 1935 he half forgot that there had been any depression at all before Roosevelt came into power, and was fully persuaded that the only wise thing for Americans to do would be—as Walter

Lippmann said bitterly in his Harvard Phi Beta Kappa address in 1935—"to sit and wait, like Chinese coolies in a famine, until, for some mysterious reason, the warm blood of confidence rises once more in the veins of bank directors and corporation executives." Another reason why the thunder on the Right was loud was that money was being widely spent by big corporations to inculcate such views among their proxy-signers and among newspaper readers. Another reason was, perhaps, that the campaigns against specific Administration measures—the attempts to prove that they would create economic havoc—intensified the alarms of conservatives generally, and thus the panic was to a considerable degree self-induced. It would be interesting, for example, to know how much of the decline in public-utility securities during 1934 and early 1935 should be ascribed to the Administration's activities, and how much should be ascribed to advertisements and circulars which sedulously disseminated the idea that Congress was about to "complete the destruction of the savings of millions of investors."

It would be far from fair, of course, to dismiss the agitation on the Right as mere "propaganda." No one who heard a banker or broker or business man inveigh against the New Deal as a compound of economic absurdities and a deterrent to recovery could doubt that these men spoke from the heart, utterly convinced that the patient who had been so ill for five long years would soon recover if only the physician in Washington would stop giving him medicine and tell him he was well. Yet one may reasonably doubt whether the "lack of confidence" which in effect kept capital on strike, year after year, was due wholly to fear or dislike of the Administration's programs. Surely it was due also to an instinctive realization, among the powerful insiders, that the American economy was still far out of balance, New Deal or no New Deal, and that the makings of a really prosperous market for new business were simply not visible.

§ 6

With cannon to left of him and cannon to right of him, and his program clearly not reaching its objective, the President showed a gradual change in temper. As the months went by and new obstacles rose up before him, he began to seem less the brilliant and decisive leader that he had been in March, 1933, and more the political opportunist that he had been as Governor of New York and Democratic candidate in 1932. As the winds of opinion shifted, so he shifted, from Left to Right and back again. (History was repeating itself: a second Roosevelt was balancing on the political tightrope.) Close observers of the New Deal noticed an increasing tendency to announce new programs with a blare of trumpets and then, as opposition developed, to moderate them. Every president has to play politics, but before long the Postmaster-General's influence upon New Deal appointments began to seem unnecessarily potent. Some of Roosevelt's plans for recovery, furthermore, began to look less like the product of disinterested economic thought than like impromptu attempts to placate this group and that—to toss a few potential silver profits here, a little conservatism there, a little social idealism elsewhere.

If one says this, however, one should in fairness add that Roosevelt had undertaken a well-nigh impossible task —that of being President of the American economy as well as of the American polity, despite the fact that his chief talents were for conciliation rather than for economic statesmanship; and that he had undertaken it at a time when the economy was undergoing changes impossible to bring under control. Since Roosevelt did not

possess dictatorial power—and did not wish to possess it—
he was bound to depend mainly upon the voluntary
coöperation of the public, and this coöperation came
hard; for although the citizen will lay down his life for
his country, apparently he will not lay down his money.
Roosevelt had to persuade, encourage, compromise, cajole.

Luckily there was one respect in which his own political advantage and the advantage of the republic were
almost identical. His instinct for the middle of the political road, his engaging smile, his appealing manner, and
even, perhaps, the compromises which made his policies
so confusing, all helped to preserve, in a time of very
severe stress, that "domestic tranquillity" for the insurance of which the people of the United States had formed
their more perfect union. Even men who abominated
Roosevelt's economic ideas and distrusted his promises
felt that at least he wanted to hold the country together.

§ 7

By the end of May, 1935, when the Supreme Court's
unanimous decision against the NRA brought the second
phase of the New Deal to a close, the condition of the
national economy was roughly as follows:

Business activity—as measured by the *Annalist's* index
—was not far from eighty per cent of the "estimated
normal."

It was being maintained at this rate with the aid of
the expenditure by the government of so many billion
dollars that the net debt of the Federal Government was
rapidly rising. (From the end of 1930 to the end of the
Hoover Administration it had risen from about 16 billions to over 21, and from the end of the Hoover Administration to the end of 1934 it had risen further to almost
26 billions.) What was going on might be described as a

race between recovery and national bankruptcy. Debt still weighed heavily upon the country: as private debt decreased a little, public debt increased.

Generally speaking, the people at the upper end of the economic scale were better off than they had been at the beginning of the New Deal. (There were numerous exceptions—men and women still struggling with debt or impoverished by the vanishing of their investments—and these exceptions were often very audible.) Big business, generally speaking, was out of the red. The combined profits of 210 large corporations for the first quarter of 1935 were 21.8 per cent bigger than for the first quarter of 1934, according to figures compiled by the National City Bank. They were not yet large, but the trend was upward—a trend revealed also in the income-tax returns for 1934, which showed noteworthy gains in the incomes of the rich. Small business, however, was (again generally speaking) still on the ragged edge. Salary-earners and wage-earners—if they still had jobs—were perhaps a little better off. The farmers—except in the drought regions—were mostly a good deal better off. But at the bottom of the economic scale the conditions were appalling.

The number of men out of work, according to most estimates, was still at least ten millions. (The situation was much better than when Roosevelt came to the White House, but had improved little if at all during the long stalemate.) Of these ten millions, some five millions had so far exhausted their resources as to need public relief. Add to these five millions another million or two of people who were on relief for reasons other than unemployment as measured in the statistical estimates—men, for example, who needed aid because their farms had been ruined by drought or because their small businesses had gone under—and then multiply the resulting figure by three, in order to include not only the men on relief but also their families, and you arrive at an explanation of the fact that over twenty millions of Americans (say one person in six in the country) were dependent upon the meager bounty of the rest of the population.

If the unemployment situation was at least holding its own, the relief situation was not; for with every month of continued depression, more people used up their savings and joined the class of economic serfs.

These serfs, scattered throughout the country, ranged in former occupation from architects to stevedores. All ages were represented among them, though most of them were young. Some of them, of course, were chronic misfits. Others had been upstanding citizens, but were now becoming chronic dependents, with such small prospect of economic independence that they accepted life on the dole as the best thing in sight—unless, perhaps, some of them could manage to draw two doles. Others were still stubbornly trying to climb back to self-support, but found the way blocked by the shortage of jobs. Not only was this group growing in numbers; inevitably it was—on the average—deteriorating in character and spirit. To use the cold-blooded language of business rather than the language of human compassion: if the members of this group could find a chance to work and earn before it was too late, they might become a body of consumers worth reckoning with; denied such a chance, they were on their way to becoming a permanent dead weight on the taxpayers. Great numbers of them were becoming potential tramps, panhandlers, gangsters, members of the mob, whether of reaction or revolution. The phrase "land of opportunity," once so great with promise, had become ironic indeed.

Furthermore, the race was not only between recovery and governmental bankruptcy, and between recovery and demoralization of the jobless, but also between recovery and technological change. I have spoken of the indices as standing at about eighty per cent of "normal." Yet it was obvious that so far had invention and mechanization and efficiency increased, that business would have to attain a volume far above "normal" to absorb even a majority of the dispossessed. New machinery was still replacing men; indeed, the depression had accelerated the process. And it was far from being at an end. To give two examples of what was in prospect, the invention of a new cotton-picking machine threatened to annihilate many of the share-croppers of the South, and chemistry was showing the way to such intensive production of foodstuffs that the days of the small farmer appeared to be numbered. All this scientific and mechanical progress opened, of course, vistas of incredible plenty—if only the distributing apparatus would work. But the distributing apparatus, as we have seen, was out of gear.

Meanwhile America's foreign trade was still out of balance, international trade barriers remained high, there was continued danger of an international contest in currency depreciation, and behind all these sources of discord stood the ugly possibility of war.

The general world-wide economic trend was upward, it was true. Probably the American economic trend was also upward. But the longer the stalemate continued, the more enormous became the difficulties to be surmounted, and the smaller became the chance that, without superlative statesmanship, the country could restore its millions of serfs to economic citizenship.

§ 8

It was a strangely altered world in which the former lords of creation now found themselves. The economic initiative had definitely passed from Wall Street to Washington—at least for the time being—and many of their one-time instruments of power had been blunted or taken away from them.

The House of Morgan, for example, was now no longer permitted to issue securities; it was simply a bank of deposit. Other private banking houses, too, had been compelled to make the choice between deposit banking and investment banking; most of them—including Kuhn, Loeb & Co. and Dillon, Read & Co.—had chosen to issue securities and forego deposits. The commercial banks were now minus their investment affiliates. The traditional machinery for issuing the common stock of new corporations to insiders and then unloading it on the stock market had apparently been somewhat crippled by the Securities Exchange Act of 1934. As for the traditional machinery for manipulating the stock market, power to cripple it had at least been lodged with the Securities and Exchange Commission. The opportunities for corporate insiders to make big profits at the expense of their corporations or their proxy-signers were likewise somewhat limited by the power of publicity: they had to report changes in their share-holdings, salaries and bonuses received, and contracts made with their companies. In many other respects, the well-traveled avenues to easy riches had been closed off or put under Federal traffic control—until it seemed to the men of Wall Street as if they could now do nothing without filling out an elaborate form and waiting until some functionary in Washington gave the word.

Commercial bankers, looking for uses to which to put their depositors' funds and unable to find many qualified commercial borrowers, were investing in more and more government bonds, until they, too, felt that their destinies were at the disposal of Washington; and now, in the spring of 1935, the federal government was threatening to concentrate more authority in the Federal Reserve Board, increasing its limited power over the volume of check-money. The commercial bankers still retained the right of individual decision about their banks' investments, but the bounds within which they might do so seemed to be contracting.

How vital and how permanent these changes would prove to be was beyond prediction. The power of governmental regulation depends upon the vigilance, imagination, and honesty of officials—very variable qualities, all of them. An indolent or unwary commission could overlook abuses or deal with them ineptly; a few venal employees in Washington could turn almost any law into a sham. The power of governmental regulation depends likewise upon public opinion—and we have seen how it fared during the seven fat years when public opinion was indulgent. Laws, furthermore, are not eternal; they may be repealed, or else distorted or overridden by the courts. New devices for financial conquest can always be forged, and the principle of community of interest can often accomplish what the law has tried to prevent. For example, to say that the House of Morgan was out of the securities business was to overlook the possibilities of effective working alliances between it and houses of issue; to say that the big New York banks were bereft of their affiliates was to overlook the possibilities of similar working alliances between such banks and investment companies.

The truth was that the extent to which the power of the financiers of Wall Street had been checked could not be measured because this power was being largely held in abeyance. Unwilling to venture into new business on any considerable scale, these men were having little opportunity to test out new methods of maintaining and

achieving influence. Broadly speaking, the game of financial conquest was not being played.

Yet it is curious to note the extent to which the fundamental trend toward concentration of economic power
was continuing. The big corporations were relatively
stronger than ever before. In 1929 the 200 biggest corporations in the country had controlled—according to
Berle and Means—some 49 per cent of all non-financial
corporate wealth. By the beginning of 1932, according to
Means's estimate, the proportion had increased to about
55 per cent. Since then the NRA had notoriously given
an advantage to big as against small corporations and had
made it difficult for new concerns to invade the territory
of the going companies. No recent comprehensive figures
were available, but the scattered evidence did not suggest that the trend was changing. For example, in Chapter VIII we noted that, in the automobile industry, the
three biggest companies had so crowded their competitors off the road during the nineteen-twenties that by
1930 they were making 83.3 per cent of all the passenger
cars newly registered. By the year 1934 these three biggest companies made, not 83.3 per cent of the passenger
cars, but 90.8 per cent of them; and in the month of
March, 1935, they made 93.4 per cent of them. The monster corporation had a bigger place than ever before in
the dim sun of American business.

The ownership of these monster corporations was
now even more widely distributed than in the years of
plenty. Here are a few figures which suggest how wide
had been the distribution since 1930. The American Telephone and Telegraph Company had 567,000 stockholders at the end of 1930; it had 675,000 at the end of 1934.
The General Motors Corporation had 263,000 at the
end of 1930, and 350,000 at the end of 1934. The United
States Steel Corporation had 145,000 in 1930, and 239,-

ooo at the end of 1934. The General Electric Company had 116,000 in 1930, and 196,000 at the end of 1934. To be sure, the movement appeared to be slackening; a good many large concerns, indeed, had fewer stockholders at the end of 1934 than at the end of 1933. But in general it was still truer in 1935 than in 1930 to say that the working control of most of the very large corporations rested in the hands of groups of insiders who owned only a fraction of the stock; that the vast majority of shareholders regarded their stock certificates as tokens of liquid wealth rather than as tokens of responsible ownership; and that the insiders were subject to very little effective check by the scattered majority owners.

They were subject, as we have noticed, to much more check by government authority than before, but government authorities have usually been amenable to pressure from people who knew exactly what they wanted—and could pay for it. Whether in the future Washington would know what it wanted, whether New York would in the course of time be discovered to be holding the Washington puppet-strings, whether some new conjunction of economic forces would alter the whole nature of the problem of control, were questions impossible to answer in 1935.

Whatever was to happen, it was clear by now that the age of American finance which had begun with the twentieth century had come to a close. Perhaps another one was to come; but if so, the circumstances which conditioned it and the instruments of which it made use would be so altered that this new age could hardly resemble closely the age which had been ushered in by Morgan the Elder in the far-off days of 1900. It would be different not merely because of the New Deal or changing political sentiment, but chiefly because of the play of economic forces beyond the sway of bankers or collectivists or Presidents.

§ 9

And for America, what lay ahead? An attempt to return to the philosophy of laissez-faire, a discarding of restrictions upon business, a new age of emprise for the controllers of property—and, perhaps, new and greater insecurity for the propertyless? A yielding to pressure from this group and that, perhaps a drift into uncontrollable inflation and further disaster? A revolution, a dictatorship, an era of mutual suspicion and bloodshed and tyranny? A new world war? Or, possibly, a not too undisciplined recovery, a relaxation of tensions, a slow approach to an era of orderly and distributed abundance?

These, too, were questions impossible to answer. But this much was sure. The problem which confronted the United States was so vast and so complex that the cries of those who shouted frantically for and against the New Deal, for and against freedom for property, for and against proletarian revolt, were like the cries of the blind men in John Godfrey Saxe's poem—the blind men who were led to an elephant and were asked to describe it, and each felt a portion of it and called out his version of what the creature was like: it was like a spear, it was like a snake, it was like a wall. The problem was nothing less than how to adjust our institutions, under the new circumstances created by the vast financial and economic changes of the past generation, so as to multiply effectively and distribute with some decent approach to fairness the products of the earth, the fruits of labor, and the unprecedented gifts of science—and to do this without destroying human liberty.

Appendix

SOURCES AND OBLIGATIONS

I should like to express, first of all, my sense of obligation to the authors of a few books of which I have made especially extended use. For facts and figures in my first seven chapters I have drawn constantly upon Alexander Dana Noyes's two concise and authoritative volumes, *Forty Years of American Finance* (G. P. Putnam's Sons, 1909) and *The War Period of American Finance, 1908-1925* (Putnam, 1926); to any student of the finance of this epoch they are invaluable. For facts with regard to the process of concentration, and still more for underlining the great importance of the topic, I am indebted to Adolf A. Berle, Jr., and Gardiner C. Means as the authors of *The Modern Corporation and Private Property* (Commerce Clearing House, Inc., 1932). I have also made use at many points of John T. Flynn's *God's Gold* (Harcourt, Brace, 1932), an excellent biography of John D. Rockefeller, and of his somewhat one-sided but penetrating *Security Speculation: Its Economic Effects* (Harcourt, 1934), and to a less extent of various magazine articles of his, and I am indebted to Mr. Flynn himself for many ideas and suggestions.

My other sources have been very numerous and varied; the chief ones may perhaps be best arranged chapter by chapter, though I have made extensive use of several of them.

In Chapter I ("Morgan Calls the Tune") my primary obligation is to Burton J. Hendrick's very interesting two-volume *Life of Andrew Carnegie* (Doubleday, Doran, 1932), a book which has not had the attention it deserves: my account of the Carnegie-Schwab-Morgan negotiations, and especially of the dinner of December 12, 1900, and the subsequent meeting at Morgan's house, is derived principally from Mr. Hendrick's narrative, as is my reference to Carnegie's later years. For the general background of this chapter, as of later chapters, I used Noyes extensively. For the account of economic developments before the twentieth century began, I made considerable use of *The United States Since 1865*, by Louis M. Hacker and Benjamin B. Kendrick (F. S. Crofts &

Co., 1932), a history which is exceptionally strong in economic analysis; of *The Rise of American Civilization*, by Charles A. Beard and Mary R. Beard (Macmillan, 1927) ; and of *God's Gold* (for Rockefeller, the South Improvement Co., and the rise of the trusts and promoters). I have taken some facts and incidents about Gary and the formation of the Steel Corporation from Ida M. Tarbell's *Life of Elbert H. Gary* (Appleton, 1925) and some stories about John W. Gates from *Bet-a-Million Gates*, by Robert Irving Warshow (Greenberg, 1932). As to Morgan the Elder, I read everything I could lay my hands on, including Lewis Corey's *The House of Morgan* (G. Howard Watt, 1930), John K. Winkler's *Morgan the Magnificent* (Garden City Publishing Co., 1930), Carl Hovey's *Life Story of J. Pierpont Morgan* (New York: Sturgis & Walton, 1911), and biographies of other men, memoirs, etc., in which he incidentally appears. My account of the financing of the Steel Corporation uses facts and figures from the *Report of the Commissioner of Corporations on the Steel Industry* (1911), which is printed with the monumental Stanley Committee hearings (*U. S. Steel Corporation: House Committee on Investigation of the U. S. Steel Corporation, House Resolution 148, 62d Congress, 1st and 2d sessions*).

In Chapter II ("The Harriman Challenge") my indebtedness is chiefly to George Kennan's *E. H. Harriman, a Biography* (Houghton Mifflin, 1922). But the story of Harriman's career and the struggle over the Northern Pacific draws also upon three other biographies: *Jacob H. Schiff, His Life and Letters*, by Cyrus Adler (Doubleday, Doran, 1928) ; *The Life of James J. Hill*, by Joseph Gilpin Pyle (Doubleday, 1917) ; and *The Portrait of a Banker: James Stillman*, by Anna Robeson Burr (Duffield, 1927) —an engagingly written book upon which I have drawn in later chapters too. (These biographies are all very favorable to their respective subjects, but illuminating, especially when compared.) The account of Harriman's talk with a New York banker was given me by the banker himself. Sterling's part in planning the Northern Pacific *coup* is from John K. Winkler's *The First Billion* (Vanguard, 1934) ; I have satisfied myself that Mr. Winkler's evidence was strong. My story of the Northern Pacific panic uses stock quotations and anecdotes from the *New York Times*; and also data from current issues of the *Commercial and Financial Chronicle*.

In Chapter III ("The Overlords") the economic history is

based largely upon Noyes, Corey, and Henry Clews's *Fifty Years in Wall Street* (New York: Irving Publishing Co., 1908). Readers who are amused at Clews's social observations should know that his enormous book, written at intervals over a long period of years, is full of delightfully naïve passages and of revealing facts about contemporary finance and financiers. For aid in understanding Roosevelt's attitude (and for the campaign contributions of 1904) I am indebted to Henry F. Pringle's judicious *Theodore Roosevelt: A Biography* (Harcourt, 1931). The Clarence W. Barron quotations are from those two volumes of the journals of a money-minded man, *They Told Barron* and *More They Told Barron*, edited and arranged by Arthur Pound and Samuel Taylor Moore (Harper, 1930 and 1931); I have quoted from these books elsewhere too. The account of the spheres of influence in the early years of the century is mostly worked out from data given in the report of the Pujo Committee (see below) and checked from other sources. The Boston manufacturer's story was told me by the man himself. As to the ten financiers, my sources are largely apparent from the text, but I might add that I made use of *God's Gold*, Kennan, Adler, and Burr (as cited above); of an article on George F. Baker in the Boston *Sunday Post* for June 15, 1924; of numerous magazine articles, and—for Morgan's religious life—of William Lawrence's *Memories of a Happy Life* (Houghton Mifflin, 1926). The Frick-Mellon conversation is from *Mellon's Millions, The Life and Times of Andrew W. Mellon*, by Harvey O'Connor (John Day Co., 1933). The quotation of Rogers in court is from an article on "The Taming of Rogers" in the *American Magazine*, July, 1906. The Crowninshield quotation is from *Vogue*, Jan., 1923. The news items at the end of the chapter are drawn mostly from the New York *Tribune* and other newspapers of the period.

In Chapter IV ("Panic") the background is from Noyes and from articles such as Edwin Lefèvre's "The Game Got Them," *Everybody's*, Jan., 1908 (from which I have quoted). The story of the Heinze collapse is mostly from the *New International Year Book* for 1907, the *Commercial and Financial Chronicle* for Nov. 2, 1907, and current issues of the New York *Tribune*. As to the subsequent banking phases of the Panic, I studied carefully the exhaustive (and conflicting) testimony of participants as given before the Stanley Committee (see above) and the Pujo Committee (*U. S. Banking and Currency Committee, House, 62.*

Money Trust Investigation. Investigation of the financial and monetary conditions in the United States under House resolutions 429 and 504). I also used Burr, Lawrence, and the interesting account in Thomas W. Lamont's *Henry P. Davison* (Harper, 1933), from all of which I have quoted. As to Roosevelt's part in the Tennessee purchase, Pringle proved especially useful. The quotation of Stillman near the end of the chapter is from John K. Winkler's *The First Billion*. For information about the Morgan Library as it was in 1907 I am indebted to Miss Belle da Costa Greene, the librarian.

In Chapter V ("Counter-Offensive") my primary obligation is to John Chamberlain for *Farewell to Reform* (John Day, 1932), from which I drew both facts and ideas. Other valuable sources were Harold Underwood Faulkner's *The Quest for Social Justice, 1898-1914* (Vol. XI of *A History of American Life*: Macmillan, 1931); Hacker and Kendrick (especially for their analysis of the position of the Supreme Court); Pringle (especially for his analysis of Roosevelt as a reformer); Roosevelt's own letters and addresses, and Wilson's addresses; and Mark Sullivan's *Our Times*, from the third volume of which, subtitled *Pre-War America* (Scribner, 1930), I took data on the Hughes investigation of the insurance companies. On the left-wing labor offensive I used Louis Adamic's *Dynamite* (Viking, 1931). I have quoted from Bliss Perry's *Henry Lee Higginson, Life and Letters* (Little, Brown, 1921).

In Chapter VI ("Pujo"), my extensive use of the report of the Pujo Committee, and of the record of the hearings before the Committee, is obvious. The data on General Motors are from Arthur Pound's *The Turning Wheel* (Doubleday, Doran, 1934); on the beginnings of the utility systems, from *The Holding Company*, by James C. Bonbright and Gardiner C. Means (McGraw, 1932), which has of course been helpful elsewhere also; on the New Haven, mostly from Faulkner, checked from other sources. The scenes in the Pujo Committee room are based on news stories in the New York *Tribune*. As to the Wilson reform legislation, *The American Leviathan: The Republic in the Machine Age*, by Charles A. Beard and William Beard (Macmillan, 1930) proved useful.

In Chapter VII ("War") I draw heavily upon the mass of information carefully assembled and clearly set forth in Noyes's admirable book on *The War Period of American Finance*. My chief sources on the beginnings of the Federal Reserve, aside from Noyes, were *The Federal Reserve System*, by Paul M. Warburg (Macmillan, 1930), and Lamont's life of Davison (cited above); the latter book was of course a prime source on the Morgan war financing. The Bryan-Morgan letter is taken from Walter Millis's *Road to War* (Houghton Mifflin, 1935). The war profit figures are from Moody's and from annual corporate reports as published with the *Commercial and Financial Chronicle*, except that the government calculation of the Steel Corporation's profits and the figures for Calumet & Hecla and Utah Copper are from the Nye Committee report of 1935, to accompany H. R. 5529 (*To Prevent Profiteering in War: 74 Congress, 1st session, Senate Report 577*). The Morgan quotation about "American principles of liberty" is from a letter to Gary, *New York Times*, Sept. 23, 1919. The labor union figures are from *Recent Social Trends in the United States*, The Report of the President's Research Committee on Social Trends (McGraw-Hill Book Co., 1933), volume 2, the chapter on labor. The estimate of the increase in the number of stockholders is from Berle and Means, p. 56 and p. 368-9.

In Chapter VIII ("The Seven Fat Years") my debt to Messrs. Berle and Means is heavy; they have contributed the best still picture, so to speak, of the process of which my book attempts to take a sort of moving picture, and I have used their figures and analyses at length. On the fortunes of the reform laws during the Seven Fat Years, my chief obligation is to Hacker and Kendrick. On codes of practice, to "Whose Child is the NRA?" by John T. Flynn, *Harper's Magazine*, Sept., 1934. On corporate publicity, to *The Propaganda Menace*, by Frederick E. Lumley (Appleton-Century, 1933). On the lot of the economic heretic, to *Middletown*, by Robert S. Lynd and Helen Merrell Lynd (Harcourt, 1929), a book which no historian of that period will be able to do without. On the nature and measurement of prosperity during the Seven Fat Years, to *Recent Economic Changes*, The Report of the Committee on Recent Economic Changes of the President's Conference on Unemployment (McGraw-Hill Book Co., 1929); to the highly useful chapter by Edwin F. Gay and Leo Wolman on "Trends in Economic Organization" in volume I of *Recent Social Trends in the United States* (see above), which was also valuable later on banking trends; and to *America's Capacity to Consume*, by Maurice Leven, Harold G. Moulton, and Clark Warburton (Brookings Institution, 1934). The estimates of the workers' share of the fruits of efficiency are derived from *Recent Economic Changes*, II, 653-654; for the cost of living meanwhile, see *Recent Social Trends*, II, 820. The figures on banking concentration are mostly from *Concentration of Control in American Industry*, by Harry W. Laidler (Crowell, 1931). The figures attributed to N. R. Danielian on holding-company domination of utilities are from an article in *Harper's Magazine*, June, 1935. The data on Dodge financing and Cities Service stock are from Berle and Means, 75-76. The reference to Delaware corporation privileges is based on a pamphlet, "Pointers on the Formation of Delaware Corporations," issued by the Delaware Registration Trust Co., 1931 edition. The data on the Milwaukee receivership are from *The Investor Pays*, by Max Lowenthal (Knopf, 1933).

In Chapter IX ("Building the Pyramids") my best source on Insull was a series of articles by John T. Flynn in *Collier's*, beginning Dec. 3, 1932. This is the basis of my account of the Middle West financing in 1912. The data on service contracts (Insull and other) are from "Certain Aspects of Utility Service Contracts," by Norman S. Buchanan, reprinted from the *Journal of Business* of the University of Chicago, Apr., 1934; the "piano-rug" incident in the Insull system is from N. R. Danielian's "From Insull to Injury," *Atlantic Monthly*, Apr., 1933. The account of the stock market operations in Insull Utility Investments is based on the analysis in Flynn's *Security Speculation* (cited above). On financial practices in the utility systems I am indebted also to William Z. Ripley's *Main Street and Wall Street* (Little, Brown, 1932). Wherever possible I have gone back of these sources to the endless evidence in that Brobdingnagian Federal Trade Commission document which goes by the gentle title of *Utility Corporations: Letter from the Chairman of the Federal Trade Commission transmitting in response to Senate Resolution No. 83 a monthly report on the electric power and gas utilities inquiry* (71 volumes from 1928 to early 1935, and more coming!). As for the Van Sweringens, my principal source, aside from magazine articles in *Fortune* and elsewhere, is a document to which I shall refer from now on simply as *SEP*: namely, *Stock Exchange Practices: Report of the Committee on Banking and Currency pursuant to S. Res. 84, 72d Congress, and S. Res. 56 and 97, 73d Congress: Report No. 1455, Senate, 73d Congress, 2d Session*. This document, which is a compact report of what is now generally called the Pecora investigation, contains a clear account of the steps in the Van Sweringen financing. My analysis of the Van Sweringen pyramid is based on a chart in Berle and Means, 74; my source for the Cleveland bank incident is *SEP*, 319; for the Missouri Pacific financial incidents, "The Story of the Missouri Pacific," by Max Lowenthal, *Harper's Magazine*, Dec., 1934.

In Chapter X ("Bankers, Salesmen, and Speculators") I have made much use of the above-mentioned chapter in *Recent Social Trends* (for the general changes in banking) and of *SEP*. For alterations in the national money supply, I drew upon Laughlin Currie's *The Supply and Control of Money in the United States* (Harvard Economic Studies, vol. XLVII, Harvard University Press). The Barton article on Charles E. Mitchell appeared in the *American Magazine* for Feb., 1923. For security selling methods, see *SEP*, 167; and *Scapegoats*, by Julian Sherrod (Brewer, Warren, & Putnam, 1931). On the facts of banking developments in California my principal source was a mimeographed report on branch banking in California prepared by the Federal Reserve Committee on Branch, Chain, and Group Banking (1932). For Detroit group banking operations, *SEP*, 247. For the story of the Bank of United States, *Little Napoleons and Dummy Directors*, a well written and clear account by M. R. Werner (Harper, 1933). For Cleveland banks in real estate, *SEP*, 295, 317. For the Wiggin transactions in Chase stock, *SEP*, 188; for his testimony, *SEP*, 184.

In Chapter XI ("Into the Stratosphere") most of the specific incidents are from *SEP*: the Pennroad financing, 113; Morgan tax payments, 321, gain in net worth, 223; U. S. and Foreign Securities, 334-348; United Corporation option warrants, 103-4, 117-8; Sinclair stock operation, 65-6; Radio, 47; General Asphalt, 67; Underwood-Elliott-Fisher, 193; brokers' loans by corporations, 16. For data on the origin of common stock of corporations, Flynn's *Security Speculation* is worth consulting; his views have been the target of much criticism, but they seem to me stronger on the admittedly partial evidence than his critics charge. For the details of the American Commercial Alcohol stock operation of 1933, I am indebted to this same book. I should have told the story of the rising bull market—and of the Panic of 1929—much more fully in these pages had I not already told it in *Only Yesterday*.

In Chapter XII ("The Overlords, 1929") much of the information about the fifty men was collected for me by Sanderson Vanderbilt. (The arrangement of it and the generalizations are of course my own.) The quotation from Mr. Justice Stone may be found in the *Harvard Law Review*, Nov., 1934.

In Chapter XIII ("Downfall and Confusion") I am under great obligation to George Soule for his acute analysis of the decline of 1929-33 and of Hoover's policy in *The Coming American Revolution* (Macmillan, 1934). The figures on dividend payments in 1932 are from an article by Stuart Chase in the *New Republic*, Jan. 9, 1935, which in turn was based on Internal Revenue figures. The data on the trend of interest payments, dividends, wages, etc., are from "National Income, 1929-1932," by Simon Kuznets, which is Bulletin 49 of the National Bureau of Economic Research; on the growth of internal debt, from *The Internal Debts of the United States*, edited by Evans Clark (published for the Twentieth Century Fund, Inc., by Macmillan, 1933) ; on liquid claims, from *Liquid Claims and National Wealth*, by Adolf A. Berle, Jr., and Victoria J. Pederson (Macmillan, 1934). Gardiner C. Means's pamphlet on industrial prices was printed as *Industrial Prices and their Relative Inflexibility: Letter from the Secretary of Agriculture transmitting in response to Sen. Res. 17, a report relating to the subject of industrial prices and their relative inflexibility, 74th Congress, 1st session, Doc. 13.* As to the banking collapse of 1933, I found *28 days: A History of the Banking Crisis*, by C. C. Colt and N. S. Keith (Greenberg, 1933), very helpful.

In the last chapter ("All Change") I do not think there are any sources which require special mention—except perhaps that the quotation about the conflict between capital and labor, in my discussion of opinion on the Left, is from *The Economic Consequences of the New Deal*, by Benjamin Stolberg and Warren Jay Vinton (Harcourt, 1935). I have not attempted to carry the story beyond the Supreme Court's decision at the end of May, 1935. Whatever was undetermined at that time—the fate of bills then pending, the results of the decision itself, and, indeed, the whole economic fate of America—is left, as it were, suspended in mid-air.

In closing this memorandum of obligations, I wish to express my particular gratitude to Anne Jones Richter for a long labor of copying; to Rollin Alger Sawyer and his aides at the New York Public Library for help at many points; and to various people for very kindly reading parts of my manuscript in first draft and suggesting corrections and revisions (they represent divergent points of view; I have not been able to carry out all their suggestions, and for this reason I am all the more anxious that none of them should be thought of as having approved what I have written) : John T. Flynn, Stuart Chase, Guy Greer, N. R. Danielian, Max Lowenthal, C. C. Colt, Donald K. Evans, and W. Rufus Brent; Junius S. Morgan, Thomas W. Lamont, and other members of the firm of J. P. Morgan & Co.; and Cass Canfield, Ordway Tead, and other associates of mine at Harper & Brothers.

For helpful criticism and encouragement by my late mother, Alberta Lewis Allen, by my wife's mother, Letitia C. Rogers, and above all by my wife, Agnes Rogers Allen, I cannot begin to express my gratitude.

FREDERICK LEWIS ALLEN

Scarsdale, New York
June 25, 1935

INDEX

QUADRANGLE PAPERBACKS

American History

Frederick Lewis Allen. *The Lords of Creation.* (QP35)
Lewis Atherton. *Main Street on the Middle Border.* (QP36)
Thomas A. Bailey. *Woodrow Wilson and the Lost Peace.* (QP1)
Thomas A. Bailey. *Woodrow Wilson and the Great Betrayal.* (QP2)
Charles A. Beard. *The Idea of National Interest.* (QP27)
Carl L. Becker. *Everyman His Own Historian.* (QP33)
Ray A. Billington. *The Protestant Crusade.* (QP12)
Allan G. Bogue. *From Prairie to Corn Belt.* (QP50)
Kenneth E. Boulding. *The Organizational Revolution.* (QP43)
David M. Chalmers. *Hooded Americanism.* (QP51)
John Chamberlain. *Farewell to Reform.* (QP19)
Alice Hamilton Cromie. *A Tour Guide to the Civil War.*
Robert D. Cross. *The Emergence of Liberal Catholicism in America.* (QP44)
Richard M. Dalfiume. *American Politics Since 1945.* (NYTimes Book, QP57)
Chester McArthur Destler. *American Radicalism, 1865-1901.* (QP30)
Robert A. Divine. *American Foreign Policy Since 1945.* (NYTimes Book, QP58)
Robert A. Divine. *The Illusion of Neutrality.* (QP45)
Elisha P. Douglass. *Rebels and Democrats.* (QP26)
Herman Finer. *Road to Reaction.* (QP5)
Felix Frankfurter. *The Commerce Clause.* (QP16)
Lloyd C. Gardner. *A Different Frontier.* (QP32)
Edwin Scott Gaustad. *The Great Awakening in New England.* (QP46)
Ray Ginger. *Altgeld's America.* (QP21)
Gerald N. Grob. *Workers and Utopia.* (QP61)
Louis Hartz. *Economic Policy and Democratic Thought.* (QP52)
William B. Hesseltine. *Lincoln's Plan of Reconstruction.* (QP41)
Granville Hicks. *The Great Tradition.* (QP62)
Dwight W. Hoover. *Understanding Negro History.* (QP49)
Stanley P. Hirshson. *Farewell to the Bloody Shirt.* (QP53)
Frederic C. Howe. *The Confessions of a Reformer.* (QP39)
Louis Joughin and Edmund M. Morgan. *The Legacy of Sacco and Vanzetti.* (QP7)
William Loren Katz. *Teachers' Guide to American Negro History.* (QP210)
Edward Chase Kirkland. *Dream and Thought in the Business Community, 1860-1900.* (QP11)
Edward Chase Kirkland. *Industry Comes of Age.* (QP42)
Adrienne Koch. *The Philosophy of Thomas Jefferson.* (QP17)
Gabriel Kolko. *The Triumph of Conservatism.* (QP40)
Walter LaFeber. *John Quincy Adams and American Continental Empire.* (QP23)
David E. Lilienthal. *TVA: Democracy on the March.* (QP28)
Arthur S. Link. *Wilson the Diplomatist.* (QP18)
Huey P. Long. *Every Man a King.* (QP8)
Gene M. Lyons. *America: Purpose and Power.* (QP24)
Jackson Turner Main. *The Antifederalists.* (QP14)
Ernest R. May. *The World War and American Isolation, 1914-1917.* (QP29)
Henry F. May. *The End of American Innocence.* (QP9)
George E. Mowry. *The California Progressives.* (QP6)
William L. O'Neill. *American Society Since 1945.* (NYTimes Book, QP59)
Frank L. Owsley. *Plain Folk of the Old South.* (QP22)
David Graham Phillips. *The Treason of the Senate.* (QP20)
Julius W. Pratt. *Expansionists of 1898.* (QP15)
Moses Rischin. *The American Gospel of Success.* (QP54)
John P. Roche. *The Quest for the Dream.* (QP47)
David A. Shannon. *The Socialist Party of America.* (QP38)
Andrew Sinclair. *The Available Man.* (QP60)
John Spargo. *The Bitter Cry of the Children.* (QP55)
Richard W. Van Alstyne. *The Rising American Empire.* (QP25)
Willard M. Wallace. *Appeal to Arms.* (QP10)
Norman Ware. *The Industrial Worker, 1840-1860.* (QP13)
Albert K. Weinberg. *Manifest Destiny.* (QP3)
Bernard A. Weisberger. *They Gathered at the River.* (QP37)
Robert H. Wiebe. *Businessmen and Reform.* (QP56)
Bell I. Wiley. *The Plain People of the Confederacy.* (QP4)
William Appleman Williams. *The Contours of American History.* (QP34)
William Appleman Williams. *The Great Evasion.* (QP48)
Esmond Wright. *Causes and Consequences of the American Revolution.* (QP31)

European History

William Sheridan Allen. *The Nazi Seizure of Power*. (QP302)
W. O. Henderson. *The Industrial Revolution in Europe*. (QP303)
Raul Hilberg. *The Destruction of the European Jews*. (QP301)
Telford Taylor. *Sword and Swastika*. (QP304)

Philosophy

F. H. Bradley. *The Presuppositions of Critical History*. (QP108)
William Earle. *Objectivity*. (QP109)
James M. Edie, James P. Scanlan, Mary-Barbara Zeldin, George L. Kline. *Russian Philosophy*.
   (3 vols, QP111, 112, 113)
James M. Edie. *An Invitation to Phenomenology*. (QP103)
James M. Edie. *Phenomenology in America*. (QP105)
Manfred S. Frings. *Heidegger and the Quest for Truth*. (QP107)
Moltke S. Gram. *Kant: Disputed Questions*. (QP104)
Lionel Rubinoff. *Faith and Reason*. (QP106)
Paul Tibbetts. *Perception*. (QP110)
Pierre Thévenaz. *What Is Phenomenology?* (QP101)

Social Science

George and Eunice Grier. *Equality and Beyond*. (QP204)
Charles O. Lerche, Jr. *Last Chance in Europe*. (QP207)
David Mitrany. *A Working Peace System*. (QP205)
Martin Oppenheimer and George Lakey. *A Manual for Direct Action*. (QP202)
Fred Powledge. *To Change a Child*. (QP209)
Lee Rainwater. *And the Poor Get Children*. (QP208)
Clarence Senior. *The Puerto Ricans*. (QP201)
Arthur L. Stinchcombe. *Rebellion in a High School*. (QP211)

330092

CS					
A425	DEWEY		PARTS	COPY	EDITION
CUTTER		VOLUMES		1	

1935 ALLEN FI

YEAR

LORDS OF C

CUTTER

DEWEY

VOLUMES

PARTS EDITION YEAR

71
72
74
76
77
79
83
85
88